The Prehistory
of Denmark

JØRGEN JENSEN

The Prehistory
of Denmark

METHUEN
LONDON AND NEW YORK

First published in 1982 by
Methuen & Co. Ltd
11 New Fetter Lane, London EC4P 4EE

Published in the USA by
Methuen & Co.
in association with Methuen, Inc.
733 Third Avenue, New York, NY 10017

Phototypeset in Linotron 202 by
Graphicraft Typesetters Hong Kong
Printed in Great Britain at the University Press, Cambridge

British Library Cataloguing in Publication Data

Jensen, Jørgen
The prehistory of Denmark.
1. Denmark–History–to 1241
I. Title
936.3   DL161
ISBN 0-416-34190-X
ISBN 0-416-34200-0 Pbk

Library of Congress Cataloging in Publication Data

Jensen, Jørgen, 1936 July 30–
The prehistory of Denmark.
Translation of: Dansk socialhistorie. v. 1.
Bibliography: p.
Includes index.
1. Man, Prehistoric–Denmark.   2. Denmark–Antiquities.
I. Title.
GN826.J4613   1982   948.9'01   82-24885
ISBN 0-416-34190-X
ISBN 0-416-34200-0 (pbk.)

To my wife Barbara

Contents

List of figures   xi
Preface   xvii
Introduction
  Archaeology in Denmark   1
  Denmark, the bridge to the north   5

PART I   THE HUNTERS AND GATHERERS 11,000–4200 BC   9

1   A changing environment   11
      After the last Ice Age   11
      The first continuous forest   15
      A new forest scene: the hazel-pine forest   16
      The stable primeval forest   17
      Man and the ecosystem   22
2   The hunting population   24
      Fertility and mortality   24
      How many were there?   29
3   Subsistence and settlement   33
      Mobility and territory   33
      Reindeer hunters   35
      Hunters and gatherers of the Boreal period   38
      Hunters and gatherers of the Atlantic period   42
      A population crisis at the end of the fifth millennium BC?   50
      Economy of the hunters and gatherers   52
4   Social structure of the hunters and gatherers   54
5   Finds and interpretations   59

PART II   THE FIRST FARMERS *c.* 4200–2800 BC   67

6   The introduction of farming in Denmark   69
    Introduction   69
    The moving frontier   71
    The farming communities and their environment   73
    The evidence of pollen analysis   75
7   Population growth and food production   78
    The growth potential of the agrarian society   78
    A theory of agricultural development under
       population pressure   79
    Fertility and mortality in the early agrarian society   81
8   Subsistence and settlement   84
    Introduction   84
    Land use of the early farming communities   85
    Settlement   90
    Subsistence patterns   98
    The circulation of goods   103
    Economy of the farming communities   107
9   Social patterns in the early farming communities   109
10 Finds and interpretations   117

PART III   TOWARDS A NEW ERA 2800–500 BC   129

11 A changing environment   131
    Farming communities in transition   131
    The changing land   132
    The changing climate   134
12 Subsistence and settlement   138
    Towards a new settlement pattern   138
    Villages and farmsteads   146
    Towards more productive agricultural forms   151
    The exchange of goods and raw materials   155
    Concepts of exchange   157
    The case of amber   161
    External and internal exchange up to 500 BC   163
13 Social patterns from 2800 to 500 BC   168
14 Finds and interpretations   179

PART IV   THE CHIEFDOMS OF THE IRON AGE 500 BC–800 AD   191

15 Environmental changes   193
    The development of the open, man-made landscape   193
    The development of the climate during the Iron Age   196

16 Subsistence and settlement   198
      Expansion of the farming communities   198
      Villages and farmsteads around the birth of Christ   204
      Farming communities in transition   214
      Subsistence patterns during the Iron Age   222
      Iron   228
17 The development of economic institutions   232
      Exchange systems   232
      Exchange until 800 AD   235
18 Political and social development   255
      Economy and social development   255
      Political and economic power concentrations   257
      Processes towards the early Danish state   267
19 Finds and interpretations   275

      Bibliography   287
      Index   322

List of Figures

1 Christian Jürgensen Thomsen. *Photo: The National Museum, Copenhagen.* 2

2 The National Museum in Copenhagen. *Photo: Jørgen Jensen.* 4

3 Geomorphological map of Denmark. *After A. Sømme (ed.):* A Geography of Norden, *1960.* 7

4 Landscape at Tollund bog, Jutland. *Photo: Inga Aistrup.* 14

5 Pollen chart of the vegetational development in Denmark. *After K. Jessen 1938.* 15

6 Map of northern Europe *c.* 8500 BC. *After J. Jensen 1979b.* 16

7 Map of Denmark *c.* 7000 BC. *After J. Jensen 1979b.* 18

8 Map of Denmark *c.* 4500 BC. *After J. Jensen 1979b.* 20

9 Landscape on the island of Ormø, southern Denmark. *Photo: Ole Akhøj.* 21

10 Mesolithic grave from Bøgebakken, Vedbæk. *After E. Brinch Petersen:* Acta Archaeologica, *vol. 47, 1976.* 25

11 Graph of fluctuating food resources compared with demographic optimum capacity. *After D. Clarke 1972.* 28

12 Survey diagram of the Danish Mesolithic period. *After E. Brinch Petersen 1973.* 31

13 Finds from the tanged-point techno-complex. *After A. Fischer in* Studies in Scandinavian Prehistory and Early History, *vol. 2 (in press).* 37

14 Maglemosian wooden arrows and spears. *After C.J. Becker 1945.* 41

15 Mesolithic fishing implements. *After E. Brinch Petersen 1979.* 47

16 Arrows and arrowheads from the Ertebølle culture. *Photo: The National Museum, Copenhagen.* 48

17 Mesolithic axes. *After E. Brinch Petersen 1979.* 48

18 Mesolithic wooden paddle. *After S.H. Andersen in* Antikvariske studier 4, 1980.   49

19 Danish Mesolithic chronology. *After E. Brinch Petersen 1973.*   63

20 Radiocarbon dates of the Danish Mesolithic period. *After E. Brinch Petersen 1973.*   64

21 Chronology of Mesolithic microliths and other lithic types. *After E. Brinch Petersen 1973.*   65

22 Survey diagram of human influence on vegetation in south Scandinavia. *After B. Berglund 1969.*   76

23 Survival chart from Swiss Neolithic communities. *After W. Scheffrahn 1967.*   82

24 Spatial distribution of Neolithic long dolmens. *After J. Bekmose 1978.*   86

25 Settlement pattern of Neolithic communities in eastern Jutland. *After T. Madsen 1978a.*   91

26 The two phases of the Neolithic Sarup complex on Funen. *After N.H. Andersen 1980.*   94

27 Plan of excavations at Toftum, Jutland. *After T. Madsen 1977.*   95

28 Hypothetical division into territories of the Neolithic settlement in the Sarup area, Funen. *After N.H. Andersen 1980.*   97

29 Neolithic flint axe from Sigerslev, Zealand. *Photo: The National Museum, Copenhagen.*   98

30 Flint mine at Hov, Jutland. *Photo: C.J. Becker.*   101

31 Situation of Danish chalk and limestone deposits. *After C.J. Becker 1951.*   102

32 Neolithic thin-butted ceremonial flint axes. *Photo: The National Museum, Copenhagen.*   105

33 Neolithic long barrow at Bygholm Nørremark, Jutland. *After P. Rønne 1979.*   112

34 Neolithic earth grave from Dragsholm, Zealand. *After E. Brinch Petersen 1974.*   118

35 Neolithic cult house at Herrup, Jutland. *After C.J. Becker 1969.*   121

36 Plough marks found under graves from the Neolithic TRB culture. *Drawing: Jørgen Jensen.*   122

37 Terminology used by E.R. Service and M.R. Fried. *After C.L. Redman 1978.*   127

38 Landscape of Bronze-Age type at Jægersborg Dyrhave, Zealand. *Photo: Jørgen Jensen.*   133

39 Climatic fluctuations during the last 5500 years. *After B. Aaby 1974.*   136

40 Distribution of the Late-Neolithic flint daggers. *After J. Jensen 1979b.*   140

41 Distribution of the Early-Bronze-Age graves. *After J. Jensen 1979b.*   141

42 Distribution of the Late-Bronze-Age graves. *After J. Jensen 1979b.*   142

43 Distribution of Bronze-Age finds in north-western Jutland. *After K. Kristiansen 1978a.*   145

44 Late-Neolithic house site at Myrhøj, Jutland. *After J. Aarup Jensen 1972.*   147

45 Early-Bronze-Age house site at Trappendal, Jutland. *After S.W. Andersen 1981.*   148

46 Reconstruction of Late-Bronze-Age longhouse excavated at Hovergårde, Jutland. *Drawing: Jørgen Jensen.*   149

47 Late-Bronze-Age settlement at Spjald, Jutland. *After C.J. Becker 1972a.*   150

48 Ard types of the Bronze Age. *Drawing: Jørgen Jensen.*   152

49 Wooden animal trap from Nisset Nørremose, Jutland. *Photo: The National Museum, Copenhagen.*   154

50 Ceremonial bronze axes from Egebak, Jutland. *Photo: The National Museum, Copenhagen.*   155

51 Weapons and ornaments from the Early Bronze Age, period II. *After Aner and Kersten, vol. 2, 1976.*   159

52 Weapons and ornaments from the Early Bronze Age, period III. *After Aner and Kersten, vol. 2, 1976.*   160

53 Central-European imported bronzes. *Photo: The National Museum, Copenhagen.*   164

54 Wheeled bronze cauldron from Skallerup, Zealand. *After Aner and Kersten, vol. 2, 1976.*   165

55 Typology of the Danish flint daggers. *After E. Lomborg 1973.*   171

56 The Egtved grave. Photo: *The National Museum, Copenhagen.*   172

57 The Borum Eshøj grave. *Photo: The National Museum, Copenhagen.*   172

58 Folding stool from Guldhøj, Jutland. *Photo: The National Museum, Copenhagen.*   173

59 Histogram indicating the amount of bronze found in Early Bronze Age graves (period II). *After K. Randsborg 1974b.*   174

60 Late-Bronze-Age hoard from Kertinge Mark, Funen. *Photo: The National Museum, Copenhagen.*   175

61 Ship motifs from the Late Bronze Age. *Drawing: Jørgen Jensen.*   177

62 Danish radiocarbon dates of the Middle Neolithic period. *After P.O. Nielsen 1977.*   184

63 Landscape of Iron-Age type at Røsnæs, Zealand. *Photo: Jørgen Jensen.*   194

64 Reconstruction of Iron-Age house at Lejre, Zealand. *Photo: Jørgen Jensen.* 205
65 Pre-Roman Iron-Age village at Grøntoft, Jutland. *After C.J. Becker 1966.* 207
66 Reconstruction of Iron-Age village at Hodde, Jutland. *Photo: The National Museum, Copenhagen.* 208
67 Distribution of Iron-Age settlements in the Ribe area, Jutland. *After S. Jensen 1980.* 211
68 Distribution of Iron-Age settlements in the Thy area, Jutland. *After S. Jensen 1976a.* 213
69 Iron-Age settlement at Vorbasse, Jutland. *After S. Hvass 1979.* 216
70 Development of the Iron-Age farmstead. *Drawing: Jørgen Jensen.* 217
71 Development of the three-aisled Iron-Age longhouse. *Drawing: Jørgen Jensen.* 219
72 Farmstead from the Vorbasse settlement, Jutland. *After S. Hvass 1976.* 219
73 Iron-Age settlements at Hodde and Vorbasse, Jutland. *Drawing: Jørgen Jensen.* 221
74 Iron-Age ard from Donneruplund, Jutland. *Drawing: Jørgen Jensen.* 225
75 Distribution of iron objects during period V-VI of the Late Bronze Age. *After F. Horst 1971.* 229
76 Schematic representation of the stages of prehistoric iron production. *After H. Hayen in* Oldenburger Jahrbuch 67, 1968. 230
77 The Gundestrup cauldron. *Photo: The National Museum, Copenhagen.* 237
78 The Dejbjerg wagon. *Photo: The National Museum, Copenhagen.* 238
79 Map of Europe north of the *Limes. After L. Hedager 1978c.* 239
80 Shortest distance to the *Limes* for finds of Roman imports. *After L. Hedager 1978c.* 240
81 Schematic representation of the commodities included in the exchange between the Roman Empire and the North. *After L. Hedager 1978c.* 243
82 Histogram indicating the proportions of wealth in graves from the Roman Iron Age. *After L. Hedager 1980.* 245
83 Distribution of Roman imports in eastern Denmark. *After L. Hedager 1980.* 246
84 The Hoby grave. *Photo: The National Museum, Copenhagen.* 247
85 The Nydam boat. *Drawing: Jørgen Jensen.* 251
86 Cross-sections of Iron-Age ships. *After O. Crumlin Petersen 1967.* 252

87 Pre-Roman neck ring from Væt, Jutland. *Photo: The National
    Museum, Copenhagen.*   258
88 The Hjortspring boat. *Drawing: Jørgen Jensen.*   259
89 Distribution of Danish Iron-Age weapon finds in bogs.   262
90 The number of objects in the weapon find at Ejsbøl, Jutland.
    After M. Ørsnes 1968.   263
91 Cross-section through the oldest part of the rampart at
    Dannevirke. *Drawing: Jørgen Jensen.*   265
92 The Kanhave canal, Samsø. *After Skalk 1960, 4.*   266
93 King Gorm's runic stone. *Photo: The National Museum,
    Copenhagen.*   273
94 The Tollund Man. *Photo: The National Museum, Copenhagen.*   280

Preface

This book was written to present a general survey of the prehistory of Denmark as it has emerged after the past decade of research. Up to the 1960s Danish archaeology was dominated by a handful of distinguished scholars: Sophus Müller, Johannes Brøndsted, Gudmund Hatt, P.V. Glob, and C.J. Becker. Moreover the discipline was strongly influenced by continental modes of thought, and the chronological problems were still the main focus of research.

However, in Denmark as in other European countries, the 1960s became a period of change. A wave of new theories did away with the old diffusionistic framework. Many scholars spoke of a crisis in the profession. But as elsewhere in the west, the 1960s also marked the beginning of a rich productivity in the field, and today we can speak of at least three contrasting theoretical perspectives in Danish archaeology: positivist, marxist and structuralist. Each one of them has been able to open up fruitful perspectives for future research.

These changes first developed after the publication of the last major survey of Danish archaeology to be translated for readers outside Denmark, Johannes Brøndsted's *Nordische Vorzeit* from 1960–3. It therefore seemed quite clear that both students and teachers in other countries would have need of a general introduction to the perspectives recently opened in Danish archaeology.

It is this need which the present book seeks to meet. To be sure, many of the conclusions are preliminary, because detailed, systematic and up-to-date studies are still required in many fields. Despite this lack, I have written the present book in the hope of providing a synthesis of the 10,000 years of Danish prehistory up to the early state formation of the Viking period.

This work could not have been written without the inspiration of many discussions with colleagues in Denmark and abroad, too numerous to be mentioned here. However, I owe special thanks to Professor Olaf Olsen, State Antiquary and Director of the National Museum of Denmark, who in 1975 encouraged me to write this book; to Professor J. Desmond Clark, University of California, Berkeley, who extended his generous hospitality to me during a stay in Berkeley in 1980; to Professor John Coles, University of Cambridge, who willingly offered advice in the preparation of this English edition; and finally to the Danish Research Council for the Humanities, which supported this project financially.

I also wish to thank my wife, Barbara Bluestone, who did the translation and without whose endless patience, support and linguistic help this work could not have been completed.

Jørgen Jensen 1982
The National Museum, Copenhagen

Introduction

Archaeology in Denmark

It all began in 1807, when the British army bombarded and burned down much of Copenhagen. Denmark found itself in the midst of one of the devastating wars of the Napoleonic period. This period also witnessed another sort of destruction. In the wake of the radical agricultural reforms of the 1780s terrible damage was wrought to thousands of prehistoric monuments in Denmark. New forms of land management led to the cultivation of regions which had not been ploughed for more than a thousand years. A profusion of buried treasures from heathen times was ploughed up from the soil – all while their hiding-places, the prehistoric monuments, were damaged.

In that catastrophic year 1807, this alarming situation led to the formation of a royal antiquities commission. The goal of this commission was primarily to save what could be saved from destruction and also to ascertain what remained of prehistoric monuments in the Danish countryside. With the formulation of this task, a new epoch was born not only in Danish archaeology but also in what later developed into European archaeology. For the first time ever in Europe, archaeology was defined as an independent discipline, focused upon prehistoric artefacts and monuments.

The next major step was taken in 1816, when the commission hired a prosperous young businessman, Christian Jürgensen Thomsen (1788–1865), to arrange its collections of prehistoric finds (Figure 1). Three years later, in 1819, the collections were presented to the public in an exhibition in which the 'antiquities' were arranged into three groups according to their material: stone, bronze and iron.

Up to 1830, C. J. Thomsen slowly developed the idea that this

Figure 1 Christian Jürgensen Thomsen (1788–1865), the creator of the three-
period system, the first technological evolutionary model in European prehistory. Drawn in 1846 by the Danish artist Magnus Petersen.

threefold division according to material was also a chronological
framework. Thus Thomsen created the three-period system with his
Stone, Bronze and Iron Ages, which became the first technological
evolutionary model in prehistory.

Thomsen's pioneering work was soon supplemented in many ways,
especially by his successor as director of the national collections, Jens
Jakob Asmussen Worsaae (1831–85). The years up to Worsaae's death in
1885 saw the founding of the entire institutional and theoretical
framework which has prevailed in Danish archaeology almost up to the
present. The National Museum in Copenhagen was founded; in addition a central registration of Danish prehistoric monuments, still one of
the essential tools for archaeological research, was established in 1873.
During these years there flourished in Copenhagen an archaeological

milieu, internationally oriented and open to related sciences as well as to amateurs. The same era saw the rise of cultural – historical diffusionism, the theoretical framework for Danish archaeology until the 1960s.

Up to the 1960s, the National Museum in Copenhagen was the focus of most archaeological activity in Denmark. The economic surge of the 1960s, however, also led to changes in the institutional structure of archaeology in Denmark. Some activities were centralized, others de-centralized and taken over by the growing number of local museums directed by professional archaeologists. A similar trend could be observed in the other Scandinavian countries. The 1960s and 1970s also saw the boom of the cities and the rapid growth of motorways, housing projects, pipe-lines, etc., all of which contributed to the widespread destruction of prehistoric monuments. Therefore one of the most significant archaeological events in Denmark during these years was the passing of a series of environmental laws under which all prehistoric monuments are protected. The term 'monument' embraces every trace of prehistoric man, be it grave, settlement or votive find. Protection of all archaeological sites in Denmark is thus ensured by law and has as a result become integrated in the long-range planning for the country as a whole. All observations of archaeological interest must be reported to the National Museum, the director of which is the leader of all antiquarian activities in Denmark.

A wide spectrum of archaeological research, including rescue excava-tions of prehistoric monuments, is carried out by three types of institutions in close co-operation: the National Museum in Copenhagen, the many smaller museums spread throughout the provinces, and the institutes of archaeology at the universities of Århus and Copenhagen.

The National Museum (Figure 2), the most venerable of these part-ners, possesses the most important prehistoric collections in Denmark. This institution is clearly a product of the liberal humanism espoused by the educated classes in the mid- and late nineteenth century. Like a number of other European museums, the National Museum was found-ed upon the vision of a grand all-inclusive universal repository. The First Department of the museum contains the prehistoric collection. Here, as we have mentioned, a unique central registration of all prehistoric finds in Denmark has been conducted since the late nineteenth century. The archives which are now in the process of being computerized include information about more than 125,000 localities. Thus they offer the natural foundation for all archaeological research in Denmark. The National Museum also houses a number of valuable laboratories for such studies as radiocarbon dating, pollen analysis, dendrochronology, etc. Other museums also contribute to the joint effort. About eighty

Figure 2 Prinsens Palæ (Palace of the Crown Prince) in Copenhagen. Built in 1742–4; it is now the main seat of the Danish National Museum.

provincial museums are officially recognized by the Danish state and twenty-two of them are directed by or include one or more university-trained archaeologists on their staff. Efforts to decentralize the system have increased the number of archaeological projects – especially rescue excavations – carried out by the local museums. Impressive archaeological collections are found in Ålborg, Århus, Haderslev and Odense.

The archaeological institutes at the universities of Copenhagen and Århus have flourished since the 1960s. Besides educating archaeologists, a process averaging six years, these institutions now also participate in research projects, often in conjunction with the National Museum or local museums. Although the institutes possess no collections, they do carry out excavations and finance much archaeological research in Denmark.

The work of these various archaeological institutions is co-ordinated by the Ancient Monument Board, established in 1977. This council was created to define guidelines for the research policy for all archaeological activity in Denmark.

The last twenty years have not only brought great changes in the external organization of Danish archaeology. There have been internal upheavals as well. Modern methods and new theoretical concepts have been introduced, and field work has been revolutionized by mechanization. Since the 1960s ambitious excavations of prehistoric settlements have been successfully completed. Entire village complexes spreading over several hectares have been uncovered, thus providing insight into the organization of prehistoric society to an extent which would have been inconceivable with the limited methods of earlier generations. These new methods have had a tremendous impact on our knowledge of, for example, the farming communities of the Iron Age. Nor has the size of the excavations been the only change. Novel excavation techniques have also entailed a wider application of scientific methods such as pollen analysis, radiocarbon dating, thermoluminescence dating, dendrochronology, etc. Equally vital developments have occurred in archaeological theory. Until the 1960s, the theoretical framework of Danish archaeology was based primarily upon diffusionistic thought from the nineteenth century. A highly mechanistic concept of cultural evolution prevailed. Evolution was viewed as a series of static phases succeeding one another as a result of invasion, climatic change, technological innovation and similar isolated factors.

In the 1960s, however, archaeologists struck out in new directions. Ecological approaches became ever more integrated into Danish archaeology. The study of man's environment became as essential as the study of his tools – somewhat later, social anthropology, particularly as practised in England and America, exerted a powerful influence. As in most western countries there was talk of a new archaeology which with more exact methods sought to determine the relationship between the various parameters in prehistoric cultural systems.

In the following account, an evolutionary perspective has been applied to the tremendous period stretching from the last Ice Age to the Vikings. This account is based upon the course of nature during the millennia following the last Ice Age. This natural process and the changes it caused in the resources accessible to man were of prime significance in determining the size of the population, its exploitation of the resources, and its social structure. In the next chapter we shall therefore attempt to trace the intimate bond which existed between man and his environment from the earliest communities of reindeer hunters to the late hunter-gatherer communities, the lives of which were completely transformed by the introduction of agriculture around the end of the fifth millennium BC.

Denmark, the bridge to the north

Perhaps it was on a winter day 12,000 years ago, at the end of the Ice

Age, when a human being gazed at the Danish landscape for the first time. It was a bare arctic land, sharp in its contours, cold and windy and with only a meagre tundra vegetation – just enough for herds of reindeer to find food here part of the year. These reindeer provided man with his first foothold in the arctic regions so far to the north. In pursuing and hunting these reindeer, man had taken the first step in what was to be 10,000 years of continuous human settlement in southern Scandinavia.

Throughout these many millennia, Denmark served as a bridge between central Europe and the Scandinavian peninsula. This continued to hold true when the land developed its present archipelago nature, about 7000 years ago. Its many islands and its shallow waters functioned as an effective link to the northernmost part of the continent.

The topography of Denmark bears witness to the fact that the land was only partially covered by the ice sheet during the last Ice Age, the Würm-Weichel glaciation. The margin of the enormous expanse of inland ice ran down through the centre of Jutland, dividing the young moraine from the old moraine landscape (Figure 3). West of the ice sheet, the edge of which formed what is today called the Main Stationary Line, there was, during the last Ice Age, an open arctic area. This was an old moraine landscape which had been created during the next-to-last Ice Age. Running water, rain, snow, wind and frost together formed its surface. Today this landscape is characterized by the so-called hill islands, the oldest feature in the Danish terrain. The gently rounded forms of these hill islands contrast greatly with the far bolder relief of the young moraine landscapes east of the Main Stationary Line. The old moraine landscape is devoid of the tunnel valleys, marginal moraine, lakes, hilly areas and undrained depressions which distinguish the young moraine landscape.

A modern traveller to west Jutland will see the hill islands rise up from the vast flatness of the outwash plains. These plains were the deposits of the meltwater rivers, sandy inland deltas created near the ice margin during the last glacial period. The outwash plains are cut by low river valleys; their flat surface is in places disturbed by circular hollows formed by subsidence when masses of dead ice melted. These hollows may be filled by lakes or bogs, those damp places which have meant so much in the prehistory of Denmark because of their remarkable preservative qualities. In north and east Denmark, the modern traveller encounters quite another sort of scenery. Here is the young moraine region with its dramatic relief. Yet in east Denmark as well, the rugged surfaces were gradually smoothed out by millennia of ploughing.

Young moraine landscapes in north and east Denmark are either hilly

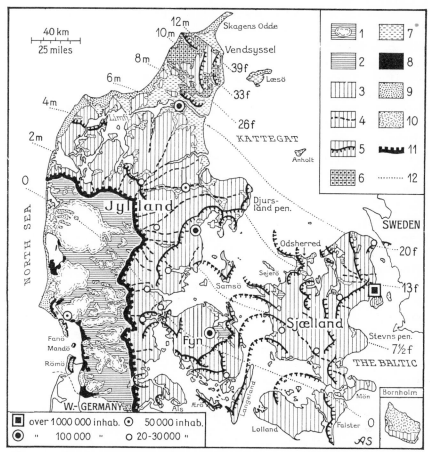

Figure 3 Geomorphological map of Denmark. 1. Old moraine landscape,
Riss-Saale glaciation. 2. Outwash plain, meltwater deposits from the Würm-
Weichsel glaciation. 3. Young moraine landscape, Würm-Weichsel glaciation.
4. Subglacial valleys with long lakes and bog depressions. 5. Significant
marginal zones, in many places forming the glacial series of landscapes:
central depressions separated by marginal moraine hills from the distally
placed outwash plains. 6. Late-glacial plateau, raised sea floor. 7. Marine
foreland. 8. Marsh plain. 9. Dune landscapes. 10. Granite landscape with
rocky coasts and joint valleys in Bornholm. 11. Main Stationary Line during
the Würm-Weichsel glaciation. 12. Isobases for the relative uplift of land since
the Litorina-Tapes transgressions.

or flat. During the last Ice Age, the hill country was created in the border
zone of the ice by the accumulation of moraine material. When the ice
moved forward, it pressed vast quantities of earlier-deposited material
together, sometimes in rampart-shaped ridges. These ridges consist of

particles of all sizes, from grains of clay to huge boulders. Today this marginal moraine has become a countryside of rounded hills hundreds of metres long. Here and there are rows of hills stretching kilometre after kilometre.

In contrast to the moraine hills, the moraine flats are normally formed where there is boulder clay. This type of terrain, exemplified by the area bordered by Copenhagen, Roskilde and Køge, is smoothly undulating. The relatively thin layer of moraine soil was left behind on an ice-eroded surface when the ice melted away 10,000 years ago. With their fertile soil and plane surface, the moraine flats are the finest agricultural land in Denmark today. Yet they were not cultivated until late in prehistory, due in part to the difficulties they presented to primitive tilling instruments. Furthermore, the moraine flats had to be laboriously drained before they could be cultivated to the extent they are now.

No matter where one travels in Denmark, the sea is always close at hand. In fact, no spot lies more than 50 kilometres from the shore. The 7000-kilometre-long coastline is marvellously varied. Places such as Møn, on Stevns in eastern Denmark, and Bulbjerg on the North Sea, boast cliff coasts carved in limestone rocks. Most of the other coasts are formed of glacial deposits, boulder clays and sand. Danish shores are usually flat and can be categorized either as beach-ridge shores or marshland shores. The former type evolves where the breaker zone sweeps in to the shoreline. Here a beach is formed of gravel and sand from the beach drift. These very wide flat shores are found along the North Sea, whereas the Baltic shores span only a few metres.

The marshland shore is found at sheltered spots such as the estuarine areas of inner bays and fjords. The south-west coast of Jutland, for example, is bordered by an almost unbroken marsh. Here, at their lowest-lying point, the outwash plains are submerged. Only here do we find a tidal range of any consequence, namely about 2 metres. Further north the tidal amplitude diminishes and in the inner Danish seas it is very slight.

The countryside of today has been moulded by man, chiefly over the past 200 years. Towards the end of the eighteenth century, radical agricultural reforms were carried out in Denmark. Land which had been untilled since the Middle Ages was reclaimed. Thus a sweeping transformation of the landscape was initiated. With it followed the dawning interest of the Romantic era in prehistoric monuments, an interest which led to the creation of Danish archaeology.

PART I

The hunters and gatherers
11,000–4200 BC

1

A changing environment

After the last Ice Age

During the Pleistocene, northern Europe underwent at least four waves of fierce, cold ice ages. During at least two of the warmer periods which intervened between the ice ages, man appears to have lived in Denmark. The oldest and best documented finds are man-made tools from Vejstrup Forest in Jutland. Through them we can trace the presence of man in Denmark more than 200,000 years back in time.

Unfortunately, our knowledge of the first appearance of man in Scandinavia is so scanty that it would be impossible to attempt to determine his behavioural patterns. Not until after the last Ice Age, the Würm-Weichsel, can we piece together a coherent picture of human evolution in Denmark.

Approximately 13,000 years ago began the climatic change which brought the last Ice Age to a close. During this glacial period, Denmark was completely covered by ice except for the western parts of Jutland. At Hald near Viborg, the edge of the ice made a sharp angle. From here it extended westwards towards Britain. To the south the ice margin extended down through mid-Jutland.

As the ice sheet retreated, vast quantities of meltwater began to flow out to the cold arctic sea, and where the ice had once lain, a barren landscape was now exposed. The most striking feature of the newly revealed land was the pale raw soil. This barren raw soil imparted to the landscape a remarkably light colour due to the fact that the soil contained no humus but much lime. Even where sparse vegetation gradually began to grow, the light colour predominated. Only after an exceedingly slow 'maturation' process lasting thousands of years was the light raw soil converted into dark fertile mould. When the ice disappeared, the land was, from a biological point of view, still young.

The first pioneer flora which spread over the barren earth, thus creating an open tundra, consisted in part of mountain avens (*Dryas octopetala*), which was conspicuous in the landscape with its ivory-white flowers on long stems. Here and there were white carpets of this flower. Dwarf willow (*Salix herbacea*), arctic willow (*Salix polaris*), dwarf birch (*Betula nana*) and sea buckthorn (*Hippophaë rhamnoides*) flourished, along with the now rare Öland rock rose (*Helianthemum oelandicum*) which tinted southern slopes yellow during the short arctic summer (Figure 4). All these immigrated pioneers were hardy and cold-tolerating. Many of them could survive under snow most of the year; all of them managed to blossom and produce seeds during the brief cool summer. These pioneer growths were characterized by their love of light and their preference for calcareous soils. During this period, the summer temperature averaged 8°–9°C.

Around 10,500 BC came one of the first brief warm phases which can so deeply disturb the delicately balanced arctic vegetation. The first Late Glacial warm phase is called the Bølling oscillation. During this short period, a park tundra developed in Denmark with light forests of birch in the warm areas. The open tundra still dominated in the cold north-facing or damp areas. The landscape became green in the summer, but the return of the night frost must have brought bright yellows and reds, followed by winter whiteness.

During the Bølling oscillation, the area which is now Denmark was freed of ice; but the mild temperature was only a brief respite. A new cold thrust around 10,000 BC (the Older Dryas) caused a major recession; the light pioneer forest was obliterated and once more the open tundra prevailed.

Then, several centuries later, a new warm phase known as the Allerød period began. Once more a park tundra grew up with birch (*Betula pubescens*) as the dominant tree. Quaking aspen (*Populis tremula*) and rowan (*Sorbus aucuparia*) also appeared together with juniper (*Juniperus communis*) and bird cherry (*Prunus padus*). The climate was so mild that presumably pine also grew.

During the Allerød period the south-eastern and north-western parts of the country contrasted sharply with one another. South-east Denmark now had a temperate climate with an average July temperature of 13°–14°C. Then around 9000 BC, a last sudden temperature drop (the Late Dryas) was felt over most of Europe north of the Alps. The climate became sub-arctic, the summer temperature sank to about 10°C. The inland ice ceased to thaw on the Scandinavian peninsula, and in Denmark trees very nearly stopped growing. The south was a park tundra, whereas in the north-west a wide open tundra dominated. The flora resembled that found today near the northern pine forest limit.

Animals as well as pioneer plants found their way to Denmark toward the close of the Ice Age. The reindeer was the characteristic tundra animal. In pursuit came its worst enemies: the wolverine and the wolf. Bison and wild horses grazed in the Late Glacial terrain, and there were also lemmings and blue hares. Fish of the Late Glacial waters included perch (*Perca fluviatilis*) and pike (*Esox lucius*).

During such mild periods as the Bølling and the Allerød, animal life grew increasingly varied. It was, from a modern viewpoint, a strangely mixed fauna. Tundra and steppe animals such as the reindeer, wild horse and bison still flourished in the milder environment. Now, however, the open forest vegetation attracted forest animals to the country. The newcomers included the now-extinct Irish elk (*Megaloceros giganteus*) and the common elk. The beaver, the brown bear and the lynx also arrived.

The Late Glacial ice sea was inhospitable to both flora and fauna. During cold periods the sea was frozen in the winter and filled with drift ice in the summer. However, whales and seals made their home in this ice sea. There are traces of the Greenland whale (*Balaena mysticetus*) and the killer whale (*Orcinus orca*); the ringed seal (*Pusa hispida*) and the walrus (*Odobenus rosmarus*) probably also lived in the glacial sea. Fish included the high arctic cod species *Gadus saida*. In warmer periods there was less drift ice. Along with the temperate mollusc fauna, new larger animals such as the rorqual (*Balaen optera physalus*) and the blue whale (*Sibbadus musculus*) also appeared. Arctic birds on the open sea included multitudes of long-tailed ducks (*Pagonetta glacialis*).

The extent of the land during the Late Glacial period is still not entirely known. At first northern Denmark was still heavily weighed down by the ice sheet masses. Northern Jutland consisted of a series of islands and the ice sea extended further eastwards, along the island of Læsø, roughly down to the present north coast of Zealand. The Baltic surface was still frozen. The land now freed from the weight of the ice gradually rose. But during the warmer periods the sea-level rose even faster then the land due to the influx of meltwater. In the end, it was the rise of the land which most influenced Denmark's geography. By the end of the Glacial period the land mass seen in Figure 6 had appeared.

This outline of the development of nature from the Late Glacial period and on through the millennia is based upon more than a century of research. Geological, pollen-botanical and zoological investigations have shed light on the migration of plants and animals to the land uncovered by the melting of the ice. Of especial importance is the relative

Figure 4 An open landscape covered with a hardy and cold-tolerating vegetation was the scene of the appearance of the first hunting groups to arrive in Denmark after the last Ice Age. The general impression may have resembled this landscape from the Tollund bog in central Jutland.

chronology of Danish vegetational history which has been described in botanist Knud Jessen's division of the pollen diagrams (Figure 5) into nine zones (I–IX). These zones can today be pinpointed chronologically by radiocarbon datings. In the main, the great drama of the development of the environment after the last Ice Age has been revealed. However, it still remains to identify the factors which set this drama into motion: the development of the climate and the soil, and not least of all man's influence on nature.

In the Late Glacial landscape just described, the first hunting communities appeared. Man's role during this period resembles that of the pioneer plants and animals. The lives of the hunting people were totally shaped by their marginal environment. Nor is it surprising that traces of the first reindeer hunters are so scarce. This reflects a tiny population, the size of which was proportional to the resources available. To be sure, the fauna of Denmark has probably never since been so varied as in the sunny Late Glacial period. But these resources were subject to extreme

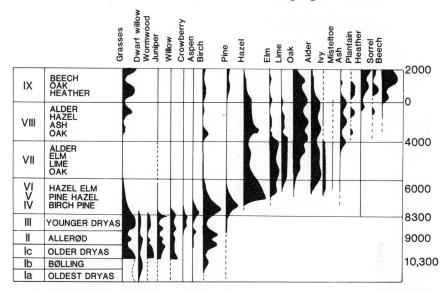

Figure 5 Pollen chart of the vegetational development in Denmark as described by botanist Knud Jessen in his division of the pollen diagrams into nine zones.

seasonal changes which determined both the size of the population and human behaviour. As will be shown, rising average temperatures in the subsequent period eased conditions for the hunting people and altered their existence.

The first continuous forest

Quite suddenly, around 8300 BC, the temperature rose drastically and in a short time the open park tundra was completely transformed. This period is termed the Pre-Boreal. Now a light and open birch forest spread over the terrain. The rapid rise in temperature encouraged the growth of trees such as aspen and birch which here and there had survived the cold period. Pine followed. All these trees were light-demanding pioneers and were the only species which survived long. They had already existed in the warm Allerød period. However, their development was irregular. Shortly after the first steep increase in temperature a brief cold period set in, delaying growth for some centuries. Then once more the temperature rose.

The continuous forest created by the warmer climate totally altered the animal life of the territory. The abundance of big game which had once roamed the open land now disappeared, to be supplanted by more localized species. The hunters' favourite game, the reindeer, vanished, and the aurochs and elk instead made the forest their home. Gradually red deer also became common in the light pioneer forest. Naturally, the presence of these meat-yielding animals strongly influenced the hunters' way of life.

During the Pre-Boreal, the land mass of Denmark looked completely different from today (Figure 6). It was then the northernmost tip of a large continent extending westward all the way to Britain. The climate was still cool, averaging about 15°C in July.

A new forest scene: the Hazel–Pine forest

After the light, open forest of the Birch–Pine period had endured for more than a thousand years, a new and more radical transformation of Denmark occurred about 7000 BC. As the summer temperature continued to rise trees appeared which later dominated the forest: oak

Figure 6 The relationship between land and sea about 8500 BC. A major part of the Scandinavian peninsula is still covered by the inland ice.

(*Quercus*), elm (*Ulmus*), hazel (*Corylus*), aspen (*Populus tremula*) and lime (*Tilia cordata*). Hazel, the first to migrate, now reigned in the forest together with pine. The appearance of hazel marks the beginning of the Boreal period. This tree thrives in the meagre shadow cast by a forest of birch, pine and aspen, where it also receives an ample quantity of sunlight. The underwood must have been rich in nuts, which became a vital supplement to the diet of the forest inhabitants.

In the Boreal hazel–pine forest, the large meat animals such as the aurochs and the elk still abounded. At the same time the red deer, the roe deer and the wild boar also became common. Compared with the wealth of game in the Late Glacial landscape, the forest of the Hazel–Pine period was nearly barren. In the poverty of its bio-mass, the Boreal forest can be compared to a desert or semi-desert. But from an ecological point of view, nature had evolved into a new stage of greater diversity and stability than before. Seasonal fluctuations in the availability of resources became less drastic. A broader spectrum of choice of existence now opened to the inhabitants of the land. The transformed environment had remoulded the life of the hunter communities. Most probably the population gradually increased due in part to a lesser dependence on seasonal variations in the access to food, the presence of large game animals, and the abundance of edible plant foods such as nuts, roots, bulbs, mushrooms, bark, fruits, plant juices, and many more. Although these plant foods have not yet been studied carefully, it is likely that gathering played an ever-increasing role in the life of human societies. In the following, the term 'hunters and gatherers' will refer to the societal form which prevailed from the Pre-Boreal period onward.

During the Boreal, Denmark was still much larger in area than it is today (Figure 7). But in both the Pre-Boreal and Boreal periods, the sea-level rose rapidly. The North Sea flooded over the land bridge between Jutland and Britain. One arm of the sea reached south of Britain, thus creating the Channel. The Baltic was turned into an enormous lake (the Baltic Ice Lake), the outlet of which was a wide river running through what is today the Storebælt. The land mass was at least one-fourth larger than modern Denmark. Today almost all the old coastlines are submerged.

The stable primeval forest

Warmth-loving trees immigrated to Denmark during the Boreal: first came hazel, later elm, ash (*Fraxinus*) and lime. No stable equilibrium among these trees existed. However, the forest slowly evolved toward

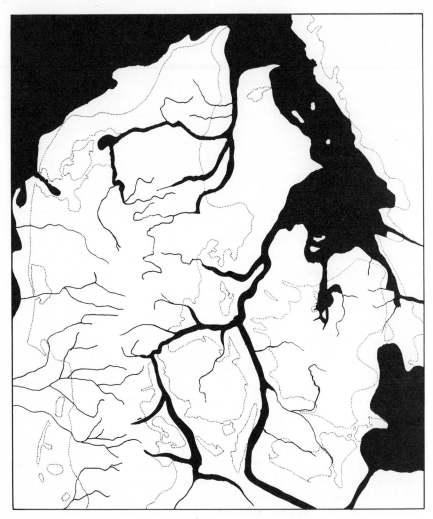

Figure 7 The relationship between land and sea about 7000 BC.

the stable primeval forest of the Post-Glacial warm period. By this is meant that the light-demanding pioneer trees of earlier times were gradually supplanted as shade trees gained ground. This process produced the equilibrium characteristic of a mature ecosystem. This period – the Allerød – saw the culmination of climatic development. Presumably the summer temperature was 2°–3°C higher than today.

At the commencement of the Hazel–Pine period, hazel competed with the pioneer trees and these were, in the long run, doomed.

Increasing warmth encouraged new shade trees to immigrate. Thus the forest moved into the phase of stable development which was to change the existence of its inhabitants so profoundly. By 6000 BC the stable primeval forest seems to have been formed. This stage was achieved at the same time as the climate changed from dry to humid; Denmark acquired an Atlantic oceanic climate. Doubtless the formation of the North Sea played its part in the increased humidity and warmth.

The dense primeval forest covering the land after 6000 BC was especially dominated by the lime, but elm and oak were also highly visible in the forest. The most striking feature of the stable primeval forest was its dense canopy. As undergrowth was relatively sparse, big game was afforded a poor selection of food. Aurochs and elk gradually died out and red deer and roe deer also decreased in number. However, the wild boar, which seeks its food in the moist forest floor, apparently survived undisturbed. In general it seems that the decrease in the bio-mass is sometimes exaggerated. A number of factors indicate that swift and synchronous alternations between dense and sparse vegetation could occur over large areas comprising whole stands of trees. Cyclic regeneration in the forest did not take place in isolation but over large areas covered by a whole stand of trees of the same age which had simultaneously been toppled by a storm. Thus the interior of the forest always included large glades which offered favourable conditions for many of the food plants of the big forest game. On the whole, however, the interior forest shows low productivity and low diversity. It is thus hardly capable of supporting year-round settlements even on a minor scale.

Out by the coasts and around the numerous inland lakes, swampy areas and streams, living conditions were much more favourable. Here the vegetation and fauna were far more richly varied than in the forest (Figure 9). Abundant sunlight provided a basis for fertile plant growth and teeming animal life. In time this situation became even more important for the population of the country.

The far north of the Scandinavian peninsula was still locked by enormous quantities of ice from the Ice Age. To the south, however, the increasing warmth continued to release great quantities of meltwater and the ocean rose. In Denmark this meant that the rise of the sea during the Atlantic period (the Litorina transgression) obliterated the coastline of the Boreal period. The land shrank considerably in size, losing an area equivalent to about one-fourth that of present-day Denmark. But what the land lost in area, it gained in an overwhelmingly long coastline. The Danish coast now consisted of deep fjords, sheltered coves and numberless small islands close to the coast (Figure 8).

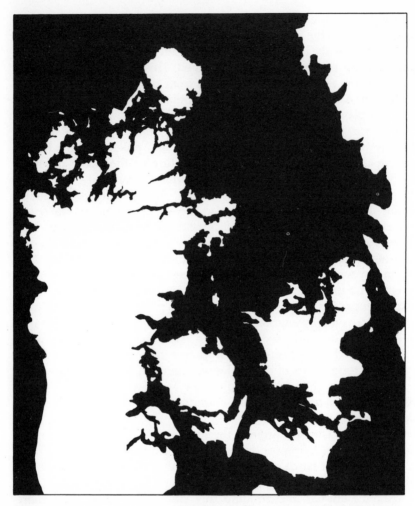

Figure 8 The relationship between land and sea about 4500 BC.

This coastal zone created the setting for a range of resources never before equalled. The high summer temperature, which resulted in a high water temperature, together with the fact that coastal erosion added many minerals to the sea, were among the factors which made the coastal zone so productive biologically.

From the viewpoint of cultural history the rise of the stable climax forest meant a basic change, as yet not entirely clarified, in the ways of adaption of the hunter–gatherer communities. A shift in the population balance may have been the result, and even if in the course of the

Figure 9 In the High Atlantic period, the Danish estuaries and the areas immediately adjacent provided living opportunities for the hunter-gatherer communities almost all year round. This type of landscape can still be found at some of the smaller Danish islands, here the island of Ormø in southern Denmark.

Atlantic virgin-forest period man made an apparently subtle adaption to the new living situation – first and foremost through an intensified exploitation of the marine zone – it can hardly be doubted that in the long run the environmental changes provoked a number of profound technological and social changes. One of the most radical changes in the living conditions of the prehistoric society began to make itself felt at the end of the fifth millennium BC: prehistoric society was slowly becoming agrarian.

Man and the ecosystem

As we have now seen, a number of remarkable environmental changes took place in Denmark in the interval between the close of the Ice Age and the end of the fifth millennium BC. The summer temperature rose from about 9°C to over 18°C – this meant a transition from a sub-arctic to a temperate climate. The summer temperature rose steadily, although it was marked by a number of small fluctuations (Figure 12). The earliest fluctuations had a notable effect on the development of the environment. In a sub-arctic climate even slight fluctuations in the average temperature may result in catastrophic changes of living conditions for both plants and animals.

Through the nearly 7000-year-long period discussed here, the Danish landscape was drastically transformed. It evolved from an open tundra vegetation to a dense stable virgin forest. Ecologically, this transformation can be termed a transition from a young ecosystem to a mature one, and the difference between the two extremes in the development was very great indeed. The young ecosystem, the tundra landscape, was exploited dynamically by a number of animal and plant species which in a short time had spread a large population throughout the area. There were, for example, plants which possessed a tremendously effective ability to spread, rapid growth and early sexual maturity, but also a relatively brief life span. This sort of ecosystem is characterized by rapid growth and high production – but it is unstable and provides poor protection for plants, animals and man. It may be seen as a system which pays high interest from a very small capital. From a biological viewpoint the young ecosystem invests in rapid growth, high production and large quantity.

In contrast, there is the mature ecosystem, which we encounter in the dense stable virgin forest which covered the country around 5000 BC. The mature ecosystem is characterized by so-called equilibrium species. For example, there are plants with a poor and ineffective ability to spread, slow growth and late sexual maturity; but in compensation they can grow very old. The equilibrium species creates a very balanced ecosystem, in which each species has its place, the boundaries of which are determined by the ecological adaptability and competitive capacity of the species. The mature ecosystem is thus characterized by great variation and stability. Due to its uninterrupted development, the mature ecosystem is adapted in all ways to the given physical–chemical conditions. It is therefore tremendously stable and well-protected from disturbances caused by natural forces. The amount of organic material produced in the ecosystem is consumed by the system itself, so that from a human viewpoint the mature ecosystem is not very productive. It invests in itself. In contrast to the young ecosystem, the mature ecosystem might be said to have a large capital but to pay little interest. In return, its range of variation is very wide.

Understanding of the development of early human societies in Denmark must be founded upon knowledge of the natural process sketched above. As will be shown, the development of the prehistoric communities was not controlled by any one factor. The decisive element was the interplay of the many factors, an interplay which was complicated and based upon mutual dependence. From an ecological viewpoint the growth of the human communities can be described as a process in which an ever larger part of the total energy flow of the ecosystem was channelled through the cultural system. To stimulate this development, human societies employed a multitude of means. The result was usually a growing labour input per unit of food gained. It is this development, the increase of the labour input of the prehistoric societies, which we shall now attempt to trace.

2
The hunting population

Fertility and mortality

The palaeodemographic material which we possess from the prehistoric hunter–gatherer communities is still very scanty. From Denmark and south Sweden together, about thirty individuals in all may with certainty be ascribed to the period. Denmark, however, has yielded one particular find which can give some idea of the mortality of the hunter population up to the introduction of agriculture. This is the find from Bøgebakken at Vedbæk, excavated in 1975 (S.E. Albrethsen *et al.*, 1976). Here a little cemetery from the end of the sixth millenium BC was found to contain twenty-two individuals. Four of these were newborn babies and one was about one year old. The ratio between the number of dead infants and dead adults is thus 5:17. However, this hardly gives a correct impression of infant mortality, which was most probably even higher, as the number of children's graves is hardly representative. Other investigations of prehistoric populations (G. Acsádi and J. Nemeskéri, 1970) indicate that an infant mortality of about 35 per cent or more is not uncommon.

At the cemetery in Vedbæk, of the seventeen individuals whose age could be determined, eight died before they attained the age of 20 years. This high figure is hardly surprising. Until late in historical times, mortality in the age group up to 20 years old was 50 to 60 per cent. This means that only about 40 per cent of the living-born individuals survived beyond 20 years of age.

Among these survivors, moreover, there was a great difference between men and women. At Bøgebakken there were nine adult men; five of them were over 40 years of age, one was 25–35 and the age of the others cannot be determined. Of the women, two died around 20 years

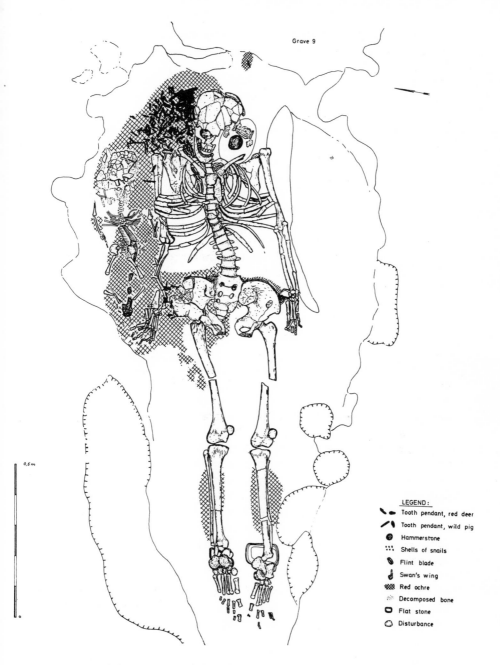

Grave 9

LEGEND:

- Tooth pendant, red deer
- Tooth pendant, wild pig
- Hammerstone
- Shells of snails
- Flint blade
- Swan's wing
- Red ochre
- Decomposed bone
- Flat stone
- Disturbance

0,5 m

Figure 10 Mesolithic grave at Bøgebakken, Vedbæk, northern Zealand. Woman buried with a new-born infant, *c.* 5000 BC.

old, three were over 40 years old, and the ages of two cannot be determined. The two young women probably exemplify the higher female mortality which can be observed in most prehistoric populations. This figure ranges up to 40 per cent higher than that of men and must represent the hard physical burden which childbirth must have been. The cemetery at Bøgebakken illustrates this in a striking way: two of the young women were buried together with their newborn babies (Figure 10).

Although the material from the hunter–gatherer society is slight, it can still give us an impression of the mortality rate. A population with such narrow chances of survival can of course grow only very slowly. Population increases are the result of a complicated interplay of many physiological and culturally determined factors.

While the above-mentioned observations on mortality seem to be representative for prehistoric hunter–gatherer communities, the fertility of the prehistoric population is far more of a puzzle. By fertility is meant the actual reproduction of the population, when the maximum reproductive capacity of a woman is considered together with the physiological and cultural factors which influence the birth rate.

With regard to the maximum reproductive capacity of women very little is known. Present-day societies with a very high fertility can, for example, be encountered in minority groups in North America, where on the average a woman gives birth to ten children. The theoretically possible figure is probably considerably higher. It is, however, impossible to form a well-founded idea of the figures for the prehistoric population. The only alternative is to refer to studies of present-day hunter–gatherer communities. In these communities the average number of children born is frequently reduced to five or six due to prolonged breast-feeding, physiological control and abortion. This figure is further reduced to from three to five children by infanticide and similar culturally determined measures. A natural infant and child mortality further reduced this figure probably by 20–50 per cent. Finally, about 5 per cent of the surviving individuals are believed to have been killed during childhood as a result of warlike activities.

The variables which determine the birth rate in a hunter–gatherer community are thus both physiological and cultural in nature. The physiological control factors are relatively easy to describe. They usually derive from the fact that the strongly seasonally determined food situation easily creates crises which result in less robust children; for example, in these periods children are deprived of sufficient nourishing milk and therefore die more easily. Poor food also leads to more birth abnormalities; fluctuations in the quantity of resources demand more labour, which in turn causes more miscarriages and unsuccessful births. The physiological factors are thus dependent upon the quantity of resources and are clearly a contributing factor in limiting extreme fluctuations of population size.

Meanwhile, many observations indicate that another set of control factors helps prevent population crises in the hunter–gatherer society. In the low-technology society, population growth results first in a certain increase in the quantity of food per individual, in so far as this is possible. This increase takes place because normally a more productive technology will come into function. However, if the population exceeds this demographic optimum, a number of culturally conditioned measures for restricting the birth rate will come into play: infanticide, for example.

However, the demographic optimum most often lies far below the number which the territory is able to carry. An exploitation of only 20–30 per cent of the maximum carrying capacity is not uncommon. It should also be added that this sort of population balance is often maintained by a daily labour input of 2–4 hours per individual. To illustrate this, the hypothetical situation set out in Figure 11a shows how the quantity of resources can fluctuate over an 80-year period within a given region, here exploited by a hunter–gatherer community. Figure 11b shows the total amount of resources within the same area over a similar length of time. It is here evident that the demographic optimum of about fourteen families is a good deal lower than the number of families able to survive by exploiting the maximum carrying capacity of the territory.

In later years, it has frequently been observed that hunter–gatherer communities, at least those in temperate and tropical zones, are adapted to their resource situation, often with a wide margin of safety. With regard to the hunter–gatherer populations in prehistory the temperate areas' abundant production of plant food has often been forgotten – though in fact this production may have given the hunter–gatherer communities the opportunity of adaption with a wide margin of safety. To some degree this sort of adaption may have allowed fluctuations in population size without the danger of destroying the economic system. Such a situation is thought to have existed during most of the Mesolithic period in Denmark. Here, however, a crisis apparently arose about the fifth millennium BC. Probably as a result of this crisis the agrarian economy was introduced.

From a biological point of view, this situation is illustrated in the so-called Liebig's law of minimums. The biologist Justus Liebig (1803–73) postulated that the degree of an organism's growth is determined

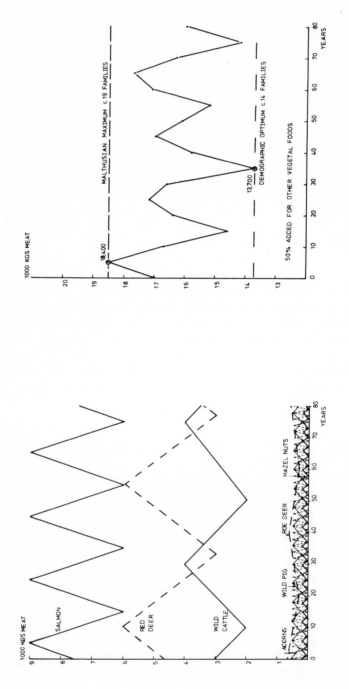

Figure 11 Hypothetical representation of how food resources in a forest area can fluctuate over an 80-year period (left). The graph (right) shows the total amount of resources compared with the demographic optimum capacity.

by the weakest link in the chain of essential life factors: plants, for example, are dependent upon the amount of water, light, nutrients, and so on. Applying this concept to human societies, it is implied that the minimum of food resources, including seasonal variation, determines the population size within a given territory.

Of course, insight into population problems in human society is not achieved by simple analogy with biological laws. The factors which catalyse the control measures must also be clarified. In relation to the hunter–gatherer communities, these measures are far from clear, but it has been indicated that the area per individual, the space between various groups, the amount of food per individual, the distance covered to obtain food and the intervals between the moving of settlements are factors which contribute to trigger off control measures. In particular the amount of labour per individual seems to be of decisive significance in establishing cultural norms for population control. It has been mentioned that the large burden of work placed upon women by most hunter–gatherer societies is one of the most efficient means of preventing uncontrolled population growth. Women's work often includes gathering great amounts of food, fetching water, collecting firewood, taking care of children, preparing food, transporting possessions when the dwelling is moved, and so on. This very burden puts a severe strain on a woman and may provoke, for example, infanticide, sexual withdrawal or miscarriage. Thus the sexual division of labour may very well have had this function in prehistoric hunter–gatherer societies.

How many were there?

We have now listed a number of factors which may have helped maintain the population balance, that is, an adaption to the food situation in Mesolithic Denmark. These remarks have been made because archaeological explanations are often based upon the theories of T.R. Malthus (1766–1834). A frequent assumption is that by itself a population will expand to the maximum which the environment can support. This sort of growth will result in a minimum of resources per individual, which in turn leads to crises resolvable only by war, epidemics, famine or the introduction of a new technology. In contrast to this viewpoint, newer population studies seem to have shown that in hunter–gatherer societies there is often a surplus of resources per individual. The implication is that the population problem can only be understood by studying the means by which the hunter–gatherer communities prevent over-exploitation of their territories.

As shown above, the ecological system in Denmark underwent

profound changes between 11,000 and 4200 BC. These changes were primarily caused by rising summer temperatures and the consequent modifications in fauna and vegetation, as well as the shifting balance between land and sea. The rises of sea-level in the Atlantic period, for example, may very well have resulted in increased population pressure, quite simply because the accessible land area was diminished. The following pages will attempt to illustrate how man responded to these changes. But first it is necessary to consider a few archaeological estimates of the relative population size during the period.

The population curve shown in Figure 12 is partially based on the number of known finds. It is therefore quite hypothetical, as the number of finds is always dependent upon the intensity of research devoted to a given region. The find quantity is also determined by the focus of the study. Thus the population curve shown here can only be regarded as a hypothetical tool based on a combination of demographic, scientific and archaeological evidence.

For the period up to c. 7500 BC, the population curve shows a number of fluctuations separated by long, seemingly empty periods. This can hardly mean that the country was uninhabited in these latter periods, but only that a low population density existed. After 7500 BC, there is a continuous rise in the curve, which culminates around 6500 BC; thereafter the curve is stabilized for a longer period before the last upward swing around 4700 BC, the period preceding the introduction of agriculture.

This graph depicts only relative population development in Denmark. No precise idea of the absolute population size can be gained, although some attempts have been made. One was made by J. Troels-Smith (1955) who compared the Palaeolithic hunters of the Late Glacial to present-day reindeer hunters living in northern Canada (Barren Grounds) in natural conditions resembling those of Late Glacial Denmark. Troels-Smith's line of thought is as follows: the Canadian Eskimos live with a population density of 0.003 per square kilometre – 'if we imagine that a ƀimilar number of people lived here in Denmark in the Late Glacial, this would correspond to about 120 people divided into 25–30 families; in other words, Denmark was divided among about 30 active hunters.'

The other alternative was suggested by J.G.D. Clark in 1975. Over the roughly 70,000 km² large area which in Late Glacial times encompassed Scania, Denmark and Schleswig-Holstein, Clark estimates that about 330,000 reindeer could live. He further estimates that to maintain an average family unit 500 reindeer per year are required. That is, that number of reindeer could support a population of about 660 family units

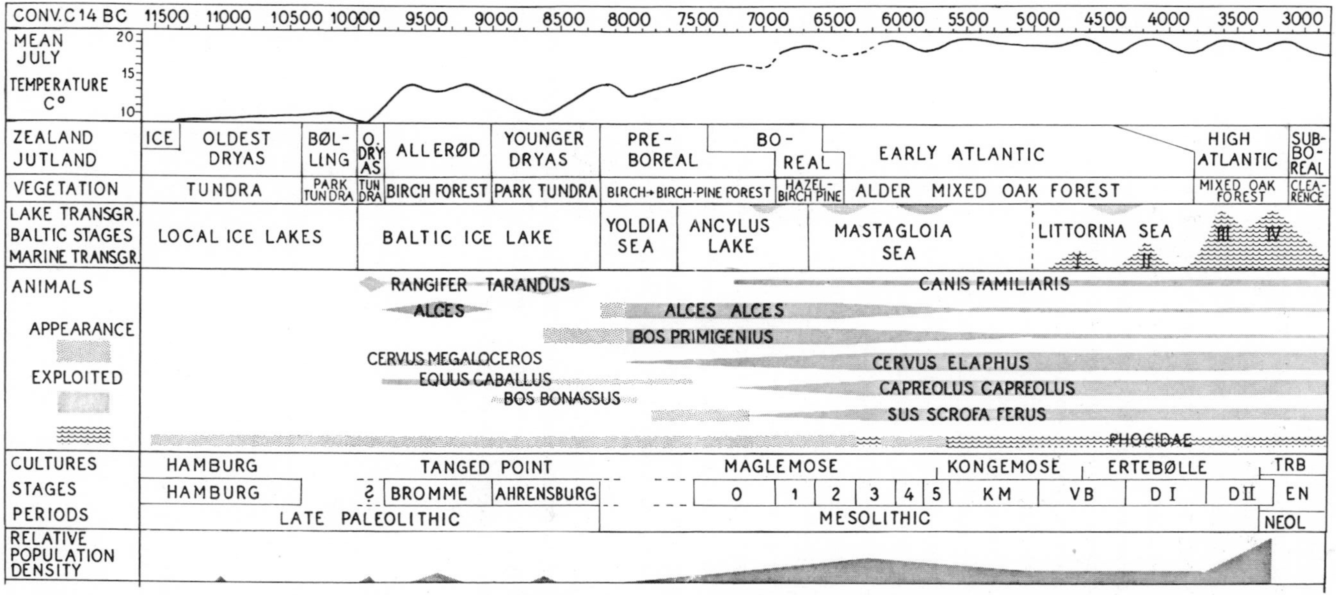

Figure 12 Survey diagram of the Danish Mesolithic period.

or 3300 individuals. Clark further suggests that the reindeer hunters lived in groups of three or four family units, which is to say that the entire area was exploited by roughly 165–220 'micro-bands'. Finding the common denominator of these calculations, we have a population ranging from 120 to 1700 individuals within what is today Denmark. It ought to be noted that J.G.D. Clark's calculations operate with a maximum exploitation of the carrying capacity of the region. As mentioned, this degree of exploitation seems improbable, so the estimate of 1700 individuals is doubtless too high.

With the widening of the food spectrum in the subsequent millennia, it becomes far more difficult to estimate how large a population the Danish territory could carry; knowledge of both the resource situation and the territorial exploitation of the hunter–gatherer societies is still sadly deficient. For the Boreal period in Denmark, a population density of about one per 20–50 km^2 has been suggested. For the Atlantic period the figures have been set even lower due to the presumed gradual decline of the bio-mass in the Atlantic climax forest. Unfortunately, no attempts have been made to determine the extent of the accessible available marine and terrestrial resources. Yet comparison with modern statistics on the quantity of big game such as red deer, roe deer and wild pig in various forest regions in the Northern hemisphere (P. Mellars, 1975) yields noticeably higher figures than suggested above. A population density of about one per 5 km^2, that is, about 8000 individuals within the Danish territory, does not seem unreasonable. This figure can probably be pushed even higher, as the calculations are based only on how much big game is shot yearly; neither fishing nor gathering of plant foods has been taken into consideration.

3
Subsistence and settlement

Mobility and territory

Investigation of man's habitat in south Scandinavia in the interval
between the melting of the ice and the beginning of agriculture seems to
show that before the High Atlantic period no single ecological zone
offered sufficient resources to provide enough food for a year-round
population group. Consequently, the hunter–gatherer societies had to
exploit not one but several ecological zones. Only in this way could they
alleviate the risk of food shortage during the critical months of the year.
An understanding of the prehistoric hunter–gatherer communities is
therefore dependent upon the extent to which it can be ascertained how
the annual territory was used season after season and what size the
hunter–gatherer groups had in the various seasons. Knowledge of these
conditions is also necessary in understanding not only the material
culture but also the organization and structure of the population of
Denmark in the millennia under discussion.

Theoretically there are many possible ways of adaption which a
hunter–gatherer community can choose. Two of these ways in particular may apply to the Danish territory in the Palaeolithic and Mesolithic
periods:

1 The base camps were moved throughout the year according to
  seasonal and ecological variations leading to the formation of an
  annual migration circuit.
2 The base camps were permanently placed in proximity to different
  ecological zones. Thus the inhabitants could exploit several biotopes
  by sending off smaller foraging units for shorter periods.

As yet our knowledge of the strategy of the hunter-gatherers in the centuries after the melting of the ice is still too limited to allow for firm conclusions. In the long perspective, however, the period up to the introduction of agriculture seems to have witnessed a gradual transition from the first alternative to the second.

In learning how the hunter–gatherer societies adapted to their physical environment the study of territorial conditions of course gains great significance. A hypothetical model has been constructed by J.G.D. Clark (1975) who distinguishes four different types of territory. The first is the territory which is exploited from the single base camp. Of course the extent of this territory cannot be determined generally. If hunting people move on foot alone, their radius will hardly exceed a walk of a couple of hours, about 10 kilometres. However, if boats or other means of transportation such as sledges or skis are used, then naturally the radius is enlarged.

The second type of territory is comprised of the area which is covered by the mobile community in the course of a single annual migration circuit. As already mentioned, before the end of the Mesolithic there was probably no ecological zone in Denmark which had sufficient available resources to secure food for a year-round population group. The hunter–gatherer societies may have moved periodically to exploit the seasonally determined foraging opportunities. This may have held true for much of the Boreal period, for example. Sometimes, such as in a winter with heavy rain or snow, the base camps must have remained at the same site for months. In such periods the group very likely increased in size. At other times of the year, the moves apparently were frequent. The group size may thus have diminished, so that a single nuclear family may have foraged alone.

The third type of territory is somewhat more intangible. It is called the social territory. This concept is based upon the realization that the exchange of goods and probably also of women plays a decisive role in most low-technology societies. Analogy with present-day societies also indicates that this sort of exchange is based upon permanent structured patterns. The exchange of goods often branches out among common descent groups, a circumstance to which we will return later. Archaeologically the social territory may be characterized as the area which the individual settlement group draws upon for raw materials and finished products. The social territory often corresponds to that which most Danish archaeologists term a cultural group.

The last territorial unit, and the most all-encompassing, is called in archaeological terminology a culture, a techno-territory or a techno-complex. This is a group of social territories sharing many common features of subsistence and economy. In the Late Glacial period, for example, most of the north European lowland constitutes a single techno-territory.

As yet the picture of man's first presence in Denmark is very unclear. A very small population leaves only a very scanty archaeological record. At the same time various geological conditions make the archaeological material appear very fragmented. In the following the evaluation of this scanty material will be approached from the viewpoint that the adaption of subsistence to environmental conditions determines the population size, the character of the settlement, the extent of the territorial units, and the relationship between these groups. In other words, the basis upon which the relationship between man and nature is to be studied is the human labour process; in the widest sense of the words, society's means of production. The social structure of the hunter–gatherer society is thus the result of a complicated interplay of factors such as natural food production, population size, and means of production.

Reindeer hunters

The Late Glacial imposed identical ecological conditions upon the vast north European lowland. Common features of the territory included the vegetation, the climate – and above all the reindeer herds which during most of the era provided the major source of protein for the mobile hunting societies which found their subsistence in the open tundra landscape. In warmer periods the number of species of wild animals was most probably changed. The food potential of the hunting communities was thus expanded; yet reindeer hunting remained essential throughout the Late Glacial period.

As a result of this ecological homogeneity many closely related hunting communities can be traced throughout the northern European lowlands in the Late Glacial period. Most likely the society functioned at such a low level of integration that single families and individuals could move over vast areas and at different times could merge into various groups, as known from present-day arctic hunting communities. This may explain the homogeneity which characterizes the material equipment of the Late Glacial society.

In a sub-arctic hunter society, where the main staff of life is reindeer hunting, the need for protein may result in a number of different hunting strategies. These differences are based upon the unique behaviour of the reindeer. Reindeer live in such large herds that they must constantly seek new grasslands. Normally a hunting community including women and children cannot follow the herds for longer periods, as the animals simply move too quickly during their seasonal migrations. This and other hunting problems are resolved by the hunter communities in diverse ways. Often they are only seasonally dependent on reindeer, as the hunting of sea mammals, for instance, may yield an alternative source of food. Elsewhere, fishing in inland waters is the modifying factor. Finally there is the possibility that year-round reindeer hunting remains the primary source of food. The hunting community then covers a wide-ranging annual territory, not by following a single herd, but by moving the camp when supplies run low and furthermore by supplementing the production from more incidental sources. This practice involves great risks for food crises and requires in all cases that the hunter groups be quite small. All of these possibilities must be weighed in the evaluation of the first human colonists which during the Late' Glacial arrived at the territory which is today Denmark.

Probably the oldest bands which moved around in what is today Denmark belonged to what is in archaeological terminology called the Hamburg culture, which most likely had already appeared in the Bølling period. In recent years the hunting strategy of these groups has been re-evaluated to some extent (see, for example, J.G.D. Clark, 1975). The northernmost settlements from the period are found near the Danish-German border. These settlements were once thought to be camps established during the summer hunts for the reindeer herds which grazed near the edge of the ice in the warm season. But this picture may have to be altered. Several factors indicate that the seasonal migrations of the reindeer were actually quite the opposite. In the winter months the snow in the northernmost part of the lowland was not deep. Thus the reindeer herds probably sought the north in the winter. Consequently the excavated settlement sites must be interpreted as settlements from which great quantities of reindeer were hunted in the cold season during their migration northward. At this time of the year, the meat could be frozen, so the hunting peoples could have remained at the same place all winter. With the coming of spring, the southward reindeer migrations were also exploited. Soon afterwards, the camp was abandoned and the hunters moved southwards, probably all the way down to the central German highland regions, where an open vegetation of birch and pine comprised the fringes of the forest.

In the following centuries the traces of the hunter communities' presence in Denmark are scattered and unrelated. First around 9700 BC – in the Allerød period – with the beginning of the so-called tanged-point techno-complex, the finds again become more informative (Figure 13). The warm climate of the Allerød period and the consequent change in the flora and fauna of the land doubtless resulted in changes in the subsistence strategy of the hunting communities: in colder periods reindeer comprised the sole source of food, whereas in the Allerød

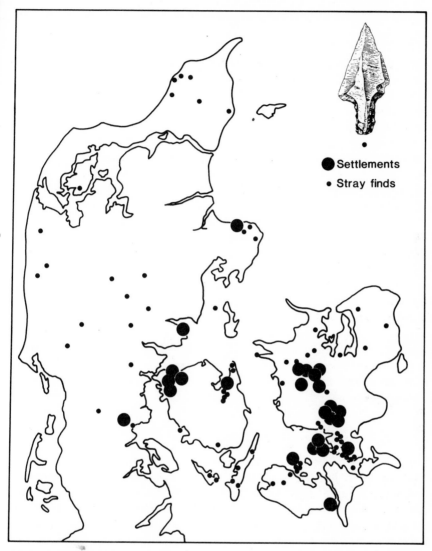

Figure 13 Stray finds and settlements from the tanged-point techno-complex.

period there was a much more varied selection of game – and also of plant foods. Yet the size of the group at the known sites, all of which were seasonal settlements, continued to be quite small. Probably the group consisted of only a single nuclear family. Of course, in certain seasons groups of nuclear families might live together. Perhaps they did so in the coastal zones during the winter.

Exactly how the hunting people in the Allerød period adapted their food strategy to the reindeer herds and at the same time exploited alternative food sources is still unclear. Coastal capture of sea mammals such as seals (through holes in the ice) may be one possibility. Stranded whales may also have turned up now and then, but there is simply no evidence for this as the coastal zone from that era is now submerged. Inland fishing may well have been practised, to judge by the location of the settlement sites in the terrain.

With the final phase of the Late Glacial, the Younger Dryas, the climate grew colder and once again the reindeer became the sole land mammal of any significance. Once again a transformation of the subsistence strategy may be presumed to have taken place, a transformation resembling that which characterized the earlier cold periods. It is true that only scattered finds from this period are known from the present-day Danish territory, but in Schleswig-Holstein the finds are more informative. As a whole they give the impression of a hunting culture which by means of seasonal migrations expertly exploited all opportunities for hunting reindeer. Among other things there is unmistakable evidence of the systematic selection of reindeer bulls as opposed to cows. The settlement sites still indicate a minimal group size, at least from the autumn to the early spring months, when the hunters probably moved up to Denmark. We are here still dealing with a society so open in character, at such a low level of integration, that single families and individuals could move over vast areas – now and again merging into various groups.

Hunters and gatherers of the Boreal period

The Post-Glacial period created changes in the flora and fauna which gradually transformed the lifeways of the first colonists. The resource spectrum became more varied as a result of a warmer climate. The reindeer, which had previously been the primary food source of the hunting communities, disappeared and was replaced by a wide range of animal species. As the newly immigrated animals were for the most part animals accustomed to living in smaller groups and collectively suited to a broader range of local environments in contrast to the migrating flock animals of earlier times, the social behaviour of the hunting people was affected to no small degree.

The archaeological record from the beginning of the Post-Glacial period is still rife with gaps. But from the end of the eighth millennium BC the sources multiply, so that through the seventh millennium a picture of the hunter–gatherer communities emerges with greater

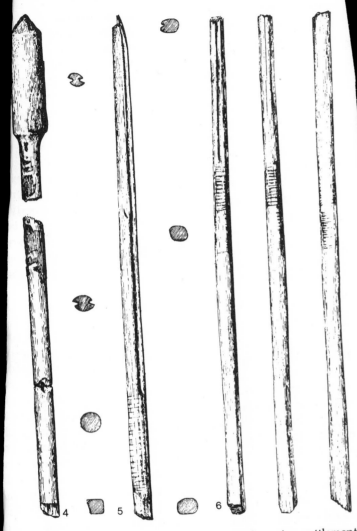

ooden arrows and spears found at the Maglemosian settlement
d IV, Zealand. Both arrows and spears have furrows intended for
of flint microliths.

put forward in older archaeological literature, we must
at the inland regions were also exploited to some degree.
as of the all-dominating role of the coastal zone for the
therer communities are due in some degree to a onesidedness
by the selection of sites chosen for excavation by earlier

clarity. The cultural region in which the hunting peoples in Denmark
were integrated expanded in comparison to that of the Late Glacial
period. In archaeological literature this territory or techno-complex is
termed the Maglemose culture. For nearly 1500 years there was a
striking unity in subsistence form and technology over much of the great
north European lowland, the area which today includes England,
Denmark, central and southern Sweden, northern Germany and parts
of northern and western Poland. In all, this region covered about
300,000 km^2. To be sure, the hunting communities varied in behavioural
forms within this vast region. The seasonally determined migrations of
the communities were of course intimately related to the meat animals
which still comprised the chief source of protein – and in fact the
movements of these animals in the terrain were determined in great part
by the topography of the country. In this regard there is a clear-cut
difference between a lowland region such as Denmark and a region with
more distinct surface relief such as England. Yet although certain
differences in the seasonal pattern of the hunting peoples are evident,
the material is too meagre to permit sweeping generalizations.

The same uncertainty also holds true of attempts to define the annual
territory. Most often, the hunter–gatherer communities of the Pre-
Boreal and Boreal are depicted as typical inland cultures. But this view
may be challenged due to the one-sidedness of the source material. The
coastlines of the Pre-Boreal and Boreal (Figure 7) lie mostly beneath the
sea today, so traces of any possible coastal settlement sites are necessarily few. Even if the coastal zone in the Pre-Boreal and Boreal period did
not offer quite the same biological richness as later during the Atlantic
with the rise of the sea level, it is logical to assume that the exploitation
of the resources of the coastal zone was also part of the seasonal life
pattern of the hunter-gatherer communities, for example during the
critical spring months; in fact, seal hunting has been documented. In
evaluating the significance of the coastal zone it must be remembered
that even in later periods, for while intensive exploitation of the coast
has been documented, we find only few traces of coastal hunting at the
inland settlement sites.

The accessible evidence of the hunter–gatherer communities' exploitation of the resources, particularly in the seventh millennium BC, shows a
broad exploitation of the biological potential of the forest. All species of
large meat animals were hunted. Among these, elk and aurochs could
yield about 500 kilogrammes of meat. Both of these large meat animals
were present from the beginning of the period but gradually played out
their role as game in the course of the following millennia in pace with
the increasing density of the forest. The plentiful red deer and roe deer

were also hunted. In fact, living conditions for these animals improved in the course of the period. The same holds true of the wild pig, which during the period played an ever-larger role as a source of protein. The preferred fur-bearing animals were the beaver, the marten, the fox and the badger. Inland fishing was dominated by the catching of pike, for which fishing spears and lines were used. There is but poor evidence of the gathering of plant foods; the gathering of hazel nuts and a few other fruits and seeds is the only indication of this vital aspect of the subsistence pattern.

Due to the marked lopsidedness of the archaeological record, knowledge of the annual migrations of the hunter-gatherer communities, and consequently of their annual territory in the Pre-Boreal and Boreal, is limited. The best-known aspects are the camps of the summer season, which were made primarily by inland fresh-water streams and lakes. From a number of these localities there are finds of small rectangular huts apparently built of branches rammed in round a floor and pulled together at the top to make a roof. These small huts were inhabited by small groups of people – probably just a single nuclear family. The summer huts were the base camp for many activities such as hunting, fishing and gathering of plant food. To judge from what we know of present-day hunting societies we can presume that gathering was largely carried out by the women.

The settlement sites of the winter months are, in contrast, virtually unknown. A few localities indicate that during the cold period settlement was made on dryer land, although still near fresh water. It is an important observation that the winter settlements seem to have been comprised of larger groups than those of the summer. Winter settlements were apparently based upon the advantages of co-operative hunting.

Little is known of how the hunter–gatherer bands moved between these two settlement types. Presumably exploitation of the coastal zone took place in the late autumn and early spring months; both periods seem to be advantageous for the hunting of sea mammals, as indicated by a few finds. Aside from the more permanent summer and winter settlements, we know of a number of specific activity camps seemingly more transitory in character, such as butchering-places, where big game such as elk and aurochs were quartered before transport back to the base camp. The fishing sites also found were probably connected to the summer settlement. Finally there are some sites which may have functioned as transit camps on the way between the seasonal settlement sites of the coast and the inland sites. The picture is still dim, but it does seem certain that the strategy of the hunter–gatherer communities

entailed a mobile settlem
off temporarily during
favourable ecological nic

The material equipmer
phase shows a varied e
hunters used the bones o
fifteen different types of to
types include spearheads,
hunting as well as fishing.
bow and arrows attest a hig
bow is accompanied by se
(Figure 14). Wooden spear
number of specialized axes
implements include paddle
hollowed-out tree trunks). T
fringes of the techno-territor
the dog, which already seer
Europe in the Late Glacial pe

Hunters and gatherers of the

Improved living conditions in
population increase which pres
the seventh millennium BC. B
dense shady virgin forest gained
a certain impoverishment of th
sixth millennium BC. Both for th
deer species, the density of the
conditions. During this period th
as a result of the rise of the sea-l
shown that this occurred in four s
in which the sea-level sank slightl
particularly extensive. It is logica
gradually encroached upon the te
resulting in both a greater perman
strain on the resources. For a time
environment at the coasts could re
sure, but in the long run the situa

If this theory is correct, it may e
behaviour of the hunter–gatherers
BC. As yet the nature of these chang
environmental situation it is underst.
tive coastal zones were thoroughly

Figure 14 W
   Holmegår
   insertion

frequently
assume th
Earlier id
hunter–g
favoured

generations of archaeologists. Today a great number of settlement sites from the sixth millennium BC are known from both the coast and inland. Zealand especially predominates, whereas not until recently have settlements been revealed on the coasts of Jutland. Inland settlement sites in Jutland have been located but not yet excavated.

In viewing the archaeological record from the sixth millennium BC, a differentiated settlement pattern may be discerned. The topographical location of the settlement sites shows that the population still exploited several ecological zones. Inland, the hunting of big game such as elk, aurochs, red deer, roe deer and boar dominated. By the coasts, sea mammals such as the seal and the porpoise were sought. At the same time fishing for piked dogfish and cod in particular was carried on, along with extensive bird hunting. But there is still no evidence of the gathering of plant products.

As the finds from the sixth millennium BC, the so-called Kongemose culture, were not distinguished in the archaeological record until fairly recently, details of the settlement pattern of the hunter–gatherer communities are very little known. No clear idea of the seasonal patterns of the bands and consequently of the extent of their annual territory can yet be obtained. Only two types of seasonal settlements are known, and strikingly enough both seem to have been summer settlements. The first type is encountered in the coastal regions, usually near sheltered coves and on islands in calm inland shallows, not surprisingly in exactly those resource areas which were characterized by the greatest biological production. The finds clearly imply an intensive exploitation of marine resources; among other things, fishing and hunting of sea mammals and coastal birds are here for the first time supplemented by the intensive gathering of shellfish. The second settlement type is found inland. Here the topographical location of the settlement sites corresponds precisely to the summer settlements made in the seventh millennium BC by inland fresh-water systems. The biological production here is second in line after the coastal estuaries. In some cases the settlement sites quite obviously seem to indicate a more intensive settlement than previously; apparently they also include a larger group size. But as yet no coherent picture of the seasonal pattern can be formed – the source material is far too scanty and incidental.

It can thus be very difficult to evaluate the presumed changes in the behaviour of the hunter–gatherer communities in the sixth millennium BC. The changes in the forest scene, the rising of the sea-level and the increased biological abundance at the coast most likely led to a transformation of the subsistence strategy of the bands and their social organization. But these changes first clearly show themselves in the archaeological record after the transformation had already occurred, when the communities seem to have sought a new equilibrium. This seems to have happened in the course of the fifth millennium BC.

The hunter–gatherer society which in this epoch exploited the potential of the country is termed in archaeological literature the 'Ertebølle culture'. The traces of Ertebølle settlements are known to a degree which indicates that population pressure had grown in the course of the fifth millennium BC. The cause of this may possibly be sought in the tendency towards a more sedentary settlement pattern which was the result of the increased coastal biological production in the High Atlantic period. In general the rise of the sea also resulted in a diminishing of the land area and consequently in an increase in population size per square kilometre.

However comprehensive the source material may be, it cannot be arranged into a complete picture of the subsistence strategy of the hunter–gatherer communities. One reason is that topographically conditioned variations in the quantity of game which have not yet been determined probably affected the behaviour of the different bands. Another explanation takes into consideration the topographically conditioned differences in preservation conditions for organic material. In fact, the presence of organic material is decisive for the understanding of the character of the individual settlement, its period of function and the extent of hunting and gathering.

Just as in the sixth millennium BC, the fifth millennium BC witnessed an intensive exploitation of both the coast and inland. The decisive factor is that in the course of the period there seems to have been a gradual transition to a more sedentary settlement pattern, that is, an exploitation of the same localities over longer periods of the year. Naturally enough, this happened particularly in the coastal zone, where the biological production was greatest. Here too arose the situation which destroyed the traditional regulation of population size and in the end led to intensified manipulation of the environment and hence a transition to food production.

To understand this development and to be able to describe the tolerance of the Ertebølle subsistence system, it is necessary to illuminate the various resource areas which were at the disposal of the hunter–gatherer cultures: the estuaries, the fresh-water systems of the inland, the islands off the coast, the exposed mainland coasts, the forest interior, and so on. Ecological studies here have shown that the resource regions can be arranged in a qualitative ranking with respect to their relative degree of productivity, diversity, seasonality and overall stability (C. Paludan-Müller, 1978).

At the top of the ranking order there are the estuaries, the average annual carrying capacity of which is higher than anywhere else. In fact, along with tropical rain-forests and coral reefs, estuaries rank as the most productive category of ecosystems in terms of primary production. In the High Atlantic period the Danish estuaries and the areas immediately adjacent must have provided living opportunities for the hunter–gatherer communities almost all year round.

Next in rank come the fresh-water systems of the inland areas. They too are characterized by high productivity and high diversity, but also by a higher degree of seasonality than the estuaries. It has therefore been concluded that they were exploited mainly from mid-spring to mid-autumn. However, a more restricted and specialized exploitation may have taken place during the rest of the year.

Next in line come the outer peninsulas and the narrow straits of the coasts as well as the small islands which were so numerous in Denmark during the Atlantic period. Here there is a more complex pattern of fluctuation of resources, often with several interrupted bulk occurrences of food resources during the year.

Finally, at the bottom of the scale of productivity we find the exposed mainland coasts and the closed forest of the inland areas. At neither of these environments can any allocation of settlements be expected beyond the level of occasional short-term camps.

Thus the settlements in the estuaries are of primary interest and this group also includes a very large portion of the well-known settlement sites from the High Atlantic period. In north-east Zealand, for example, a large number of settlements are concentrated in the four fjord regions by Villingebæk, Nivå, Vedbæk and Klampenborg. A fifth settlement concentration is found on the island of Amager. From these five settlement concentrations, with transportation ranges rarely exceeding 10 kilometres, it was possible to control a territory of about 600 km² with a coastline of about 170 kilometres.

The large coastal settlements are frequently distinguished by considerable layers of shells, the striking remains of an intensive food-gathering. The gathering of molluscs played a major role especially in the Limfjord regions, along the east coast of Jutland, and in the northern parts of Funen and Zealand. The gathering was carried out together with a wide-ranging exploitation of both the terrestrial and the marine fauna.

In the inland forests, red deer, roe deer and wild pig were hunted along with a broad selection of fur-bearing animals. Marine mammals, fish, molluscs and a plentiful variety of birds were hunted and gathered on the open sea and by the coast.

Few of the settlement sites have been carefully studied. However, a number of investigations of one of the classic coastal settlement sites, Mejlgaard on Djursland, resulted in the hypothesis that the shell mound was used by a community of approximately forty people on a prolonged seasonal or mobile-cum-sedentary basis; that it was repeatedly occupied from year to year; and that it was dependent on a diversity of resources, among which both the molluscs and the non-molluscan marine resources contributed at least as much to the site economy as the terrestrial resources.

Unfortunately our knowledge of the large coastal settlements suffers from many gaps. The remains of dwellings are very meagre and little is known as to how long the various settlements were in function. If the large coastal settlements do in fact represent the transition to a more sedentary settlement form – and there is much to indicate that this is the case – then they must have played a role in the transformation of the population situation. In a settlement pattern with a large annual territory and short-term stays at the individual settlement sites, the number of infants to be transported will always be low. But when the annual territory and hence also migratory distances are diminished, so that the women, at least, remain longer in one place, then improved living conditions are created for children and population growth is encouraged. It may be concluded that the altered circumstances in the fifth millennium BC led the hunter–gatherer communities towards a changed strategy. But in the long run this strategy may have destroyed the equilibrium of the subsistence system and resulted in an increasing population pressure, which around the close of the fifth millennium BC impelled the inhabitants of Denmark to introduce an agrarian economy.

Whereas the large coastal settlements probably represented a more permanent settlement form, the small seasonal camps were still established on the coast. These were intended to exploit only certain resources. Late autumn settlements have been found which were intended to exploit the migrations of sea mammals such as the grey seal (*Halichoeru grypus*). While awaiting the favourable migration of seals, other food, such as cod, could be caught. This fish (*Gadus morrhua*) may have been subsequently dried and stored as a food reserve.

Not surprisingly, inland seasonal camps are also known from both the summer and winter seasons. Most often these were founded on islets or by the shores of inland fresh-water systems. In some cases the local fauna was exploited to the fullest – in other cases hunting was focused on just a few species such as boar and fur-bearing animals. Finds of the bones of sea mammals at inland settlement sites demonstrate that the inhabitants had contact with the coast, although details of the migrations of the hunter–gatherer bands cannot be known. The role of gathering is indicated by finds of an abundance of seeds and fruits, but the extent to which their presence is coincidental is still unclear. The great variation of edible plants, herbs, bulbs, fruits, berries, nuts, bark, shoots, as well as insects and small animals, which the Atlantic forest offered in the summer, doubtless constituted a vital percentage of the food, though how much cannot be known.

The material equipment of the late hunter–gatherer communities was not great but in relation to earlier times it is clear that more effective hunting methods were being sought. The fish trap was an example of this (Figure 15). The trap is a labour-saving device used for both coastal and fresh-water fishing. Net fishing now also appears as well as the

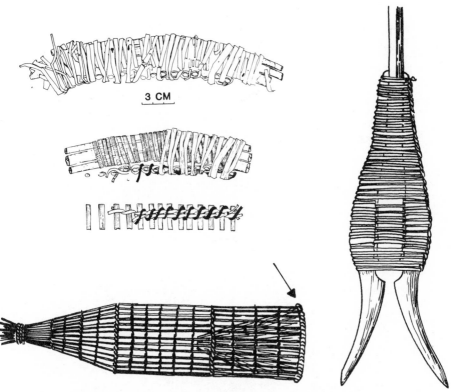

Figure 15 Mesolithic fishing implements. Left top: fragments of fish trap from Maglemosegårds Vænge, Zealand; bottom: reconstruction. Right: Fishing spear found at a submerged Mesolithic settlement off the island of Ærø, southern Denmark.

capture of fur-bearing animals in traps. An important innovation is the use of pottery which was included in the equipment of the hunter–gatherer communities about 4700–4600 BC. The pottery technique was

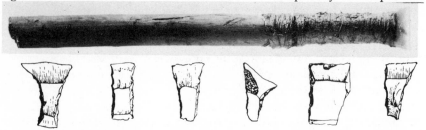

Figure 16 During the Atlantic period a large selection of arrow types was used by the Ertebølle hunters. The most common type had a transverse arrowhead, as seen on an arrow found in a bog in Ejsing parish, Jutland (above). Below: typical Ertebølle transverse arrowheads made of flint.

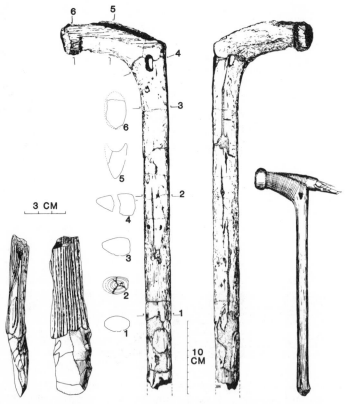

Figure 17 Axe shaft found at a Mesolithic settlement, Maglemosegårds Vænge, Zealand, and axe head found at Kolding Fjord, Jutland. Right: reconstruction.

used for the production of blubber lamps and of containers for the preparation and storage of food.

This increased need to preserve food ought to be viewed in connection with the introduction of the agrarian economy from the south. In the period around 4700 BC there were agrarian cultures in northern Germany and Poland, not far distant from Denmark. It is likely that the hunter–gatherers' familiarity with, for example, pottery technique may be ascribed to contact with the agrarian cultures in the south.

The material equipment also included harpoons, fish hooks, bows, and arrows (Figure 16), boomerangs, wooden spears, and clubs, together with a large selection of special axe types (Figure 17). Finds of paddles (Figure 18) indicate that just as in the foregoing period, boats were used not only for inland sailing but also, to judge by the fauna, for hunting on the open sea. Finally, it should be remembered that nets, pit traps, poison, and many other devices do not leave visible traces. The dog is still the only domesticated animal which has been documented.

A population crisis at the end of the fifth millennium BC?

The still rather fragmentary picture of the economy of the hunter–gatherer communities in the fifth millennium BC leaves us with many unanswered questions. These questions are mostly related to the profound transformation of the subsistence strategy of the prehistoric population which set in at the end of the fifth millennium BC with the beginning of agriculture.

In the period after 6000 BC the altered environmental situation must have created a number of marked consequences for the hunter–gatherer communities either in the form of an altered demographic situation and/or as changes in the subsistence and settlement pattern. The first possibility is difficult to evaluate, but again the population size may have stagnated in the course of the sixth and the beginning of the fifth millennia BC. But after this, there again seems to have been a rise, in fact a striking one. This increase may have been indirectly triggered by an environmental transformation caused by the rising sea-level in the Atlantic period. If this is the case, and if the population balance had been shifted, then it is not surprising that during the fifth millennium BC the hunter–gatherer communities apparently exceeded the tolerance of their subsistence system. With the introduction of technological innovations they began an intensified manipulation of their environment.

The decisive factor in this process is the greater permanence of settlement observable especially in the period after 4700 BC. After this time we can expect to find proof that the inhabitants of the country

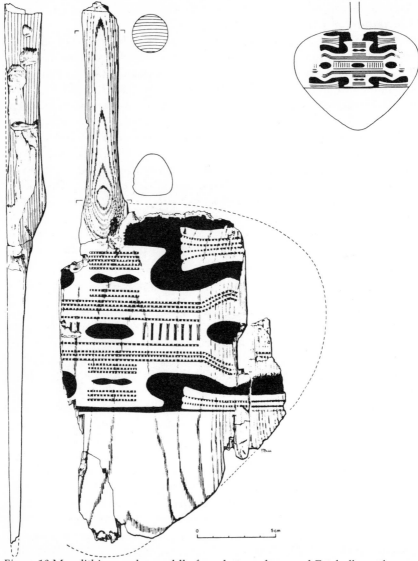

Figure 18 Mesolithic wooden paddle found at a submerged Ertebølle settlement at Tybrind Vig in Lille Bælt.

began to employ new supplementary subsistence forms – namely a sort of agrarian economy.

The first indirect traces of the presence of agriculture, according to radiocarbon dates, come from about 4200 BC. At this time, the archaeological finds yield for the first time the thin-walled pottery which is thought to represent the earliest agrarian cultures, the so-called 'Funnel-Necked Beaker culture.' The direct traces of agriculture, impressions of grain in pottery, cereal pollen, and bones of domesticated animals, however, first turn up at a slightly later point in time, namely around 3900–3800 BC. Already prior to 4200 BC, however, the prehistoric inhabitants seem to have established contact with the agrarian cultures which flourished just a few hundred kilometres south of what is now Denmark. Knowledge of pottery-making, which may have been sought due to increased demands for storing food, turns up around 4700 BC. The tempering, shaping and firing of clay are accomplishments which clearly derive from foreign impulses, more specifically from the contemporaneous cultures in north-west Germany.

The material equipment of the late hunter–gatherer society also includes features which point to a connection with the agrarian cultures in north-west Germany. Certain new tool types, especially those made of bone and antler, seem best explained by this postulated contact. Similarly, there are features in the technological development which placed new demands upon tools. As a case in point, certain changes in flint techniques indicate a more advanced woodcutting technique. It is not unlikely that future research will demonstrate even more profound influences from the southern agrarian cultures in the period 4700–4200BC.

Still, the hypotheses about the rise of agriculture in Denmark are very tentative. One possible explanation is presented in L.R. Binford's comprehensive Post-Pleistocene theory (L.R. Binford, 1968a). According to this theory, the Post-Glacial formation of certain rich environments where sedentarism became possible destroyed the traditional regulation of the population size, so that population growth was triggered off, and surplus population budded off and resettled in less favourable areas.

Danish archaeologists have long been aware of the fact that the estuarine resource space of the High Atlantic period in Denmark provided just such a rich environment where sedentarism may have been possible. This theory has recently been formulated thus (C. Paludan-Müller, 1978):

With the beginning of the High Atlantic period (c. 5000 BC) the carrying capacity of the estuaries increased considerably so as to permit permanent residence within the same area for the first time. Constraints on the reproduction of the population occupying the estuarine resource space became insufficient or non-existent. Around the middle of the fifth millennium BC the estuarine areas began acting as 'propulsive areas' in the sense that they began to produce a population surplus. The

budding-off of the surplus population resulted in an increasing exploitation of the inland fresh waters and the seaward islands on a seasonal
basis. After some time, however, the natural optimal carrying capacity
for food gatherers in the inner fresh waters and the seaward islands had
been achieved. This situation necessitated an increase in the carrying
capacity of the area as a whole, which meant a more effective human
manipulation of the environment in order to boost the productivity of
organisms of economic significance.

The only ecosystem which would lend itself to this sort of manipulation was the climax forest. And the best place to manipulate the climax
forest would be inland. A site here could encompass more forest within
its home range than at an estuarine site, where population density
figures would already range near the 'social carrying capacity', or at an
island site, where there would be little forest to manipulate.

The manipulation could entail, for example, that the large trees were
ringed in order to create clearings in the forest in which could grow
edible plants such as hazel and eagle fern. These clearings were also
good browsing areas for game. The next step in the manipulative
process inland would be the introduction of more efficiently controlled
resource species such as domesticated cattle and eventually domesticated plants.

This sort of model can explain some of the changes which occur in
man's bio-environment in Denmark during the fifth millennium BC and
the beginning of the fourth millennium BC, changes which gradually led
to a semi-agrarian economy.

But it must be emphasized that this theory is built on a shaky
foundation. First and foremost, it lacks the detailed chronological
framework within which the data of the settlement finds can be
grouped. Not until we have many more radiocarbon dates than we have
today will we be able to test the validity of the theory. Until then, the
centuries which witnessed the transition to a semi-agrarian economy are
still among the most poorly illuminated centuries in Danish prehistory.

Economy of the hunters and gatherers

After this description of environmental development since the last Ice
Age, demographic changes and the evidence of the archaeological record
regarding subsistence and settlement patterns, it is logical to seek a
synthesis of the economy of the hunter–gatherers. Economy is here
defined as that part of social life which includes production, distribution
and consumption of goods and services. Our present focus will be on
production.

Flexibility and mobility, the main characteristics of the hunter–gatherer communities, were evident in the description of the interplay of the natural food situation, the population size and the means of production of the bands. By means of production we mean a process in which both man and nature participate, a process in which man on his own initiative establishes, regulates and controls his metabolism with nature.

The previous sections described the factors which constitute and determine this process. These factors are: 1) the labour input, which depends upon the population density and the quantity of resources; 2) the labour object, that is nature, the finished products of which are appropriated by society; and 3) the tools of production, that is, the material equipment or capital of the hunter–gatherer communities.

The tools of production fall into two categories: capital goods and consumer goods. The first category includes mainly the hunting implements of the hunter–gatherer communities, from their bows and arrows to the boats from which hunting took place. These capital goods were quite modest, as befits the virtual inability of the hunter–gatherer communities to accumulate capital.

In the prehistoric hunter–gatherer communities, production consisted of goods which could not be conserved. There are very few exceptions to this rule prior to the beginning of agriculture. A general conclusion is that the hunter–gatherer communities have a very poor ability to save, that is, to postpone consumption. This inability to accumulate capital means that improvements of the production apparatus can only to a slight extent be based upon this ability.

As a general rule, the hunter–gatherer communities' difficulty in postponing consumption prevents their economy from becoming dynamic. As a result, very little economic growth can occur. This is one of the basic reasons why the societal form survived relatively unchanged through the millennia following the melting of the ice from Denmark and up to the beginning of food production around 4200 BC. In other words, this means that we can determine how the production tools in the hunter–gatherer communities can be termed aids in appropriating the finished products of nature. In this way the resources strongly influence the very type of organization and labour practices of the hunter–gatherer communities. For example, we have seen how the type of food resources and the forms of technology by which the biota are exploited are the most important determinants of local group size and composition. In sum: the labour form made possible by the environment as well as by the population size determined the economic and social organization of the hunter–gatherer society.

4

Social structure of the hunters and gatherers

The archaeological record which can illuminate the social structure of the early hunter–gatherer society in Denmark is very slender indeed. Comparisons with present-day hunter–gatherer societies can to some degree expand our ideas of the societal forms in Denmark before the introduction of agriculture, but such comparisons will always be problematic; present-day hunters and gatherers are usually dependent upon other societal forms or have been forced into marginal areas, thereby experiencing a modification of their original culture features.

The patrilocal or patrilineal band has been considered the most 'typical' form of social organization before the beginning of agriculture. As often pointed out, the band society seems to have existed under extremely varied natural conditions everywhere on earth. It seems to be the most effective social organizational form in regions with low population density. It is also thought to be the oldest form because it can be adapted to areas with widely differing natural conditions.

A band society is comprised of a number of small, usually mobile groups. Each group is self-sufficient and the subsistence form is generally hunting and gathering. The only known division of labour is based upon age and sex. As a rule, the society is egalitarian in its social organization, that is, there is no regulated inequality in the access to economic resources and to social status positions. Consequently there are no specialized political positions. In the individual hunter–gatherer group social authority is normally in the hands of the oldest male members of the group.

A number of features of the band society are regarded by evolutionistic anthropology as being quite ancient in the history of human societies. The first feature of interest here is the group division and the rules controlling the relationships among the various social groups. More theoretical speculations as to why man, like many primates, lives in groups, will not be examined here. The need for food and shelter and the fact that the sexual behaviour of most primates is not seasonal have been suggested to explain why man primarily lives in groups all year round.

In establishing the most elementary rules of group behaviour, social anthropology has emphasized the role which sharing must have played for the earliest forms of society. Why this mutuality arose is not clear. In the hundreds of thousands of years which it has taken mankind to spread out over the earth, the exchange of women has been one of the earliest features. The French anthropologist Claude Lévi-Strauss, for example, has described how in primitive society a woman is often regarded as a gift, and how a man and his group are the recipients of this gift. This sort of mutual exchange between human groups transforms simple couple relationship to 'marriage alliances', as the exchange involves one or another relative stability in the couple relationship. It is also frequently observed that in present-day hunter–gatherer societies monogamy is the dominant form of common life. Thus monogamy is not the late form of marriage implied in many older evolutionary theories.

The nuclear family was probably also stabilized by the division of labour between the sexes. In a hunter–gatherer society hunting usually requires that men can roam far and wide, whereas at any given time there will always be women who are prevented from doing so. The monogamous relationship thus provides many economic advantages. The men participate in the hunt, which in a society with poor technological equipment frequently demands the collaboration of several men, whereas women, due to pregnancies and child-care, are less mobile and hunt small animals, gather plant food and carry out more localized activities such as food preparation, childbirth and child-care. As pointed out above, this division of labour also favours population control.

The advantages of marriage rules are also obvious for the group or society as a whole. Marriage outside the group, exogamy, has a vital function in the eyes of society: it establishes ties among groups and thus diminishes the potential for conflict. The exchange of men is rare in a hunter–gatherer society because collective hunting is more effective if a man belongs to the territory. A woman, on the other hand, can more easily transfer to another group without weakening her original group. The men's permanent sense of belonging to the group can thus in a low-technology society be of crucial importance for co-operation and group solidarity.

Of course, this description can only offer generalities on the societal basis for the hunter–gatherer communities which existed in Denmark from the melting of the ice to the beginning of agriculture. The intention here has been to demonstrate that social organization can hardly be based upon the nuclear family, because this family was presumably created by society and not vice versa. This line of thought bears a number of structural consequences for the hunter–gatherer societies. If exogamy was the basis for couple relationship and the woman usually followed the man, then every group included married women from another group and at the same time gave away some of its own marriageable women. In this way the individual band was integrated into a larger whole, namely the group of bands which comprised the social territory. These bands were related by genealogical ties and probably also by forms of co-operation such as the exchange of goods. The social structure thus comprised of the following groups: 1) nuclear families; 2) extended families consisting of more or less permanent associations of adult males and their nuclear families; and 3) the territorial society, the group of bands which constituted the social territory.

Of the groups listed, the nuclear family made up of father, mother, offspring, and perhaps elderly relatives, was the most cohesive unit in the hunter–gatherer society. The division of labour based upon age and sex which exists within the nuclear family is the only essential one in the hunter–gatherer society. This means that in periods the nuclear family could forage alone if the resource situation allowed. It is precisely this flexibility which seems to be discernible in, for example, the settlement pattern of the Boreal period.

This leads us to the size of the hunter–gatherer communities, which seems to vary over a relatively narrow range. Groups of up to eight or ten men are very common, that is, the community will often be comprised of about thirty or forty persons. In fact, this is the group size estimated for the coastal settlements of the Atlantic period. The social territory of a group of genealogically related communities rarely exceeds one thousand persons. But it is important to bear in mind that we are not dealing here with a tribe in the sense which the word acquires later in the discussion of the first agricultural communities.

If, as suggested above, not only the size but also the topographic distribution of the communities is directly related to the quantity, seasonality and stability of the food resources, a number of general features of this form of organization are given. These features are: low population density, geographic mobility, flexible group structure and small group size. Wherever hunting, for example, demands the co-operation of many people and the game captured can feed everyone at one time, the group size will normally be large. In other periods, however, the food situation can compel the nuclear family to obtain its food alone. This seems to have been the case in periods of the annual cycle in the Boreal and perhaps also in the Atlantic period. These variables are noted to emphasize that the nuclear families which comprise the extended band do not necessarily live together all the time, or even much of the time, in order to be perceived as such. To judge by our knowledge of present-day band societies, we know that such factors as shared mythology, common ceremonies and kinship relationships may integrate nuclear families in periods of wide geographical distribution.

Finally, it should be mentioned that the annual territory exploited by the hunter–gatherer community is not necessarily enclosed by boundaries. One of the chief functions of marriage outside the group seems to be that it opens the group for territorial exploitation so that larger variations of natural resources can be utilized by related groups.

Naturally this description can only serve as a hypothetical framework for understanding the prehistoric hunter–gatherer society. However, as we have mentioned, the most striking feature of the subsistence form and settlement pattern in the period after the melting of the ice from Denmark is the flexibility of the group size. The summer camps of the Boreal period, for instance, seem to reflect a seasonally conditioned division into nuclear families and a correspondingly large group size in the winter period. This sort of strategy seems best explained by the ecological situation in which the hunter–gatherer communities existed.

It is considerably more difficult to explain the settlement concentrations of the Atlantic period – for example in the Zealand fjords. Do they represent a larger group formation which moved around together in the fjord region – or were they several scattered contemporary settlements? Both strategies had advantages but only future research will be able to answer the question. There is yet another related question: did the hunter–gatherer communities during the High Atlantic develop higher forms of social integration than the band society? Did the hunting societies at the end of the fifth millennium BC operate on a tribal level such as has been suggested for other areas of Europe (R.B. Lee, 1968)?

In any case, the archaeological finds from the period predating the introduction of agriculture do not indicate specialized forms of labour. We can thus hardly expect to find social organization forms beyond the egalitarian. In this connection it is important to remember that egalitarian does not necessarily mean that all members of a social unit are equal. In modern egalitarian societies it may be seen that a prestige position achieved through recognized status, such as that of a good hunter, cannot be transferred by inheritance or in any other way. Just because a man is a good hunter, his sons are not necessarily good hunters. The egalitarian social forms thus restrict social inequalities to a minimum.

In summary it may be said that the momentary character of the labour processes, the hunter–gatherer communities' lack of ability to postpone consumption and accumulate capital, the limiting of division of labour to age and sex – all of these factors place the early hunter–gatherer society at the level of social organization labelled the band society. With the apparent restructuring of the subsistence strategy in the course of the fifth millennium BC, a new situation must have been created. The more sedentary settlement pattern and the presumed change in productivity may have created higher forms of integration. The problem is as yet unresolved and demands first and foremost many new finds from the important transitional phase between the late hunter–gatherer society and the semi-agrarian society of the fourth millennium BC.

5

Finds and interpretations

Most of our knowledge about the Palaeolithic and Mesolithic cultures during the Late and Post-Glacial period up to about 4200 BC derives from excavated settlements of the hunter–gatherer communities. As yet the archaeological record includes very few grave finds.

The study of the settlements of the hunter–gatherer communities in Denmark is seriously hindered by the inconsistency with which the source material has been analysed. To analyse finds from a Palaeolithic or Mesolithic settlement, the collaboration of many scientific disciplines is demanded. Unfortunately, many of the principal settlements of the period are accessible only in the form of preliminary reports. These include such noteworthy finds *as Holmegård* (C.J. Becker, 1945); *Åmosen* (K. Andersen, 1951); and *Kongemosen* (S. Jørgensen, 1956). Other finds, such as the important settlement of *Lundby* on Zealand, excavated in 1928–31, have never even been published. Yet another lack is that the archaeological record is so little representative. As a case in point, study of the settlement pattern of the hunter–gatherer communities has made it evident that many of the known settlements must have functioned as a base camp for specific activity camps, in which the hunter–gatherer communities carried out strictly seasonal activities. This group of finds is badly under-represented in the archaeological record.

Little of the source material which has turned up in the past hundred years can fulfil the demands of modern archaeological research. However, since the 1940s improved excavation methods have remedied many problems. We can hope that the detailed regional investigations now in progress will be able to shed some light on the representativeness of older source material. In this connection investigations now underway in the Øresund region, i.e. north-eastern Zealand and western Scania, are particularly significant. Nowhere else in Europe do we have such a rich and varied concentration of Mesolithic settlements representing a long uninterrupted coastal settlement.

The first excavation of a Mesolithic settlement on the Zealand side of the Øresund took place in 1912. Since then a number of excavations have been made here, but the enormous potential of the area first became evident with the start of the so-called Vedbæk project in 1975 (E. Brinch Petersen, 1979; K. Aaris-Sørensen, 1980b). This project includes investigation of the unique Mesolithic cemetery Bøgebakken (E. Brinch Petersen, 1976b).

The goal of the Vedbæk project is to study cultural and environmental changes by a Stone Age fjord during the Atlantic period. Here, the collaboration of archaeologists and researchers from many branches of natural science has, among other things, revealed the influence which changes in the water-level of the Litorina sea had on such factors as the location of the settlements, their preservation, their tool kits and their chronology. Thus the project can also help evaluate the representativeness of the finds made earlier. A similar project is underway on the east coast of Jutland (S.H. Andersen, 1976).

Older archaeological literature describes many significant excavations. However, there are but few published reports on settlements from the Palaeolithic, that is settlements which predate the transition between K. Jessen's pollen zones III and IV (T. Mathiassen, 1946; S.H. Andersen, 1972). Yet we can anticipate an increase in the archaeological record (for example, see A. Fischer, 1978).

The most important works on the Mesolithic Maglemose culture include, in chronological order from the Pre-Boreal period up to the transition to the Kongemose culture of the Atlantic period: *Klosterlund* (E. Brinch Petersen, 1966); *Holmegård VI* (C.J. Becker, 1945); *Sønder Hadsund* (E. Brinch Petersen, 1966); *Verup* (K. Andersen, 1960); *Mullerup* (G.F.L. Sarauw, 1903); *Ulkestrup* (K. Andersen, 1951); *Holmegård V* (C.J. Becker, 1945); *Sværdborg I* (K. Friis Johansen, 1919); *Stallerupholm* (R.E. Blankholm and S.H. Andersen, 1967); *Ulkestrup II* (K. Andersen, 1951); *Sværdborg II* (E. Brinch Petersen, 1971); *Holmegård I–II* (H.C. Broholm, 1924); *Sværdborg I* (B. Bille Henriksen, 1976).

The subsequent Kongemose culture yields very few finds; these include *Kongemosen* (S. Jørgensen, 1956); *Vedbæk Boldbaner* (T. Mathiassen, 1946); and *Brovst* and *Øster Jølby* (S.H. Andersen, 1969).

From the last part of the period, the Ertebølle culture, there is an abundance of sites. These sites often show traces of repeated settlements, the youngest of which have been interpreted as specific activity camps for the first farming communities (J. Skårup, 1973). Among the most noteworthy of these are: *Dyrholm* and *Kolind* (T. Mathiassen, 1942); *Norslund* (S.H. Andersen and C. Malmros, 1965); *Ertebølle* (A.P. Madsen, 1900); *Mejlgård* (H. Hellmuth Andersen, 1960; G.N. Bailey, 1978); *Sølager* (J. Skårup, 1973); *Aggersund* (S.H. Andersen 1978); *Bloksbjerg* (E. Westerby, 1927); *Ølby Lyng* (E. Brinch Petersen, 1970a); and *Ring Kloster* (S.H. Andersen, 1974).

Grave finds from the Mesolithic period in Denmark have until recently been very rare (H. Norling-Christensen, 1945; U.L. Hansen, 1972a; E. Brinch Petersen, 1976b). The excavations at Bøgebakken near Vedbæk have augmented the material considerably and also provided us with insight into Mesolithic anthropology (S.E. Albrethsen *et al.*, 1976). All the Danish finds have recently been published in conjunction with other European Mesolithic finds (R.R. Newell *et al.*, 1979).

Familiarity with environmental history is a necessary prerequisite for understanding the development of the hunter–gatherer communities, especially in a territory such as Denmark where ecological changes are most clearly marked. Thus a close collaboration with the natural sciences has been maintained in Danish archaeology since the mid-nineteenth century, when the early settlements in Denmark were first studied. In particular, the results of the so-called 'kitchen-midden commission' (published by A.P. Madsen in 1900) served as a forerunner for modern research. A history of investigation can be found in E. Brinch Petersen (1973).

Studies of the Late and Post-Glacial vegetational history of Denmark and south Sweden have been summarized by J. Iversen (1973) and B.E. Berglund (1966 a and b). Detailed knowledge of the various phases of vegetational history derives first and foremost from K. Jessen's zone classification (1935, 1937, 1938); later modifications were made by J. Iversen (1941) and S. Jørgensen (1963). Climatic history was reconstructed (Figure 12) on the basis of evidence of the immigration of animals and plants; see, for example, studies by J. Iversen (1954, 1973) and B.E. Berglund (1966 a and b, 1968, 1969), whereas the relationship between the land and the sea has been illuminated by studies of J. Iversen (1937), K. Jessen (1938) and J. Troels-Smith (1942). Of particular importance are recent Swedish investigations which correlate datings for the Litorina transgressions (changes of the ocean level) with pollen evidence and radiocarbon datings (B.E. Berglund, 1971b).

From the abundant literature on Late and Post-Glacial fauna, only the most important works will be cited. A useful overview of the animal species represented at the Palaeolithic and Mesolithic settlements is provided by E. Brinch Petersen (1973); whereas C. Paludan-Müller (1978) has produced a summary of the food potential of the various biotopes in the Atlantic period. Of particular relevance for the study of faunal conditions are, furthermore, works of M. Degerbøl (1933), U. Møhl (1970), B. Løppenthin (1967), M. Degerbøl and B. Fredskild (1970) and K. Aaris-Sørensen (1980 a and b). See also D.A. Sturdy's important study (1975).

Unfortunately few detailed statistics have been compiled on the quantitative relationship of the various animal species represented at the settlements; however, see important studies by C.G.J. Petersen (1922), J.L. Bay-Petersen (1978), K. Aaris-Sørensen (1980 a and b) and E. Brinch Petersen (1970a). The problems concerning the representativeness of the faunal remains are well illustrated in a study on the Mejlgård shell mound by G.N. Bailey (1978). Piecing together a complete picture of the diet of the hunter–gatherer communities is also difficult due to problems in demonstrating the extent of gathering of plant products (R.W. Dennell, 1979). Perhaps in the future, isotopic analysis of prehistoric bones will bring us closer to illuminating these problems (A.B. Brown, 1974). For a discussion, see Boaz and Hampel (1978).

In recent years there has been a growing tendency to take an ecological approach to the study of the Palaeolithic and Mesolithic societies; see, for example, works by E. Brinch Petersen (1973) and C. Paludan-Müller (1978). Stimulating works from the field of social anthropology which have influenced Danish archaeologists include publications of R.B. Lee and I. DeVore (1968) and A. Leeds and A.P. Vayda (1965).

Another major trend in newer archaeological research is the interest in demographic factors. A survey of the development of this field has been published by Philip E.L. Smith (1970). Publications which have had relevance for Danish conditions include Brian Spooner (1972), Brian Hayden (1972) and P.R. Ehrlich and J.P. Holdren (1971). As a consequence of the interest in demography in recent years, attention has been focused on the significance of the carrying capacity of the various ecological zones. This concern may be found in several more recent studies, for example C. Paludan-Müller (1978). An estimate of the relative population size in Denmark during the Late and Post-Glacial periods has been attempted by E. Brinch Petersen (1973), whereas the absolute population size has been estimated by J. Troels-Smith (1955, 1960a) and J.G.D. Clark (1975).

An important part of Danish Mesolithic archaeology has been concentrated on chronological studies. Over the years, many attempts have been made to establish a functional chronological framework (E. Brinch Petersen, 1973). These attempts have sometimes resulted in most complicated schemes (Figure 19). The relatively new radiocarbon dates

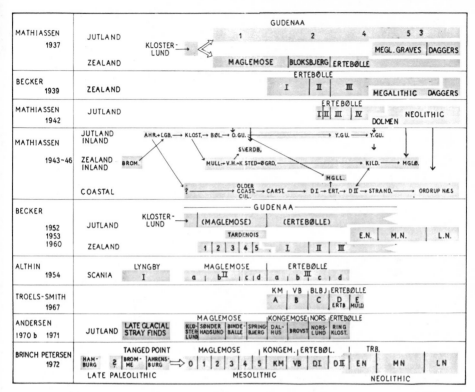

Figure 19 Danish Mesolithic chronology, research history.

have contributed to an altered and partially simplified conception (Figure 20). The radiocarbon dates used below are based on a number of corrections of older conventional dates. These so-called calibrated radiocarbon datings have in recent years led to a radical re-evaluation of north European prehistory (C. Renfrew, 1973b). Among other things, the introduction of agriculture to Denmark has been pushed back 1700 years earlier than the date which scholars only twenty years ago accepted.

From the period between the close of the Ice Age and the introduction of agriculture there are now (1981) more than one hundred radiocarbon datings of the Danish Mesolithic period at our disposal (Figure 20). Together with improved archaeological methods, these datings help create a firmer basis for chronological discussions. Most significantly, the postulate of the complete or partial contemporaneity of a number of 'cultures' has been rejected. For example, the term 'Gudenå culture' (T. Mathiassen, 1937) has been abandoned (S.H. Andersen, 1971). Instead,

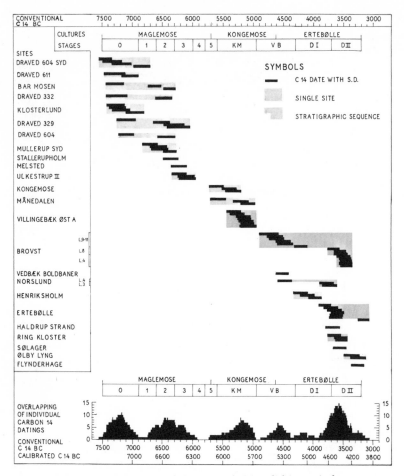

Figure 20 Radiocarbon dates of the Danish Mesolithic period.

a unilinear cultural development has been proposed (E. Brinch Petersen, 1973; S.H. Andersen, 1971; A. Fischer, 1978) in which the various phases succeed one another in a simple chronological progression.

General surveys of the period as a whole are relatively rare; one of them, published by J.G.D. Clark in 1975, offers a number of astute observations pertaining especially to the early part of the period. For the Late Glacial period (the Palaeolithic) there is a popular summary by J. Troels-Smith, 1955. For many years, the few Danish Palaeolithic stray finds could only be illuminated through a number of excavated settlements from northern Germany (A. Rust, 1937, 1943). After excavation of the Palaeolithic Bromme site on Zealand (T. Mathiassen, 1946a), the

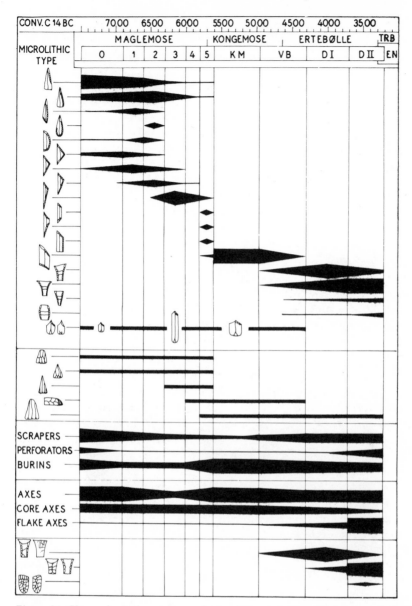

Figure 21 Chronological sequence of microliths and other lithic types during the Mesolithic period in Denmark.

Danish material has also been augmented (S.H. Andersen, 1970); equally important finds have been made in Scania (B. Salmonsson,

1964). Noteworthy contributions to the discussion also include works of E. Brinch Petersen (1970b), C.J. Becker (1971c) and A. Fischer (1978).

With the more ample archaeological record from the Pre-Boreal period and thereafter (the Mesolithic period), a clearer picture is also drawn of the individual cultural phases. From an archaeological viewpoint, each stage is defined through the composition of its tool kit. The Mesolithic Maglemose culture is characterized by various microlithic points and triangles, whereas the rhombic arrowhead typifies the Kongemose, and the transverse arrowhead the Ertebølle (Figure 21). A cultural designation thus defined can consequently only be taken as a functional unit for the archaeologist. The border between two 'cultures' will logically have to be drawn where the new microlithic type appears in numbers exceeding 50 per cent of the total microlithic tool kit (E. Brinch Petersen, 1973). On the basis of the successive transformations of tool types, the entire Mesolithic period, including the Maglemose, Kongemose and Ertebølle cultures, can be divided into ten chronological stages. However, there is no obvious correlation between archaeological and vegetational stages. The archaeological cultural terms refer exclusively to the development of the tool tradition. In so doing, the often very rigid approach of earlier Mesolithic archaeology has been radically modified (E. Brinch Petersen, 1973).

The methodological views described have been employed in a number of vital new works. For the Maglemose culture, reference is made to publications of E. Brinch Petersen (1966, 1971), R.E. Blankholm and S.H. Andersen (1967) and B. Bille Henriksen (1976). Finds from the Kongemose culture have only been described to a small degree – S.H. Andersen (1969b) and S. Jørgensen (1956, 1961) – whereas the Ertebølle culture has been a subject of growing interest in recent years; see, for example, works of J. Troels-Smith (1953, 1960a, 1966, 1967), C.J. Becker (1954), E.. Brinch Petersen (1970a) and S.H. Andersen (1973, 1974). An important part of the debate has dealt with the finds from the final Ertebølle phase and their relationship to the finds from the first farming communities (C. Paludan-Müller, 1978).

PART II

The first farmers
c. 4200–2800 BC

6

The introduction of farming
in Denmark

Introduction

In the period after *c.* 4200 BC it is possible to observe a number of decisive changes in the economy of the prehistoric population in Denmark: the first signs of a new subsistence form, agriculture, now appear. The early archaeological evidence for the incipient food production is very sparse, but after the middle of the fourth millennium BC the innovations appear in their full range. This radical transformation of the economic structure of prehistoric society seems, as already mentioned, to be very complicated and is still far from clarified. Formerly the process was considered in Danish archaeology to have occurred quite suddenly and to have manifested itself as an economically, technologically, chronologically and demographically distinct transition. Nowadays, there is much to indicate that a far more complex view of this vital transitional phase must be employed. One fact, however, is indisputable: the incipient food production, meaning stock-rearing and grain-cultivation, gradually came to exercise a profound influence on all areas of the population's mode of living. Yet we must remember that early farming hardly revealed itself immediately as a great blessing to its first practitioners. There is good reason to presume that at first farming was only a modest supplement to normal activities. Most of the food probably still had to be obtained by hunting and gathering.

In a social regard, the new economy which distinguished early food production gradually caused a transition from one type of society to another. The band society, which had been the hunter–gatherers' organizational form, was very likely replaced by a more complex social pattern. Probably new societal forms now grew forth within a tribal mode of organization. The reason for this was that the new agrarian economy could not operate under the social and religious structure of earlier Mesolithic societies. In the beginning the agrarian economy probably diminished the pressure on the resources which had created it, resulting in a loosened social organization. Agriculture, however, probably also destroyed the traditional regulation of the population size so that a population growth was triggered off. Consequently more or less marked changes had to occur in the economic and social structures, allowing increased densities of population and precipitating changes in the settlement pattern. At present the archaeological evidence of this transition is meagre, but as will be described below, a number of observations indicate sweeping transformations in the course of the fourth millennium BC.

To understand the background for this lengthy course of development a number of factors must be clarified. On the whole very few of the material prerequisites for the beginning of agriculture in Denmark can be discerned in the period predating 4200 BC. A multitude of elements in the new cultural form had to be introduced from abroad. Such elements included domesticated animals, cultivated cereal types, and vital aspects of the technology inherent in the new subsistence form. Certainly, there had been contact between the late hunter–gatherer communities and the agrarian communities to the south – but this contact alone cannot explain the introduction of an agrarian economy about 4200 BC. So it is necessary to consider some possible causes of the origin of agriculture and its dissemination throughout Europe.

It is also important to emphasize that the prehistoric population could hardly have chosen the new subsistence strategy voluntarily. Compared with the existence of the hunter–gatherers, the introduction of stock-rearing and cereal cultivation meant that prehistoric man had to furnish a greater input of labour. An agrarian-based economy offered greater potential for growth than an economy based solely on hunting, fishing and food-gathering; but in return agriculture demanded a higher labour input per unit of food gained. This changed subsistence strategy may be viewed as the hunter–gatherers' response to a falling living standard. This view is justified by the fact that a low-technology society normally strives to employ the subsistence strategy which can nourish the population at the cost of a minimal input of labour. Meanwhile, it is possible that, as already mentioned, near the close of the fifth millennium BC a resource crisis threatened the Danish prehistoric population. This crisis may have hastened the introduction of domesticated plants and animals into the prehistoric society. Finally, it is important to emphasize that inherent in the transition to a subsistence form mainly based upon domesticated animals and cereal cultivation were hitherto unknown possibilities for economic and demographic growth. The root of this growth lay in the relative flexibility of the resources. Precisely for this reason, agriculture as a means of subsistence entails a constant demand for technological innovation. The factors named here will be described in more detail below.

The moving frontier

In recent decades, investigations of the origins of agriculture in the Middle East have shown that the understanding of this revolutionary step in the history of mankind must be sought in a study of the lifeways and adaptions of the inhabitants of the area during the Pleistocene. Many modern investigations seem to indicate that the introduction of agriculture was the result of a certain hunting and food-gathering strategy developed by hunters and gatherers by the late Pleistocene – and that the catalyst for change was a demographic one.

At the heart of modern research lie questions such as: what made agriculture advantageous and what helped stimulate changes in the early domesticates in the Middle East? A variety of hypotheses have been formulated to explain these developments. One of the most frequently cited hypotheses (K.V. Flannery, 1969) suggests that population growth in certain areas of the Zagros Mountains had begun already 20,000 years ago due to the so-called broad spectrum revolution. This change consisted of a significant broadening of the subsistence base to include ever greater amounts of fish, crabs, shellfish, birds and possibly plant food. Reliance on a broad range of food sources encouraged a sedentary settlement pattern which in turn stimulated population growth. This caused the surplus population to move into more marginal environments, taking with them wild forms of sheep, goats, wheat and barley.

The marginal zone hypothesis cannot be fully tested with data from the archaeological record in the Near East. But no matter how one explains the origin of the agricultural economy there is hardly any doubt that it arose as a result of a growing strain on the resources in the region of origin. The critical point seems to have been reached when a society of hunters and food-gatherers attained the population level on which resource scarcity forced the population to supplement gathering with, for example, cultivation of plants, and hunting with animal husbandry. In the beginning these new strategies were relatively restricted in relation to the traditional mode of obtaining food. But in time they increased, as the new strategies which provided an opportunity for an increase in the food production stimulated a population growth at the same time.

Many thousands of years intervened between the rise of agriculture in the Middle East and the first signs of agriculture in southern Scandinavia. Between these two events the dissemination of agriculture followed paths which over the past few decades archaeological research has been able to determine with a good deal of certainty. The process seems to have been characterized by a pattern of rapid spread and relatively low population density, as the surplus population of the farming communities had apparently expanded to ecological niches resembling the original territory as much as possible. Radiocarbon dates reveal that in the seventh and sixth millennia the agrarian economy spread from Anatolia to the Balkan peninsula and hence via the lower and middle Danube to central Europe.

The first European farming societies on the Balkan peninsula branched out by means of the network of fertile river valleys on the peninsula. From the Balkan peninsula the moving frontier continued via the loess regions along the lower and middle Danube. This final spreading in the loess plains of Europe betokens the transition from a frontal to an axially orientated distribution pattern. From north-west Hungary, there was a spread via the loess-covered areas up to the upper Danube, the lower Rhine and the lower Oder. These regions were then covered by a light open mixed oak forest and comprised a relatively unexploited ecological niche. The composition of the forest doubtless determined the farmers' choice of arable land.

The distribution of the early agrarian societies has been described as a wave of advance which progressed with an average speed of about one kilometre each year. Settlements were always made in regions with high agricultural potential. Probably the rise in temperature in the Atlantic period also favoured the spread – in any case, it can be observed that the great spread out over Europe began in the seventh millennium, that is, at the beginning of the Atlantic period. In the fifth millennium BC the wave of advance had reached the earlier ice-locked regions on the north European lowland. Then the colonization shifted in character, as the agrarian culture now confronted regions with soil types which were either unexploitable or less productive. Archaeological terminology distinguishes between a central European so-called 'Linear Pottery culture', associated with the loess regions, and a north European 'Funnel-Necked Beaker culture'.

Whereas the spread of the 'Linear Pottery culture' could be described as a wave of advance, which seemed to force the surplus population forward in an axial distribution pattern, another explanation must probably be sought for the rise of the agrarian economy within the great lowland region of northern Europe. The consistent preference earlier shown for certain soil types within the 'Linear Pottery culture' does not exist in north-west Germany and southern Scandinavia. The neolithiza-tion of this area has therefore been termed a secondary phenomenon as it apparently had a different background from the early neolithization of central Europe. This background has already been touched upon above. To delve further into the problem, we shall now seek to illuminate the environmental conditions which characterized Denmark at the end of the fifth millennium BC.

The farming communities and their environment

The High Atlantic period was the warmest of the great Post-Pleistocene periods. In the fifth millennium BC, in the last phase of the Atlantic, the rise in temperature in Denmark culminated. The climate was now warm and moist: the summer temperature was at least 2°, more probably 3°, higher than today. This favourable climate continued into the succeed-ing period, during which the agrarian communities began in earnest to make their mark on the environment.

The fifth millennium BC also witnessed the culmination of the Litorina transgression, possibly resulting in a shift in the population equilibrium. If this is the case, it may explain why at the end of the High Atlantic period the first signs of a true agricultural economy can be observed in Denmark. From this time, the relationship between the prehistoric society and its environment acquired a completely new dimension: man's manipulation of the fauna and the vegetation now became a vital factor. However, the influence of a primitive agricultural system on the forest is difficult to identify in the beginning. Consequently, up to the middle of the fourth millennium BC, the changes observed are difficult to interpret.

The natural environment which was the scene of the first farming communities in Denmark was above all dominated by the climax forest. Through the foregoing millennia, the vegetation had tended towards a climax stage. The stable virgin forest had formed and conditioned the development potential of the newly established subsistence strategy. The agrarian economy demanded new forms of labour, the most important of which was forest clearance.

The forest which confronted the first farming society represented a climax stage in the great ecological succession. It was a stable virgin forest; when trees died, new trees of the same type grew up in their place; no longer did forests of pioneer trees encroach. The virgin forest of the Sub-Boreal period covered all of Denmark, interrupted only by the many lakes and swampy areas. The lime seems to have been the predominant forest tree. On poor dry sandy soil such as that in west Jutland, oak rivalled the lime. Elm too was common, although it suffered a decline around 3800 BC. This decline will later be examined more carefully. The role of the ash was not large, but it did grow around the beginning of the fourth millennium BC. By the shores of streams and lakes the alder was the leading tree.

Within the various landscapes, the composition of this dark, shady virgin forest was naturally varied. On high, well-watered ground the lime predominated. On moister ground there was a more varied forest – a mixed oak forest. Here lime, elm and ash grew, with the oak as the predominant tree. In the moist swampy regions the alder reigned, whereas birch alone was found near the moist deep peat bogs.

The interior of the virgin forest was murky. Tree trunks were far more massive than is normal for modern forests. The underbrush-vegetation on the forest floor was scanty as a result of the dense canopy, and the forest floor was full of mouldering wood.

The small farming communities which arose around 4000 BC seem primarily to have been located on the border between high well-watered ground and low ground where the moist forest floor could provide nourishment for domesticated pigs. On the high ground small clearings were established by burning the forest, the heat of which released nutrients in the upper few centimetres of the forest soil. However, ash had only a slight effect as a fertilizer. The burning also rinsed the forest floor of competing growths and weed-like vegetation. All of these results bettered growing conditions for cereal.

The stationary condition which characterized the forest meant that the amount of humus mineralized each year corresponded to the amount formed by the dead organic materials which were left. This process is most noticeable on soil which is rich in nutrients and it increases with the rising temperature. In short, the mould production of the Atlantic climax forest must have been great, a factor which benefited agriculture tremendously.

This process was a link in a much greater cycle, the course of which has been described in conjunction with the environmental development in the Post-Pleistocene. A similar cycle can also be shown to have existed between the glaciations. The cycle commences with a glacial period, in which solifluction prevents the formation of a stable plant growth. Then comes the formation of a soil rich in lime and minerals which is neutral or slightly sour, and at some places soil exhaustion begins. This stage corresponds to the climax forest in the climatic optimum of the Atlantic period. At last, when the temperature again begins to drop, comes an increased exhaustion of the soil with an increasing degree of sourness and podsolization as a consequence (J. Iversen, 1969).

As evident, there was a large production of mould in the dense climax forest during the transition between the High Atlantic and the Sub-Boreal periods. The natural deterioration of the soil was as yet slight but the impact of man hastened it considerably synchronous with the earliest agrarian cultures. The spread of agriculture in Denmark thus rapidly became an irreversible process.

The extensive swiddening practised by the first farmers destroyed large areas of forest. As we will see later, the exhausted fields were abandoned after a brief period of cultivation. Thus more ways for exhausting the soil were created. In particular the light forest with scrub pasture here and there which resulted from cattle grazing must have suffered rapid soil deterioration, a condition which is also familiar from more recent times (S.T. Andersen, 1979). On hilly terrain the destruction of the natural vegetation could also be accompanied by soil erosion when the mould was no longer anchored by the roots of the plants.

So there is good reason to believe that the mould of the forest floor which must have existed when agriculture was introduced degenerated badly quite early. This factor, in addition to the negative effect of ard ploughing see pp. 99 ff, 143 ff, and 222 ff) and the lack of manuring, seems to have had a decisive impact on the future course of agriculture. We will return to these circumstances later.

The evidence of pollen analysis

An understanding of this process and of the existence of the first farming society in the dense climax forest is first and foremost conveyed by the natural sciences and in particular by pollen analysis. This discipline determines the quantitative relationship of the pollen of various plants. By analysing samples from all layers in a number of bogs, it has been possible to establish a relative chronology for the vegetational development in southern Scandinavia. This development is marked by a number of expansion stages caused by the intrusion of the farming communities into nature. Four stages have been identified. The first stage began during the fourth millennium BC and represents the 'landnam' of the first farmer. After some centuries, this first human intrusion into the forest is supplanted by a new expansion period which set in somewhat after the beginning of the third millennium BC at approximately the same time as the so-called 'Single Grave culture'. In the centuries predating the birth of Christ an increase in human activity is again apparent, but dwindles somewhat about 400–500 AD. A last expansion phase begins in the Viking period – and again lessens in the late Middle Ages (Figure 22).

Of these four expansion stages which have been determined on a very general basis, our interest is focused primarily on the first stage. Often this first landnam phase is divided into two parts: an A-landnam corresponding to the so-called elm fall, marked by a drastic fall in the pollen curve of the elm at the transition to the Sub-Boreal; and a B-landnam, which very clearly shows the effect on the vegetational

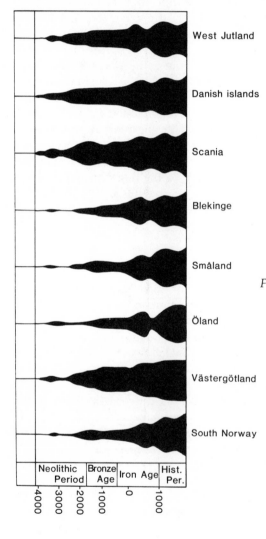

West Jutland

Danish islands

Scania

Blekinge

Småland

Öland

Västergötland

South Norway

Neolithic Period	Bronze Age	Iron Age	Hist. Per.

-4000 -3000 -2000 -1000 0 1000

Figure 22 Survey diagram illustrating human influence on the vegetation in eight areas of south Scandinavia. The chart attempts to illustrate the four general expansion stages of farming and stock-raising during the prehistoric period. 1. The early Neolithic 'landnam' (*c.* 4000–3200 BC). 2. The late Neolithic and early Bronze Age expansion (*c.* 2800–1000 BC). 3. The expansion of the early Iron Age (*c.* 200 BC–400 AD). 4. The expansion of the Viking period (*c.* 800–1000 AD).

development of the primitive swidden farming of the early farming communities.

The elm fall or the A-landnam is the first change in the vegetational development which may be attributed to human activity. Whether this holds true, however, is very uncertain. On the border between the Atlantic and the Sub-Boreal, the pollen curve of the elm falls noticeably. A corresponding fall can in fact be observed over all of north-western Europe. The elm fall has been explained climatically with regard to the so-called elm disease which has also ravaged Europe and North America in our century.

However, a number of scholars have persuasively argued that the elm fall is the result of primitive agriculture. It has been pointed out that in a deciduous forest region such as Denmark, primitive stock-raising must be based upon leaf fodder. Ecologically the elm fall can be perfectly well explained as the result of a primitive agricultural economy with husbandry. But it is difficult to integrate this theory with the conclusions which can be drawn from archaeological investigations of contemporary settlements. Whether or not the elm fall was the result of the encroachment of the first farming communities in the forest is a question which must hang in abeyance. In the meantime the existence of the farming communities prior to the elm fall may be traced in other ways. Finds of pottery assignable to the first agrarian communities have been radio-carbon-dated to the period immediately preceding the elm fall.

Around 3200 BC – here and there even earlier – that is, one thousand years after the first archaeological evidence of the slow advance of the agricultural economy, we find a number of vegetational changes – the B-landnam – which quite clearly can be ascribed to an agrarian culture. The specifics of these changes will not be discussed here. However, it may be mentioned that in the detailed pollen diagrams, this landnam phase may be divided into three stages. The first stage corresponds to the forest clearance of the agrarian communities. This clearance has been interpreted as having entailed a swiddening or burning-off of the trees and bushes growing on the land intended for cultivation. After a fairly brief period of cultivation follows another stage which, according to the pollen analysts, is the result of cattle grazing on the abandoned fields. The third stage represents the regeneration of the forest after the cessation of cattle grazing. After a certain development this phase ends with the forest strangling all other plant species in its growing density.

Early agriculture had but a limited effect on the dense virgin forest. Throughout the fourth millennium BC Denmark was still dominated by dense forest and underbrush. Not until the third millennium BC did the scrub pastures gradually grow in importance.

7

Population growth and food production

The growth potential of the agrarian society

The beginning of agriculture has often been claimed to be one of the most revolutionary steps in the history of mankind. The beginning of food production is said to have created the potential for economic and demographic growth of previously unequalled extent. However, it is not until recently that Danish archaeologists have delved more deeply into these problems. Whilst the modern world is increasingly confronted with population problems, prehistoric archaeology has sought to gain insight into the societal mechanisms which lead to population growth.

In older research the problem could be defined fairly simply. Population growth was frequently regarded as the direct result of technological innovation. Today there is a more pronounced tendency to see population pressure as an independent variable affecting other cultural and environmental factors, a view which requires a re-evaluation of many archaeological hypotheses.

An attempt has been made above to demonstrate that the cause of agriculture in southern Scandinavia should possibly be sought in the demographic situation. An attempt will now be made to determine whether this basic viewpoint can also be maintained in relation to further agricultural development in Danish prehistory. It may be asked whether this hypothesis can explain the expansion stages indicated, for example, by pollen analysis.

As suggested earlier, we must presume that seasonal fluctuations in the amount of resources were of crucial importance in establishing the optimal population size of the hunter–gatherer communities. The population size had to be adapted to the resources in the poorest seasons and to fluctuations in the resources over the years. With the introduction of the agrarian economy the effect of such fluctuations is diminished by such innovations as the development of methods of preserving and storing. Above all, however, agrarian societies are characterized by the emphasis they place on resources with a high potential for expansion. Animal husbandry combined with plant cultivation entails just such a potential. Each of the two subsistence strategies has its own characteristics. The holding of domestic animals is less productive than plant cultivation, as animals rank more highly in the food chain than plants. But domesticated animals are mobile, and herds can be led to where there is a sufficiency of food. However, a significant expansion of stock-holding demands drastic changes in the ecosystem. Obtaining a larger grazing area in a terrain of virgin forest, for example, demands an enormous investment of labour. Cereal cultivation also demands a considerable investment of labour. The cultivated area can be enlarged fairly easily although it requires an increase in regular labour to care for the fields. In return even quite small technological changes often deeply affect the yield. In conjunction the two subsistence forms have a high potential for expansion, depending of course upon the possibilities for an increased investment of labour.

Thus there exists a wide difference between societies based wholly or partially on agriculture and all other societal forms. In agrarian society demographic control is not so crucial as in the hunter–gatherer society due to this growth potential. But at the same time this growth potential is accompanied by a constant demand for technological innovation. It is the nature of this innovation which we shall now attempt to illuminate.

A theory of agricultural development under population pressure

The Danish economist Esther Boserup's studies of present-day low-technological societies have had tremendous significance for the understanding of the development of early agriculture in Denmark. Her point of departure is the fact that in a primitive agriculture much of the arable land must lie fallow most of the time to regain its fertility.

To begin with slash-and-burn farming, which is the most economical agricultural system in a sparsely populated area, a series of stages can be observed. These stages occur as the fallow period is increasingly shortened as a consequence of the intensified harvesting necessitated by growing population pressure. To counteract a fall in the yield, farmers are continually forced to employ new means. The introduction of the plough to Denmark during the third millennium BC and perhaps even earlier thus represents the next stage in the process. The technology of the agrarian society must of necessity be modified in each new developmental stage to ensure a sufficiently high yield.

However, the development of the agrarian society demands an ever growing investment of labour, that is the growth of the population results in an increased labour input per food unit gained. Production rises but the product per labour unit falls. It is this fall in productivity which sheds doubt on older theories which instead viewed population increase as the direct result of technological innovations. Contrary to this viewpoint, Esther Boserup claims that an agrarian population does not naturally increase its labour input voluntarily, even if this input is very small, as in the earliest agriculture. Growing population pressure provoked by the tendency toward sedentarism can, however, force the agrarian society to increase its labour input. Harder and more efficient work also raises effectiveness in other areas, greater population density allows more specialized divisions of labour, and the process is thus set in motion.

As we have said, Esther Boserup points out that with a low population density an extensive agriculture based upon slash-and-burn is the most economic agricultural system, as regards the investment of labour. This system has various consequences. First of all, farming with long fallow periods demands but little preparation of the soil because cultivation only occurs for a short length of time. Nor is it necessary to maintain fertility by fertilizing during the cultivation period; it is hardly worth the effort to clear tree trunks out of the way. Therefore the use of a plough is unnecessary and the cultivated area can be abandoned when the weeds begin to compete seriously with the cultivated species, and when the nutrients released by the swiddening diminish. In short, a relatively small labour input is sufficient to ensure a good yield. However, slash-and-burn farming demands large areas per family when the fallow areas are taken into consideration. Slash-and-burn cannot therefore be maintained when the population exceeds a certain point when there would no longer be enough land to continue with the long fallow periods.

As remarked above, the population increase gradually necessitates an abandonment of slash-and-burn and the introduction of agricultural systems which exploit the area more effectively. In return, there is a lower yield per working hour; more work is required. In Denmark, the first step in this direction seems to have occurred at the end of the fourth millennium and throughout the third millennium BC. Traces of ard-ploughing are more frequent in this period; animal husbandry continues to expand. Both of these changes demand an increased labour input: the draught animals must be fed, fodder must be gathered, the fields must be cleared, weeded and enclosed; therefore the various amounts of invested labour rise. It is not possible to trace this process in detail by means of the archaeological record. The process probably occurred at a different pace in various regions. After the introduction of ard-ploughing, however, the expansion of productivity seems to have occurred primarily by means of the raising of domestic animals. This situation will be examined later.

The hypothesis suggested here is on several counts an extension of the views proposed above regarding the development of the hunter–gatherer communities up to c. 4200 BC. Here too an attempt has been made to show how the continued effort to adapt to the food situation entailed the use of a number of culturally conditioned means to control population size. The incipient food production around 4200 BC has been seen in the same perspective and explained as the response of the population to a falling living standard. This sort of explanation makes it possible to reject the invasion hypotheses which formerly played an exaggerated role in European archaeological literature. To explain the rise of agricultural economy by simply suggesting a massive invasion of foreign peoples is in reality no explanation at all, as the economic analysis which provides an understanding of the dynamics of further cultural development is thereby often neglected. In the same way the hypothesis of the 'filtering in' of foreign ethnic groups and their assimilation with the local population cannot be supported on chronological grounds. Determining the primary catalyst in the set of factors which led to the introduction of agriculture demands a deeper understanding of the complicated interrelationship of the food situation, the population size and society's means of production. With the introduction of the agricultural economy, the population size once more fell far below the limit imposed by the previous subsistence form. For more than a thousand years, the population grew again, until a new maximum was reached – a development which will be treated in the following chapters.

Fertility and mortality in the early agrarian society

In the discussion of demographic conditions in the hunter–gatherer communities, reference was made to a number of more general results which in part pertained to the prehistoric population's chances of survival. Many of these results were obtained by comparison with present-day low-technology societies. With the beginning of the agricultural economy around 4200 BC, we have more concrete evidence regarding the individual's chances of survival. A number of results from early Swiss agrarian communities, for example, confirm the statistics mentioned above; moreover, they seem to have validity for the Danish situation.

A survival chart for individuals from a number of contemporaneous Swiss farming communities is shown in Figure 23. The extremely high mortality in the younger age groups is clearly evident – indeed it is probably even higher, because the skeletons of infants cannot be well preserved. The survival chart shows that after 13 years only about 40–45

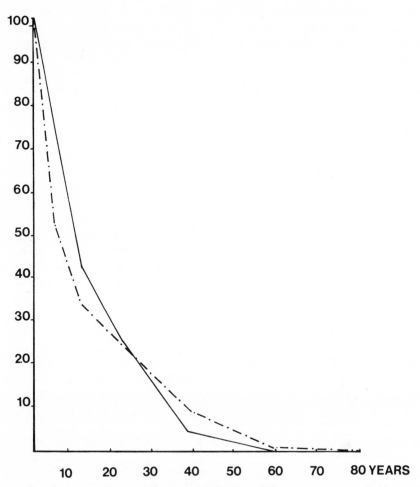

Figure 23 A survival chart from a number of Swiss Neolithic communities. The height of the curve above the horizontal axis indicates how large a percentage of a generation survived in each age group.

per cent of the living-born individuals are still alive. After 22 years, more than 70 per cent of the individuals are dead – the average life expectancy for living-born individuals is between 20 and 25 years. This implies that only about 30 per cent of those born attained adulthood.

The distribution of the two sexes also shows some striking features, in particular men's distinctly better chances of survival. In general only very few changes in mortality can be expected in the course of prehistory. Swedish investigations of the medieval population in Jämtland in Sweden (N.-G. Gejvall, 1960) show a noteworthy correspondence with the observations in Figure 23. Infant mortality for the first year of life of over 30 per cent does not seem to have been uncommon. Similarly, observations of the high mortality in the young age groups and women's poor chances of survival in comparison to those of men seem to be applicable to all prehistoric periods (G. Acsádi and J. Nemeskéri, 1970).

These factors naturally had great significance for the composition of the individual populations. The farming communities must have possessed a sizeable surplus of men. The number of individuals in the younger age groups was only slightly larger than the number in the mature age groups. Population growth must have occurred extremely slowly, and even though 'over-population' is a relative phenomenon, it seems only to a limited extent applicable as an explanatory basis in the hypotheses of invasions with which earlier archaeology operated.

Regarding the health conditions of the prehistoric population after the introduction of agricultural economy, only a few factors will be mentioned here. The wide-spectred subsistence strategy which characterized the early farming communities would hardly have caused any major changes. Growing dependence upon cereal food, which came to characterize the farming communities, may in periods have been accompanied by a lack of proteins and fat. It is very possible that vitamin deficiency, especially in the vitamin groups A, B and D, and the consequent deficiency diseases existed in the population after c. 4200 BC. In fact, rachitis has been identified on skeletons from the the Neolithic period in Denmark. Despite the fact that food could now be produced in hitherto unimagined quantities, deficiency diseases and food crises may paradoxically have been the result of the introduction of agriculture. This situation will be studied more closely in the following chapter.

8

Subsistence and settlement

Introduction

The first expansion of agriculture in Denmark extended over a period of about 1500 years. In archaeological literature this period is referred to by the rather unfortunate name, 'the Funnel-Necked Beaker culture'. After the latest calibrated radiocarbon dates this period is believed to have begun about 4200 BC, which is 1700 years earlier than was believed just twenty years ago.

In the same way, various hypotheses regarding the period have had to be modified. It was formerly thought that several hundred years after the introduction of agriculture a new ethnic group, the so-called 'Single Grave people', invaded Denmark. The oldest agrarian population of the country was hence thought to have lived alongside this new ethnic element until the two groups merged after some centuries. Again, radiocarbon datings have modified earlier theories. The parallelism alluded to between the two population groups has not been confirmed by either archaeological or scientific studies. A more logical hypothesis is that in the course of the third millennium BC, especially after c. 2800 BC, a number of profound economic and social changes occurred within the agrarian communities. In the archaeological literature this new develop-mental stage is termed the 'Single Grave culture'. The entire problem is still under debate and will be described more thoroughly in the next chapter.

Through nearly 1500 years the first agricultural culture evolved relatively undisturbed in Denmark. The archaeological remains which can provide information on the trends of the period are, to be sure, quite abundant in the latter half, when a series of environmental, cultural and organizational factors favoured a rapid growth of the agricultural communities. In general, however, one gains the impression of great continuity in societal development during the whole period.

Land use of the early farming communities

The subsistence form practised in the fourth millennium BC in Denmark is rather obscure. This is because the settlement pattern of the first agrarian communities is still a neglected area of research. Up to the present, very few settlements have been studied for the purpose of gaining an overall picture of the nature of a settlement site. The same neglect holds true of ecological studies, which could, among other things, describe the relationship of the settlement to the biological zones exploitable by an individual village. Knowledge of the geographic distribution of the early farming communities also leaves much to be desired. In this regard, however, a single valuable study has been made, based upon the preserved and protected grave monuments (J. Bekmose, 1978).

The point of departure for this latter investigation consisted of the protected megalith graves from the end of the fourth millennium BC, the well-known dolmens and passage graves. Of these, only the rectangular type of dolmen without passage can be dated to the earliest farming communities, whereas there is a growing body of information dating most other types to a period of only a few centuries around 3200 BC.

By means of a statistical study it was concluded that the preserved megalith structures could be presumed to constitute a representative sample. The monuments should therefore prove useful as a basis for conclusions regarding the geographic distribution of the agrarian communities, the selection of settlement areas within the arable regions of the country, and the relative population situation of the period.

The point of departure is naturally the extent of the country in the period under discussion. North of a line which runs diagonally from Nissum Bredning in the west of Jutland to northern Falster in the east of Denmark, the land was then considerably lower than today. The fjords of northern Zealand were considerably wider, Djursland was divided by the now dry Kolind fjord, and northern Jutland was broken up into numerous islands. South of the line, however, the land was higher. Tåsinge, Ærø and Falster comprised one island. This also held true of Lolland and Falster, just as the islands of the Wadden Sea were connected with southern Jutland.

On the map of Denmark, Figure 24, which shows the present-day coastline of the country, the spatial distribution of the dolmens in long barrows is illustrated through a trend-surface analysis. The dolmens in

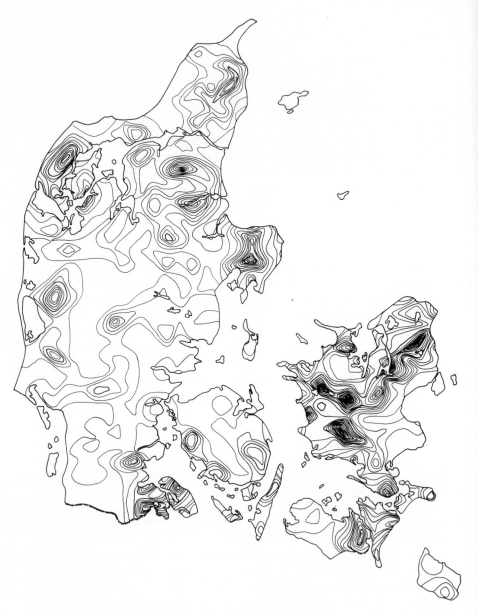

Figure 24 The spatial distribution of Neolithic dolmens in long barrows, illustrated by a trend surface analysis.

long barrows are a group of monuments which is spread throughout the country, although there are areas which are strikingly poor in finds in central, western and eastern Jutland. The same holds true of Funen, just as there are small areas which are poor in finds on western Lolland and eastern Zealand. The geography of the Atlantic period naturally plays a role for the understanding of the distribution pattern, but as a whole concentrations can be observed around what was once a series of archipelago-like coastal regions. The concentrations lie in northern Zealand, on Lolland, Falster, southern Zealand and eastern Funen with connection to the eastern part of south Jutland. Finally there are concentrations on Djursland, in Himmerland and in the western Limfjord area together with a less noteworthy one by Ringkøbing fjord.

In general it can be observed that the early agrarian communities showed a preference for high-lying well-drained ground. But the distribution of the settlements can hardly be explained on this basis alone. The relationship with the archipelago regions of the time and their multitude of various biological zones must have been just as decisive. As will later be seen, this corresponds to the wide-spectred subsistence strategy practised by the early farming communities.

The map on which the geographic distribution of the dolmens in long barrows is plotted helps provide an idea of the basic pattern in the geographic distribution of the early agrarian communities. Supplementing this picture with, for example, the distribution of the dolmens in round barrows, few important exceptions can be noted. To be sure, the dolmens in round barrows have a more limited distribution than dolmens in long barrows but still many of the groupings which characterize the distribution of long dolmens are present. In the main, the passage graves also correspond to the map in Figure 24. The passage graves, however, are primarily an east Danish phenomenon and are often associated with the distribution areas of dolmens.

The great significance ascribed to the megalithic monuments such as dolmens and passage graves is due to the role which they must have played in the territorial patterns of the agrarian communities. If it is presumed that as a result of swidden agriculture settlement was moved at regular intervals within a defined territory, then the great stone graves in contrast must have been among the few permanent elements in the existence of the farming communities. This view has been expressed by Colin Renfrew (1976) as follows: that for the individual community the grave monument was not merely the grave of the forefathers; it was also a permanent symbol of continuity in the possession of the surrounding territory.

This situation will be studied more closely later. Here it will only be suggested that the distribution of the large stone graves seems to indicate the settlement pattern of the farming communities. This pattern is not necessarily completely valid, as the stone graves are not the sole grave form of the epoch. The picture which can be glimpsed about 1000 years after the first traces of an agrarian economy appear are settlements which, particularly in southern Denmark, were established with a certain preference for the heavy soils, primarily of glacial clay, and – of perhaps even greater importance – situated around a number of archipelago-like coastal regions where the variation of resources was especially great.

Within the individual settlement areas, development assumed a number of forms. The correspondence between the multitude of biological zones and benign soils seems to have provided the south Danish settlements in particular with the opportunity for great expansion at the beginning of the third millennium BC. Here, in fact, new settlement concentrations arose, for example on northern Funen, where a new archipelago settlement appeared. In northern and central Jutland development seems to have stagnated to a certain degree after an initial establishment phase; demographic concentrations similar to those seen in southern Denmark never seem to have been achieved.

We have now considered the overall picture of the settlement of the farming communities as it appeared in the final centuries of the fourth millennium BC. This is the period during which the megalith constructions were erected, called in archaeological terminology the end of the Early Neolithic and the beginning of the Middle Neolithic. Unfortunately it is very difficult to determine the long-term trends in the development of the settlement. This is due chiefly to the fact that the archaeological sources which illuminate the so-called Single Grave culture, the period after 2800 BC, occur scattered and by chance. Not even the intensive regional surveys carried out by the Danish National Museum in the 1940s and 1950s can provide any unambiguous picture. However, some long-term tendencies can be glimpsed.

The intensive regional surveys mentioned were carried out both in north-west Zealand and in north-west Jutland. In the former area, where the quality of the soil is quite homogeneous, settlement in the first millennium of the existence of the farming communities shows a relatively even spreading over the entire area. For instance, the central parts of Zealand were also the location of a relatively intensive exploitation. The regions near the coast, however, seem to have had the largest population concentration. It also appears that the exploitation of the inland diminished somewhat after c. 3000 BC. An expansion of the settlement in the coastal regions and a certain thinning out in the inland regions seem evident. This marked tendency continued with growing force in the succeeding millennia.

The explanation for this situation should hardly be sought in a decreasing population. In fact, quite the opposite may have been the case. The shift was presumably related to changes in the agricultural system. Whereas the earliest slash-and-burn agriculture probably compelled the farming communities to a high degree of mobility, the gradual introduction of the plough and perhaps especially the expansion of stock-raising observable in the course of the period may thus have favoured a more sedentary settlement pattern. The farming communities may thus have preferred different types of soil and especially vegetation than previously. The dense virgin forest in the interior of the island may no longer have been so attractive. Instead growth gradually took place in a terrain where more intensive settlement had created a more open vegetation and thus better conditions for an expansion of animal husbandry.

This tendency may also be evident in the other area which has been thoroughly studied, the north-western part of Jutland. The settlement here shows in the first phases an even distribution over the moraine regions along the southern part of the Limfjord. The sandy regions of the outwash plains in the south, on the other hand, show a far more scattered settlement. As on Zealand, the farming communities seem at first to have sought the dense forest areas which were necessary for swidden agriculture. But in time the lighter soils seem to have been preferred rather than the heavy moraine soil. This tendency gained great impetus in the following millennia, and at the same time the open forest vegetation on the present-day heathy plains were to an increasing degree taken over for settlement. Again it can be presumed that the development from swidden agriculture to an agriculture with growing emphasis on cattle was the reason for the shift in settlement. In these areas of Jutland a major change in the settlement pattern seems to have taken place around 2800 BC. The attempts of the communities to expand production, especially by increasing stock-breeding, may well have been directed toward the more open vegetation forms in preference to the dense forest areas on the heavy moraine ground.

These two examples perhaps describe the beginning of the settlement type which can be distinctly observed in the second millennium BC: in Jutland, settlement seems to be concentrated with growing intensity on the lighter, although not the very lightest, soils whereas the dense forests growing, for example, on the moraine soil of eastern Jutland seem to have been avoided. On Zealand the moraine areas in the interior of the island seem to have been gradually abandoned. Instead, settlement was concentrated in the regions near the coast where a relatively large population gradually created a countryside with a quite open forest. The extensive swidden agriculture accompanied by a mobile settlement pattern seems to have been gradually replaced by a more sedentary settlement pattern. The prerequisite for this may have been the growing importance of the plough and the increase in stock-rearing, with the consequent greater need for grazing areas. As yet this process cannot be followed in detail, but it became distinct in the course of the second millennium BC.

Settlement

The picture which can be drawn of the settlement pattern of the early farming communities on the macro-level seems also to be repeated on the micro-level. The very wide-spectred subsistence strategy practised by the farming communities through the fourth millennium BC explains why settlement took place especially in areas with a great environmental variation. The same pattern is also evident in more restricted settlement areas and in the study of individual settlement sites. Here it is also seen that every single community adapted itself in all details to the ecological niche in which it existed. For example, the composition of the livestock was determined by the specific ecological advantages offered by the environment. Access to grazing areas, to fresh water, to hunting, and so on, seems to have deeply influenced the character of the individual settlement site.

The study of the first farming communities' settlement pattern in Denmark is, however, still in its infancy. As yet very few settlement sites have been excavated, so it has not been possible to gain an impression of, for example, the house-types – and consequently of the size of the individual settlement. The structures which were once considered typical of the dwelling form of the farming communities, the so-called longhouses from Barkær in Jutland, have been proved in recent studies to be enormous grave structures, probably long barrows. Intensive investigations of small defined areas are also very few. Yet a single newer investigation made within a 1600 km² area on the east coast of Jutland (T. Madsen, 1978a) has yielded significant results which can serve as a guide for future research.

The area investigated in this latter study (Figure 25) is a tremendously varied hilly moraine landscape traversed by numerous wide valleys with lakes and streams at their bottom. During the marine transgression in the fourth millennium BC the inhabitable area was somewhat smaller than it is today; it was also more emphatically divided

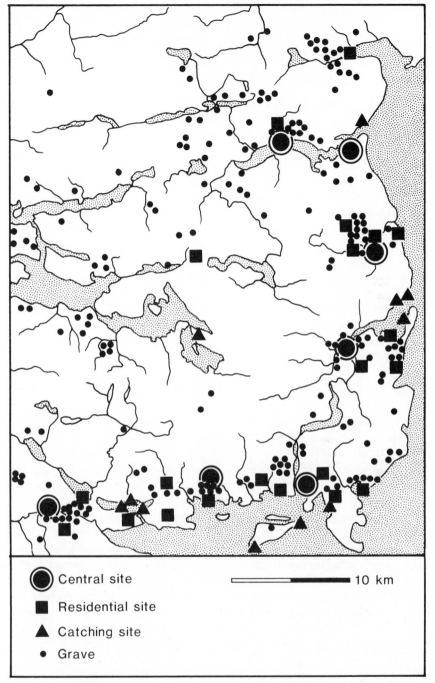

Figure 25 Settlement pattern of Neolithic communities in a hilly moraine landscape in the central part of eastern Jutland. The megalith graves, central sites, and settlements are mostly clustered around the swampy valleys a few kilometres behind the coastline.

by watercourses. First, the settlements of the region and the graves (megalith graves and so-called earth graves) were plotted and a distinct pattern thus emerged. Of particular note are the small clusters of megalith graves and settlement sites which, just a few kilometres behind the coastline, are concentrated around the moist valleys which at that time were quite marked. On the high moraine ground between the valleys and in the interior there are practically no traces of either settlements or graves. In the interior of the land the traces of the early farming communities are concentrated chiefly around lakes and the stream system to which they are associated. Distribution here seems to have occurred mainly where the large water systems lead inland. A typical feature of the settlement pattern is thus the intimate connection to the river valleys with their lake- and bog-basins, together with the fact that the most pronounced concentrations are all near the coast. Quite clearly the preferred areas were those with a large variation of resources and a location close to the low-lying areas with a high water-table and open water (sea, lakes or major watercourses).

Through analysis of the settlements of the region it has been possible to distinguish a number of different categories, namely the so-called maintenance sites, specific activity camps and so-called central sites, of which the latter were shared by an undetermined number of communities.

The so-called maintenance sites comprise the most poorly illuminated aspect of the settlement pattern. This is partially due to the fact that many of the sites which were earlier thought to be maintenance sites have instead proved to be central sites, i.e. causewayed camps, and thus to have had a different function in the settlement pattern from that presumed earlier. Other sites, such as the well-known Barkær on Djursland, have, as already mentioned, proved to be grave complexes, the timber constructions of which may have had a certain resemblance to the dwellings of the farming communities, although they did not serve as actual dwellings. What is left is a group of sites, each of which was probably the centre of agricultural activities within its individual terri-tory. Their location often seems to be on the border between high, well-drained ground and low-lying moist land. This location has been explained as a response to the wish to exploit the high-lying ground for swidden agriculture and the moist damp forest regions for pig-raising. It also seems incontestable that these sites were moved at intervals when necessitated by the resource situation. This corresponds well to the picture of swidden agriculture suggested by pollen analysis.

Moreover, there are vague indications that the size of these main-tenance sites increased in time. At the beginning of the fourth millennium BC they seem to have been quite small, perhaps serving only a single extended family. Over the centuries however, they grew in size, which may be the beginning of the more sedentary settlement pattern which is the prerequisite for the changes of subsistence which occurred in the course of the third millennium BC.

Near the maintenance sites are the hunting places, a site category which has recently been acknowledged as part of the settlement pattern. These are small sites of seemingly very temporary character. Very frequently the same localities were used over and over again; often the Neolithic settlement layer lies directly on top of a Mesolithic one. This continuity in the use of the hunting sites supports the thesis that the transition from the hunting society of the fifth millennium to the agrarian society of the fourth millennium BC occurred very gradually. This means that at first farming was only a modest supplement to the traditional subsistence activities. A major proportion of food probably still had to be obtained by hunting and gathering.

The hunting sites are located in both coastal and inland areas, sometimes on small isolated islands. Seal hunting may have been the purpose of some of these brief stays. Other sites lie near narrow passages in the fjords where the shifting tides created enormous shell banks and where net fishing could be carried out with favourable results. It was earlier thought that the significance of the hunting places diminished in the course of the fourth millennium BC. But this can hardly be the case. Judging by the archaeological record, hunting and gathering seem to have continued as a significant part of the subsistence pattern of the farming communities for a very long time.

Thus it is possible to discern a detailed pattern for the exploitation of the natural resources. The general impression which emerges shows a very wide-spectred subsistence strategy in which hunting, fishing and food-gathering were practised in conjunction with primitive swidden agriculture. Not until sometime in the third millennium BC did this pattern start changing as cattle-raising was gradually given primary emphasis.

The central sites or causewayed camps are the last category of settlements within the Neolithic settlement pattern. These peculiar complexes have been known to Danish archaeology for very few years. But already a great number of finds have been made, and there is no doubt that in Denmark the causewayed camps are an integral part of the settlement pattern of the farming communities. As yet, only the localities Sarup on Funen and Toftum in east Jutland have been the subjects of larger investigations. The size of the complexes seems to have been impressive. The cultural traces at Sarup (Figure 26) cover an

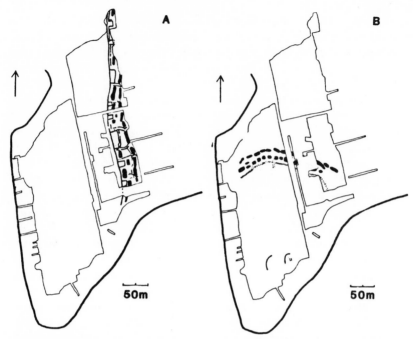

Figure 26 The two phases of the Sarup complex. A: The first phase radiocarbon-
  dated to about 3250 BC (calibrated). B: The second phase radiocarbon-dated to
  about 3150 BC (calibrated).

area of about 4 hectares, and at Toftum (Figure 27) about 3 hectares.

A common feature of these sites is that they are often located on small
promontories surrounded on three sides by watercourses and meadows. The overall appearance of the complexes is not yet known but
they are frequently enclosed by palisades and rows of short ditches
interrupted by earthen bridges.

The Sarup complex (Figure 26) is, as already mentioned, one of the
most thoroughly studied complexes. It contains traces of construction
from a long period of the Neolithic, but the most important settlement
phases are those from the final 200–300 years of the fourth millennium
BC. From the first of these phases, radiocarbon-dated to *c.* 3250 BC, there
is a palisade ditch at least 250 metres long and 1 metre deep, in which
there once stood a fence consisting of oak posts 3–4 metres long. Next to
this palisade fence, there was a series of outbuildings, each 6 × 7 metres,
flanking a larger outbuilding measuring 7 × 20 metres. Between and in
front of these there were moat-like depressions and at the extreme east
there was yet another moat with numerous earthen bridges. At one
place in the palisade fence there was an entrance enclosed by posts.

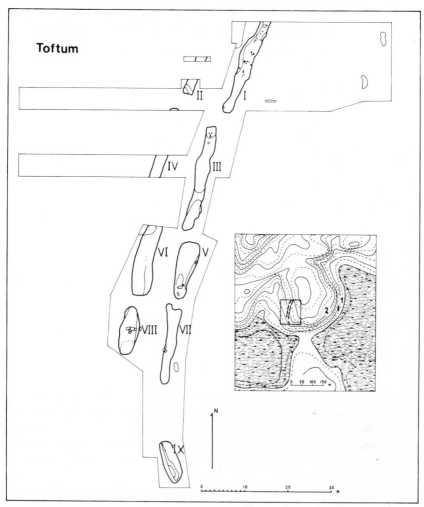

Figure 27 Plan of excavations at Toftum, a Neolithic central site in eastern Jutland. Insert: contour map of the locality (contour intervals 2.5 metres).

The bottoms of the so-called moats contained intact clay vessels, fragmented human skeletons and traces of fire. The moats had been filled in manually very quickly, possibly even the same year that they were dug. In the areas enclosed by the palisade, finds have been made of unbroken clay vessels, some of which contained grain. From a similar, as yet unexcavated, causewayed camp at Årupgård in Jutland there is still another find of a clay vessel containing numerous pieces of amber and metal.

About one hundred years later, another palisade structure was erected at Sarup, radiocarbon-dated to about 3150 BC. However, this structure was only half as large as the older one and consisted of a double row of moats 1 metre deep, together with a palisade fence. In the area thus enclosed, pits have been found with whole clay vessels or flint axes, all of which indicate that this complex, just as the one a century earlier, served a ritual purpose.

Here and there in central and north Europe, similar complexes from about the same period are quite common. The determination of their function, however, is not yet conclusive. They have been interpreted as temporary defence structures and as cattle folds, in which the separation and marking of calves and the winter slaughter were carried out. But it is more probable that these huge enclosures were meeting-places which served social as well as economic and ritual purposes.

This interpretation is confirmed in part by calculations of the labour necessary to erect the complex (N.H. Andersen, 1980). The palisade fence of the Sarup complex required at least 1800 oak logs 3–4 metres long and about 42 centimetres thick, in all about 800 cubic metres of oak. If the chopping and transportation of each log took three working days, then the palisade fence would have taken about 5400 man-days. The digging of about 5000 cubic metres of earth from the moat required about 2500 man-days. Thus the complex as a whole took 7900 man-days. As the complex was used only for a very short time, probably only a single season, its erection may have required 110 men working for three months, a figure which clearly indicates that the complex must have been the result of a co-ordinated effort by several settlement units.

A locational analysis in the south-western part of Funen, where the Sarup complex lies, has shown the existence here of 108 identifiable and probably contemporaneous megalith graves. These graves clearly lie in clusters, as confirmed by statistical analysis. With the help of the so-called Theissen polygons, an attempt has been made to define the territories which belong to the individual clusters of megalith graves (N.H. Andersen, 1980). It appears that there were probably sixteen nearly identical territories or settlement units (Figure 28). There is still uncertainty as to how the individual households were situated within the settlement units, as the habitation sites are still only known in very few cases. But there is reason to believe that the various households lived scattered, gradually moving as the soil became exhausted. Precisely such a dispersed settlement and the labour tasks related to the farming economy would have created the need for an integration of the various settlement units. The central sites of the type to which the Sarup complex belongs seem to be an expression of this integration.

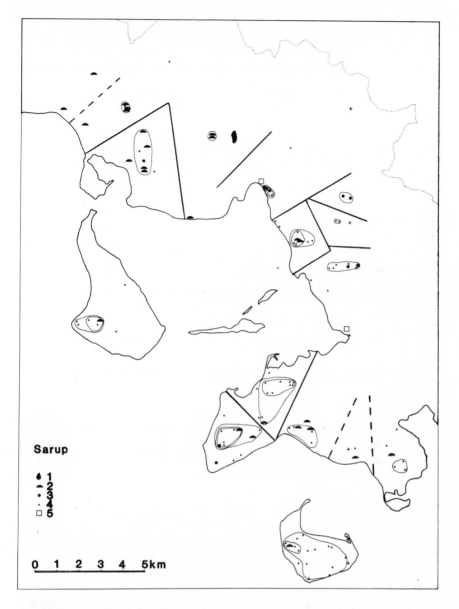

Figure 28 Hypothetical division into territories of the settlements around the Sarup complex. 1. Central site. 2. Long dolmen. 3. Round dolmen. 4. Single megalith grave. 5. Settlement site.

Subsistence patterns

After the prehistoric population had begun to exploit the soil produc-
tively around 4200 BC, there arose labour tasks which demanded an
investment of human labour to a hitherto unequalled degree. Pollen
analysis can provide an impression of the impact which forest clearance
had on the vegetation and can thus lead to conclusions from which the
main features of the new production form can be deduced. The first
stage is obscure, but in the course of the fourth millennium a picture
emerges of a swidden agriculture based upon the burning-off of the
forest. The traces of this extensive subsistence form seem particularly
apparent in the pollen diagrams from the end of the fourth millennium
BC but may go back even further in time.

As mentioned above, the landnam phase typically appears in three
stages in the pollen diagrams. The first stage represents the forest
clearance. The second stage shows cattle grazing on the abandoned
land, and the third stage shows how the high forest returned, although
in a changed form. At the end of this phase, the dense virgin forest
again closed in. We do not know how large the cleared area was. One
can only imagine how clearance was carried out in the early spring as a
collective effort. It has been calculated that with the techniques available, chopping with polished flint axes (Figure 29), an area of about 1
hectare could be cleared by five men in less than fourteen days.

In burning, the heat released nutrients in the upper centimetres of the

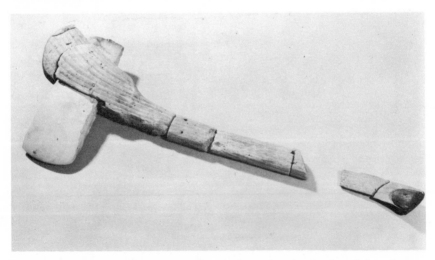

Figure 29 Thin-butted flint axe with a haft made of ash, found in a bog at
Sigerslev, eastern Zealand.

soil and at the same time cleared the soil of competing plants. Weeding the crops was therefore hardly necessary.

It seems that monocultures were raised, but as yet very little is known about the relative proportions of grain types raised. But it is possible that wheat types dominated through the fourth millennium, whereas in the course of the third millennium there was a certain shift to barley, which remained the leading grain type throughout the rest of pre-history.

The methods of cultivation are shrouded in uncertainty. It has been suggested that grain was raised near the settlement on small areas tilled with a spade-like tool. This supposition appears likely, but it should also be added that this cultivation form was probably mainly associated with swidden agriculture. It has already been described how population growth and probably also the increasing exhaustion of the soil quite early led to a gradual decrease of the slash-and-burn technique and a transition to a more sedentary agriculture based on ard-ploughing.

The oldest traces of ploughing in Denmark date from the end of the fourth millennium BC (see figure 36); throughout the third millennium and thereafter they become ever more frequent. The significance of this development will be described in the following chapter. Here we can only list some of the observations which have been made with imitative experiments in ard-ploughing (H.O. Hansen, 1969).

In ard-ploughing, the soil is loosened but not at all (or only very slightly) turned. The ard can be used to plough down grain, but it cannot be used to plough down weeds, a plant growth which otherwise could be transformed to humus.

Another negative effect of ard-ploughing results from the fact that the furrows are narrow and quite shallow. This yields an insufficient airing of the soil and a poor water balance. This effect is unfortunate, as plant roots use oxygen and eliminate carbon dioxide. If the soil is not sufficiently porous, plant growth is hindered by the accumulated carbon dioxide and living conditions are poor for worms and micro-organisms.

This situation inevitably leads to soil exhaustion. New mould formation occurs only to a very slight degree and erosion becomes an active factor in soil exhaustion. These negative effects were not counteracted until the introduction of manuring. It must therefore be concluded that the ard was not a particularly suitable implement – indeed it contributed to the soil exhaustion which in the course of the third millennium must have considerably weakened the subsistence economy of the farming communities (S. Nielsen, 1980).

With regard to the size of the crops there is naturally also a scarcity of information. Imitative experiments have been able to show that with slash-and-burn quite large yields can be achieved – probably as high as thirteen-fold. But these yields must have been very brief, lasting probably only a couple of years. Ard-ploughing produced a considerably lower yield – at the most from twofold to fourfold. This helps to explain why in the long run an expansion of productivity could not be achieved by cultivation but instead had to take place via expansion of stock-raising.

Aside from the cultivation of small fields close to the settlements, a considerable amount of labour must have gone into gathering the leafy fodder consumed by the cattle during the winter months. Elm and ash were very valuable as fodder. This also held true of the leaves of other sorts of trees, especially of the lime, which was a favourite of cattle.

As yet our knowledge of the domestic animals in the first farming communities is relatively limited, but from the latter half of the period, around 3200 BC, evidence from a number of the large settlements in general seems to show that a settlement adapted itself in all details to the ecological niche in which it was located. If a village lay near suitable pastures, perhaps near the coast, then this situation would be reflected in an emphasis on sheep-raising.

However, the dominant activity at the sites was the raising of pigs, which doubtless provided the major source of protein. This situation is easy to understand when it is considered that the pig is, in fact, biologically adapted to areas of dense leafy forests where the production of mast is ample and where it can thrive with a minimum of care. Pigs demand practically no investment of human labour, in buildings for example. Furthermore, pigherds can easily be adapted to human needs if other sources of food fail.

Sheep and goats also played an important role. Their ratio was probably about 5:1. As mentioned, the holding of sheep increased in relation to the proximity to natural pastures such as shore meadows. Like pigs, sheep offer a number of easily achieved economic advantages. Sheep place far fewer demands on the investment of human labour than do cattle. Moreover, sheep can eat grass throughout the growth period and require relatively little investment of labour in the form of gathering winter fodder. Sheep meat is also well-suited for wind-drying and thus constitutes a major meat reserve in lean seasons. The holding of sheep in the early farming communities seems to have been intended for meat production. A few mature goats were probably kept at the settlements – mainly to ensure supplies of dairy products.

The role of cattle-raising in the early farming economy is not yet particularly well illuminated. Cattle herds consisted of mature breeding cows and a few bulls. Steers were raised for meat and heifers to renew the stock of breeding animals. No traces have been observed of the use of bullocks, which bears out the assumption of the minor role of the plough in early agriculture. The slaughtering age was normally 3–4 years, which may indicate that the gathering of winter fodder was not such a burdensome investment of labour; had it been burdensome, slaughtering would have been carried out earlier. The relatively mild and short winters in the fourth and third millennia BC must have been favourable for cattle-raising.

Yet the role of stock-raising in the early agrarian economy raises a number of important problems. The herd could hardly have produced dairy products to any significant degree. But whereas the raising of meat cattle probably entailed a multitude of economic advantages, it should also be kept in mind that cattle require more labour than other domestic animals. The herd could be radically expanded only if increased pasture

Figure 30 Early Neolithic flint mine at Hov, northern Jutland.

was obtained and this land had to be taken primarily from the forest. It is therefore natural that the significance of cattle-raising was relatively slight during the fourth millennium BC. But it is also noteworthy that already in the beginning of the third millennium BC a change can be glimpsed: stock-raising seems to increase in importance as the once so wide-spectred subsistence strategy seems to narrow. It is conceivable that we have here one of the leading factors in the process which in coming centuries caused such profound modifications in the economic subsistence situation of the agrarian communities.

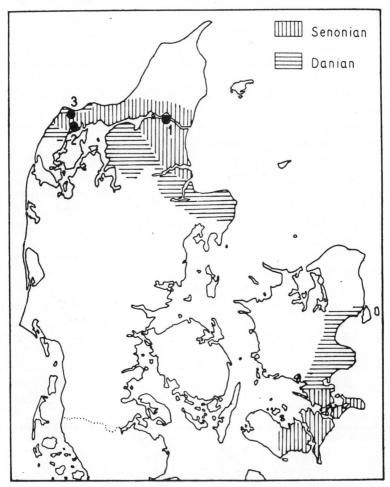

Figure 31 Situation of Danish chalk and limestone deposits with Neolithic flint mines indicated: 1. Alborg. 2. Hov. 3. Bjerre.

Although food production in the early agrarian communities is relatively clear, very little is known about other types of production. In the foreground there is the flint-mining industry at such places as the great hilly areas of northern Jutland, where cretaceous limestone and with it the coveted black or grey Senon flint is found nearly up at the surface. At Sennels, north of Thisted, numerous flint mines have been excavated (Figures 30 and 31). The shafts are shaped like inverted cones, roughly 4–5 metres wide at the surface of the earth. At Sennels the flint is deposited in horizontal layers 3–4 metres deep in the limestone. The mining of the flint took place from galleries hewn out from the bottom of the shaft with deer-antler picks 3–5 metres into the limestone. The abandoned shafts were filled up with chalk from the functioning mines next to the emptied ones.

At the flint-chopping sites between the shafts the flint-smith carried out the initial shaping of the fresh flint; the 'crust' was removed and the flint pieces were made into half-finished goods which were given a final fashioning elsewhere.

Another raw material which played an important part in the economy of the early Neolithic communities was amber. As today, amber in prehistory was found everywhere in Denmark. The North Sea coast of Jutland yielded the greatest quantities. But the coasts of the Kattegat – and in the east of the Baltic – also furnish rich amber finds. Outside Denmark, amber can be found along the German, Dutch and English coasts of the North Sea. And to the east, amber can be found along the Baltic coasts over to the largest amber deposits in the world, in Samland.

In the fourth and early third millennia BC the circulation of amber was confined to the Baltic zone, which included Denmark. Not until later did it spread further south, a story that will be related in the following chapters. In the early agrarian society, however, amber, together with axes made of the coveted Senon flint, seems to have been part of a special group of particularly valuable goods which played a dominant role in the social and political life of the farming communities. The exchange of these goods, probably in ceremonial rituals, seems to have played a central role in social competition. At the same time, both amber and flint were probably necessary for binding and maintaining social relations, just as they very likely also had a sort of fly-wheel effect which served to hold an even wider exchange of goods in motion.

The circulation of goods

The distribution of flint and amber is probably one of the earliest and most striking examples of the production and circulation of goods which increasingly contributed to socio-economic development throughout prehistory. It has long been acknowledged that there was a close relationship between the organization and control of exchange and the development of ranking in prehistoric societies. With this in mind, it is interesting to see that in the course of the fourth millennium BC the archaeological finds in Denmark show an increase in the appearance of non-utilitarian objects such as oversized flint axes, metal ornaments and great quantities of amber (K. Randsborg, 1979).

Regarding amber, there are a number of interesting aspects in the geographic distribution. Far into the fourth millennium its distribution is a simple fall-off pattern with the largest concentrations in the western parts of the country, which also contained the largest natural deposits. In the latter half of the fourth millennium and in the third millennium BC, however, this pattern was disturbed. Instead there were now a number of concentrations at some distance from the richest source areas. Amber concentrations now lay primarily in the rich and economically expansive megalith settlements in eastern Denmark, where amber to a great degree was included in grave-goods. Thus there is much to indicate that amber was increasingly regarded as a material with symbolic value and as such was included in ranked contexts in Denmark. Outside Denmark, or rather outside the Baltic zone, the circulation of amber was still very limited.

A pattern which is similar in many ways can also be observed in the distribution of the thin-butted flint axes. The differences are probably to be ascribed to the fact that this material possessed great utilitarian value besides its symbolic value. This is manifest in the fact that it is not possible to divide the flint axes into two groups, one with technological functions and one with social functions. The types form a sequence ranging from small axes, 15–20 centimetres long, to the imposing oversized 'ceremonial axes' almost 50 centimetres long (Figure 32).

A similar phenomenon can be observed in a more modern context. In an interesting study of the significance of stone axes as prestige symbols in a tribal society in the highland of New Guinea (F. Højlund, 1979), it has been shown how the various axe types had several different potential functions which could be activated in the proper social connection. One and the same axe type could be for the prosperous man primarily a work tool, whereas for the less prosperous man, who did not own special ceremonial axes, it could also possess a ceremonial value.

F. Højlund's study is also a model example of the role which the production and distribution of valuable objects can have for the reproduction of a tribal society. Among the tribal societies in New Guinea's highland the most important prerequisite for power and position was

Figure 32 Thin-butted ceremonial flint axes of the Neolithic period.

not the control of the land. Instead it was the direct control of people and thereby of their labour. This control was exercised by control of the exchange of valuable objects which were indispensable for binding and maintaining social relationships. A common factor in the exchange of valuable objects was that they primarily took place between neighbouring clans which were bound to one another by marriage alliances. In the highland there was no developed social stratification by which birth or descent gave a person right to a defined position. Instead the manipulation of the exchange of particularly valuable objects with symbolic worth provided the opportunity for the rise of so-called Big Men. By creating a situation of dependency, for example by investing in the bride price required of young men, a Big Man could build a group of 'satellites' around him, bound by personal bonds of dependency, who could provide support in discussions or armed combat.

The production and distribution of the valuable objects also seems in a wider sense to have had significance for the reproductive basis of the highland societies. Groups which controlled many valuable objects were able to marry more women into their group than they gave away to other groups. Thus on a regional plan centres were created with many polygamous marriages and a periphery arose in which there was a lack of women and a surplus of unmarried men. By incorporating both marriageable women and unmarried (or exiled) men from the peripheral groups, the centres increased their control over the labour force. In this way further expansion was made possible – perhaps tending towards a higher degree of political stratification similar to the true chiefdoms in, for example, Polynesia.

Of course, the example described here cannot be transferred directly to the situation in Denmark in the fourth millennium BC. But it can help describe the relationship which always exists between the circulation of valuable objects and the incipient development of ranking in a society at the tribal level of integration. In Denmark this sort of accelerated circulation and concurrent accumulation of wealth in, for example, the funerary cult can be observed. The circulation of symbolic objects, metal ornaments, ceremonial weapons, and so on, thus seems to have had a sort of fly-wheel effect on the establishment of social relations – and on the increased hierarchization within the early agrarian society.

In a more narrow utilitarian perspective, the exchange of goods may also have had the function of preventing sorely needed raw materials such as flint from being underexploited due to lack of direct connections between the areas of production and consumption. In fact, something of the sort has been observed in the highlands of New Guinea (Rappaport, 1968) and may also have been valid during the Neolithic in Denmark with the country's geographically concentrated flint-mine industry. In such a situation, valuable objects such as items of adornment often become trade goods because they may be exchanged for essential raw materials. They may thus stimulate production and at the same time have a fly-wheel effect on the whole system of circulating goods.

The valuable objects could also have functioned in other ways, for example in establishing social relations. Possibly they aided in organizing a labour force of a size which a single society by itself could not muster. The erection of the presumed central sites may be viewed with this in mind.

Economy of the farming communities

After the discussion of the subsistence and settlement pattern of the early farming communities, the main economic trends in the period *c.* 4200–2800 BC will be briefly summarized. A characteristic difference in relation to the hunter–gatherer communities in the foregoing period was that the spontaneous nature of work was now disappearing. In the farming communities most natural products were gathered in the form of a harvest. So to some degree the direct connection between labour and consumption which previously characterized the subsistence form was now ended. At the same time many new forms of work were introduced: forest clearance, fencing of fields, sowing, weeding, harvesting, and storing of supplies. These tasks demanded the co-ordinated labour of many people within a relatively limited period of time. The new tasks also demanded a linking of the labour processes over longer periods, thus causing the disappearance of the spontaneous character of work; instead the typical annual cycle of the farming society appeared.

Beyond these general features the development of the early agrarian society was marked by a number of unique features in the means of production. The early agrarian society may be said to have regulated its balance with nature by a broad-spectred production form. By this is meant a production form which, in contrast to more intensive agricultural forms, sought to ensure the survival of society by including as many forms of production as possible. Each form was to require minimal labour. The composition of the animal husbandry, the extensive practice of slash-and-burn and the continued importance of hunting and gathering were on the whole a manifestation of this. This subsistence form can reasonably be termed a semi-agrarian culture. Towards the end of the period a shift in the subsistence pattern seems to have taken place. The result is an increased emphasis on stock-raising, possibly caused by the growing population pressure.

This shift became ever more distinct in the following millennia. This tendency points to one of the most decisive differences between the hunter–gatherer societies and the organizational form of the agrarian communities. Whereas the hunter–gatherer society probably exercised strict demographic control, the agrarian society apparently slackened control due to its potential for economic expansion. In agrarian society there is a constant need for technological innovation to solve the problems posed by a growing population. At the same time this expansion potential is accompanied by a growing risk of resource crises, because the population more easily reaches the maximum limit which the resources set for growth.

Frequently European archaeologists have sought to explain such crises by proposing the invasion of foreign ethnic groups; the so-called Single Grave culture is an example of this. However, another explanation is also possible: the change in the settlement pattern which can be observed in the course of the third millennium BC may be explained as the farming communities' attempt to heighten productivity, among other things on the basis of increased population pressure. However this may be, the transition of the prehistoric society to an agrarian economy around 4200 BC gradually created unprecedented opportunities for economic growth.

9

Social patterns in the early farming communities

As shown above, the early agrarian communities in Denmark ensured their survival via a broad-spectred subsistence form which, in the beginning at least, can be termed semi-agrarian. The procural of food was for a good part based on a true agricultural economy, but beside this, other subsistence forms such as hunting, fishing and gathering were also practised. The presence of the agricultural economy in this broad spectrum – and its potential for economic and demographic growth, its greater complexity regarding labour processes and the increased demands for co-operation – created the basis for an economic and social development of prehistoric society which distinguished it from earlier stages of development.

There can hardly be any doubt that with the beginning of the fourth millennium BC, the formation of more complex societal forms in Denmark was in full swing. Already quite early, the increased productivity evident in food production and the consequent rise in population density led the agrarian society up to the socio-cultural integration level which is called the tribal society (E.R. Service, 1971). Quite soon, as can be seen from the increased circulation of goods, the tribal society evolved into a ranked society (M.H. Fried, 1960) (Figure 37).

The term 'development of ranking' implies that society develops limitations on the access to status. The reason for viewing the circulation of coveted valuable objects such as flint axes, amber, ornaments and tools of metal and the like as a possible cause of such a system is that this circulation is always dependent upon economic or other external factors.

The application of the term 'tribal society' in Service's sense of the word to the early farming agrarian society in Denmark is somewhat more problematic. The term has been hotly debated and several scholars have claimed that the phenomenon exists only on the fringes of more developed cultural systems, for example as a response to neighbouring militaristic states (M.H. Fried, 1968). With reference to Danish Neolithic society the term is used only to distinguish it from the Mesolithic egalitarian band society. Thus the term is used to characterize society with an incipient ranking, at a stage in which leadership is still very weakly developed and there is a low degree of political integration.

From a socio-economic point of view, the tribal societies known from anthropological literature vary widely. This is due quite simply to the fact that as the labour processes are very divergent they pose different demands to the structure of society. Among the common features of tribal societies which distinguish them from the band society is the fact that the settlement groups as well as the general population density are greater than in the hunter–gatherer communities; moreover, productivity is proportionately larger. The continuous or regularly recurring use of settlement areas results in a stronger territorial binding. In turn, this binding, together with the linking of the labour processes over longer periods (the production cycle) creates a greater stability in the social structure. Political differentiation in the tribal society, however, has not reached the point at which political control is institutionalized. Nor has social and economic specialization attained the stage in which there may be professional religious groups such as priesthoods, although there are religious specialists. Nor has economic specialization become more than part-time.

To be sure, all conclusions regarding socio-economic development from the end of the fifth millennium BC and far into the third millennium BC still rest upon a fragile foundation. Earlier Danish archaeologists viewed the appearance of the megalith graves at the end of the fourth millennium as one of the major climaxes in the Neolithic development. The megalith graves were associated with a complex worship of the dead in contrast to what was thought to precede it: the practice of simple inhumation to dispose of the deceased. The underlying opinion was that both stages represented an egalitarian society and the megalith graves were perceived as burial places for families or the inhabitants of entire villages. But recent investigations of such structures as the early Neolithic grave forms and revised views of the Neolithic chronology have led to new interpretations.

The evaluation of the socio-economic development is based partly on studies of the exchange of goods, partly on the study of the graves and so-called central sites of the agrarian society. There seems to be no doubt that the construction of the graves and their contents in some way reveal the social position of the buried person. However, interpretation of these circumstances is seriously hindered by the frequent lack of skeletal remains, so that the age and sex of the dead person can rarely be determined. Yet in cases where the grave equipment consists of more than pottery for food, there are indications of a heavy overrepresentation of male graves in relation to female graves.

Another difficulty is our ignorance of the burial customs of the early farming communities. The picture which has emerged after recent investigations is as follows: already from their formation, the farming communities practised complicated funerary rites which were no doubt related to an ancestor cult. The oldest grave monuments are complicated long barrows with a great diversity of timber structures. These graves could contain one or more persons.

Around the middle of the fourth millennium the first megalith graves (small rectangular dolmens) were erected on Zealand. From here they slowly spread to the rest of the country, where several different types evolved. The majority of the dolmens known were built in a relatively brief period during the last centuries of the fourth millennium BC. At the same time, the building of the great passage graves began.

The tradition of building 'non-megalith' graves, the so-called 'earth graves', in the meantime continued in both eastern and western Denmark. There are signs that the so-called 'mortuary houses' which came into use at the transition from the fourth to the third millennia BC were simply an offshoot of the long barrow timber structures of the earliest farming communities.

None of these complicated burial forms can be termed true communal graves in the sense of continuous use over an extended period. To be sure, both the early and the late graves can contain several people, but as we shall later see, this is hardly evidence of a so-called communal grave tradition. Presumably the graves were originally erected to contain people who had attained a certain rank and hence were buried with material goods and with elaborate ceremony.

Not until quite late in the Neolithic did the grave customs change. As described below, many of the great megalith monuments were now used for repeated burials, or for the deposition of bones. Even so, this is not sufficient reason to speak of a true communal grave form.

As yet, the earliest grave forms of the agrarian society are relatively little known. One of the most thoroughly studied structures is a long barrow at Bygholm Nørremark in Jutland (P. Rønne, 1979), which will here be discussed in more detail as an example of the burial customs of the period.

The structure (Figure 33) was slightly trapezoidal in form, 60 metres long and surrounded by a post-bedding trench. In the eastern end there

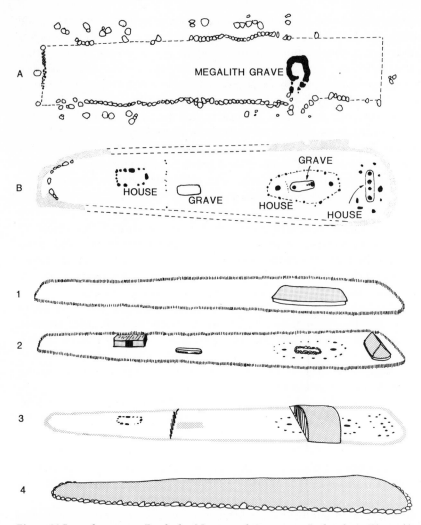

Figure 33 Long barrow at Bygholm Nørremark in eastern Jutland. A. Plan of long
   dolmen with barrow containing a megalith grave. B. Plan of non-megalithic
   grave complex found under A. Numbers 1–4 illustrate the four different
   stages in the construction of the non-megalithic long barrow.

was a façade with traces of an elaborate timber construction. Immediately west of the façade there were traces of two 'houses', one of them
with a grave, which probably consisted originally of a wooden coffin. All
that was left of the corpse was a greasy black substance together with
some tooth-enamel, which was enough to identify the dead as only

13–15 years old. An amber bead by the waist of the dead had probably been mounted on a belt. Near the chest there was an arrowhead, perhaps the cause of death.

Further to the west in the structure lay yet another grave, which contained four people. The dead lay in pairs, two with heads to the east, two to the west. There were no grave goods, neither ornaments, pottery, weapons nor tools.

Finally, furthest to the west there was a little square post-built building. Transverse rows of poles were observed at three places within the enclosure.

Somewhat later than this grave complex there was an extension of the barrow and the construction of a megalith grave in the now 80-metre-long barrow.

The course of events in this imposing and complicated burial can be reconstructed something like this: a young high-ranking individual, possibly killed by an arrow, was laid on his death bier in a house surrounded by a large trapezoidal enclosure. After the corpse had lain there for some time, the mortuary house was torn down and at the site the clothed corpse was placed in a stone-set wooden coffin. Another house, open at one side, was erected; here a ceremonial meal was held. At the same time something similar was taking place in the west part of the enclosed area. Here a grave for four dead adults was dug and a little ritual house was built. After a certain period the space was cleared of enclosures and houses and the earthen barrow was built. This was carried out in stages, as the barrow form was determined by the transverse rows of poles. The intervals between these were filled with soil and a stone-setting was placed around the foot of the barrow.

This grave type, the long barrow with timber structures, is found with many variations – especially in the west of Denmark. As already mentioned, the timber structures from Barkær, once interpreted as longhouses, should most likely be ascribed to this grave type. In fact, this type has parallels over a far greater area, namely over all the northern European lowland, including England. Even with all the variations, they are apparently the result of structurally similar solutions to religious, ritual and socio-political problems common to the Neolithic societies in the great northern European techno-complex of the fourth millennium BC (T. Madsen, 1979a).

A multitude of details in this early Neolithic burial practice anticipates later practices in the megalith graves. Both earth graves and megalith graves were built sequentially into the same barrows – and the megalith graves are not necessarily the latest. 'Purification' fires have also been burnt in both grave types, and similarly the great quantities of pottery found by the façades of the long barrows indicate that rituals took place here just as by the entrance to the megalith graves. The similarities between the form of the earth graves and that of the megalith graves can be demonstrated on many other counts.

These similarities have cast doubt upon earlier ideas of the megalith graves as expressions of a communal burial custom practised by an egalitarian society, and representing a continuous use over an extended period. Newer investigations seem to confirm this doubt. Instead, the picture now emerges of a burial practice, common for both the earth graves and the dolmens, in which individuals or a few together were buried simultaneously with elaborate ceremonies, including lengthy stays or great funeral feasts at the site.

Not until the construction of the so-called passage graves do essential changes seem to have occurred. The lack of small bones among the often large mass of bones found in the passage graves indicate that the dead were skeletalized before deposition in the passage graves. That is, the grave cult called for the deposition of bones in the passage graves and not for proper burials (S. Thorsen, 1980). These depositions should correspond to the high incidence of secondary burials which took place synchronously in the dolmens due to the easier accessibility of these grave monuments. It is also probable that there is a connection with the burials in the so-called stone-heap graves in Jutland. Here excavations have demonstrated that skeletalization of the dead may have occurred prior to actual deposition in the earth.

Finally, finds of fragmented human skeletons in the great ceremonial central sites of the Sarup type can also be fitted into the new hypothesis of the burial customs of Neolithic society. The central sites may have been where the skeletalization of the dead took place before the deposition in the large permanent grave monuments. This new interpretation is still based upon very slight evidence and requires further proof.

The description of the early farming communities in Denmark drew tentatively upon two concepts derived from ethnographic studies: ranked societies and tribal organization. These two concepts have been used here as a kind of heuristic tool. This has been done in the belief that there exists a relationship between the nature and disposition of the archaeological record on one hand and the organization of prehistoric society on the other. The problem, however, is that this relationship is not direct – and that in Danish archaeology the attempts to clarify this relationship have to date been few and uncertain.

As shown, however, interpretations of the archaeological record often entail theories of the social structure of prehistoric society. The earlier assumption of the appearance of a communal burial custom in agrarian society around the end of the fourth millennium BC was an example of this. An attempt has therefore been made to show how many newer investigations of the burial practice in the early farming communities have been able to change that assumption. Today, then, we must presume that already from the beginning of the fourth millennium BC, and possibly even earlier, society tended toward a non-egalitarian ranked society, probably within a tribal form of organization. The large labour-demanding grave structures intended for a minority of people, the imposing central sites which were presumably ceremonial, and finally the network of connections which disseminated prestige goods such as axes, amber and metal – all of this indicates that the process was already well underway quite early in the existence of the farming communities.

With the transition to an agricultural economy, prehistoric society had to face a set of problems which could not be solved within the organizational form of the band society. One of these problems must have been that the numerous new settlement groups were all expanding and therefore could only to a slight degree form an economically integrated society. And in fact it is a frequent observation that tribal societies often live in a permanent state of war. Conflicts in tribal society have a clear tendency to develop into feuds – and feuds tend to continue indefinitely, as regular warfare and the conquering of enemy territory is seldom possible. Psychological warfare, involving practices such as head-hunting, cannibalism and massacres, therefore often typify societies organized on the tribal level. The existence of central sites, traces of cannibalism, the use of such objects as battle-axes for status symbols, all known from Neolithic Denmark, are therefore important elements in the definition of the societal form of the early farming communities. It is also important to investigate how tribal societies can be expected to respond to problems of the sort described.

In order to stabilize potential dangerous relationships among the local groups, tribal society often establishes various institutions: clans, age groups, religious or military societies comprising larger or smaller segments of the settlement group. Concretely, there may be communal religious ceremonies at the great central sites, exchange of gifts, and so on. Such institutions may create a certain integration among the various local groups. But this integration is seldom long-lasting. Frequently the institutions listed only come into play if an external crisis threatens. If the crisis is averted, there is often a reversion to the relatively closed local community.

However weak this form of organization may appear, it does signify a considerable rise of the integration level in comparison with the organizational form of the hunter–gatherer society. This sort of integration, which can be brought into play at any time, does not normally exist in the band society.

Of course, these institutions are very difficult to trace in the archaeological record. But they can explain in theory how the early farming communities functioned in the first thousand years of their existence. At the same time they can also provide a clue to why the development, with its growing population pressure in the following millennia, tended towards a more hierarchical form of organization with a stabilizing of certain status functions as a consequence.

10

Finds and interpretations

The archaeological record which illuminates the first farming communities ranges over a number of main areas, the chief of which are settlements and graves. There also exists an important material of primary ritual deposits in bogs together with a number of significant traces of flint mining in the early agrarian society.

Settlement finds from the prehistory of Denmark have of late been the object of renewed interest. New excavation methods are being used to uncover enormous excavation surfaces because the more limited investigations of earlier times proved insufficient in relation to the framework of problems proposed by modern archaeological research. But on the whole, the comprehensive investigations of recent years have been concentrated on finds from the later periods of prehistory (the Bronze and Iron Ages). So with few exceptions the study of the settlement pattern of the early farming communities in Denmark must be based upon old and often inadequate investigations (Figure 34). Among the localities studied in recent years are *Stengade* on Langeland (J. Skårup, 1975) together with a number of smaller excavations (E. Johansen, 1975; and K. Davidsen, 1978). Important older investigations include *Troldebjerg*, *Blandebjerg*, and *Lindø* (J. Winther, 1926–8, 1935, 1943), *Bundsø* (T. Mathiassen, 1939), and *Klintebakken* (H. Berg, 1951).

None of these older investigations could incontestably determine house remains. To be sure, the Troldebjerg settlement is believed by several scholars to have consisted of about twenty-five house sites, both large longhouses and horseshoe-shaped huts. The character of the large complex at Troldebjerg, which is about 250 metres long and 100 metres wide, is still a puzzle. Its topographical situation greatly resembles the large central sites of the Sarup type. Meanwhile, new excavations will be able to shed light upon the function of the complex.

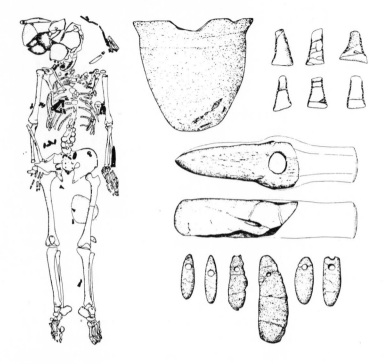

Figure 34 Early Neolithic so-called earth grave with transverse arrowheads, battle axe, amber pendants, and clay vessel found at Dragsholm, Zealand.

Like Troldebjerg, the settlement sites Klintebakken, Blandebjerg and Lindø lie on the island of Langeland in southern Denmark. All these settlement sites are characterized by thick cultural layers, although no house sites have been determined with certainty. On the Lindø settlement, however, there were a couple of rectangular structures which have been interpreted as house remains.

The Bundsø settlement site lies on the island of Als, also in southern Denmark. Thick cultural layers and extensive stone pavings attest a considerable settlement, but not even here has it been possible to identify the nature of the place more precisely. Probably it is a central site of the Sarup type. All the sites mentioned are of great importance for the Neolithic chronology. Each one has yielded finds which represent brief stages in the middle Neolithic development.

In archaeological literature, a particularly dominating role has been played by *Barkær* on Djursland (P.V. Glob, 1949). However, the find has never been published in its entirety, and it must be noted that it has recently been reinterpreted and is now regarded by its excavator as a grave complex (P.V. Glob, 1975). The same interpretation has also been suggested for the Langeland locality *Stengade* (P.V. Glob, 1975).

There are also unique problems associated with the small settlements which have recently been identified as seasonal hunting places for the first agriculturists. This is the case with *Hesselø, Sølager*, and a number of other smaller sites which were all published in 1973 (J. Skårup). Of particular interest in this connection is *Muldbjerg* on Zealand. No proper report on this important and very carefully excavated site has yet been published (Troels-Smith, 1957b, 1959a). The settlement site, which has been completely excavated, lies on a little island in the large Åmose bog. The centre of the settlement was a large hut, 7 × 3 metres, with a bark floor. The finds of pottery in particular date the site to the earliest phase of the Neolithic. Apparently this was one of the small specific activity camps established in conjunction with the large all-year-round settlements.

Excavations of the large presumed central sites can be expected to shed new light on the settlement pattern of the early farming communities. The most comprehensive investigations have been in *Sarup* on southern Funen (N.H. Andersen, 1974, 1975, 1976). *Toftum* near Horsens (T. Madsen, 1977, 1978a) can also be expected to gain great significance. Excavations at these places correspond in many respects to the work at *Büdelsdorf* by the Eider River (H. Hingst, 1971) – but it is still too early to undertake an overall evaluation of this important group of finds.

The total number of settlements from the first phase of the farming society is as yet quite small. Most of the excavations have only studied parts of the settlement areas, so there is still much doubt with regard to the structure of the village complexes, the house types and the settlement pattern in the wide sense. Comprehensive study of this important source area is sorely needed.

Grave finds from the early farming communities also comprise a rather inaccessible find group. General surveys are few (J. Brøndsted, 1957) and often outdated (C.A. Nordman, 1917 a and b).

Of the many grave types, the so-called megalith graves, dolmens and passage graves have long been studied. Regarding the dolmens, there is a 1941 survey with the majority of the finds (K. Thorvildsen), whereas a classification of the numerous construction forms was attempted by E. Aner in 1963 – see further C.J. Becker (1947). Of the more important special studies, there is only room to mention the works of H. Berg of 1951 and 1956, together with S. Thorsen's study of 1980. This latter article demonstrates certain similarities between the dolmens and the early Neolithic earth graves.

Gaps are also apparent in the material on the passage graves, aside from older partially outdated publications by C.A. Nordman (1917 a and b) and G. Rosenberg (1929). Special investigations have been published by such scholars as K. Ebbesen (1975), E. Jørgensen (1977a), P. Kjærum (1957, 1969), K. Thorvildsen (1946), and M. Ørsnes (1956). A number of more general evaluations are presented in works by P. Kjærum (1967) and L. Kaelas (1967). Dating is carefully treated in H. Berg's work of 1951. A number of important Swedish investigations relevant to the Danish situation are found in publications by A. Bagge and L. Kaelas (1950) together with M. Strömberg (1968, 1971b).

The group of non-megalith graves also forms a rather obscure picture (Figure 33). The grave type was first identified by K. Friis Johansen in 1917. A comprehensive up-to-date survey of the early Neolithic structures was published by Torsten Madsen (1979a). This important work discusses newer excavations by E. Jørgensen (1977b), Preben Rønne (1979), David Liversage (1970), Bjørn Stürup (1965), C. Fischer (1975), P.V. Glob (1975), and O. Faber (1976). Views of the relationship of the early Neolithic grave structures throughout the northern European lowland have been offered by S. Piggott (1966) and K. Jazdzewski (1973). The 'unchambered' long barrows from Bygholm Nørregaard described in detail here (see pp. 111 ff) have been excavated and published in a preliminary report by Preben Rønne (1979).

The works mentioned above all treat early finds, whereas U.L. Hansen (1972b) has described a number of late variations of the type. In yet another unresolved relationship to the 'non-megalith graves' are the so-called 'stone packing graves', a grave type first identified in the 1950s (C.J. Becker, 1959; E. Jørgensen, 1977a; T. Madsen, 1975). Since then, about 500 structures have been excavated, but this number is simply the result of a goal-oriented research effort (see E. Jørgensen, 1977a). Almost all the structures are found in a belt stretching from the Ringkøbing region to the west part of Himmerland, but it is not insignificant that research activity has been primarily concentrated in the areas where the graves were first found in abundance. The possibility cannot therefore be ignored that the original distribution covered a larger part of the country.

A still puzzling manifestation of the ritual practices of the early farming communities consists of the so-called 'cult houses' (Figure 35) – a type of structure which has first been demonstrated within the last generation (P. Kjærum, 1967). Reports on cult houses have been published by C.J. Becker (1969), O. Marseen (1960) and P. Kjærum (1955).

The ritual practice of the first agrarian society with special focus upon

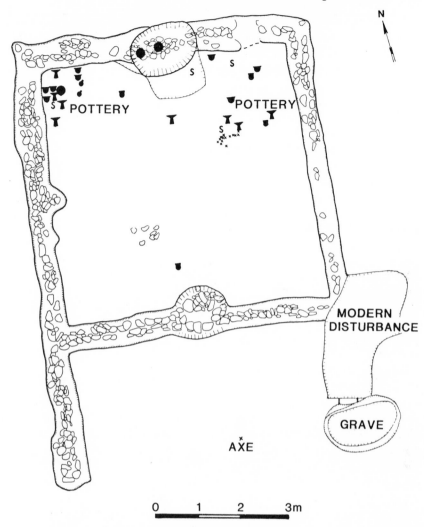

Figure 35 Plan of so-called cult-house, excavated at Herrup, northern Jutland.

the deposits in moist ground is illuminated by one comprehensive work, C.J. Becker's thesis of 1947. The important material of votive finds, that is deposits of valuable objects, especially flint axes, has in recent years been the object of increased interest. A valuable survey of a part of the finds was published by P.O. Nielsen (1977b). Here the find group was perceived as an expression of the development of ranking in the farming communities described above.

Problems related to the origin of agriculture in the Middle East have,

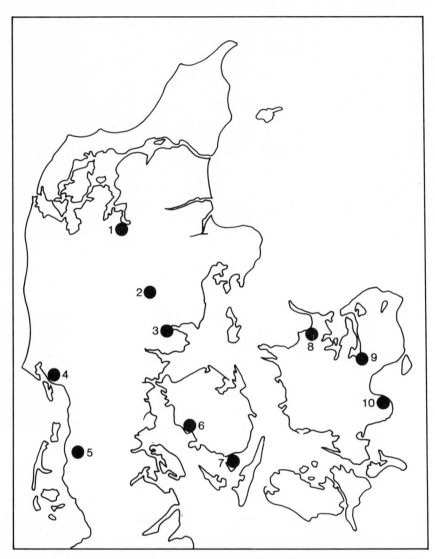

Figure 36 Plough marks found under graves from the Funnel-Necked Beaker culture. 1. Skibshøj, Viborg county. 2. Brendekroggård, Skanderborg county. 3. Præstehøj, Vejle county. 4. Nygård, Ribe county. 5. Steneng, Ribe county. 6. Snave, Svendborg county. 7. Capeshøj, Svendborg county. 8. Blomster-vænget, Holbæk county. 9. Himmelev, Copenhagen county. 10. Fuglebæks-banken, Præstø county.

since Gordon Childe's work in the 1930s, been the object of lively debate. From the abundance of recent literature, only a few works shall be mentioned which described the 'neolithization' on the basis of demographic views, namely K.V. Flannery and F. Hole (1969); a survey of the total material has been published by Charles L. Redman (1978). An interesting attempt to examine the validity of this demographic explanation has been carried out in the USA (Michael J. Harner, 1970). On the basis of a very comprehensive ethnographic material, a model has been set up which suggests that the transition to food production normally occurs in a hunter–gatherer society when it has exploited its resources to the limit of population density. Some social and demographic consequences of this have also been the subject of studies (R. Sussmann, 1972) whose results fully bear out the views expressed above. Related theories may be found in the works of S. Struever (1971) and B. Spooner (1972).

With regard to works on the neolithization of Europe, archaeological literature is very extensive. One example of a newer survey is by H. Müller-Karpe (1968). The ecological and demographic factors behind the dispersion of the farming economy, however, have only been studied to a minor degree. Exceptions to this include works of A.J. Ammermann and L.L. Cavalli-Sforza (1973), A.P. Phillips (1973) and A.G. Sherratt (1972).

Literature treating the first agriculture in Denmark is very extensive and presents extremely divergent interpretations of the archaeological record. A good deal of the literature is devoted to chronological studies, which naturally enough hold an important position in research. However, in later years chronological studies have been enriched with a new dimension through the development of scientific methods. Only twenty years ago, estimates based upon conventional archaeological methods set the beginning of agriculture in Denmark at about 2500 BC. With the first radiocarbon dates, this limit was moved to about 3000 BC. New finds pushed the beginning of agriculture back 300 years more in time. However, calibrations of the radiocarbon dates have set the beginning of agriculture in Denmark to about 4200 BC – that is about 1700 years further back in time than had been imagined just twenty years ago (H. Tauber, 1972). These calibrated radiocarbon dates from the basis of the present work (H.E. Suess, 1970).

Not until recently has Danish archaeology adjusted itself to the new and surprising set of dates. Danish archaeologists have traditionally presented two alternative interpretations: agriculture has been thought to have arisen either as the result of the invasion of a foreign ethnic element (C.J. Becker, 1947) or else as a consequence of a number of modifications in the subsistence strategy of the local hunter–gatherer population (J. Troels-Smith, 1960a, 1966; H. Schwabedissen, 1968). New archaeological arguments (J. Skårup, 1973; S.H. Andersen, 1973) have to some degree brought new elements to this debate, but at the same time the calibrated radiocarbon dates have revealed the paucity of the archaeological record, especially from the first centuries after the introduction of the farming economy in Denmark. This deficiency is also noticeable in newer works which seek to view the process on the basis of theories derived from L.R. Binford's Post-Pleistocene Adaption theory (C. Paludan-Müller, 1978).

The specific chronology within the early and middle Neolithic period has hitherto been based upon two artefact groups: pottery and axe types (C.J. Becker, 1947, 1954, 1957a). On this basis, the period has been divided into two main phases, early and middle Neolithic time (EN = Early Neolithic, MN A = Middle Neolithic Funnel-Necked Beaker Culture). In 1947 C.J. Becker divided the Early Neolithic into phases A, B and C, each of which represented successive stages in a chronological development. This derivative system is still practical for the general categorization of the site inventories, but newer radiocarbon dates have shown that A, B and so-called non-megalithic C pottery are generally contemporaneous (T. Madsen, 1979a).

In conclusion the following can be said about the neolithization in Denmark: the first traces of the early Neolithic farming communities turn up around 4200 BC. In the early period, till about 3600 BC, sites containing A, B and non-megalithic C pottery occur. The A-sites are mainly known in east Denmark, whereas the B-sites are more evenly spread. Non-megalithic C-sites especially are concentrated in Jutland. At the time when megalithic C pottery turns up on the Danish islands, the non-megalithic C pottery continues in Jutland. The megalithic C pottery gradually spread all over Denmark (K. Ebbesen and D. Mahler, 1979) and at the beginning of the MN A, c. 3200 BC, only faint traces of the non-megalithic styles are still present in northern Jutland (T. Madsen, 1979a). The suggestion by Jan Lichardus (1976) that the B pottery is the earliest stage of the agrarian culture in Denmark seems unfounded.

The Middle Neolithic period (MN A) is divided into phases I–V on the basis of the pottery from a number of the largest settlement finds of the period (C.J. Becker, 1947, 1954). The flint axes too have been used to support the division mentioned (C.J. Becker, 1959). Here, however, newer studies (P.O. Nielsen, 1977a) seem to indicate that this find group is not well suited for the purpose. The thick-butted flint axes from the Middle Neolithic range in fact over a far longer period of time, MN A and MN B, than earlier assumed.

Recent contributions to the chronological discussion also include works of K. Ebbesen (1979) and K. Davidsen (1975). The problems related to the end of the period and the transition to the so-called Single Grave culture (C.J. Becker, 1967a; K. Davidsen, 1975; C. Malmros and H. Tauber, 1975; P.O. Nielsen, 1977 a and b) will be discussed in more detail in the following section.

One noteworthy problem deals with the so-called Pitted Ware culture (C.J. Becker, 1950a). This has often been interpreted as an independent ethnic group which appeared in Denmark during the Middle Neolithic. But the Danish finds from the Pitted Ware culture may represent nothing other than specific activity camps founded by the agrarian communities. This problem demands new investigations and will not be examined here (S. Nielsen, 1979).

The profile of the natural environment in which the first farming society arose is based primarily upon the studies which were carried out in Denmark by scholars such as K. Jessen and J. Iversen. A summary of the results of pollen analysts was presented in 1967 by J. Iversen who concluded:

> By and large, the great developmental drama of the vegetation after the Ice Age is now known. What remains is to distinguish the factors which set this whole drama and its various phases into motion – climatic fluctuations, the development of the soil, and in the later millennia not least of all the many kinds of human influence during prehistoric and historic times.

This ecological analysis is still in its infancy and depends upon the continued co-operation of a great many disciplines – including prehistoric archaeology. Many of the results so far have been obtained through this sort of collaboration carried out in Draved Forest near Løgum Kloster in Jutland. Here, a series of practical experiments has led to a widened understanding of such factors as the influence of early agriculture upon the forest (J. Iversen, 1967; A. Steensberg, 1979; S. Jørgensen, 1953; A. Andersen, 1966). Danish pollen analysts have concentrated particularly on an interpretation of the local pollen diagrams, whereas in Sweden (B.E. Berglund, 1969) the attempt has been made to synthesize the many detailed investigations into a comprehensive picture of the vegetational history of southern Scandinavia. This total picture is still rife with uncertainty but there is reason to anticipate great progress in this field.

With regard to the relationship between food production and demographic development, archaeological studies are still in their infancy. Inspiration for new sorts of questions derives first of all from the works of Esther Boserup, which have in later years played a growing role in archaeological literature (P.E.L. Smith, 1970). Debate as to the application of these theories in historic and prehistoric research is still very lively (the Boserup Symposium, 1972; G.L. Cowgill, 1975).

The anthropological material which forms the foundation for conclusions regarding Danish conditions has been published by K. Brøste and J.B. Jørgensen (1956). The above-named studies of Swiss examples were made by W. Scheffrahn (1967). Surveys of the subject are found in such works as H.V. Vallois (1960), as well as G. Acsádi and J. Nemeskéri (1970).

Studies of the economic structure underlying the earliest farming communities are based upon a very slender source material. Generalizations about the settlement pattern have been made by T. Mathiassen in 1948 and 1959 in two studies; the result of these studies have only to a small degree been exploited in Danish archaeology. A number of weaknesses in the classification of the registered finds have contributed to this. Surveys of the subsistence strategy of the early farming communities have been carried out by J. Troels-Smith (1953, 1960) and by C.J. Becker (1954); see also works by K. Jessen (1951) and G. Jørgensen (1976, 1977). An important sketch for the understanding of the role of domesticated animals in the Middle Neolithic has been published by C.F.W. Higham (1969). For a more general survey, see M. Degerbøl's study from 1933.

As yet, no exhaustive study exists of the plough marks from the Stone Age through the Bronze Age, although this would be most helpful. Therefore the history of the use of the plough (ard) can only be followed sporadically through the Neolithic. The earliest plough marks hitherto date from the fourth millennium BC and were revealed during excavation of a long barrow in Steneng, southern Jutland (O. Voss, 1966). With regard to details of the farming techniques in the first phase of the Neolithic, general reference is made to the work of J. Iversen of 1967 and A. Steensberg of 1979. An important survey of a number of pedological problems is provided by S. Nielsen (1980).

Investigations of the role of hunting and gathering in the Danish Neolithic are quite new. This particular aspect of the economy of the farming communities is the topic of J. Skårup's study of 1973. Studies of flint-mining in the Neolithic have been generally treated by C.J. Becker (1951, 1958), whereas a number of more theoretical considerations on the exchange of goods, seen against a European background, were presented by A.G. Sherratt in 1976.

Attempts to determine organizational aspects of the early food-producing communities in Denmark are rare (K. Randsborg, 1975). The relating of the development of prehistoric society to concepts derived from ethnographic literature relies mainly upon works of Morton H. Fried (1960, 1967) and Elman R. Service (1966, 1971, 1975). Here there are two different models of societal organization. The first (M.H. Fried) focuses on the vertical relations between members of a society by describing ways in which societies differentiate their members. Fried distinguishes four different types of society: egalitarian, ranked and stratified societies, together with states. The second model (E.R. Service) describes the development of community organization in terms of a growing socio-cultural integration. Service also distinguishes four different types of society: band societies, tribes, chiefdoms and states (Figure 37).

The two models are not parallel, but they are both useful heuristic tools for studies of social evolution in primitive societies. They have therefore in recent years achieved an ever wider applicability. For example, they have been used by Charles L. Redman (1978) to describe

Morton Fried's terminology	Elman Service's terminology
State society	State organisation
Stratified society	
Ranked society	Chiefdom organisation
	Tribal organisation
Egalitarian society	Band organisation

Figure 37 Terminology used by Elman R. Service (1971) and Morton H. Fried (1967).

the development from early farming to urban society in the Near East. As in Redman's work the two models are in the present work contrasted with one another and moreover are related to the development of the prehistoric communities in southern Scandinavia.

The earliest agrarian communities in Denmark are here assigned to the level which in E.R. Service's model is called the tribe. This refers to a society whose political and economic organization is based on local production organized along lines of kinship. The tribal society distinguishes itself from the band society in its having developed a higher degree of integration. This was achieved by the help of factors such as sodalities which cross-cut local groups, clans, age groups, secret societies, and so on – all phenomena which are practically impossible to distinguish in the archaeological record.

The description of early Danish agrarian society as a tribal society is due above all to the assumption that the growth of the agricultural economy must have confronted society with necessary tasks which could hardly have been solved on a band level of organization. This holds true first and foremost of the subsistence form, but also of some of the socio-cultural phenomena described: the construction of the large labour-demanding grave monuments and the central sites, for example. Some of these phenomena are also viewed as a manifestation of the incipient ranking of society. In relation to M.H. Fried's model, the early farming communities are therefore placed at the transition between the egalitarian and the ranked type of society. This development seems to have commenced quite early in the Neolithic. Once more the question arises of whether the hunter–gatherer society of the Atlantic period managed to develop higher forms of integration than the band society (see p. 57).

No definitive answer can yet be given, but as pointed out, the relating of the archaeological record to the more theoretically oriented models of community organization will have an important heuristic function in future research on the introduction of agriculture in southern Scandinavia. Thus an alternative can be created to earlier research, which has hitherto unsuccessfully sought to explain this revolution on the basis of ethnic concepts and invasion theories.

PART III

Towards a new era
2800–500 BC

11

A changing environment

Farming communities in transition

The third and second millennia BC seem to have witnessed three major developments. First, farming communities gradually abandoned their wide-spectred subsistence strategy for the development of transhumance, a process with parallels over most of northern Europe (C.F.W. Higham, 1967). Second, the growth of non-egalitarian ranked societies accelerated, ending with the emergence of so-called chiefdoms. The most impressive result of this development was the ambitious barrow-building of the second millennium BC. Third, interregional contacts grew in intensity. The archaeological record reflects this phenomenon in the widespread distribution of metal objects, which also reveal the presence of complex sumptuary rules within the developing chiefdoms.

These three developments took place in a period which in many respects is highly problematic as regards the archaeological record. This holds true for the first four or five centuries of the period, the era of the so-called Single Grave culture. However, much of the problem stems from the invasion hypothesis so dear to earlier generations of European archaeologists. A hypothetical invasion of the so-called Single Grave people was proposed to explain the onesidedness of the archaeological record, namely the fact that the majority of finds from the period were made in west Denmark.

In recent years, however, calibrated radiocarbon dates have toppled this early theory. No longer can the Single Grave culture be considered a foreign ethnic group partially overlapping the so-called Funnel-Necked Beaker culture; we now know that the latter phenomenon quite simply succeeded the former. What actually did happen during the third millennium BC was probably a radical change in the subsistence strategy of the early farming communities. None the less, the period covering approximately 2800–2400 BC is still one of the most obscure in the prehistory of Denmark.

Following the end of the Single Grave culture around 2400 BC, our picture again begins to come into focus. The centuries up to *c.* 1800 BC comprise the Late Neolithic period. During this time, the farming communities expanded rapidly. The changes in the subsistence pattern which had taken place in the foregoing centuries now emerged clearly. Man's impact on the ecosystem became considerable.

Economic and technological breakthroughs took place from the beginning of the second millennium BC. In particular, the new metal technology was a catalyst for economic development in the farming communities. Thus, from about 1800 BC, we can speak of a Danish or 'Nordic' Bronze Age. We can trace up to *c.* 500 BC an agrarian society ever more dependent on interregional contacts. Denmark now became an integral part of a large area consisting of southern Scandinavia, northern Germany and Poland. This vast cultural region was loosely held together by shifting exchange systems determined by the productive capacity of each area.

The changing land

During the fourth millennium BC the first farming communities of Denmark made their mark on the virgin forest. But as yet the impact of man on the vegetation was slight. The Danish landscape was still dominated by shady forest and scrub. Only in the more densely populated areas which were formed during the fourth millennium BC was the landscape gradually becoming more open.

As the land was exploited more and more, this picture began to change drastically. In the third millennium BC light forest and scrub could be seen throughout Denmark as a landscape with extensive pastures was created. Widespread grazing, severe exhaustion of the soil, the spread of a new settlement pattern and the increasing use of the ard for ploughing were factors which in the long run affected the entire ecosystem. The result was the creation of a landscape with gradual transition between light forest, scrub pasture and extensive grass pasture (Figure 38). According to the pollen spectra, this type of landscape existed not only in Denmark but over much of the north European lowland.

This development was based on a new ecological situation which necessitated new types of land management. In eastern Denmark the changes may have been introduced even earlier. In any case, Denmark

Figure 38 The typical Danish Bronze-Age landscape was characterized by light forest, scrub pasture, and extensive grass pasture.

seems to have been the scene of an agricultural expansion from the middle of the third millennium BC. Pollen diagrams for that time show, for example, far-reaching forest clearance on Djursland in eastern Jutland. Forest clearance and cattle grazing were now more prevalent than ever. As cattle retarded the regeneration of the lime forest and hazel groves, there were now spacious grass pastures nearly devoid of hazel scrub. This trend continued into the second and first millennia BC. Man's impact on the Danish countryside had become evident indeed.

However, few details are known of the settlement pattern and its ecological background during the third millennium BC. Pollen analyses are unfortunately few in number. Yet all over southern Scandinavia they show the same general pattern, namely a lively agricultural expansion beginning with the so-called Single Grave culture, shortly before the middle of the third millennium BC and persisting throughout the next thousand years.

There were many regional variations. In central Jutland the light sandy soils were preferred because their original open forest vegetation must have been especially well-suited for extensive grazing. In eastern Jutland, however, the boulder clay soils were still quite unsettled. Here lay rich potential for settlement expansion. Yet this potential was not exploited until the last few centuries BC. On the poor sandy soils in west Jutland, deterioration must already have been quite advanced due to human interference. Already at the beginning of the second millennium BC barrows were built on deserted arable land which heavy grazing had converted to poor pasture. In fact, at some places burial mounds were erected on heathland, a vegetation form directly resulting from human exploitation. Already here was the genesis of the process culminating in the last centuries BC when the lightest soils in westernmost Denmark had exhausted their potential for population increase.

The changing climate

Ever since the introduction of farming in Denmark, climatic shifts had affected the subsistence strategy of the agrarian communities and with it the shifting frontier between the forest and the man-made landscape. A long-standing assumption of climatologists has been that from 2800 BC up to the beginning of the Sub-Atlantic period around 600–500 BC the climate was warm and dry with an average summer temperature slightly higher than it is today. The long-term development, however, showed a falling trend towards that of the present-day climate. Around 600–500 BC a drastic change to a cooler and more humid climate marked the close of the Post-Glacial warm period.

In general this picture is still valid. But recent investigations have proved that the process was more complicated. No doubt the average temperature showed a slight decrease during the period 2800–500 BC, but this course was irregular, as it was disturbed by a series of fluctuations. Many opinions held by older generations of archaeologists about the climatic change at the transition from the Sub-Boreal to the Sub-Atlantic period around 600 BC must therefore be revised.

For many years archaeologists, supported by climatological evidence, have claimed that the climatic change around 600 BC (observable in peat bogs as a boundary horizon, the so-called RY III) had a catastrophic impact on the agrarian societies in northern Europe. Perhaps there is a connection between climate and changes in land management in this period. Even so, the catastrophe theory ought to be rejected. On the contrary, the archaeological record indicates that around the middle of the first millennium BC agrarian societies were expanding to a degree hitherto unequalled in the prehistory of northern Europe.

Knowledge of climatic development in the last five or six millennia stems primarily from intensive research on the north European raised bogs. Valuable studies have been made in Sweden in particular. But even in Denmark, where peat digging has unfortunately obliterated the majority of raised bogs, vital information has been gleaned.

The raised bog has been compared to a huge sponge saturated with rainwater. It possesses a completely independent aquatic balance as it is not affected by the ground-water level under the bog. The moisture of the raised bog is obtained exclusively from the atmosphere, so that the growth rate and structure of the peat reflect climatic conditions at the time of its formation. Thus a raised bog can act as a self-registering climatograph for millennia. In dry warm conditions, a dark-brown nearly structureless peat is formed. A cool damp climate results in a light, somewhat decomposed peat of well-preserved sphagnum shoots. The boundary between dark and light peat is called a recurrence level or boundary horizon.

The stratification of the peat bog thus registers general long-term trends in the climate. One boundary horizon in particular has been singled out, the one which marks the dividing line between the Sub-Boreal and the Sub-Atlantic periods, about 600 BC. Recently, however, it has been demonstrated that the boundary horizons in different bogs are not always comparable. Furthermore it appears that the climatic development in the past five or six millennia has had a fluctuation course. New studies based on radiocarbon dates indicate possible cyclical climatic variations lasting about 260 years (B. Aaby, 1974). This periodicity, though, is not general, as in some cases there is a double distance between the registrations of climatic changes (Figure 39). Whether this is due to faulty observation or to an actual absence of change is not entirely certain. Similarly, not all climatic oscillations produce equally noticeable effects in various raised bogs.

Nor is it entirely clear what the boundary horizons signify. To be sure, they demonstrate a transition to a moister environment. But increased moisture can be caused both by reduced evaporation, i.e. a fall in temperature, and by increased precipitation. It is difficult to distinguish between the two causes. Nevertheless, there is biological evidence of a falling trend in the summer temperature from the fourth to the first millennia BC. Consequently Danish scientists have been inclined to

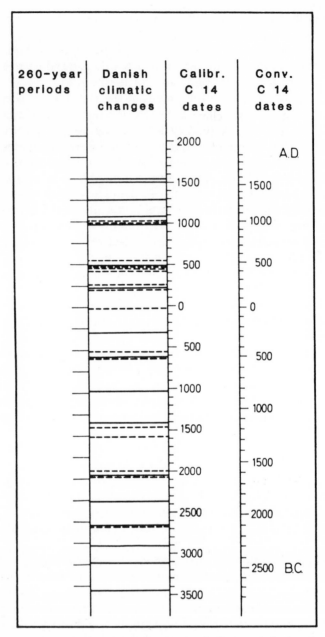

Figure 39 Observed climatic changes in Denmark during the last 5500 years. The radiocarbon dates seem to indicate cyclical variations lasting about 260 years.

regard the major cause of the formation of the boundary horizons as being a wave-like fall in temperature.

For the period spanning 2800–500 BC, this means that changes to moister and colder conditions must have occurred around the beginning of the period, *c.* 2700 BC. The next oscillation came around 2350 BC, followed by yet another one around 2100 BC. At this stage a hiatus occurred and subsequent climatic changes are registered around 1600 BC, 1400 BC, and 1050 BC. A final change, noted around 600–500 BC, is identical with the so-called classic boundary horizon (RY III) which was earlier credited with the catastrophic significance of having led to the breakdown of Bronze Age society and the rise of Iron Age society.

Today we must acknowledge that climatic changes were far more frequent than has earlier been assumed. Consequently it has become impossible to demonstrate a clear correlation between changes in climatic conditions and changes in the subsistence strategy of agrarian societies of the past.

12

Subsistence and settlement

Towards a new settlement pattern

During the third millennium BC a series of changes in Denmark resulted in a settlement pattern which lasted about 2500 years. Unfortunately the archaeological record reflecting this period is rife with problems. The first difficulty concerns the time span, *c.* 2800–2400 BC, the time of the Single Grave culture. Most of the archaeological finds from that period were excavated in the west of Denmark, in Jutland. On the islands in eastern Denmark, finds are rare.

This unbalanced find distribution has long been used as one of the strongest arguments in favour of the theory of an invasion of the so-called Single Grave people at the beginning of the third millennium BC. This invasion theory postulated that an ethnic group called the Single Grave people settled on the light sandy soils of western Jutland, whereas the original agrarian population still resided on the moraine soils in the east. The Single Grave people were thought to have spread gradually onto these heavier soils in east Denmark, so that by the end of the third millennium BC they were supposed to have established themselves as an 'upper class' in relation to the subjugated 'Funnel-Beaker people'.

Today the entire invasion theory has collapsed under the weighty evidence of modern radiocarbon dating. Consequently recent research has been concentrated on the archaeological record from eastern Denmark. Surprisingly, it has been demonstrated that contrary to earlier theories there was a continuous settlement here from the fourth millennium far into the third millennium BC, that is into a period once thought to be devoid of archaeological remains (P.O. Nielsen, 1977a). For example, it has been shown that the large megalith graves on the

Danish islands were still in use after *c.* 2800 BC. At the same time a remarkable quantity of sacrificial deposits, flint axes for example, were being deposited in lakes and bogs (P.O. Nielsen 1977b). Thus, in contrast to earlier hypotheses, eastern Denmark is far from lacking in finds during the Single Grave period (2800–2400 BC). Even so, it is still impossible to explain the peculiar difference in find quantity between west and east Denmark. One likely cause is the intensive cultivation of later epochs which obliterated earlier remains. Subsequent periods of prehistory, such as the final half of the first millennium BC, also exhibit a similar dearth of finds in eastern Denmark.

Meanwhile, a comparison between the settlement areas of the first farming communities (Figure 27) and the settlement areas which developed towards the end of the third millennium BC testifies to significant changes in the settlement pattern in the intervening period. This may be demonstrated by the map, Figure 40, which conveys some idea of the major settlement features during the Late Neolithic period (2400–1800 BC). The tendencies observed become even more evident in a comparison between the map in Figure 40 and the maps showing settlement in the Bronze Age (1800–500 BC) (Figures 41 and 42). The maps are based upon the distribution of approximately 4000 Bronze Age graves and there is reason to believe that the number of graves within a reasonably large area reflects the relative population density. The overall picture emerging from Figure 42 clearly shows the main settlement features resulting from the changes which occurred in the third millennium BC. At the same time it appears that this new pattern remained virtually unchanged from the Late Neolithic period down to the Iron Age, *c.* 500 BC.

In Jutland, the most striking fact is that settlement apparently avoided the heavy moraine soils of the eastern region as well as the light sandy soils in the west. Population concentrations can be observed in central Vendsyssel, western Himmerland, the westernmost part of the Limfjord, and further south along the ridge of Jutland with extensions toward the west coast. The picture is somewhat blurred regarding the island of Funen, but on Zealand there is a clear-cut tendency to avoid the centre of the island. This tendency is already evident from the start of the third millennium BC. Sizeable concentrations of population existed in the north-west and west of Zealand, in the region surrounding the Isefjord and Roskilde fjord, and in the south on the islands of Møn and Falster.

In the course of nearly 2000 years, as shown by the maps, only small changes occurred either as an expansion of settlement or as an increased tendency to form clusters. These shifts probably resulted in changes of

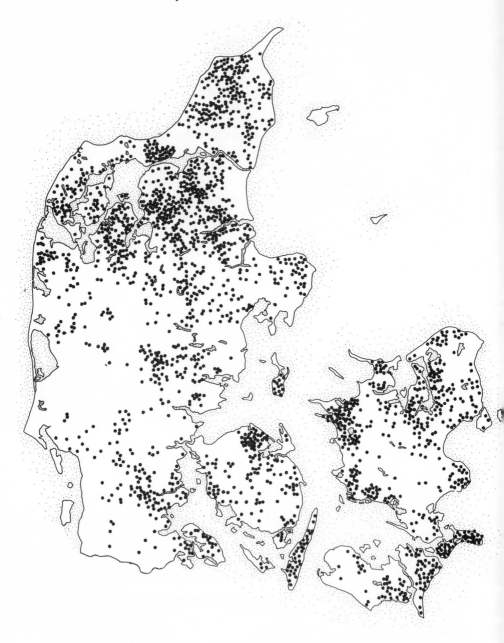

Figure 40 Distribution of the late Neolithic flint daggers, type I–V (*cf*. fig. 55) from *c*. 2400–1800 BC.

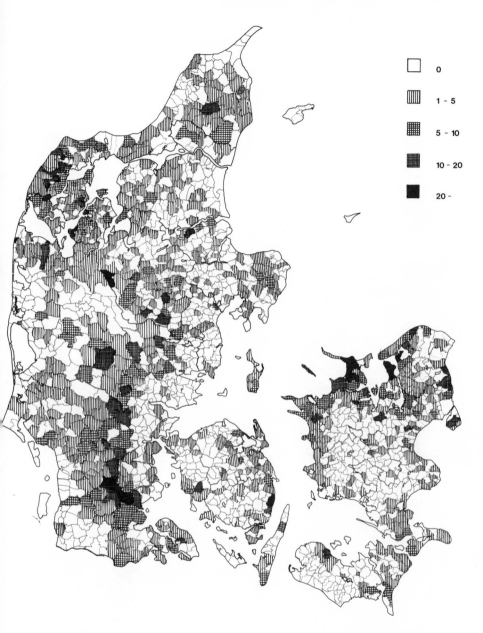

Figure 41 Distribution of grave finds from the Early Bronze Age mapped by parishes. The various signatures indicate the number of graves found within each parish.

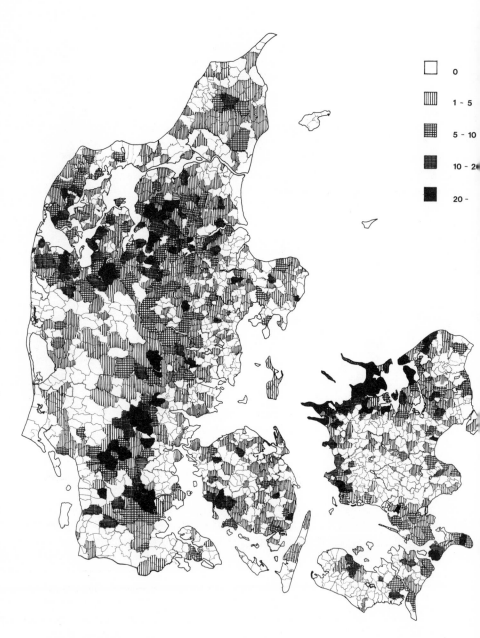

	0
	1 - 5
	5 - 10
	10 - 2●
	20 -

Figure 42 Distribution of grave finds from the Late Bronze Age mapped by parishes. The various signatures indicate the number of graves found within each parish.

socio-economic conditions, a supposition that is supported by the archaeological record. In the long run, however, increased settlement in west Jutland during the first millennium BC is more important. The expanding settlement westward prefigured the expansion which we can observe during the first centuries of the Iron Age, after 500 BC. Perhaps the more abundant precipitation of the first millennium BC improved agricultural conditions in west Jutland for a few centuries. On the whole, though, settlement was strikingly stationary from 2400–500 BC.

The cause of the change in settlement pattern during the third millennium BC has already been touched upon. Apparently the subsistence pattern of the earliest farming communities was a wide-spectred one which demanded a certain mobility. As a result of population pressure, many modifications were introduced during the third millennium BC. The wide-spectred subsistence strategy seems to have been abandoned; instead ard-ploughing became more accepted and greater emphasis was given to stock-raising. As a matter of fact, there seems to have been a similar trend in many areas of central and northern Europe in the same period (A.G. Sherratt, 1980). Here too the dramatic invasion theories of earlier generations have been abandoned of late. Instead, interest has been focused on evidence of technological innovations, intensified forest clearance and expansion of grasslands. These observations point to the development of new subsistence strategies by the farming communities.

To elucidate this process we shall briefly examine some of the few fragments of pedological evidence from early times. It has already been shown how the extensive swidden agriculture practised by the first farmers washed iron and mineral nutrients out of the upper layers of the forest floor, thus exhausting the soil. How long this process took cannot be known. But there is much to indicate that the natural forest mould from the beginning of the Sub-Boreal period, during which agriculture was introduced, deteriorated rapidly.

Prehistoric cultivation horizons confirm this swift degeneration. Buried soils may be found, for example, beneath Bronze Age barrows. Not only do these buried soils, through pollen analysis, testify to the local vegetation when the barrow was built; they can also inform us about the pedogenetic stage of development of the soil, its content of mineral nutrients and its ability to supply plants with water. Compared with modern soil at the same sites, buried soils are storehouses of information which until recently have hardly been exploited (S. Nielsen, 1980).

The emerging impression of agriculture in Denmark up to the beginning of the Iron Age is that of a farming system which hastened the deterioration of the ecological system and contributed to the rapid spread of the heathland, especially in western Jutland.

The buried soil underlying Bronze Age barrows nearly always consists of a poor, very thin layer of mould in which cereal crops, for example, would hardly have produced more than threefold, or at the utmost fourfold. With the technology available to the farming communities, only a very modest layer of mould could be formed. This situation was not bettered until the introduction of manuring during the Iron Age.

Naturally the physical composition of the subsoil was an essential factor in forming the mould layer resulting from continuous cultivation. The heavy boulder clay in east Denmark, for example, resulted in a better mould layer than the light sandy soil of west Denmark. But the present-day layer of mould cannot directly provide information on cultivation at a certain site thousands of years ago. The mould layer in a modern ploughed field is primarily the result of modern methods of cultivation. Therefore, recent studies (K. Kristiansen, 1978a; K. Randsborg, 1974a and b) which have attempted to relate the distribution of wealth in the Bronze Age to measurements of modern soil quality must be taken with a grain of salt. At the most, they can provide very rough generalizations about the varying conditions of farming in various parts of prehistoric Denmark.

On the whole, we can assume that the lightest soils in west Jutland can hardly have been suitable for cereal cultivation until late in prehistory. Thus we have no impressions of grain in the pottery of the so-called Single Grave culture in these regions. Here the major type of subsistence was probably the raising of sheep and cattle.

Even elsewhere in Denmark, where the mould was richer, cereal cultivation played only a modest role in the subsistence strategy. A threefold harvest was probably common; even in the Middle Ages yields in northern Europe were rarely higher. In addition, fields must have been quite small owing to the input of work required. So even on the good lands of east Denmark, stock-breeding, supplemented with food-gathering from marine and other sources, must have constituted the most important part of the subsistence pattern.

These factors help explain the settlement pattern which emerged during the third and second millennia BC. The land which the farming communities selected for settlement was usually what is today considered soil of medium quality. Four thousand years ago this meant areas with a rather open forest vegetation which could easily be exploited for cattle grazing. What we today consider high-quality soils, such as those in east Jutland, would not have been especially attractive due to their far denser forest vegetation. This preference for lighter soils, for areas

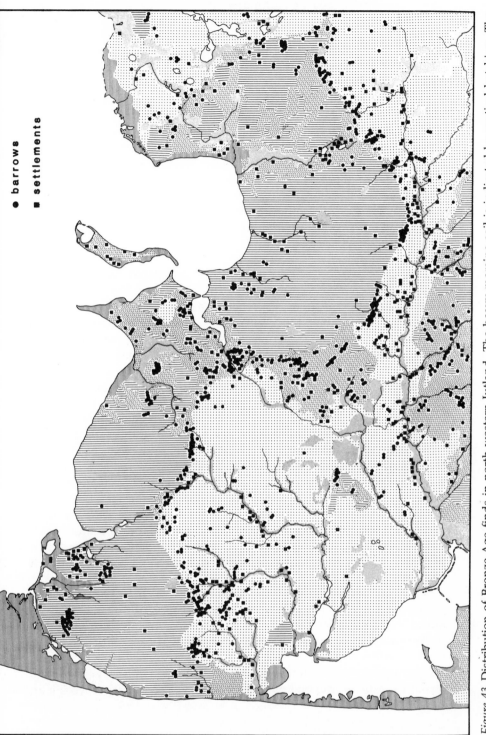

● barrows

■ settlements

Figure 43 Distribution of Bronze-Age finds in north-western Jutland. The heavy moraine soil is indicated by vertical hatching. The dotted areas indicate the sandy soils of the outwash plains.

which were open oak woodlands with heathy clearings, is for example reflected in the distribution of Bronze Age finds in north-west Jutland (Figure 43) (K. Kristiansen, 1978a).

Often this pattern was adapted to local conditions. In north-west Zealand, which was one of the most populous settled areas from the third to the first millennia BC, topography played a more crucial role than in north-west Jutland. So far, no pollen analyses have been made in this region, but the distribution of the finds together with the topographical situation indicates that large areas were covered with an open forest with abundant grasslands and denser forest in the uninhabited regions. This type of pasture is extremely productive when grazed by cattle. Furthermore the clay soil stimulated reproduction of the vegetation better here than in west Jutland. Marine resources may also have been a vital alternative source of food.

Villages and farmsteads

Recent Jutland excavations, especially those in the western part of the peninsula, have unearthed numerous settlements from the Late Neolithic and the Bronze Age. Large-scale excavations have uncovered whole village complexes consisting of up to fifty houses. The earliest sites date from the beginning of the Neolithic (c. 2400 BC). Unfortunately, the settlement type of the Single Grave culture from the middle of the third millennium BC remains a puzzle. Yet there are hints that the type of settlement which can be glimpsed at the end of the third millennium BC may reach further back in time, in fact to the Single Grave culture.

The excavated sites reveal that around 2400 BC settlements consisted of small clusters of farmsteads, each housing a single family. The typical house is a relatively short rectangular construction, 12 to 20 metres long and 6 or 7 metres wide with a partially sunken floor (Figure 44). The roof is supported by a single row of posts. This house type seems to have been built some centuries into the second millennium BC, after which new types of houses appeared. A common architectural tradition prevailed throughout much of southern Scandinavia and northern Germany.

Sometime in the middle of the second millennium BC the archaeological record shows that a new, well-defined type of house was introduced. Large sturdy three-aisled longhouses now appeared at the settlements. These houses were always oriented east–west, and their roofs were supported by two rows of interior posts (Figure 45). A number of constructional modifications were made in this type over the centuries. Most of the buildings were spacious, frequently covering an

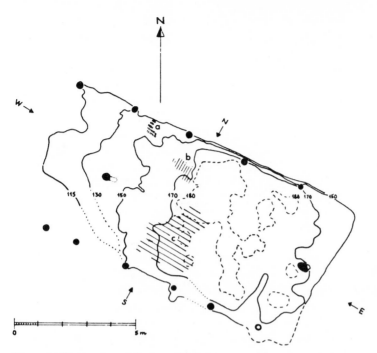

Figure 44 House site of the Late Neolithic period found at Myrhøj,
western Jutland.

area of 60–150 m². Some houses actually measure up to 250 m².
Variations in size may be related to the differences in wealth observed in
contemporaneous graves.

The large houses of the second and first millennia BC are most often
bisected by two entrances (Figure 46). The west half was the dwelling
area, but the function of the east end is still a puzzle. In some cases,
boxes for large animals have been discovered. But if the east end was a
stall, then the livestock must have been positioned in a way somewhat
different from the position in the Iron Age houses. Together with the
longhouses, smaller storehouses have also been found. These are
normally from 6 to 7 metres in length and 3 or 4 metres in width.

The origin of the three-aisled longhouses is unclear. In the second
millennium BC they may be found side by side with another house type
with turf walls. Certain similarities do exist between the house types,
but as yet the turf-built houses are sparsely documented in the
archaeological record and their function is still obscure.

Architecture followed the same general pattern throughout Denmark
in the second and first millennia BC. In fact, congruence in building

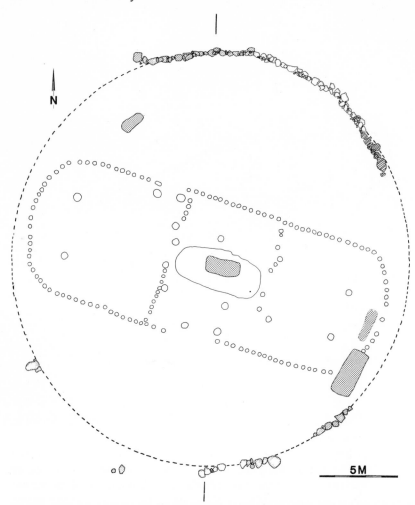

Figure 45 House site of the Early Bronze Age, Montelius period II, found under a
Bronze-Age barrow at Trappendal, southern Jutland.

traditions stretched even further. From around the middle of the second
millennium BC houses based upon the same constructional principles as
those in Jutland can be traced in the lowland region south of the North
Sea, all the way down to the mouth of the Rhine. The structures are
three-aisled longhouses and, like the Danish ones, are usually divided
into two parts, of which one is for dwelling. The other half can
sometimes be identified as a stall from finds of stall partitions. Dutch
longhouses from the second millennium BC could shelter up to thirty

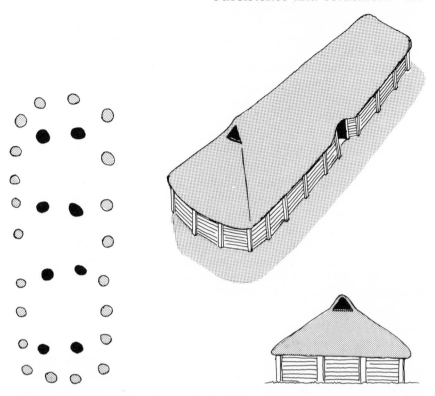

Figure 46 Reconstruction of a typical three-aisled longhouse of the Late Bronze
Age. Reconstructed after a house site found at Hovergårde, western Jutland.

head of livestock. Together with the oblong houses, storehouses are
often found. Although this type is most common in Holland, it has, as
already mentioned, also turned up in Jutland. Radio-carbon dates prove
the Dutch houses to be contemporary with the oldest Danish three-
aisled houses.

In Denmark and abroad, these structures raise the question of
whether the settlements consisted of large and small clusters of independent households or whether they were single farmsteads. This
subject has long been debated in Danish archaeology (S. Müller, 1904).
In Denmark the question remains unanswered despite the more than
one hundred house sites which have been unearthed during the last
decade. The crux of the problem is the impossibility of determining how
many houses stood at the same site at the same time. No doubt
settlements of the Bronze Age differed from those at the end of the first
millennium BC. But just what are those differences and how general are

they? Does the archaeological record indicate a contraction of the settlement, i.e. a development from individual farmsteads to regular villages during the second and first millennia BC in Denmark?

The oldest-known settlement from the period in question is Myrhøj in northern Jutland, radiocarbon-dated to c. 2400 BC. This settlement included only three houses. However there may still be unexcavated houses on the site. This also holds true of another settlement, Egehøj in eastern Jutland, radiocarbon-dated to about 1800 BC. Of the three house sites excavated here, the largest was 19 × 6 metres. But again the limits of the settlement are unknown. At Vadgård in northern Jutland, a settlement radiocarbon-dated to 1350–1200 BC, excavations have revealed a rather large, partially enclosed complex centred around a sacred structure. This can clearly be called a village similar to those encountered later in the Iron Age.

Some of the late finds, such as settlements from the first half of the first millennium BC, also seem to have been comprised of many households. At Spjald in western Jutland, about thirty-three houses were excavated, within an area of about 350 × 70 metres (Figure 47). Even though it can by no means be proved that all of these houses stood simultaneously, the multitude of house sites cannot be interpreted as representing various stages in the existence of one or more farmsteads. The Spjald settlement must have formed a regular village community even if its structure cannot be defined. A similar situation is found at several other localities. At Bjerg, only 7 kilometres from the Spjald settlement, about fifty-five house sites were found, divided into two main groups. Again it is impossible to ascertain the size or structure of

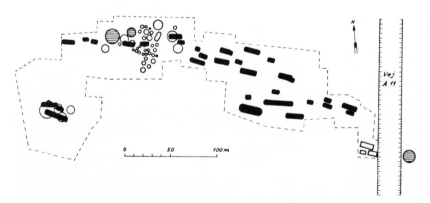

Figure 47 Simplified plan of the Late Bronze-Age settlement at Spjald, western Jutland. The house sites of the Late Bronze Age are indicated in black, later graves and house sites with open contours.

the community at any given stage of its existence. Nor can it be directly compared to the Iron Age village at Grøntoft (Figure 65), only a few centuries younger. Nonetheless there is reason to believe that both individual farmsteads and more extensive village communities existed in western Jutland during the early first millennium BC. The same situation prevailed through the latter half of the millennium, into the early Iron Age.

In east Denmark, only a few house sites have been excavated. Very little is therefore known of the site structure. Refuse layers several metres thick found at the settlement Voldtofte on Funen may indicate that large long-lived villages existed here during the first millennium BC.

But what exactly is a village? In Denmark the village has been the most widespread settlement form for centuries, from the Viking Age up to the agricultural reforms at the end of the eighteenth century. Throughout Danish history, village communities which were collectively supervised possessed formal and informal bodies which administered the rules of husbandry, protected local customs, and enforced peace and order. A village was thus a nuclear settlement forming a system comprised of elements of economic, social and cultural character. However, the definition of a village in historical times is not applicable to prehistory. Here a more simple definition of a village must suffice: a topographical unit comprised of a cluster of three or more independent households. Other features, such as the social, economic and cultural forms of co-operation are of secondary importance. Of course, various forms of co-operation existed in prehistoric villages. But the nature of these forms is unknown and therefore cannot be included in the archaeological definition of a village.

Towards more productive agricultural forms

Throughout the third millennium BC the farming communities in Denmark had slowly abandoned their wide-spectred subsistence strategy. An altered ecological situation and growing population pressure had little by little forced them into new types of land management based upon more extensive stock-raising and a different use of the arable land. Ard-ploughing was now widespread (Figure 48). No doubt these innovations swelled the agricultural output of the farming communities in Denmark. There were, however, serious restraints such as the necessity of a higher input of labour required for working the land. Expansion of the cultivated area was thus strictly limited. Consequently, expansion of pasture and cattle holdings offered the best ways of augmenting agricultural income. This development cannot be closely stu-

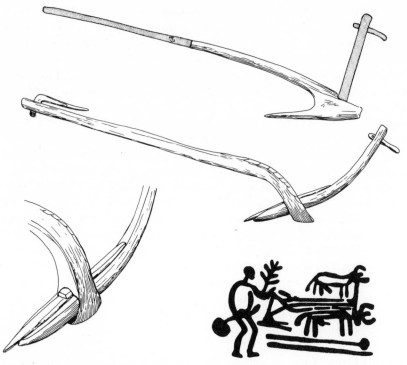

Figure 48 The two different ard types of the Bronze Age. Above: crook ard found at Hvorslev, Viborg county. Below: bow ard found at Døstrup, Ålborg county. Bottom: Bronze Age rock carving with ploughing scene from Listleby, Bohuslän, Sweden.

died from the third to the first millennia BC but its results are obvious in the Late Bronze Age (1000–500 BC).

Regarding the earliest periods, up to the start of the Bronze Age, most theories on the subsistence strategy of the farming communities were once based upon the hypothetical invasion of the Single Grave people, who were seen as nomadic pastoralists. However, the archaeological record from that period presents unmistakable evidence of both stock-breeding and cereal cultivation. The latter is documented by grain impressions in pottery and finds of ard furrows, as well as finds of querns and harvest implements at the settlements. In a few cases, finds of animal bones shed some light on the role of animal husbandry. Pollen diagrams display the effects of man's ever more profound impact on vegetation caused primarily by expansive cattle grazing. In the culturally related areas outside Denmark, the archaeological record reflects the same trend. Furthermore, during the Early Bronze Age (1800–1000 BC) archaeological evidence of the subsistence strategy of the farming communities is scarce. But it is important that aside from countless finds of ard furrows under barrows, the oldest ards themselves, radiocarbon-dated to about 1500 BC, are being discovered in Danish bogs.

During the Late Bronze Age (1000–500 BC) the archaeological record becomes more informative. Hundreds of settlements are known from that period, and almost everywhere they display the same basic features: the primary meat producer, at least on the more benign lands, was the ox. The horse also supplied a good deal of meat, often about as much as sheep and pigs, although the prevalence of these latter animals varies greatly according to physical and biological conditions in the various regions. On the second-rate lands in western Denmark, sheep were probably the most important livestock. The meagre archaeological record cannot yet indicate how the farming communities exploited the various ecological zones. Similarly the age distribution of the cattle does not testify to the overwintering strategy employed by the farming communities. Some finds indicate that winter slaughtering was considerable but no generalizations can be drawn.

Cereal cultivation during the late Bronze Age is noteworthy for the decreasing importance of wheat, especially of emmer. Barley, particularly naked barley, increased correspondingly in importance. When this cropping change occurred is not clear. It seems that the role played by barley had already increased in the third millennium BC. Another improvement which apparently did not take place until the first millennium BC was the introduction of oats and millet. Other cultivated plants included peas (*Pisum*), bean (*Vicia faba*) and perhaps also the oil plant gold of pleasure (*Camelina sativa*).

The role of hunting and food-gathering in the farming communities of the third to the first millennia BC is still very poorly documented in the archaeological record (Figure 49). There are indications that throughout the period marine resources were still exploited. Seasonal camps from the early first millennium BC show that in certain coastal regions fishing, especially for cod, haddock and flounder, supplemented agricultural incomes. The gathering of marine molluscs and the hunting of sea mammals apparently also played a certain role in the subsistence economy.

No matter how minute the changes that the farming communities underwent from the third to the first millennia BC, they all contributed to an altered subsistence strategy. Increased population pressure was probably the prime cause of this process, during which the farming communities gradually abandoned their wide-spectred subsistence pattern. Agriculture became more labour-intensive, leading to heightened

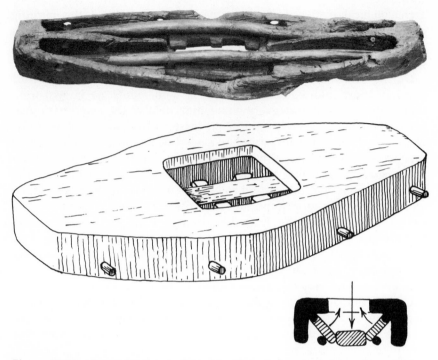

Figure 49 Wooden animal trap from the Bronze Age found in a bog, Nisset
Nørremose, Viborg county. Two massive oak flaps are held by a beechwood
spring. The merest pressure on the trap would release it.

exploitation of the settled area, a lower degree of mobility of the
individual communities, greater emphasis on ard ploughing and a rise
in the importance of animal husbandry. Although this development can
only be traced sporadically in the archaeological record, it does constitute an alternative to the conventional invasion hypotheses of continental archaeology. However, the greatest limitation of the archaeological
record is that most settlements are found on the second-rate soils of
Jutland. The paucity of settlement finds on more benign soils calls the
representativeness of the Jutland finds into question. Similarly it is most
unfortunate that the subsistence strategy of the farming communities
first comes into focus in the last thousand years of the period, when the
strategy had already been transformed.

In any case, there seem to have been few major technological
innovations during the third and second millennia BC. The introduction
of metal technology around 2000 BC does not seem to have altered the
subsistence strategy to any great degree. Metal was in demand not so

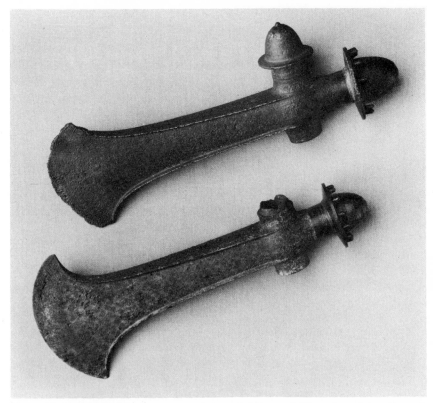

Figure 50 Ceremonial bronze axes, each weighing *c*. 7 kilos, found together at Egebak, Hjørring county.

much for its utilitarian merits as for its symbolic value as an indicator of status and wealth (Figure 50). Thus its effect on the socio-economic development of the farming communities was secondary. As will presently be shown, its importance lay in the reproduction of the social structure.

The exchange of goods and raw materials

In the hunter–gatherer societies of the Palaeolithic and Mesolithic periods, the exchange of certain raw materials already played an important role in defining social territories. Later, in the fourth millennium BC, when the first farming communities developed, the exchange of goods and raw materials became increasingly significant. During the following millennia a close correlation between exchange and the development of ranking can be observed within the individual settlement areas in Denmark.

In all so-called primitive societies, goods and services are distributed via institutional forms which may vary enormously. They may also be incomprehensible from the viewpoint of modern economics. Economic transactions are difficult to isolate in societies which have not yet developed a market economy. It is a well-known fact that in such societies an economic transaction is always the manifestation of an underlying social relation such as friendship, kinship and political or religious obligations. This implies that the exchange of goods and services in a primitive society is normally a brief episode in a more comprehensive social relationship. The study of the exchange of goods is thus vital to the understanding of social organization in prehistoric societies.

Already with the incipient development of ranked societies in Denmark in the course of the fourth millennium BC, a large-scale exchange of goods took place. Flint from northern Jutland was distributed over large areas of southern Scandinavia. Far-reaching exchange of amber also began. In the most prosperous settlement regions, both amber and flint played a prominent part in ranked contexts.

Around 2000 BC the exchange systems flourished. Amber turns up at this time in central European finds. Just before the middle of the second millennium BC its expansion culminated. Baltic amber now appeared as far south as the Mediterranean in the Mycenaean shaft graves.

Concurrently metal objects circulated widely among the farming communities in the north European lowland. Obviously some kind of relationship bound the simultaneous development of metal technology, the increased exchange of raw materials, and changes in societal organization.

In Denmark the transformation around 2000 BC has often been explained by the postulated invasion of the Single Grave people several centuries earlier. It was thought that at the end of the third millennium BC the two presumed ethnic groups merged so that the Single Grave people formed an 'aristocratic warrior class' which owned the means of production and controlled the interregional exchange (J. Brøndsted, 1957). Meanwhile a 'peasant class', the Funnel-Necked Beaker people, were thought to have created the economic surplus by which the supposed warrior class acquired imported metal. Thus the period around 2000 BC was considered crucial in leading to a kind of 'feudal' Bronze Age society.

This theory, which was modelled on the Viking period 3000 years later, was founded on the belief that history develops cyclically.

Consequently Bronze Age society was attributed with institutional forms which were in fact foreign to its social structure. Recently, though, many Danish archaeologists have sought other paths. The new concepts employed may lead to a more realistic evaluation of the processes underlying the exchange systems of the third to the first millennia BC.

Concepts of exchange

The theoretical framework used here to describe the basic principles of distribution in primitive society was proposed by economist Karl Polanyi. His three basic concepts of economic life are 1) reciprocity, in which goods and services are exchanged between equal partners without the use of money; 2) redistribution, in which goods and services are brought to a centre from which they are redistributed; and 3) market economy, in which the exchange of goods is regulated by prices varying according to supply and demand. Often these principles exist simultaneously in the same system. The dominant principle is determined by the level of production in the individual society.

Older studies discussing the exchange of goods in the Danish Bronze Age often employ concepts more or less directly derived from a market economy. This is due to the explanation models which have been used to describe socio-economic development in the Bronze Age. The use of concepts originating in later historical periods ignores the fact that a market economy is always related to economic specialization and regional divisions of labour which again are stimulated by the demands of urban centres. As with reciprocity and redistribution, a market economy can be described as a means of distributing surplus. But in contrast to the other exchange forms, the market principle is a brief profit-controlled and socially non-obligating form of exchange. Furthermore it is often (but not always) connected with the centralized authority which lies in the formation of the state. In fact, one of the primary functions of centralized authority is to ensure unhindered transportation within the territory.

This latter function has often been ignored in Scandinavian literature on prehistoric trade. Where administration is weak, unhindered transportation can hardly be relied upon. Moreover, the presence of 'markets' or 'market-places' does not necessarily mean that the market principle has been in function. Reciprocity and redistribution may just as well have created these centres of trade.

The extent to which goods were exchanged during the third to the first millennia BC is still little known. However, it seems likely that foodstuffs were inconsequential both as internal and as external exchange. The bulk of goods exchanged probably consisted of objects such as raw materials, craft products and foreign prestige goods which were needed for cementing social relations and competitions between different descent groups.

The relationship between the production and circulation of goods on the one hand and prehistoric socio-economic development on the other hand can best be understood by a more general theory dealing with so-called prestige-goods economies. Several modern studies have pointed out a number of socio-economic consequences of control over access to resources obtained through external trade (M.D. Sahlins, 1963, 1965, 1968, 1974; R.A. Rappaport, 1968; K. Ekholm, 1972; J. Friedman and M.J. Rowlands, 1978; S. Frankenstein and M.J. Rowlands, 1978). Neolithic flint and amber trade has been examined in the light of just such a model. This model helps explain some of the typical features of the development in northern Europe from the fourth millennium BC onward.

The earliest stage in this process has already been discussed (see p. 103 ff). Here we saw how an incipient control of the exchange of raw materials and prestige goods could have demographic consequences resulting within a larger area in a differential growth in size and dominance of the various groups. In the long run, this could lead to the emergence of chiefdoms. This is probably what happened at the end of the third millennium BC in several regions of the north European lowland.

At this stage the élite of the emergent chiefdoms may have reinforced their control over the circulation of goods by limiting the use of domestic goods and replacing them with foreign wealth objects. The growing circulation of bronze weapons, ornaments and implements, along with the expanding amber trade from the beginning of the second millennium BC, is here seen in this light. Most probably the numerous wealth objects (Figures 51 and 52) reflect complex sumptuary rules in north European Bronze Age society. A redistributive economic system was now evolving, causing domestic goods to be filtered up through the system in the form of tribute. These goods were used by the élite for external exchanges by which foreign prestige goods or craft products were attained. The foreign goods were then redistributed, serving as bride wealth, funerary goods, status insignias, etc.

Accelerating attempts to regulate the circulation of wealth objects were also manifest in the growth of specialist skills such as metal-casting. Specialized workshops made it easier for the élite to control production of status symbols. This probably explains the existence of highly skilled

Figure 51 Wealth objects, weapons, and ornaments from the Early Bronze Age, Montelius period II.

Figure 52 Wealth objects, weapons, and ornaments from the Early Bronze Age, Montelius period III.

bronze craftsmanship in Denmark around the mid-second millennium BC.

According to the more general theory an equilibrium may occur at this stage. And in fact this does seem to be the case in southern Scandinavia in the second millennium BC. Despite fluctuations in the quantity of bronze coming into Denmark, this equilibrium presumably prevailed over the next thousand years. Around 500 BC, however, the influx of foreign prestige goods shrank remarkably. Some sort of crisis must have shaken the formerly so stable exchange system.

The case of amber

The exchange of amber is a revealing example of the magnitude which the exchange of goods could attain during the Neolithic and Bronze Age of northern Europe. The concept of an 'amber trade' as well as of 'amber routes' is one of the oldest notions of European archaeology and has played a tremendous part in the diffusionist theories of earlier generations. In recent years, however, the analytical work of the American chemist Curt W. Beck has clarified a number of hitherto unsolved problems related to the distribution of the so-called Baltic amber. Using infra-red spectroscopy, Beck has demonstrated that a great deal of the amber from central and southern Europe in the Bronze Age and the early Iron Age is of 'Baltic' origin. By 'Baltic amber' is meant amber derived from natural deposits extending from Britain in the west to the Soviet Union in the east. Although more precise origins cannot be pinpointed, the results unequivocally show that central and south European amber was not local but had a northern origin. The archaeological record confirms that from the end of the third millennium BC north European amber was disseminated ever further southwards by means of a vast network.

As already mentioned, amber distribution before 2000 BC was restricted to more closed exchange systems along the North Sea and the Baltic. However, the launching of bronze technology in northern Europe (around 2000 BC) radically altered this situation. Baltic amber now turned up as an indicator of wealth in rich burials far from its origin: in Brittany, southern Britain, central Germany and Poland. At the same time amber finds vanish from the Baltic zone. Through subsequent millennia the graves and sacrificial deposits of Denmark, southern Sweden and the coastal regions along the southern part of the Baltic contain remarkably little amber.

There are many indications that this shift in the distribution pattern was linked to the flourishing metal import in the north. Throughout the second and most of the first millennia BC bronze objects in northern Europe were prized first and foremost as prestige indicators. The usefulness of metal was clearly secondary. As will later be shown, analysis of the quantity of imported metal in Danish Bronze Age graves clearly proves the simultaneous rise of ranking within the agrarian communities. Nevertheless throughout the Baltic zone, amber seems to only a very minor degree to have been used in a ranked context. Instead it was channelled into the far-reaching network of trade relations by which the coveted metal was obtained.

Amber which was gathered along the coasts was treasured in the north. Minute quantities of amber may be found in otherwise richly equipped graves from the second millennium BC. Magical powers were attributed to amber, as is often shown by its find context. Outside the Baltic zone, amber appears chiefly in the wealthiest graves. Thus along with other treasures, amber spread by means of the élite. This sort of exchange, which was probably carried out via prestige chains, most logically explains the distribution pattern around the mid-second millennium BC. At this time the quantity of amber in central and southern Europe reached a peak, and concurrently there seems to have been a culmination of wealth over much of the Baltic zone.

South of the Baltic, amber can be traced, often in conjunction with glass beads, in rich graves from Mecklenburg and downwards to southern Germany, eastern France and the mouth of the Rhône. Perhaps this latter area controlled the final distribution to such élite as those buried in the Mycenaean shaft graves, the amber beads of which have been identified by infra-red spectroscopy as Baltic.

These hypothetical prestige chains traversed Europe to the Mediterranean, where contact may have been established with freelance traders from the Mycenaean cultural area (C. Renfrew, 1972). Thus the wide distribution not only of amber but also of many other prestige goods can be explained. Most likely such exchanges took place among centres prospering from control of foreign goods.

This was probably also the case at the end of the eighth century BC and up to the fifth century BC. A strong socio-economic development within central Europe bolstered distribution. The prestige-goods economy which evolved around the north Balkan and central European chiefdoms in the early Iron Age must have played a critical role in maintaining a vast trade network. However, turmoil in the Mediterranean area at the end of the fifth century BC caused profound disturbances within the central European chiefdoms, which depended heavily upon the influx of foreign prestige goods (S. Frankenstein and M.J. Rowlands, 1978). And as a result of this unrest, the flow of amber from the north dried up. Not until central European urban manufacturing centres arose at the end of the second century BC did conditions for large-scale trading of amber again develop.

External and internal exchange up to 500 BC

Our overall view of the exchange of goods in the so-called Single Grave period is still indistinct, due in part to the striking imbalance of the archaeological record. Even so, we know that amber and flint were widely distributed in this period as elements in a status-motivated exchange manifest above all in male graves and to a lesser degree in female graves.

After 2400 BC, in the Late Neolithic, the exchange of goods was intensified. Status symbols in the male graves were now daggers and spears. These weapons bear witness to far-reaching contacts from southern Scandinavia northwards. Probably, the hundreds of daggers as well as sickles and other flint implements found along the Norwegian west coast were produced in northern Jutland. The most distant outposts of this diffusion are in the Swedish Norrland. However, the greatest abundance of items appears in Denmark. This corresponds to the demand created by the rise of ranking in the late Neolithic communities.

Around 2000 BC metal objects went into circulation and slowly supplanted flint in the exchange system. Metal weapons and implements from western and central Europe in particular increased. Prestige objects from the central and upper Danube region were channelled through the extensive exchange system all the way up to Denmark. Throughout the second millennium and up to about 500 BC, this great net of contacts ensured an ample influx of metal objects to southern Scandinavia. Subsequently trade was disrupted, as will be seen in the next chapter.

Metal objects were apparently exchanged in the form of finished goods; the Danish finds include no metal ingots. However, metal objects were only some of the goods used for exchange. Other commodities probably included leather wares, wax (for bronze-casting), honey, salt, textiles and many other things. But only objects of bronze, gold and pottery are preserved in the archaeological record.

A remarkable feature of the exchange system is that the majority of central European metal objects belonged to the man's sphere. Weapons and tools are clearly predominant (Figure 53). Women's ornaments rarely seem to have been exchanged. The man's sphere probably also encompassed the important group of beaten bronze cups and buckets.

Figure 53 Imported central European bronze shields and swords from the Late Bronze Age. The shield to the left is from Sørup, Ålborg county, the one to the right is of unknown provenance. The sword to the left is from Sønderup, Sorø county, the one to the right from Østerå, Vejle county.

Like other foreign goods, these ought to be interpreted as prestige objects used by the élite. The cups and buckets were probably drinking equipment which functioned in ritual contexts (Figure 54). Although they are primarily found in the so-called votive finds in peat bogs, in certain cases they also figure in the graves of people with high social status.

However, the bronze objects produced outside southern Scandinavia and parts of northern Germany constitute but a limited part of the overall exchange of goods. Far more intensive was the exchange of local so-called Nordic bronzes: weapons, implements and ornaments made in the north of bronze from central Europe. From the beginning of the second millennium BC a uniform art style – which especially characterized the specialized bronze workshops – bound the southern Scandinavian–northern German area. Within this social territory a lively exchange of status objects, craft products and probably also raw materials took place. But in contrast to the circulation of foreign goods, this geographically restricted exchange also embraced objects from both the male and the female sphere. Women's ornaments were scattered

Figure 54 Wheeled bronze cauldron, probably meant for ritual purposes, found in a richly equipped Early Bronze Age grave (Montelius period III) at Skallerup, southern Zealand.

throughout the aforementioned region as widely as, for example, weapons.

Notwithstanding the abundance of evidence for the exchange of goods and raw materials between 2800–500 BC, we are still left with innumerable unsolved problems. However, detailed studies of the provenance of metal objects and the composition of, for example, the votive finds – the so-called hoards – have definitely refuted most older theories of the Bronze Age 'long-distance trade'. The context in which foreign goods are found in Denmark clearly opposes the idea of direct transport via traders from central Europe to the Baltic area. Similarly, older theories of the amber trade and related hypothetical long-distance trade routes crossing the European continent must be rejected. As yet, only few exchange centres have been located. However, several combined archaeological and topographical studies carried out in Denmark have given encouraging results. A survey on the island of Funen has revealed an impressive concentration of wealth in the late Bronze Age. Immense and richly furnished barrows in the Voldtofte region (H. Thrane, 1976) clearly betoken a political and economic centre which must have played a key role in the exchange of prestige goods around 800 BC. A contemporary centre is found in Brandenburg, south of the Baltic, in the Seddin region (H. Wüstemann, 1974). Doubtless these localities were vital nodes in the north European network of exchange systems through which goods travelled vast distances, linking the élites of the agrarian societies.

Diverse ways of interpreting the exchange of goods up to 500 BC have been proposed. Different degrees of hierarchization within the various communities – as yet of unknown geographical extent – were probably manifest in a redistributive economic system. This system ensured both the production of specialized products (as evident in the fine bronze-work) and the continuous circulation of goods and services. Externally, these societies practised manifold forms of reciprocity, such as exchange, to cement relationships. Kinship alliances, bride purchase and similar exchange forms observed by the upper social strata may explain the diffusion of such objects as bronzes throughout the vast region of south Scandinavia and north Germany.

As stable as this system seems to have been, geographical variations through the centuries imply that the exchange of goods was controlled by centres of fluctuating political importance. Around the middle of the second millennium BC foreign goods were by and large concentrated in west Denmark. Most of the imports derived from south Germany. The prominent nodal centre in the exchange network encompassed the areas around the mouth of the Elbe and Schleswig-Holstein. From here, foreign goods travelled primarily to western Denmark and to a lesser degree to Zealand. Gold too is mainly found in the west. This implies that the goods carried to Denmark from Schleswig-Holstein came via the Weser region with the Lüneburg area as an important station towards southern Germany.

This pattern endured up to the end of the second millennium BC. Slowly it was replaced by a new pattern, according to which a centre in Mecklenburg controlled the influx of prestige goods from Europe. Much of this influx was still channelled to Denmark, but gradually an alternative network to east Denmark and south Sweden was building up. This eastward shift culminated around 1000 BC when connections from east Denmark over the Baltic to the mouth of the Oder River can be distinctly seen in the archaeological record. These connections also seem to have conducted quantities of southern European gold into Denmark.

The centres south of the Baltic have not yet been localized, although Mecklenburg and the regions south of the knee of the Elbe are known to have been crucial nodes in the network. From here, central European goods were also channelled to west Denmark.

Centuries later the same centres still functioned and the eastern parts of Denmark continued to receive most of the central European prestige goods. A more western-oriented exchange system with contacts to Jutland seems to have existed concurrently, although it was of minor economic significance compared to the eastern network. As late as the mid-first millennium BC both of these networks seem to have been intact, but new connections were established to the Polish Baltic regions. However, at that time the northward flow of metal objects was drying up and around 500 BC it seems to have ceased entirely.

Fluctuations in the import of bronze are also reflected in the circulation time of the prestige goods. Variations in circulation time can be observed from wear analysis of the bronzes (K. Kristiansen, 1978b) and in external supplies. This situation is particularly obvious around the middle of the first millennium BC, when socio-economic changes swept central Europe as a result of contact with Mediterranean civilizations which tapped the central and northern European exchange network for certain goods. These changes will be examined in the next chapter.

13

Social patterns from 2800 to 500 BC

During the fourth millennium BC, the growing complexity in production and the consequent need for co-ordination laid the foundations for a rudimentary form of ranking in the early farming communities of Denmark. These tendencies emerged distinctly at the end of the fourth and the beginning of the third millennia BC. Obviously there was now a decided emphasis on vertical relations within the communities. Through the following millennia, this emphasis became more pronounced as a result of attempts at augmenting productivity. There were severe restraints on these attempts. As the socio-economic system permitted only a slight differentiation of production, the agrarian society from 2800 to 500 BC was fairly static.

As shown in the foregoing chapter on the settlement and subsistence pattern during this period, the archaeological record – particularly that from the third millennium BC in Denmark – suffers from many critical gaps. None the less there is reason to presume that single households merged into more complex village communities as early as the third millennium BC. Throughout the period we find impressive monuments which must have demanded large-scale co-operation within the village communities. The most striking examples are the thousands of Bronze Age barrows. These barrows must have mobilized an enormous amount of labour, organized by the élite of the farming communities. In contrast to the large central sites from the fourth millennium BC this sort of mobilization indicates a more person-oriented cult. This corresponds to our impression of socio-economic development, at least from the second millennium BC.

The archaeological record from the period 2800–500 BC indicates that there existed a far-reaching exchange system ever more firmly based upon a redistributive economy within the various local regions. Thus it has been presumed that the various communities gradually became so thoroughly integrated that they developed into chiefdoms, a more complex form of the ranked type of tribal society from previous centuries. Chiefdoms are typified by 'specialization and redistribution; they are no longer merely adjunctive to a few particular endeavours, but continuously characterize a large part of the activity of the society' (E.R. Service, 1971).

Chiefdoms, however, are still recognized by the variations in rank which are the primary means to social integration. At the top of the hierarchy is the chieftain. His role is to redistribute: to plan, organize and deploy public labour and to be responsible for system-preserving religious functions. The chieftain's authority ensures integration among the various groups. Descent in relation to the chieftain normally decides the relative position of individuals and kin groups within the community.

It is also significant that even in the developed ranked society which seems to have existed in Denmark throughout the Bronze Age, social control must have been based upon enculturation and internalized sanction. Late in the existence of the prehistoric chiefdoms, during the Iron Age, mechanisms for adjudicating and enforcing more formal rules of social control were developed. This, then, is the social and political framework of the chiefdom level of organization to which Danish society belonged from about 2800 to 500 BC. A parallel development apparently took place throughout much of northern and central Europe.

Concerning the archaeological evidence of the settlement and subsistence patterns from 2800 to 500 BC, only a few conclusions can be drawn regarding the social organization of the farming communities. The grave finds, though, can provide more detailed insight into the social sphere. As mentioned, the graves can to some extent help determine the relative population density within the various regions of the country. The question which arises is, how representative are the graves as reflectors of social stratification? Danish archaeological literature often suggests that the graves of the Bronze Age in particular compose a representative sample of the entire population. This claim has been challenged in recent years but final conclusions are difficult to draw because skeletons are rarely preserved. In most graves, the sex of the deceased can be identified by the accompanying artefacts, although some small objects are common to both sexes. Between 2800 and 500 BC, male graves outnumbered female graves; children's graves are very rare. Obviously, then, the graves cannot be representative of the population as a whole. For the so-called Single Grave culture (2800–2400 BC), 75 per cent of the approximately 500 graves known in Denmark are male graves, to judge by the grave-goods. The Late Neolithic period (2400–1800 BC) also seems to exhibit a dominance of male graves. Unfortunately no usable calculations for this period have been made. But for the subsequent period, the Early Bronze Age (up to c. 1000 BC), detailed studies do exist. Out of a total of roughly 1000 graves, female graves are only half as common as male graves; children's graves are almost non-existent. The number of female graves and their contents seems to be based upon the relative population size and is thus decided by regional and chronological conditions. In the second half of the Bronze Age (1000–500 BC) identification is hindered by the introduction of cremation and the general paucity of grave goods. Very few analyses of cremated bones from the urn graves of the Late Bronze Age have been made.

We can therefore conclude that the grave finds hardly constitute a representative sample of the general population but are defined by various cultural norms, most of them related to the social status of the dead. A formalized grave cult can betoken the cause of death, place of death, age, sex, social position, group membership, and so on. More general social anthropological studies of societies which have not reached the state level (L.R. Binford, 1971) have shown that there is often a connection between the degree of social complexity and the quantity of symbolizing factors. There is therefore good reason to suppose that essential features of the social organization would be reflected in the Danish graves from about 2800 to 500 BC.

As yet, very few studies have been made of the distribution of wealth and status symbols in the graves of that period. The four centuries of the so-called Single Grave culture are further obscured by the very uneven geographic distribution of the grave finds. It is known that polished flint axes are replaced by battle axes as status symbols. Battle axes now appear in about half of the known graves. Around 2400 BC the flint dagger replaced the battle axe as the male status symbol (Figure 55).

Around 1800 BC the farming communities gradually began to integrate imported metal into their grave rites. It thus becomes possible to make quantitative evaluations of the distribution of mortuary wealth. Recent studies within this field have offered promising results for the Early Bronze Age (1800–1000 BC) (K. Randsborg, 1973, 1974b and c).

These studies have been based upon the assumption that the amount of metal in the graves of the period can be taken as an index for social stratification. Gold and bronze objects from about 1000 Danish Bronze Age graves were weighed and the ratio in value between the two metals was determined by various quantitative experiments to about 1:100. As an example, Figure 59 shows the distribution of bronze within the groups of male and female graves in the Bronze Age period II, i.e. two or

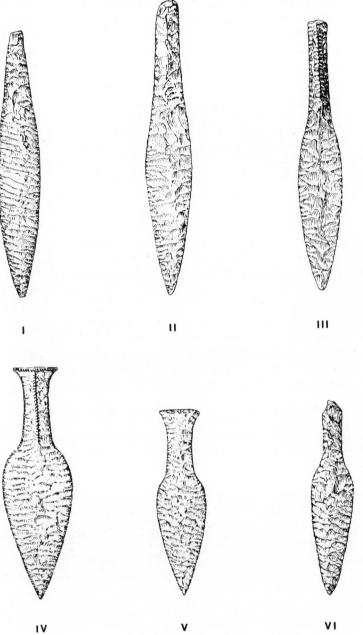

I	II	III

IV	V	VI

Figure 55 Typology of the Danish flint daggers. Types I–V are Late Neolithic; type VI belongs exclusively to the Early Bronze Age.

three centuries around the mid-second millennium BC. Male graves are seen to be abundant and more elaborate than female graves (Figures 56 and 57). In both groups, poor graves predominate. From these observations a series of conclusions have been drawn.

In the course of the second millennium BC a society emerged in which

Figure 56 A woman, about 18–20 years old, buried in an oak coffin in a barrow at Egtved, Jutland. Early Bronze Age, Montelius period II. The body was found fully dressed on a cowhide in the coffin. A shirt with elbow-length sleeves covered the upper part of the woman's body. She also wore a string skirt. Before the coffin was closed the body had been covered with a blanket.

Figure 57 A man, about 20 years old, buried in an oak coffin in a barrow, Borum Eshøj, in eastern Jutland. Early Bronze Age, Montelius period II. The young man was dressed in a loincloth held together by a leather belt. The body had been laid on a cowhide and covered with a woollen cloak. A sword scabbard containing only a little bronze dagger was found on the cloak.

wealth and status were distributed unequally. The graves hold both men and women from the upper stratum of society who, in contrast to the 'commoners', were buried with mortuary gifts of costly metal objects and, at least as regards the men, with wealth objects which can be interpreted as symbols of permanent status positions. It is also possible to observe great but graded distinctions in wealth and status in the graves of both men and women. The graves of high-ranking men contain the personal equipment of the dead, their magnificent weapons and sometimes their work axes. The poorer male graves contain merely a knife each. Gold objects appear chiefly in the rich graves, which also frequently contain objects of symbolic character and which thus can be interpreted as signs of authority. Such objects include folding stools (Figure 58), wooden bowls, staves and badges with metal mountings, and similar objects which are virtually absent from the poorer graves. In the graves of high-ranking women, these presumed symbols of authority are very rare – here high social position is betokened by heavy bronze ornaments and daggers.

The male–female status relationship is implied by the quantitative distribution of the graves. There are usually only half as many high-status female graves as graves containing men of similar rank (Figure 59). In general, the men are clearly superior as regards status positions. Yet the social hierarchy as a whole shows no sharp contrasts. The gap between rich and poor in the agrarian society was hardly wide. It is possible to link the high-status women to the richer half of the men

Figure 58 Folding stool, probably a status symbol, found in an oak-coffin grave at Guldhøj, southern Jutland.

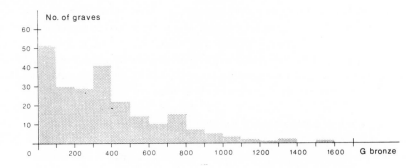

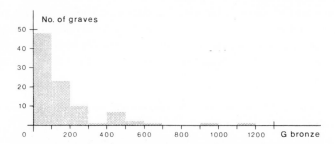

Figure 59 Histogram indicating the amounts of bronze found in men's graves
(above) and women's graves (below) during period II (Montelius) of the Early
Bronze Age.

represented in the barrows (Figure 60). Consequently the rest of the
high-ranking men must have been related to 'commoners', to women
whose status was not indicated by the mortuary rituals. The system has
therefore been interpreted as a graduated system characteristic of the
kinship-based chiefdoms.

Towards the end of the second millennium BC, a new mortuary
practice can be discerned. Status symbols are now rarely invested in the
graves. Instead the metal objects are laid in sacrificial deposits, the
so-called 'hoards'. This shift coincides by and large with a transition
from inhumation graves to cremation. Throughout the first millennium
BC graves are not particularly helpful as indicators of social ranking.
However, the graves still give a profile of the relative population density
in various parts of Denmark (Figure 42).

Over the first millennium BC, as the graves decreased in value as
indicators of social inequality, the hoards instead took over the role as
investments of objects denoting the social status of the owner(s). These
objects were chiefly massive bronze ornaments and weapons. The
plentiful group of such finds may thus be considered the remains of a

Figure 60 The hoards from the Late Bronze Age are most often found in wetlands such as bogs or meadows. A hoard may consist of one or two complete sets of women's ornaments, as was the case in this period V hoard which was found at Kertinge Mark on the island of Funen.

so-called social production withdrawal system (W.L. Rathje, 1975), in which the social élite transformed wealth into prestige by forcing large quantities of precious metal out of circulation – quite simply by depositing the metal at remote spots, never to be retrieved. The underlying idea must have been that the withdrawal of wealth served to legitimize the hierarchical order and authority of the élite.

Sacrificial deposits constitute one of the richest find groups from the period. This group includes primarily ornaments, tools and weapons. Deposits might consist of complete sets of women's ornaments or of several identical objects such as swords. The find group also includes countless single bronze objects which, like the composite finds, are often found in swampy areas or by large stones.

It is not easy to categorize the sacrificial deposits according to their content. All conceivable combinations of objects are found. The crucial factor for deposition seems to have been the value of the metal. Deposits were usually made on the fringes of a settlement, for example in the swampy lands separating the territories of the villages. With the decline of bronze imports to the north about 500 BC, the amount of bronze deposited dwindles, but sacrificial deposits were still made by the farming communities up to the birth of Christ.

The importance of sacrificial finds in the first half of the first millennium BC seems to be based on a cult focused on authority positions. Along with the personal possessions earlier deposited in the graves, sacrificial deposits now often included ritual objects which must have been related to the élite's practice of rituals: lurs, drinking sets with golden bowls and religious symbols such as figurines.

Throughout the second and most of the first millennia BC, religious symbolism was surprisingly uniform, as was, no doubt, the mythology which integrated each farming community. This homogeneity applied both geographically and chronologically. Many mythological motifs of the north European Bronze Age, such as the ship, the chariot of the sun, the fish and the horse (Figure 61), survived largely unchanged for more than a thousand years. Their dissemination throughout the north European lowland exemplifies the lively communication which existed from region to region.

The investment of wealth in mortuary rituals diminished during the first millennium BC. This decline, along with the predominant custom of cremation, makes it necessary for us to develop new methods to demonstrate social stratification in Bronze Age Denmark. In any case, it is certain that great social inequality still existed, as seen both by the sacrificial deposits and here and there also by the grave finds. Towards the close of the period, around 800 BC, a sizeable population concentration can be observed, on southern Funen for example. The population density here apparently necessitated advanced social stratification. Rich graves increased in number; some of the most imposing barrows of the period are also found here. To erect Lusehøj, the largest barrow in the

Figure 61 Ship motifs engraved on razors from the Late Bronze Age, Montelius periods IV–V.

Voldtofte area, about 3200 cubic metres of turf were required, which meant that 7 hectares of land had to be stripped. These monuments were erected over graves in which the social status of the dead was displayed by a rich equipment of wagons and drinking vessels – status symbols similar in character to those known from the hoards.

Through studies of the investment of wealth in graves and hoards, a picture emerges of the social organization from 2800 to 500 BC. These studies have uncovered the evolutionary potential of the farming communities along with some of the systematic variability in the operative cultural, biological and physical factors. Here and there are indications of a connection between population growth and increased social stratification. Social inequalities seem to have kept pace with population density, as a consequence of the demands created by the expansion and distribution of production. Similarly, the ratio between male and female status seems to have depended upon the same factors. As a working hypothesis it may be presumed that the position of a man was affected by the size of the male-dominated stock-raising, whereas a woman's status was related to the extent of field work. The archaeological record has provided some indications in this direction but more thorough studies are required as proof.

Although the archaeological record is meagre, it still confirms a relationship among the operative cultural, biological and physical factors. From an economic viewpoint, the bond between increased production and enhanced authority indicates that, as already suggested, redistributive and reciprocal economic patterns dominated in the settlement units. Analyses of the exchange system, mortuary rituals and sacrificial deposits make it probable that at the end of the third millennium BC the farming communities attained the chiefdom level of socio-cultural integration. A leading characteristic of the chiefdoms was that they were founded upon the so-called social production withdrawal system, in which the élite demonstrated its status by a tremendous mobilization of labour, such as that invested in the mortuary practices and by a correspondingly large consumption of exotic materials such as gold and bronze in the grave cult and sacrificial rites.

As regards religious practices, society at this time presumably witnessed the introduction of permanent religious positions. In a chiefdom society, these priestly offices are often passed down in a family line just as secular offices are; in fact, the 'priest' and the 'chieftain' are often one and the same person. Judging by both sacrificial deposits and graves, this situation is likely to have endured over more than one thousand years of the Bronze Age.

So far, the evolution of agrarian society from the third to the first millennia BC has been revealed in brief glimpses only. The most striking feature is that the communities seem to have been so static. Yet there is some evidence that, particularly from the end of the second millennium BC, larger concentrations of population developed in certain regions of Denmark, where the emphasis on vertical social relations also increased. One example is from south-western Funen around 800 BC, where the concentration of wealth and population was manifest in the erection of some of the most remarkable structures of the period. It is, however, peculiar that these concentrations were so short-lived. Several generations later they seem to have been dissolved. Apparently the area still offered potential for an expansion of settlement.

14

Finds and interpretations

The archaeological record covering the period *c.* 2800–500 BC falls into three categories: 1) settlements; 2) graves; and 3) sacrificial finds and hoards. In addition there are a number of other categories of finds such as roads, flint mines, etc.

Settlements. Of the above-named find categories, that of settlements at present constitutes the major area of concentration. Danish archaeology has a long tradition of settlement excavations. Already in the 1920s large-scale excavations of prehistoric villages had been carried out. At that time the primary goal was to excavate house sites so as to ascertain the function and construction of the individual house. But after the Second World War new methods were developed, such as the mechanical uncoverage of larger areas. Village communities could now be studied in their entirety.

However, settlement excavations have mainly been devoted to single prehistoric periods. The Iron Age in particular has been the focus of numerous large projects, whereas Bronze Age villages were first excavated in the 1960s. From the so-called Single Grave period and the Late Neolithic, about 2800–1800 BC, very few settlement sites have been excavated. The same holds true of the Early Bronze Age, about 1800–1000 BC. Starting from the Late Bronze Age, *c.* 1000–500 BC, enough excavations have been made to create a more distinct impression of the settlement structure in the farming communities.

The chronological imbalance of the Danish material is supplemented by a geographical one. Most of the excavations have been made on the light sandy soils of west Denmark. Here modern agricultural activity began rather late. Thus this is the region offering the best opportunities for making relatively undisturbed finds. In eastern Denmark there is still a dearth of settlement finds from most periods.

But serious dangers threaten. To be sure, all prehistoric monuments in Denmark are protected by the law for the protection of nature, ancient monuments and sites, which permits the temporary halt of constructional work for the purpose of carrying out archaeological investigations. But settlements especially are endangered by modern types of agricultural machines. Formerly the normal ploughing depth of a tractor-pulled plough was about 30–40 centimetres. The same layer of mould was turned year after year, and the plough did not reach layers which might contain undisturbed traces of prehistoric activity. But since the 1960s many farmers have introduced new types of ploughs which cut far deeper, thus disturbing the previously untouched layer of virgin soil. As a result, a multitude of settlement finds have been reported, far more than archaeologists have the capacity to investigate. This technological development is one of the factors which has compelled archaeologists to employ more efficient methods of excavation.

In many cases settlements have been localized from the air, as the rather homogeneous Danish countryside is well suited for air reconnaissance. But most frequently settlements are recognized when dark soil, charcoal and potsherds are brought up to the surface by ploughing. A trial excavation is then often initiated, and if promising results are obtained a major excavation may be launched. A tractor shovel scrapes off the upper layer of dark ploughed mould, thus uncovering a large area of light subsoil which the plough could not reach. Often up to 2000 m^2 can be excavated in a week. In some places settlement traces covering up to 100,000 m^2 have been investigated.

It is important to realize that the vestiges of a typical prehistoric settlement in Denmark consist merely of the bottom layers of the settlement. Preserved pavings, floors and hearths are rare. All such house traces have usually been removed by ploughing long before. Potsherds and other objects from the settlement are very few, as they have also been destroyed by ploughing. The 'finds' are thus merely vague dark discolourations in the subsoil which represent the bottom of the pits into which the house posts were rammed. Even so, these bare traces are often sufficient to permit determination of the size, shape and basic constructional details of a house.

The earliest settlement studies were carried out as early as the turn of the century (S. Müller, 1904). Bronze Age settlement studies were taken up at the end of the 1960s on the basis of earlier excavations (J. Jensen, 1967a) and newer investigations (H. Thrane, 1971, 1973b; C.J. Becker, 1968c and e, 1976; B. Stjernqvist, 1969). Even so, no definite conclusions were reached as to the settlement form of the era. More recently a goal-oriented research initiative has improved this picture. (C.J. Becker, 1980b).

For the period *c.* 2800–2400 BC, the so-called Single Grave period (MN B), the results are, as already mentioned, still meagre. Yet unpublished studies hint at a kinship with the settlement form of the Late Neolithic period (LN) which succeeded it. As for the era 2400–1800 BC, reference ought to be made first of all to the *Myrhøj* excavation (J. Årup Jensen, 1972) which includes what appears to have been the leading house type of the period (compare for example M. Strömberg, 1971). This construction type is also found in the Early Bronze Age (N.A. Boas, 1980). Knowledge of the settlement pattern in this period has been augmented mainly by the excavation of the large village complex *Vadgård* by the Limfjord (E. Lomborg, 1973b, 1977).

In the course of the Early Bronze Age new house types gained ground. The three-aisled longhouse turns up as early as the middle of the second millennium BC (S.W. Andersen, 1981). Throughout the rest of the period, this house type predominates in what has become a large group of excavated village complexes. Among these, special mention ought to be made of the as yet unpublished finds from *Fragtrup* (J. Jensen, 1970), as well as the excavations in *Ristoft* (C.J. Becker, 1968e), *Spjald, Bjerg, Kærholm* (C.J. Becker, 1972a and b, 1976, 1980b) and *Hovergårde* (J. Jensen, 1971) – all of which are from northern and western Jutland. Similar village complexes are at present being studied in east Denmark; these include the excavations at *Skamlebæk* on Sejrø Bay (E. Lomborg, 1977) and excavations of three-aisled longhouses at *Jersie* on east Zealand (unpublished). See furthermore the excavations of a house site under a Bronze Age barrow at Trappendal, east Jutland (S.W. Andersen, 1981).

The settlement excavations raise many questions pertaining chiefly to the total extent of the settlements and to houses the number of which functioned synchronously. The latter question results from the frequently poor conditions for dating the various house construction. As a rule the only basis for dating is a relative dating based on construction details of the house types.

Graves: The so-called Single Grave culture from roughly 2800–2400 BC is represented at Danish museums by nearly 1000 grave finds, mainly from Jutland. A good part of these graves were found as a result of one of the most goal-oriented research projects ever carried out in Danish archaeology. The grave form of the period was first recognized in the 1880s, and by the time the first general survey was published in 1898 (S. Müller) over 300 barrows had been investigated. In the following years the number of finds continued to rise. A general survey of the 'single graves' in Jutland was published by P.V. Glob in 1944, whereas the finds from the Danish islands had already been presented in 1936 (C.J.

Becker). Finds south of the Danish border were published by K.W. Struve in 1955. Recent decades have produced only stray publications of new source material (see, for example, H. Andersen, 1952; S.E. Albrethsen and J. Street Jensen, 1964; H.J. Madsen 1970; H. Thrane, 1967a). One of the most serious problems in connection with the graves of the period is that the skeletal remains were poorly preserved. Determination of the sex of the deceased therefore depends most often upon the grave-goods. Noteworthy new theories on their function as prestige objects have been suggested by F. Højlund (1974).

From the period *c*. 2400–1800 BC, the Late Neolithic, about 1000 graves are known. A very great part of these contained flint daggers. This period displays a wide range of burial customs. Graves in barrows dominate in west Denmark, where about 300 finds are known. In east Denmark stone cists and graves without barrows predominate, as somewhat over 100 finds of this group have been made. Moreover, secondary burials in the grave structures of earlier periods are very common, with about 300 cases known. The Late Neolithic graves have hardly been studied systematically at all. However, the majority of the known finds are registered in E. Lomborg's work (1973a) on the Late Neolithic flint daggers. Nor has the anthropological material been systematically studied. As a comparison with the presumed overrepresentation of men in graves from the preceding period, a single example from the Late Neolithic will be mentioned, a stone cist from Gerdrup on Zealand (D. Liversage, 1964). The sixteen individuals buried included five children of indeterminable sex. Of the rest, eight were men and three were women – which is to say that this Late Neolithic find also shows a clear overrepresentation of men.

From the Bronze Age, *c*. 1800–500 BC, about 4000 graves are known. More than 1000 of these date from the Early Bronze Age. Most of these early graves are inhumation graves, whereas the graves from the Late Bronze Age are all cremation graves. Most of the Bronze Age graves were registered, although frequently unsatisfactorily, by H.C. Broholm in 1943–9. Since 1973, an impressive and ambitious project has been underway, namely the complete publication of the finds of the Early Bronze Age (E. Aner and K. Kersten). This work, which includes very fine graphic illustrations, so far covers the Danish islands. For the Late Bronze Age, a valuable supplement to H.C. Broholm's catalogues was published by E. Baudou in 1960. But as yet no exhaustive publication of the graves of the Late Bronze Age exists. One of the reasons for this lack is that the numerous graves which contain only pottery still cannot be dated with certainty. Determinations of the age and sex of the buried individuals have thus only occasionally been attempted (N.-J. Gejvall,

1968). A vast material which has not yet been studied is kept at the National Museum in Copenhagen.

Sacrificial finds and hoards. During the first millennium of agriculture in Denmark the number of ritual bog finds is considerable (C.J. Becker, 1947). But in the following period this group of finds plays an even greater role. In particular the deposits of precious flint and bronze objects become numerous. The finds from the first two phases of the period, however, have not yet been treated comprehensively, due in part to a number of dating problems. A catalogue of a large part of the hoards from the Late Neolithic period may, however, be found in E. Lomborg's work (1973a).

Bronze Age sacrificial finds and hoards are covered in a catalogue in H.C. Broholm's survey from 1943–9 as well as in the publications of E. Aner and K. Kersten from 1973. Important supplements may also be found in E. Baudou's work of 1960. For the Late Bronze Age a catalogue has been published on a number of the single finds from Danish bogs which should probably be interpreted along the same lines as the large hoards (J. Jensen, 1972). For an important source criticism of the find group, see K. Kristiansen (1974), who has proved that the known finds constitute a representative sample of the original find quantity.

Miscellaneous finds. This group does not include many finds from the period 2800–500 BC. Yet there are interesting traces of an extensive flint-mining industry from the Late Neolithic (C.J. Becker, 1951) near Aalborg. From the Bronze Age there is a presumed ritual site at Boeslunde, which in older literature (H. Kjær, 1928b) was considered to be one of the few central sites from that era. However, recent excavations have not been able to substantiate this theory.

Of the three phases which constitute the period from 2800–500 BC, the first phase, the so-called Single Grave culture, is the most problematic. Before the calibrated radiocarbon dates cast serious doubt upon traditional views (H. Tauber, 1972), some of the finds from the Single Grave period were thought to be partially contemporary with the finds from the late Funnel-Necked Beaker culture (see for example C.J. Becker, 1954). On the basis of topographical observations, S. Müller in 1898 suggested that some time after the 'invasion' of the first farming culture there occurred yet another invasion of a foreign ethnic group, the 'Single Grave culture'. This postulate was still accepted in P.V. Glob's work (1944) on the Single Grave culture and in fact even today it thrives in archaeological literature. Even though a number of earlier theories were radically modified during the 1950s (C.J. Becker, 1959) very few scholars challenged the invasion hypothesis (M.P. Malmer, 1962). But radiocarbon datings (Figure 62) from the 1970s (H. Tauber, 1972) have since

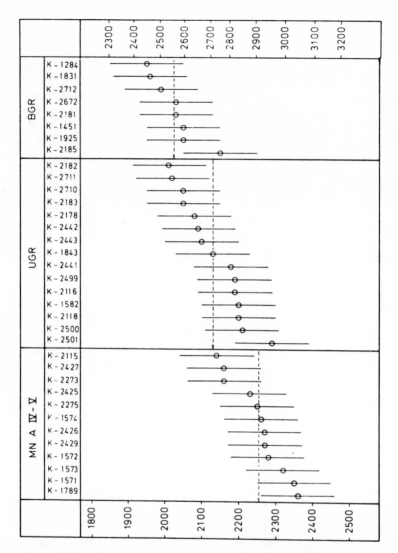

Figure 62 Danish radiocarbon dates of the two last phases of the Funnel-Necked
Beaker culture (MN A IV–V) and the two first phases of the Single Grave culture
(MN B I–II = UGR and BGR). Even though there are minor overlappings of the
datings, the average value of the samples indicates that the late finds from the
Funnel-Necked Beaker culture must be dated earlier than 2700 BC, whereas the
early finds from the Single Grave culture seem to belong to a later era. Below:
conventional radiocarbon datings. Above: calibrated radiocarbon datings.

made it clear that the late finds from the so-called Funnel-Necked Beaker culture must be dated earlier than 2700 BC, whereas the finds from the so-called Single Grave culture mainly date from a later era (C. Malmros and H. Tauber, 1975; K. Davidsen, 1975; H. Rostholm, 1977). The minor overlapping of the datings seems to be due to the usual margin of error of the method, ± 100 years. For this reason in part, it is logical to reject the invasion hypothesis and instead to view the difference between the two find complexes as the result of a chronological development. Due to the slight chronological overlapping, the division line between the two phases, which are called Middle Neolithic A (MN A) and Middle Neolithic B (MN B), is here drawn at about 2800 BC. A renewed critical evaluation of the archaeological record (see for instance N. Sterum, 1978) and the inclusion of settlement excavations are the prerequisites for maintaining the interpretation suggested. Such analyses have begun to appear in recent years (see for example P.O. Nielsen, 1977a).

The Late Neolithic period, 2400–1800 BC, presents a somewhat more favourable set of circumstances. A comprehensive evaluation of the problems of the period was formulated in 1964 (C.J. Becker); since then E. Lomborg's works of 1973a and 1975 have been able to shed light on a number of chronological problems in particular (see also T. Madsen, 1978b). E. Lomborg's results can also substantiate the idea of a unilinear development throughout the third millennium BC.

As we have shown, the two later phases have been somewhat neglected in newer Danish archaeology. The Bronze Age, on the other hand, has been the focus of considerable research activity. The division of the Bronze Age into six periods is based upon the work of O. Montelius in 1885 (see furthermore B. Gräslund, 1974b). This division is still used, although with certain modifications (E. Lomborg, 1968; K. Randsborg, 1968, 1972; G. Jacob-Friesen, 1967). Studies of the relationship between the chronology system of northern Europe and that of central Europe have been undertaken by the three scholars named as well as by H. Thrane (1975) and J. Jensen (1972). General surveys of the approximately 1300-year-long span of the Bronze Age have been published by J. Brøndsted (1958) and H.C. Broholm (1943–9) as well as in a more popular form by J. Jensen (1979a). With regard to the Late Bronze Age, mention ought to be made of E. Baudou's 1960 study.

It holds true of all three phases that until late in the 1960s the archaeological record was restricted almost exclusively to grave finds as well as votive and sacrificial finds. Therefore most conclusions dealing with economic, social, religious and political content have been based on a most lopsided foundation. In the past decade excavations, especially settlement excavations, and new working methods in archaeology and related fields have been able to shed light upon the gradual transformation of agrarian society from *c*. 2800–500 BC.

Yet insight into the ecological situation in this period is still limited. The most comprehensive survey of the environmental situation is that of J. Iversen of 1973. A number of older detailed investigations of the vegetation beneath barrows in Jutland was published in 1939 (H.C. Broholm); and a significant *landnam* on Djursland in the third millennium BC was pointed out in 1942 (T. Mathiassen). A recent attempt to combine investigations in the natural sciences with the archaeological record may be found in a study by K. Kristiansen (1978a), which treats the period *c*. 1500–500 BC. A key source here was that of tax evaluations of the quality of the arable land. For a discussion of the applicability of this method, see S. Nielsen (1980). Both works betoken an important step forward in the attempt to combine such fields as pedology and pollen analysis with the archaeological record.

Knowledge of climatic development in the Post-Glacial period is based upon R. Sernander's (1910) classical investigations of the Swedish bogs. In a number of late works by such scholars as E. Granlund, Sernander's interpretation of prehistoric climatic development has been modified. Important surveys of the archaeological and scientific problems have been published by T. Bergeron in 1956 as well as by G. Sörbom in 1966. Investigations in recent decades of the boundary horizons in Danish raised bogs, chiefly in Draved bog in south-west Jutland, have yielded noteworthy results which have been described in a preliminary report published by B. Aaby in 1974. For a more general survey, see for instance the work of R. Claiborne from 1970.

Formerly, the geographical distribution of the finds from the period 2800–500 BC was surprisingly little studied. However, a number of essential detailed studies were terminated in 1948 and 1959 with the publication of T. Mathiassen's works on the prehistoric settlement of north-west Jutland and north-west Zealand. Unfortunately a number of source problems of a technical nature (see H. Thrane, 1973b) weakened T. Mathiassen's conclusions with regard to the Single Grave culture and the Late Neolithic. For the Single Grave culture finds in Jutland, the major source remains P.V. Glob's study of 1944; but the finds from east Denmark have not been treated as a whole since 1936 (C.J. Becker). Discussions of the peculiar imbalance of the distribution picture may be found in the 1962 study of M.P. Malmer. The map in Figure 40 showing the settled areas in the Late Neolithic was made by combining the distribution maps for flint daggers from the work of E. Lomborg (1973a). Maps 41–2 showing the distribution of Bronze Age finds are based upon the present author's own registration of grave finds in the National Museum as well as in the majority of the Danish local museums, carried out from 1965–72. As already mentioned, an evaluation of the problem has been published by K. Kristiansen (1978a). For settlement studies in a north European perspective, see such works as those of C.F.W. Higham (1967) and A. Fleming (1972).

Only twenty years ago, Danish archaeologists had very vague ideas of the settlement pattern of the farming communities in the period 2800–500 BC. However, the ambitious settlement excavations of recent years have, as we have already pointed out, changed this situation dramatically. To be sure, the archaeological record is still diffuse, and in particular we lack finds from the Single Grave culture. On the other hand, settlements from the Late Neolithic and Bronze Age have become more numerous during the later years. Evaluation of the settlement pattern of the Bronze Age in particular has, since S. Müller's classic work of 1904, been dominated by the discussion on the extent to which settlement consisted of single farmsteads or of regular village complexes (J. Jensen, 1967a). After the first extensive excavations of Bronze Age settlements in Jutland at the end of the 1960s, the question was once again raised (C.J. Becker, 1968e). It was presumed that the village as a settlement form first arose in the period following 500 BC. Now that a richer source material has been revealed, the picture is more distinct. For the Early Bronze Age (E. Lomborg, 1973b) as well as the Late Bronze Age (C. J. Becker, 1972a, 1976, 1980b) it seems fully justifiable to speak of true villages, by which term is meant no more than a cluster of contemporaneous households, consisting of at least two or three farmsteads.

Problems related to the exchange system of prehistoric society have traditionally been granted an important position in archaeological literature. In general, however, efforts have been bent to the determination of 'trade routes'. Not until recently has it been possible to observe attempts to achieve an understanding of the underlying economic institutions (B. Stjernqvist, 1966). Yet within the economic sector of social anthropology, such studies have long played a major role based on the works of Karl Polanyi from the end of the 1950s. Characteristic manifestations of the discussion generated by Polanyi's works include works of G. Dalton (1961, 1965, 1967, 1969), M.D. Sahlins (1965, 1974) and H.K. Schneider (1974). In later years there has been a noticeable tendency to apply the theories of social anthropology to archaeology (see for example T. Earle and J. Ericson, 1977). In a series of newer Scandinavian surveys (C.-A. Moberg and U. Olsson, 1973; K. Lunden, 1972; J. Jensen et al., 1978) there are brief introductions to the ideas of

Karl Polanyi. These ideas have also been hotly debated within Norwegian archaeology (K. Odner, 1974).

In older archaeological literature, the relatively undefined phenomenon 'trade' has often been presumed to have been the catalyst for social changes in prehistoric society, especially after the appearance of metal technology. This holds true of the hypothesis suggested by J. Brøndsted (1958) with regard to cultural development in the period after c. 2000 BC. Brøndsted believed that the economic and social background for Bronze Age culture evinced distinct analogies with cultural conditions in the Viking Age. In recent studies on phenomena such as the exchange of goods and the supply of raw materials, wholly new views (described above) have been suggested with regard to the evaluation of the character of the exchange systems and their significance for general cultural development (C. Renfrew, 1975).

In Scandinavia, a number of comprehensive studies have shed light on various aspects of the exchange of goods, although most authors have limited themselves to speaking of 'cultural connections' in general. For the Late Neolithic, special mention should be made of works of E. Lomborg (1973a) and J.J. Butler (1963); for the Early Bronze Age, works of C.J. Becker (1964b), E. Lomborg (1960), K. Randsborg (1967, 1968, 1970, 1972) and H. Thrane (1975); for the Late Bronze Age, works of H. Thrane (1975) and J. Jensen (1965, 1966a, 1969, 1972). Only some of these works (H. Thrane, 1975) present a more theoretical discussion of trade and the exchange of goods in prehistoric society.

In connection with the exchange of goods in the Bronze Age, theories on amber trade have traditionally played a large role. These theories were based upon the 1925 work of de Navarro, in which 'trade routes' of amber across Europe were postulated. However, a number of publications in the 1960s have raised doubts about de Navarro's interpretation of the dissemination of amber (J. Jensen, 1965, 1968; B. Stjernqvist, 1966). In later years the results of C.W. Beck's analyses (1965, 1970, 1975, 1978) have brought a sorely needed clarity to many questions of provenance. Newer investigations of the guidelines sketched above have recently been published (J. Jensen, 1982).

For the period 2800–500 BC, archaeological literature includes only scattered attempts at a comprehensive evaluation of the economic and social development of the farming communities. As pointed out, the older writings postulated an invasion of the Single Grave people as a prerequisite for the formation of a class-divided Bronze Age society; see for instance J.E. Forssander (1936) and J. Brøndsted (1958). Under the influence of social anthropology and with the corroboration of radiocarbon datings, the modern archaeology has begun to seek alternative explanations for the development of the subsistence economy up to the beginning of the Iron Age (see S. Welinder, 1977; K. Kristiansen, 1978a). In this way, a more precise impression of social development can be achieved. Understanding of the early Bronze Age society has been enhanced by the works of K. Randsborg, but as yet there is a dearth of revised interpretations for both the early and the late phases. But however slight the results so far achieved by such methods as quantitative analysis (K. Randsborg, 1974a and b), they do indicate a fruitful direction.

PART IV

The chiefdoms of the Iron Age
500 BC–800 AD

15

Environmental changes

The development of the open, man-made landscape

Momentous changes took place in Denmark from the middle of the first millennium BC. Around 500 BC the widespread prestige-goods economy of which Denmark had been a part for nearly 2000 years seems to have suffered a considerable set-back. Perhaps this crisis was only transitory, for in the next few centuries there emerged a new agrarian society with a considerable potential for expansion. Everywhere in Denmark around the time of the birth of Christ, there are unmistakable indications of economic growth. This first stage culminated in the third and fourth centuries with the appearance of villages consisting of large farmsteads with a differentiated economy providing opportunities for vital secondary occupations. Agriculture now achieved a productivity hitherto unequalled in prehistoric Denmark. The stage was set for sweeping socio-economic changes which in future centuries would lead the archaic chiefdoms to pre-feudalism.

To grasp these fundamental transformations of agrarian society, we must understand the ecological milieu in which they took place. The few centuries just before the birth of Christ witnessed a profound change in the environment. In many places agriculture had completely stripped the land of forest (Figure 63). Instead there were vast stretches of grassland, small cultivated areas and unpopulated swampy areas. The population gradually increased and so did the destruction of the ancient dense forests, especially those found on heavy moraine soils. Slowly but surely the settlement pattern which had endured for over 2000 years was transformed.

Pollen diagrams sketch the general outline of this process. As already mentioned, the diagrams from *c.* 200 BC to the fifth century AD show how

Figure 63 The landscape of the Early Iron Age in Denmark was characterized by open grassland, small cultivated areas around the settlements, and between the latter vast stretches of unpopulated swampy areas. This type of landscape can still be found in isolated parts of Denmark, as shown here at Røsnæs, western Zealand.

human activity increased throughout most of south Scandinavia. This impression accords with the expansion of settlement onto the heavy soils which earlier agrarian communities had exploited only slightly. From the fifth century BC a sort of stagnation persisted up to a new expansion, the extensive *landnam* of the Viking Age in the eighth century. This presumed stagnation cannot be fully explained. Around the mid-first millennium AD the population of Europe declined markedly, but whether this also held true of south Scandinavia is not certain. In the sixth century the Justinian bubonic plague ravaged much of the continent. According to some calculations, it reduced the population by one-third or one-half (J.C. Russel, 1968). Although there is no concrete evidence of the plague in northern Europe, it may help explain certain symptoms of decline in the sixth century especially. We do not know whether these symptoms were general for south Scandinavia or even whether they were contemporaneous at the various places where they have been observed. Local conditions may very well affect, for example, the picture we have from the pollen diagrams.

Man came to have a profound impact on the composition of the forest. The lime tree had been menaced by the agricultural forms practised in

Denmark since the fourth millennium BC, which instead favoured mast trees and hazel. In the last millennium of prehistory, the lime forest suffered nearly everywhere in Denmark.

This process had several causes. The drop in summer temperature from the climatic maximum of the Atlantic period had weakened the ability of the lime to compete with other forest trees by lowering its resistance to winter cold. On the meagre soils, the deterioration of the soil had also undermined the lime in relation to the beech and the oak. Last but not least, population pressure, especially in the centuries just before and after the birth of Christ, along with the resulting expansion of settlement, set its unmistakable stamp on the forest. For example, the village communities used enormous amounts of wood as building timber and as fuel (also for iron extraction). In the lighter, more open forest where the cattle browsed and on abandoned agricultural land – especially high-lying well-drained soil – conditions for the beech were now bettered. This may particularly be seen in the boulder clay regions in east Jutland and on the islands. On the meagre soil of west Jutland, the beech was scarce up to the end of prehistory. Heavy moraine soils and a high water-table also hindered the immigration of the beech. This held true of places on south-east Zealand and on Lolland, where the oak forest still prevailed.

Together with these changes in the composition of the forest on the benign soils of east Jutland and on the islands, there was a change in the vegetation profile in west Denmark. During the Late Neolithic and Bronze Age, the farming communities preferred relatively light soils. On these soils, agriculture could be expanded by deforestation, which required a minimum of labour. In the centuries just before the birth of Christ, settlement continued to expand on the light soils in west Jutland, which still must have boasted great expanses of light open oak forest. But now the deterioration of the soil became sadly evident. The destruction of the forest caused by cattle grazing and unrestrained forest clearance washed the nutrients out of the soil. Erosion caused by the dry spring wind helped destroy the thin layer of mould on the many fields where trees and all other shelter had been chopped down. These factors, coupled with increased moisture, stimulated the spread of heather. Around the time of the birth of Christ further expansion became impossible.

Even if there is no reason to propose dramatic catastrophe theories to explain the many abandoned 'celtic fields' of western Jutland in the early Iron Age, we cannot doubt that agrarian conditions in these regions took a turn for the worse in the period preceding the birth of Christ. This development is sometimes described as a radical change in the settlement pattern. The fact is that the potential of the poor lands for population expansion had been gradually exhausted and that from now on agricultural expansion chiefly occurred in regions with better soil. South of the Danish–German border, a parallel process is evident. Here in the south, a new biotope was taken over for settlement: the marsh on the coast of the North Sea came into use as grasslands. The overall settlement picture which characterizes the closing centuries of prehistory and the beginning of historical times was thus slowly taking shape in the first centuries after the birth of Christ.

At the same time a new landscape type was being created: the hay meadows. In the pollen diagrams this man-made landscape type is manifest as a decline in the pollen of the alder. A likely interpretation of this phenomenon is that alder in the damp areas had been chopped down when the areas were converted to moist hay meadows. The use of meadows must have been a vital prerequisite for the overwintering of the cattle, an observation which is borne out by the way villages were situated in the countryside.

The development of the climate during the Iron Age

As has been stated, recent investigations of Danish raised bogs have shown that the climate has fluctuated over the past 5500 years and that these fluctuations have lasted about 260 years. New light is thus shed on the relationship between culture and climate. Climatic changes in the final phase of prehistory can be pinpointed with great accuracy. A trend toward increased precipitation and lower summer temperature set in around 600 BC, just before the transition to the Iron Age. The next fluctuation took place around 300 BC, and yet another one took place just before the birth of Christ. In the first millennium AD there are fluctuations around 200 and 500. A last fluctuation follows around 1000 AD. According to the presumed periodicity, we would expect a change around the close of the Germanic Iron Age, in the eighth century, but no evidence of this change has yet been found.

Comparison of these climatic fluctuations with the archaeological record shows surprisingly little analogy. As was the case in the period 2800–500 BC, there is no clear parallel with changes in the development of the agrarian communities in the final centuries of prehistory. This problem is especially perplexing at the beginning of the period, where the climatic fluctuation around 600 BC was earlier ascribed a considerable impact on the environmental situation of the agrarian communities. The centuries following this fluctuation have been described thus: 'The first centuries must have been hard and severe, with crop failure and famine when the flooded fields were unusable and the cattle froze' (J. Brønd-sted, 1960). Yet new studies show that at that very time, around the mid-first century BC, the agrarian communities actually expanded, at least in Jutland. Early research was often based upon a very shaky foundation. Intense research in connection with major excavations, particularly in Jutland and on Funen, have led to a more detailed view of the relationship between climatic development and the lifeways of prehistoric man. Future work must evaluate the extent to which the archaeological record can inform us about the settlement and sub-sistence patterns of prehistoric man.

16

Subsistence and settlement

Expansion of the farming communities

In the five centuries preceding the birth of Christ, a wave of settlement expansion swept over Denmark. The introduction of new types of land management created in the course of a few centuries countless changes in the old settlement pattern which had endured for almost 2000 years. This expansion trend continued up to about the middle of the first millennium AD, after which a stagnation apparently set in. Then, in the seventh and eighth centuries AD, the process again accelerated. During the last centuries of prehistory, socio-economic conditions slowly created the foundation for a development which achieved its full flowering in medieval feudal society.

Indications of this lengthy process must be sought first and foremost in the new methods of production of the agrarian communities. Therefore the archaeological record which tells about the geographic expansion of settlement both on the macro- and the micro-levels, the structure of the village communities and land management itself will be a principal focus of interest.

Archaeologists are, however, badly hindered in determining the geographical extent of settlement in the period from 500 BC to 800 AD. Few regions in Denmark have been systematically researched, so the representativeness of the archaeological record is quite uncertain. By far the majority of maps show only a more or less accidentally found material, grave finds especially. At the same time, these grave finds may represent the most widely differing historical realities, manifested by changing burial customs through the thirteen centuries of the period.

In some periods, the geographical distribution of the grave finds does seem to reflect the prevalent political and social patterns. This holds true of Zealand in the first four centuries AD. In other regions, for example on Funen, the distribution of the graves in the same period provides a better impression of the general extent and continuity of settlement, based very much on the dominant burial customs. In other periods, for example from 500–800 AD, the archaeological record is inexplicably slight. Modern archaeologists are grappling with some of these problems. As the results are preliminary, the problems will only be sketched here.

On Funen, the island in the centre of Denmark, intensive research has resulted in a most informative archaeological record. Both general and more regional surveys have been carried out. One major problem is that the quantity of finds varies considerably throughout the centuries. There is a scarcity of both graves and settlements from 500–200 BC, i.e. periods I–II of the Pre-Roman Iron Age. Thereafter the finds increase considerably in number up to the fifth century AD. More than 500 localities are known from a period lasting 600 years. Following this, the quantity is sharply reduced, with the exception of certain find categories, namely the gold finds. Not until the tenth century is there again an increase in quantity.

If the Funen finds from c. 200 BC to 400 AD are divided into three phases, each lasting 200 years, then we see that the finds from all three periods are geographically distributed in a similar way. This consistency and the congruity between the geographical extent of the graves and the settlements indicate that the finds are in fact representative for the demographic pattern on the island as a whole.

The most interesting results so far derive from studies of agrarian settlement development within narrowly defined regions. A little area on north-east Funen encompassing just a few parishes has been the scene of systematic excavations, aerial photography and field reconnaissance studies. The intention has been to illuminate the relationship between the prehistoric and the medieval settlement in order to see whether or not there had been a gap in the continuity.

The investigations were carried out on two levels. On one level, excavations were undertaken in a number of medieval villages; on the other level, attempts were made to define the resource territories within which the prehistoric settlements functioned in the centuries prior to the Middle Ages. Similar investigations have also been made in Jutland and north-west Germany. Identification of these resource territories is vitally important for the understanding of the settlement pattern throughout the Iron Age and the Middle Ages. In most cases, the resource territories were bordered by streams, meadows or swampy areas. The size of the territories varies greatly, depending upon the available resources. Within the investigation area on Funen, the maximum size of the individual resource territories did not exceed 2 km².

The preliminary investigations have given the interesting result that the medieval villages which still exist must have been founded in the period c. 1000–1200 AD: traces of older settlements were not found within the villages proper. Consequently a change in the settlement pattern seems to have occurred during the transition from prehistory to the Middle Ages. The prehistoric villages, however, are often found at a distance not exceeding 400–500 metres from the medieval villages. Thus, underlying the settlement pattern of the late Viking Age and the Middle Ages there is an older, completely different, pattern. Moreover, scattered observations from both Jutland and Zealand seem to indicate a similar discontinuity. The explanation may be that at the transition between the Late Iron Age and the Middle Ages, land management underwent a transformation. This may explain why in historical times the location of the villages within the individual resource territories were so different from the location of the prehistoric villages.

Everywhere in western Europe from the ninth up to the thirteenth centuries AD, agrarian communities accelerated in productivity. The same tendency also took place in Denmark, though slightly later. In fact, the increased productivity may explain the observed shift in the settlement pattern in Denmark between c. 1000 and 1200 AD. The prime cause of the production increase seems to have been the introduction of a new type of land management, the three-field system (E.P. Christensen, 1979). By this is meant a system according to which crops succeeded one another in a regular sequence interrupted by equally regular fallow periods. One-third of the land was thus left fallow while the rest was apportioned into winter and spring fields. Rye or wheat was sown on the winter fields; oats or barley on the spring fields. The three-field system also made use of the heavy-wheel plough. All these factors helped transform agriculture from an archaic type dominated by animal husbandry to a different type dominated by a more intensive cultivation of cereals such as is known from historical sources in the Middle Ages. The location requirements for a medieval village thus differed radically from those of a prehistoric village with its demand for productive grazing areas, especially meadows.

Thus medieval villages in Denmark cannot be traced further back in time than c. 1000–1200 AD. However, there are indications that during the final millennium of prehistory, far into the Viking Age, there existed continuous but *mobile* settlements within the naturally restricted resource areas to which later villages were also related. Here and there we can observe how Iron Age villages were oriented with easy access to meadowland. This location implies that Iron Age agriculture laid great emphasis on animal husbandry.

In much of Jutland and adjacent regions of northern Germany, at least up to the sixth century, a similar placing of settlements with regard for pastures seems to have been common. It is a shame, however, that the archaeological record on Funen from about 400 AD up to the Viking Age is so poor. Even so the preliminary investigations help suggest the following hypothesis: that in the Pre-Roman and Roman Iron Age, Funen and other parts of the country experienced a period of explosive population growth. From a Bronze Age foundation, settlement expanded steadily and achieved a temporary climax in the first two or three centuries AD. Agriculture in this period was typified by extensive stock-breeding with relatively little emphasis on cultivation of cereals. Thereafter settlement may have contracted, possibly in connection with a restructuring of the settlement pattern, although no clear reason for this can be given. During the Viking Age, another expansion took place. Throughout the Iron Age each village was moved about at certain intervals within its naturally delimited resource territory, but a territorial continuity may be presumed to have persisted up to the Viking Age and later periods. However, an actual continuity of place, that is a habitation at one and the same spot, does not seem to have emerged until sometime during the Viking Age and the early Middle Ages.

As only very few Iron Age settlements have been excavated on Funen, little is known about whether or not the break between prehistory and the Middle Ages signifies a more general change in the settlement form, for example from individual farmsteads to villages. However, it is more than likely that throughout the Iron Age settlement on Funen was chiefly organized into village communities. The changes around 1000–1200 AD can probably be ascribed to a restructuring of the village society which took place in connection with the introduction of new forms of land management.

Bornholm, the little Danish island in the Baltic, has also been studied in this regard. Here the size and geographical distribution of the Iron Age cemeteries indicate that up to about 400 AD the island was characterized by village settlement. Thereafter the individual farmstead became dominant and remained so through the Middle Ages and up to modern times. But conditions on Bornholm are quite unique; culturally the island most closely resembles the other Baltic islands of Gotland and Öland.

For Zealand and the surrounding islands, the picture is far more vague. Very few finds are known from the first 500 years of the period. The find quantity rises considerably from 0–400 AD. In the first two centuries AD there is a preponderance of finds in the south, on the neighbouring islands Lolland-Falster and Møn. Zealand shows a more even distribution. In relation to the Bronze Age, a settlement expansion is evident. The central part of the island was now put under the plough. In the third and fourth centuries this tendency continued, but now the focal point was the southern half of Zealand. The finds cluster around Stevns, in fact where the construction of the road network also reached a high point (H. Nielsen and V. Hansen, 1977). In the following centuries the find quantity again falls sharply; the concentrations are dissolved and, as was the case on Funen, it also becomes impossible on Zealand to determine which changes of the general settlement pattern took place in the centuries immediately preceding the Viking Age.

How representative, then, is the picture drawn by the Zealand finds? For the period from 500 BC to 0 absolutely no conclusions can be drawn; there are simply too few finds. The centuries after the birth of Christ, however, provide some basis for speculation. But here we must note a number of problems which partially derive from the fact that the distribution of wealth in the graves in the east Danish regions seems to represent the social and political groupings of the population far more clearly than on Funen. The cause is the predominant burial customs. In particular, the distribution of precious imported goods reflects quite clearly the location of the economic centres. In the first and second centuries AD the focal point was on Lolland. In the third and fourth centuries AD this focus was shifted northwards to east Zealand and the surrounding islands. In these key centuries just after the birth of Christ we must follow an uncharted route.

Since the end of the last century it has been commonly accepted that Danish place-names may be classified according to their suffixes and that certain chronological facts may be deduced from this. Place-names with the endings -inge, -lev, -løse and -sted (for example Sengeløse, Herlev and Alsted) have been thought to comprise the earliest group, the origin of which goes back even further than the Viking Age. These villages were assumed to be the remains of the old settlement pattern prior to the changes in land management in the Viking period and the Middle Ages. Other types of names, for example those ending in -by and -torp, were thought to form a more recent group, mainly from the Viking Age, and still others were thought to stem from the early Middle Ages (H.V. Clausen, 1916). Although many complex theories about prehistoric settlement have been based on these ideas, the reliability of the place-names has been exaggerated. The last couple of generations have evaluated this source group far more realistically.

On Funen, the place-name question has justifiably faded into the background after evidence from the recent field surveys. For Zealand the use of the oldest name types (names ending in -inge, -lev, -løse and -sted) is also problematic, as type identification of the individual names can be very uncertain. A number of statistical calculations of the archaeological find distribution both on Zealand and on Funen, however, ought to dissuade us from completely denying the value of the place-names as a source of settlement history (H. Nielsen, 1978, 1979). These statistics have shown that there is quite a clear tendency for grave finds from the Roman Iron Age to be concentrated around present-day villages bearing old place-names (with the exception of -inge). To judge from observations from Funen, which, to be sure, were made on another basis than those from Zealand, we can presume a continuity of settlement – not a continuity within the existing villages but perhaps rather a continuity within the resource territories related to place-names of the old type.

This could lead to the assumption that continuous, that is mostly deforested, settlement areas existed in the Iron Age in north-west and west Zealand and east and south Zealand. The central part of the island and the Roskilde–Copenhagen area, called 'the heath', may be presumed to have formed unified settlement areas. Despite our ignorance, we do know that we are here dealing with a situation quite different from that of the Bronze Age.

As on Funen, this situation may be seen as the result of the agricultural expansion which must have been in full swing in the centuries just after the birth of Christ. At a later phase in this process, which still parallels conditions on Funen, there apparently was a certain contraction of settlement after 400 AD, although regional continuity around localities with names of the old type was maintained up to the Viking Age.

In Jutland as well, the settlement pattern in the closing millennium of prehistory is tremendously difficult to sketch. The point of departure must be the settlement map, Figure 42, which shows the cultivated areas up to about 500 BC. This picture seems to have persisted right down to the final two centuries BC, although in the west there is an increase of settlement. Somewhat prior to the birth of Christ, expanding settlement is encountered all over the peninsula. In the first centuries of the Iron Age the lighter soils seem to have been the preferred object of increased exploitation but gradually the heavy moraine soils were also taken over. This expansion is most evident in northern Jutland and in the coastal regions by the Danish–German border.

In north-west Jutland, intensive surveys in the 1940s (T. Mathiassen, 1948) emphasized the same tendencies. Iron Age settlement spread both on the lighter soils and especially on the heavy moraine lands.

This circumstance can be most clearly observed in the fertile moraine areas around the west Limfjord. Here investigations in recent years have demonstrated a surprisingly intensive exploitation of the heavier soils from around the birth of Christ and several centuries afterwards. In many areas there are villages every two or three kilometres (Figure 68), a clear illustration of the agricultural expansion which took place around the beginning of our era – the period in which the open Danish cultural landscape truly took form.

As for the size of the population in the final millennium of prehistory, it has not yet been possible to make realistic calculations. However, estimates can be made for thirteenth-century Denmark (including Scania), the population of which is believed to have been about one million. For the period around 1645 AD, that is after the population crises of the late Middle Ages, the same area is believed to have been inhabited by about 800,000 people (E. Ladewig Petersen, 1980). As far as may be concluded from the population growth in western Europe in the centuries around the Viking Age, the population of Denmark towards the end of the Viking Age could hardly have exceeded 700,000. This implies that, in view of the explosive growth of the Viking Age, we can hardly figure on more than about 500,000 inhabitants in all of Denmark in the closing phase of the Iron Age.

Villages and farmsteads around the birth of Christ

Among the many changes which the agrarian society underwent during the Iron Age, some of the most important took place in the structure of the villages. Two observations in particular are of crucial importance for the understanding of the settlement pattern. One of them is that prehistoric settlement was mobile in character, that is the villages were moved at certain intervals, possibly with a long-range tendency to remain for increasingly longer periods at the same place. The other major observation is that the villages were moved within well-defined resource territories.

These two observations have now made it possible to bring a hitherto unachievable chronological dimension into the study of the development of village societies in Denmark. Intensive investigations of various resource areas have thus made it possible to trace individual village communities through as many as 900 years. The great expense of excavations, of course, sets limits for how detailed a picture can be drawn.

The greater or lesser mobility of the village communities in the Iron

Age was first revealed in connection with the extensive excavations at
Grøntoft in west Jutland. These excavations traced the existence of a
single 'wandering village' through about 300 years within one and the
same resource territory. The history of the village lasts from *c*. 500 BC to
some time in the third century BC. The number of building phases is not
certain, as it has not been easy to define the limits of the resource
territory. It is possible that the many excavated houses may have
belonged to two neighbouring villages.

The houses of the Grøntoft village are of the three-aisled construction
which is found at all of the Danish Iron Age settlements (Figure 64). This
construction has roots far back in time, to the middle of the second
millennium BC (see p. 146 ff). Around 500 BC it evolved into a rectangular
house shape, unvaryingly oriented east–west and with a roof supported
by two parallel rows of interior posts. At Iron Age settlements, the
length of the houses may vary from just a few metres to twenty metres.
The construction dictated that the width was nearly always 5–6 metres.
Entrances were found in both of the long sides of the house. The walls of
the houses might be timber, either massive or light, with wattle and clay
daubing. Massive earthen and turf walls are also known. The houses
were often divided into two sections: the east end sheltered cattle; the

Figure 64 Reconstruction of the typical three-aisled Early Iron-Age house at the
   Historical Archaeological Experimental Centre at Lejre, outside of
   Copenhagen.

west end with the hearth was for human dwelling. The dwelling section often had a clay floor while the byre may have had a stone-paved gutter and stall partitions.

In three hundred years, the Grøntoft society 'consumed' about 250 of these longhouses. At all stages, the village economy strongly emphasized animal husbandry. However, houses without stalls did exist. When the houses had been used for perhaps only one generation, they were torn down and moved to another site within the village territory. The old sites were ploughed over and the soil was again tilled. The constant moving shifted the original field boundaries marked by balks as well. The balks (forming so-called Celtic fields) which could be observed at the excavations thus stem from many phases of cultivation, possibly separated by fallow periods.

It is difficult to distinguish the various phases of the wandering village and to determine the size of the settlement site at any given time. Yet it is possible to note, for example, that around the third century BC the village was fenced in, probably to protect the houses from the cattle (Figure 65). At that time the village consisted of twelve buildings, as follows: five larger farmsteads, each housing 8–18 heads of cattle; two smaller farmsteads, each with 3–4 heads of cattle; and three longhouses (farmsteads) apparently lacking cattle in a byre; and finally a couple of storehouses.

In total, the third-century BC village must have contained about 8–10 households with somewhat more than fifty individuals. In addition there were about 70–80 heads of larger cattle. In estimating these sizes, we must remember that Grøntoft was a community which in agricultural terms existed on marginal soil. In fact, there is evidence that the village in some cases cultivated moor land. It is also noteworthy that the varying sizes of the households may indicate graduated differences in the distribution of wealth.

Grøntoft in western Jutland is so far the only wandering village in Denmark which has been traced from as early as 500 BC. Nowhere else has a community from the middle of the first millennium BC been studied so thoroughly. Later, in the centuries around the birth of Christ, other finds are known. The mobile village from this period is best documented in the excavations made in the 1970s of Hodde in southwestern Jutland.

In Hodde, the main lines of the history of the mobile village community can be traced through five centuries. All the successive villages lie on the eastern edge of a little hill island at intervals of 300–400 metres. To the north, west and south the hill island is bordered by river valleys. On the east side, where the settlements lie, there are large open stretches of

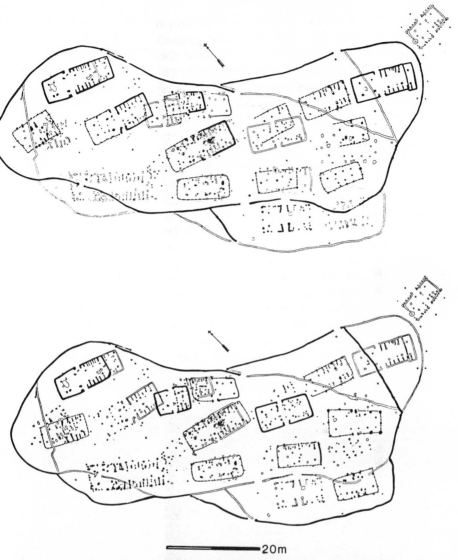

Figure 65 Two phases of the Pre-Roman Iron-Age village at Grøntoft, Jutland.
   Above: oldest phase with 13 farmhouses. Below: the younger phase with 12
   farmhouses and with a partly rebuilt surrounding palisade.

meadow. The settlements are located within this well-defined resource
territory in such a way that on one side the land of the hill island could
be used for agriculture, while the other side with the large meadows
could serve as pasture. In all, three successive villages have been found,

along with a cemetery which seems to represent a fourth, as yet undiscovered, village. When this last village is revealed, we will have a continuous settlement with its resource territory dating from the first century BC up to the fourth century AD.

Only one of these village societies, the earliest one, has been fully excavated so far. The village, which covered an area of roughly 11,000 m², was encircled by a fence and had an open commons in the centre (Figure 66).

The many fences of the village, along with stratigraphical observations, allow us to follow the development of the village through many stages. The earliest stage seems to have been the erection of the largest farmstead and its enclosure. Soon after the enclosure was built, the large fence surrounding the village area was erected, thus indicating that the later extent of the village had already been planned. Gradually other farmsteads were constructed until the enclosed area contained a total of fifty-three buildings, which can be separated into twenty-seven units. A unit invariably consisted of one longhouse either alone or together with one or two smaller houses. Twenty-two of the twenty-seven units are farmsteads with a byre at one end of the longhouse, while the remaining have no byre. The house type is identical to those of other contemporary villages.

Most of the farmsteads were situated along the north and south sides of the village, so that each farmstead had its own entrance through the surrounding fence. Most individual farms had room for 14–16 large

Figure 66 Reconstruction of the Iron Age village at Hodde from the 1st century BC. The village, which covered an area *c.* 11,000 m², is characterized by the open commons in the centre. The enclosed area contained a total of 53 buildings.

animals. Some could house more; the oldest farmstead had the greatest capacity, up to 28 large animals. At its most populous, the village housed about 200 people and 300–500 head of cattle. An unequal distribution of wealth, a very marked emphasis on animal husbandry and a seemingly slight occupational differentiation comprise the chief characteristics of this village. Another striking feature is the large open area (the commons) in the centre. Here the animals were probably herded at night during the season when they grazed outside. The noteworthy fact is that the open area seems to have been communal. The excavator describes the village thus: the independently fenced-in farmsteads correspond in principle to the medieval type of farmstead and the open space in the middle can be compared to the commons, which was shared by all the inhabitants (S. Hvass, 1976).

In the final years of the community, at least six farmsteads were torn down until at last the entire village was destroyed by fire.

The subsistence of the village can be deduced from its location in the terrain: on the boundary between field and meadow. This location is typical for most of the known Iron Age villages and probably implies that animal husbandry was the primary subsistence factor. Grazing and abundant water were basic needs which dictated the location and structure of the village.

As already remarked, the size of the palisade indicates that the gradual construction of new farmsteads seems to have been planned already at the founding of the village. In the same way, farmsteads were torn down in the late years of the village's existence – seemingly they were moved to a succeeding settlement only 400 metres away. By and large the village seems to have been moved in stages – and it seems that the life-span of the village was four or five generations, between 100 and 150 years. This was longer than the village community in Grøntoft, which existed three or four hundred years earlier. This tendency became more pronounced through the centuries.

We have noted that the successive Hodde villages have been localized up to the fourth century AD. Trial excavations in the village from the third and fourth centuries AD have shown that the house type here varies from that of the older villages. Now large multi-functional farmsteads completely dominated. An identical development took place in contemporary villages throughout western Denmark.

Excavation of the village community at Hodde has yielded the first glimpse of the settlement pattern within a single resource territory in the Early Iron Age. The constant moving may be ascribed to aspect of land management or there may have been other causes. In several places it can be documented that the abandoned village sites were taken over for cereal cultivation and naturally the soil quality was far higher at sites where a village had existed for several centuries. Still it is hard to believe that this rather limited gain was the sole cause of moving. As yet no other explanation can be suggested.

Other finds from Jutland show that Hodde was not unique. Østerbølle in northern Jutland includes house sites of large longhouses as well as smaller houses lacking byres, which form a village plan with a central commons similar to Hodde.

Information on the mobility of Iron Age village society can also be gleaned elsewhere in Denmark, for example in the low marsh regions by the North Sea in the south of Jutland (S. Jensen, 1980). Here the villages lie clustered along the edge of the so-called 'Geest' out to the low marshes in the west (Figure 67). The location of the villages is most telling. The primary location factor was the large marsh meadows, which were suited for cattle-grazing and for hay-making. The inland villages, which were considerably more scattered than the villages in the west, also existed on their large herds of cattle, as indicated by their proximity to the largest meadow areas.

None of the settlements in this south-west Jutland region date back more than a century before the birth of Christ. This holds true for the entire coastal region to the south and much of the German marsh. The marshes by the North Sea could probably not have been exploited as pasture prior to this. Thus this region is most indisputable evidence of the explosive expansion of settlement which took place in the centuries around the birth of Christ.

Here and there along this coast it has been possible to find villages which 'wandered' for centuries within one and the same resource territory. At Drengsted, for example, a rather small area was found to contain a series of settlements, some with cemeteries dating from the first century BC to the fifth century AD.

At Dankirke in south-west Jutland, a small area was found to contain several settlements with their cemeteries dating from the first century BC to the fifth century AD. Considering the existence of stray finds from as yet undiscovered settlements in the Dankirke region, there may be said to have been a continuity of settlement up to c. 700 AD, a period of 800 or 900 years.

So far the basic pattern seems to have been identical, whether in Grøntoft, Hodde, Drengsted or Dankirke. Over the centuries, mobile village communities based upon large herds of cattle moved around within narrowly defined resource territories. Part of the basic pattern also seems to be that in time the villages developed larger farmstead units and that secondary occupations gained in importance. This

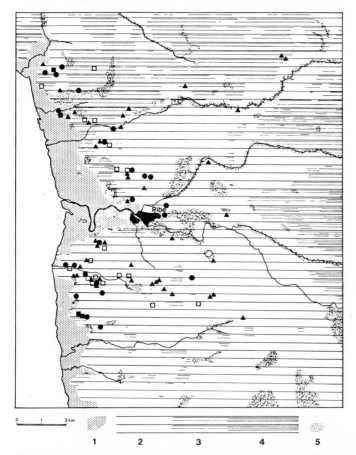

Figure 67 Distribution of the Iron Age settlements in the Ribe area in south-west Jutland. 1: Marshlands. 2: Sandy soil. 3: Clayey sandy soil. 4: Sandy clayey soil. 5: Meadows and bogs. Triangles: Pre-Roman and Early Roman Iron Age. Circles: Late Roman Iron Age, Germanic Iron Age and Viking period. Squares: Early and Late Iron Age. Open squares: undated Iron Age finds.

development truly accelerated in the third and fourth centuries AD. In this connection it may be asked what degree of economic differentiation existed among the villages as a whole in the centuries just before and after the birth of Christ? Only one area of the country offers an archaeological record sufficiently complete to answer this question. This is the north-westernmost part of Jutland in the Thy region, the area of Denmark in which the greatest number of settlements have been found. It is also an area in which the settlement pattern seems to have been less mobile than hitherto seen.

Within an area of barely 500 km², by the western part of the Limfjord, there is a dense network of approximately forty-six contemporaneous villages from the period just before the birth of Christ and up to the third century AD (Figure 68). Judging by the density of settlement in the terrain, it must be assumed that most of the villages from that period have been discovered. About 70 per cent of the villages lie only 2.5 kilometres from one another.

Most of the villages are characterized by a sort of city mound consisting of refuse layers up to several metres thick. The thickness of these layers is primarily due to the regional architectural tradition of using turf walls up to 1.5 metres thick. New houses were repeatedly built on the sites of older houses, whose rubble or turf walls formed thick refuse layers. Thus, settlement did not move about but remained at the same site.

At Grøntoft and Hodde we can distinguish several phases in the history of a single village community. But in northern Jutland, matters are quite otherwise. Here no village has been thoroughly excavated. Yet even the relatively superficial investigations carried out at Hurup, Vestervig, Mariesminde and Ginnerup are sufficiently comprehensive to permit an attempt to determine whether the lay-out of the villages reveals an economically determined pattern.

Within the area investigated, a total of thirty-three village mounds has been revealed with settlement lasting two or three centuries; at thirteen localities, less permanent settlements which did not lead to the formation of village mounds have been identified (Figure 68). The location in relation to the terrain and soil does not seem to reveal any crucial difference between the two village types.

As yet, the limits of the resource territories in which the various settlements were situated have not been determined. However, various observations may be interpreted to indicate a subsistence differentiation underlying the settlement pattern in the 500 km² area. All the villages seem to have included two house types: a short and a long one. The longhouse type combined byre and dwelling under one roof, whereas the short one lacked a byre. These latter houses were used solely for dwelling and working. The ratio between the two house types seems to vary widely from village to village. In the west part of the region, the short type predominated, but in the east part, the opposite holds true. The difference has been explained as one of subsistence economy. In the west, there was an emphasis on sheep-breeding, possibly supplemented by fishing, whereas in the east, cattle breeding and cereal cultivation were practised to a greater degree.

A related pattern can be glimpsed in the large village Nørre Fjand by

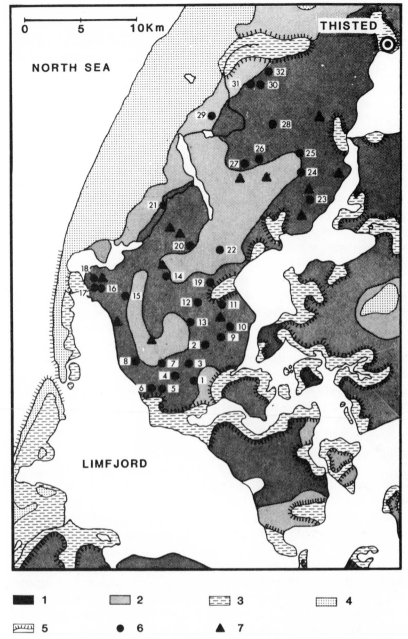

Figure 68 Early Iron Age settlements in the Thy region, north-western Jutland. 1: young moraine landscapes, predominantly clayey soil. 2: young moraine landscapes, predominantly sandy soil. 3: marine foreland. 4: dune land-scapes. 5: raised coastlines from the Stone Age. 6: village mounds from the Early Iron Age. 7: ordinary settlements from the Early Iron Age.

Ringkøbing in west Jutland. Here the subsistence pattern was dominated by fjord fishing and sheep-breeding. The production of this village was probably integrated into a larger, as yet unknown, whole.

The economic differentiation in the villages as a whole was still very slight. This is also the case with various crafts practised in the villages. Excavations in Hodde, however, indicate that smithing was a part-time speciality, and the same observation has been made for other Early Iron-Age settlements.

We can thus conclude that up to the first two centuries AD the village communities still showed very little sign of economic differentiation. On the other hand, many of the villages evidence an unequal internal distribution of wealth. The clearest example of this is in Hodde, where a social hierarchy appears with the farmstead of an apparently high-ranking man with many head of cattle at the top and small farmsteads, apparently lacking cattle, at the bottom; in between these extremes are the many medium-sized farmsteads. Naturally the functions of the village demanded a certain degree of co-operation. Aside from the apparently planned periodic moves of the village, there are such indications as the large open 'commons' in the Hodde village, the locations of the farmsteads in relation to this commons, and the extensive fencing. Even the farmsteads of the élite may be explained by the fact that the demographic and economic subsistence situation necessitated positions of authority to administer the co-operative functions of the village by leading and assigning work.

Farming communities in transition

The transformation of the village communities accelerated around the third and fourth centuries AD. Excavations in Hodde, Dankirke and Drengsted in west Denmark have revealed some of these changes. They were manifest especially in the introduction of a new type of farmstead, much larger and with many more functions than the farmsteads from the centuries just before and after the birth of Christ.

This development can be distinctly observed in the village community recently under excavation at Vorbasse in southern Jutland. This settlement, which can be dated to the first to fifth centuries AD, lies like many other Iron Age villages on the edge of a little hill island facing a large meadow area.

The history of the village goes back to the first century AD. Here some enclosed farmsteads were constructed, each consisting of an east–west oriented longhouse with a small rectangular house. The cemetery of this little hamlet is not far away and the graves indicate that the settlement originally consisted of three households.

In the second century AD, the settlement was moved 600 metres to the east, where it evolved into a village settlement covering an area of about 150 × 150 metres. This settlement, as yet known only from trial excavations, still existed at the beginning of the third century AD. The village was then moved back to the site of the original farmsteads. But now the farm type was completely different. To be sure, it still consisted of a single longhouse together with one or two small houses, all standing on an enclosed plot. But the longhouses were now far longer than those of the first century AD. The plot of the farmstead had also been enlarged a good deal. The village still consisted of individual farmsteads separated from one another by sturdy fences. There seems to have been no preconceived plan.

Yet such a plan does seem to have arisen in connection with a regulation of the settlement in the fourth century AD (Figure 69). The old farmsteads were torn down and this time three enclosed farmsteads were erected at a distance of about 100 metres from each other, apparently with an eye to further building. And indeed this expectation was realized. The spaces between the three farmsteads were soon filled in, thus making a row of farmsteads 350 metres long.

Somewhat to the east, yet another row of farmsteads was built, this one 250 metres long; furthest to the east there were still two more farmsteads with a total length of 125 metres. One of these latter farmsteads was the largest in the village. It is noteworthy that it was erected at the spot where a century earlier another very large farmstead had stood. The enclosed area of the new farmstead was 74 × 54 metres, i.e. almost 4000 m^2. It was thus much larger than the other farms in the village, which averaged about 2000 m^2. Comparison of this average size with the size of the enclosed areas of the farmsteads 300–400 years earlier in the village of Hodde show that the area of the farmsteads had grown considerably (Figure 70). Their enclosed plots had almost quadrupled. There can be no doubt that the explosive growth of the farmsteads is to be ascribed to an increase in production.

In this phase, there are also indications that secondary occupations began to play a larger role. Indications have been found that a specialized production of, for example, quernstones took place in the village. There are also traces of iron production: furnaces and a smithy were found in one of the small houses belonging to the largest farmstead.

In the fourth century AD, the village was comprised of twenty large farmsteads with a total area of 400 × 250 metres. This was the apex of its development – already a century later, in the fifth century AD, the

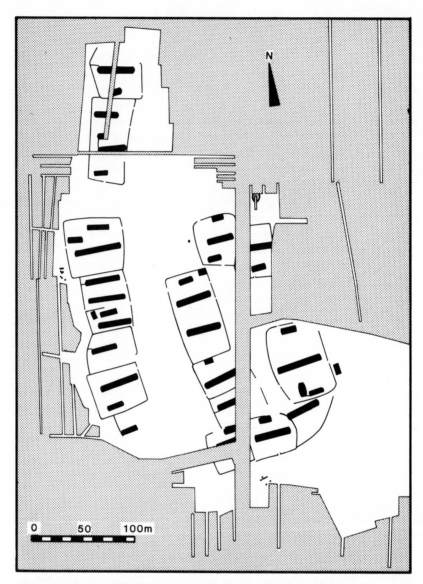

Figure 69 The Vorbasse settlement in the 4th century AD. During this period the village contained about 20 farmsteads. On average, the fence round the farmsteads enclosed an area of *c*. 2000 m².

1st cent. AD.

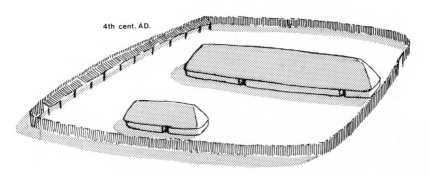

4th cent. AD.

Figure 70 During the first centuries AD the enclosed plot of the typical Danish farmstead grew considerably in size. Above: a farmstead from the Hodde settlement, 1st century AD. Below: a farmstead from the Vorbasse settlement, 4th century AD.

signs of decline are obvious. This final phase of the existence of the village shows that many of the farmsteads from the fourth century AD continued to exist but that they shrank as the cattle population diminished. Other farmsteads were torn down or moved and now at last the settlement clustered around an open area, 150 × 120 metres, maybe a commons as at the 400-years older Hodde village. In the final phase of the Vorbasse village, the largest farmstead from the fourth century AD, which had been rebuilt, still existed. This farm seems to have constituted a sort of core for the settlement during approximately 200 years.

A novel feature of this closing phase of the village was that each of the individual farmsteads now possessed their own small workshops, so-called pithouses, mostly situated at the edge of the large open central area. The presence of these small workshops may indicate that the secondary occupations had now truly been integrated into the subsistence pattern. This feature clearly presages the settlements of the eighth century and later.

The village was torn down at some point in the fifth century, and its further fate cannot be traced. As traces of later cultivation can be seen in the area, we know that an Iron Age community still existed here and that the land was tilled. But a regular settlement at the site cannot be ascertained again until the eighth century AD. And this time it was a thriving Viking settlement.

The Vorbasse village is the youngest link so far known in the evolution of a settlement pattern which can now be followed through more than 1000 years of the Iron Age. Going back in time, the kinship with earlier settlement traditions is unmistakable. This may be seen by a comparison with the Hodde village, nearly 400 years older. The placement of the two villages in relation to fields and meadows is the same. The orientation of the villages with their length perpendicular to the adjacent meadows was also the same. In both villages, animal husbandry apparently was the chief occupation. Obviously the location and plan of the village were chosen with regard to the access to grazing.

In both Hodde and Vorbasse, we can trace from the founding of the village a gradual influx of farmsteads – and in both villages it has been revealed that this influx had already been planned from the beginning. Both settlements lasted for one or two centuries, after which the gradual vacating of the settlement was initiated. Besides an open commons, both villages contained enclosed farmsteads, which constituted independent economic units. The Vorbasse settlement shows that in the course of time the central farmstead building, the longhouse, underwent major changes – as did the enclosed plot and its buildings (Figure 71). In Hodde the length of the longhouse is between 12 and 16 metres. In Vorbasse the average length is over 30 metres. This development of the longhouse can in fact be traced elsewhere in Denmark and abroad.

With this house type, which apparently evolved around the third century AD, a more differentiated division of functions than earlier becomes evident. Figure 72, for example, shows a 38-metre-long farmstead from Vorbasse with roughly 200 m^2 under one roof. Comparisons with related farmsteads found outside Denmark make it likely that the house was divided into five rooms. The westernmost room was the living room and here too food was prepared. The function of Room 2 is unknown but doubtless it was also for dwelling. Room 3 was the entrance room, probably used for the storage of tools and implements. Room 4 was a byre and Room 5 was probably used as a barn, threshing floor or the like. The question remains whether the size of the house can be taken to mean that the number of persons in each household had been increased. That is not unlikely in view of the fact that in time the secondary occupations also seemed to have increased in importance. This development is manifest in the building of the so-called pithouses. These houses were workshops with various functions: weaving, smi-

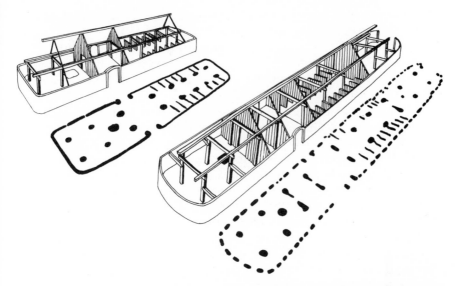

Figure 71 Schematic representation of the constructional and functional changes of the three-aisled Iron Age longhouse from the 1st century AD to the 4th century AD.

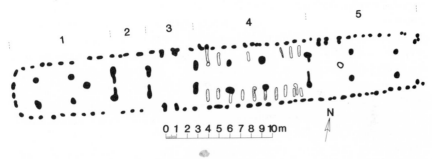

Figure 72 Thirty-eight-metre-long farmstead from the Vorbasse settlement. In contrast to earlier house types, the farmstead has now been divided up into five different rooms indicating a more differentiated function of the house.

thing, pottery-making and other specialized production probably took place here. In general, the village seems to be a forerunner of the farmsteads consisting of separate buildings, each with its own function, as known from the great farms of the Viking Age and on into the Middle Ages.

Villages such as Vorbasse seem to have been common, at least in west Denmark. Similar complexes have been found here and there in south-west Jutland. In Drengsted, where settlement can be traced back to the first century BC, excavations have been made of about fifty longhouses and twenty pithouses which are contemporary with the latest settlement in Vorbasse. In the case of Drengsted it is not possible to ascertain whether or not the houses belong to various successive phases of one and the same village.

Villages of this type are also known elsewhere in the large lowland region by the North Sea, in north-west Germany and Holland. In Flögeln (P. Schmid and W.H. Zimmermann, 1976) there is a village which in the course of three or four hundred years was re-established several times at the same spot, just as in Vorbasse. The Dutch village Wijster also displays many similarities with the Vorbasse village (W.A. van Es, 1967). This applies both to the layout of the farmstead and to the general restructuring of the village about the third or fourth century AD.

After c. 500 AD the archaeological record completely fails us, and as yet no villages from the sixth and seventh centuries have been found in Denmark. We can pick up the thread again in the course of the eighth century, after which further evolution leads to the great village complexes of the Viking Age. This unfortunate gap in the archaeological record makes it impossible to demonstrate a direct connection between the settlement pattern of the fifth century and that of the Viking Age. Yet it is certain that the leap was not a large one. Many of the features which existed in the villages around 500 AD may be recognized in the villages and great farmsteads of the Viking era. These features include the enclosed plots of the farmsteads with a centrally placed longhouse and the small workshops clustered around the main building. This also holds true of the layout of the farmsteads around an open area, and the location of the village in the terrain on the boundary of meadows which could be used for cattle grazing. Presumably no really profound changes in agrarian technology took place in the two or three hundred years from which no settlements have been found. However, it is significant that in the eighth century, along with the village societies, there were now settlements such as Ribe and Hedeby which evolved into more townlike structures in the course of the ninth century.

A general survey of agrarian development up to the Viking Age thus suffers from a number of gaps. But if one were to outline the presumed course of development, it must be assumed that the features which characterize village society up to about 500 AD endured without significant disturbances. Throughout the roughly 1300 years of the Iron Age, agricultural productivity slowly rose; the greatest step occurred around the third or fourth century AD, to judge by the appearance of the village societies (Figure 73). At the same time, the differentiation of production

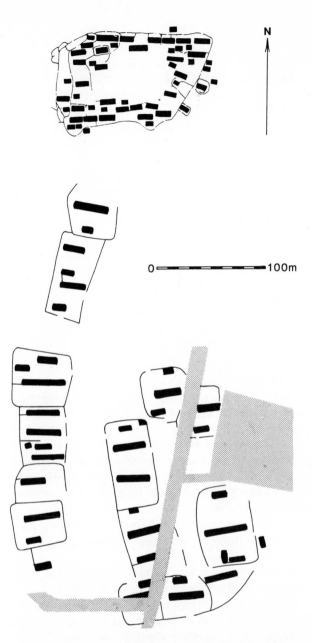

N

0 ⸺⸺⸺ 100m

Figure 73 Total view of the layout of the Hodde village
(above) and the Vorbasse village (below). The difference in size between the two complexes is probably
an indication of the growth of agricultural productivity which took place during the 3rd and 4th
centuries AD.

commenced, which in the eighth century resulted in the growth of a population of craftsmen; concurrently town-like settlements started developing. In Ribe such traces as tools and production refuse have been found from several workshops: beadmakers and metalcasters are seen to have worked here. There are also signs of a specialized production of combs and leather goods. Presumably the production exceeded that which the local population could consume; thus it is indirect evidence of a growing circulation of domestic goods.

At many places in southern Scandinavia and northern Germany, this incipient differentiation of occupation set in from the second to fourth centuries AD. However, not until some time in the eighth century, stimulated in part by an increasing hierarchization in the agrarian society, did it lead to the formation of the urban communities which would later play so important a role in the incipient state formation of the Viking Age and the early Middle Ages. But these are events which lie beyond the range of the present work.

Subsistence patterns during the Iron Age

A study of the village societies offers a glimpse of some of the changes which the agrarian society underwent in the period up to the agricultural expansion of the Viking Age and the early Middle Ages. At this late time another agricultural revolution took place, probably provoked by the population growth in the last centuries of prehistory. What lay ahead of this seemingly radical change was an agricultural system with roots all the way back to the third millennium BC – a system which through the Iron Age had slowly increased productivity by embracing ever more production-stimulating technological methods. This change seems to have occurred extremely slowly and also at different times in various regions in Denmark. At the threshold between the Viking Age and the early Middle Ages, this development seems to have accelerated in earnest.

The thirteen centuries of the Iron Age saw several changes in the type of cultivation, apparently intended to hinder ruinous soil erosion and to improve the quality of the mould, partially by use of manuring. Moreover these changes meant that an ever-larger number of animals were kept indoors in the winter, a tendency which may have begun already in the second millennium BC, but which first gained a foothold around 500 BC.

We have earlier seen how it was quite late before the prehistoric agricultural system managed to create a reasonably good layer of mould on the tilled fields. Aside from the natural washing-out of the soil, ard-ploughing and an extensive erosion exhausted the soil, especially the lighter soils. Not only has soil erosion often been observed at archaeological excavations but it also frequently appears in Danish raised bogs. Here there is such a large fall-out of soil particles that it must point to an explosive intensification of agriculture in the centuries around the birth of Christ. This observation corresponds to both pollen-analytical evidence and to the archaeological record.

Soil erosion must have been a serious problem for this expanding agriculture. The means by which the Iron Age farmers attempted to solve this problem may be apparent in the so-called Celtic fields, the remains of the prehistoric field systems. Many of these Celtic fields are known in Denmark. The majority of them are found in the western part of the country, where they were preserved thanks to the less intensive cultivation of historical times. But the balks of the Celtic fields are also known from eastern Denmark, especially Zealand and Bornholm. Here they are usually found in forests, where they were protected from cultivation in more recent times.

The Celtic fields were probably first established around the middle of the first millennium BC. How long they were in use is another question; probably only up to the mid-first millennium AD. Most frequently the Celtic fields are situated on moraine formations, especially in lighter sand-mixed soils. But as the Jutland examples have shown, also heathy areas were cultivated in the Iron Age, resulting in the formation of Celtic fields. The field systems are often naturally delimited by meadows and bogs.

The Celtic fields are bordered by low balks up to 1 metre high. The balks enclose small fields averaging between 1000 and 3000 m^2 and form a net-like pattern in the terrain. It has been suggested that the balks were covered with a hedge-like vegetation intended to shelter the fields from wind erosion. Experience has shown that this sort of net-like system of wind-breaks provides good protection against wind erosion regardless of the wind direction.

Unfortunately, there is no certain pollen-analytical evidence that the balks were in fact covered with these hedges. Hawthorn, which would be a natural form of vegetation, produces very little pollen and is therefore difficult to discern. Yet at one single spot, namely the Pre-Roman Iron Age village in Grøntoft in west Jutland, a vegetation layer found under one of the balks included the pollen of nearby scrub – a dense underbrush – of birch, alder and hazel. Perhaps these are the vestiges of a hedge-like vegetation. The hedges would then help explain the rise of the balks, as the live underbrush would have intercepted the uppermost eroded layer of soil in untilled periods. This helps explain the high content of phosphate sometimes observed in the balks. Other factors such as the moving of soil by ploughing and the removal of stones from the fields undoubtedly also contributed to the growth of the balks.

In sum, it is possible that the balks were formed as a result of several factors; soil erosion before the hedges were sufficiently high; ploughing when the field was under cultivation; soil erosion when the field lay fallow; and wind action through holes in the hedge made by grazing cattle (W. Groenmann-van Waateringe, 1979).

It is thus likely that the Celtic fields are the remains of small cultivated plots, the enclosed character of which was emphasized by a hedge-like vegetation. Most probably, after a field had been cultivated for a period, cattle were allowed to graze on it. The cattle were protected behind the hedge and at the same time the small fields were naturally manured so they could be used later for cereal cultivation.

This continuous use of the land, however, raises the question to what extent manuring was practised on Iron Age fields in order to maintain soil fertility. The introduction of manuring is a major turning-point in agrarian history, as manuring can hinder or at least significantly diminish exhaustion of the soil. As a result, the mould layer will slowly increase in thickness.

It would seem logical that the introduction of manuring would have resulted from the keeping of cattle indoors. When a byre was mucked out, the beneficial influence of the manure on plant growth would have been obvious. And indeed some early Iron Age houses have yielded traces of mucking out. In the Celtic field systems preserved at Grøntoft from the centuries just preceding the birth of Christ, there are also indications of manuring. Similar observations have been made in Holland. Here, however, it has been concluded that fields were sometimes fertilized with peat. Still other similar observations have been made on the island of Sild just south of the Danish border (H.J. Kroll, 1975).

There are thus a number of indications that manuring was practised quite early in the Iron Age. We cannot know its extent, but there is reason to believe that the technique was widespread a couple of centuries after the birth of Christ. At this time there begins to be in the archaeological record a striking lack of the rubbish pits always previously found at prehistoric settlements. We can now assume that the refuse was simply collected at dung heaps near the farmsteads.

The tilling of the fields has been to some degree illuminated by finds of ard furrows and ard parts. Ard types, more developed than the simple hook ards, were in use as early as 700 BC (Figure 74). But there is

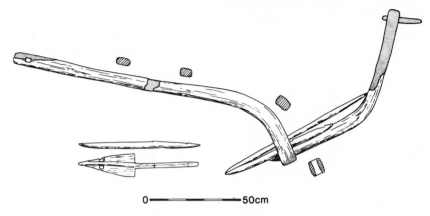

Figure 74 Iron Age ard found at Donneruplund, Vejle county.

also reason to believe that the ard was still in use as late as in the Viking period. However, recent finds just south of the Danish border indicate that more advanced plough types were in use as early as the first century BC (K.R. Schultz-Klinken, 1976). There is still some uncertainty about the interpretation of these finds, and it is usually thought that the mouldboard plough was first used in western Europe after the sixth century AD. The heavy wheel plough with a mouldboard first achieved importance in Denmark with the agricultural revolution during the early Middle Ages.

However, it is not certain that the earliest mouldboard plough was wheel-driven. Thus it cannot be denied that more advanced plough types which could turn the soil may have come to Denmark during the Iron Age. But when this transition would have occurred is completely indeterminable. We must still assume that the rather ineffective ard with its very limited effect on mould formation (see p. 99) was the most widespread ploughing implement during the Iron Age.

As for the composition of the crops, there seem to have been no changes between *c.* 500 BC and 800 AD. Since the third millennium BC field husbandry must have been based primarily on barley. Only small amounts of other grains were raised. In the first millennium BC wheat suffered a drastic decline, due probably to the climatic worsening which gradually made an impact. At the same time oats were introduced, though only to a small degree, as a cultivated plant. Rye could also be seen on the tilled fields in the period around the birth of Christ, but it was hardly a true cultivated plant in Denmark; the cultivation of rye seems to have been mainly confined to the region south of present-day Denmark. In Holland, rye is known from settlements from the fifth and sixth centuries AD. In Denmark, it was first widely cultivated in the course of the Viking Age. Thus it may be presumed that, together with the introduction of the wheel plough and the three-field system, rye was part of the agricultural revolution which occurred just after the close of prehistory.

We do not know whether some kind of crop rotation was practised on Iron Age fields or whether there existed a fixed cultivation/fallow cycle. This sort of land management would be difficult to prove pollen-analytically, as pollen samples yield a mixture of pollen from the entire cultivation period. Actual three-field farming, which decreased the risk of crop failure by dividing the crops into winter crops and spring crops and which increased production by shortening the fallow periods, is not known until the eighth or ninth centuries in western Europe. Therefore it cannot even be considered for the early Iron Age in Denmark.

Although we lack knowledge of a number of essential technological factors we can conclude that around the birth of Christ, agriculture was not very productive. In the second and third centuries AD productivity began to rise due to the expansion of animal husbandry, but the greatest leap forward seems to have taken place from the ninth to thirteenth centuries, just as elsewhere in Europe. This increase seems to have resulted from the introduction of a new form of land management, namely the three-field system with the technological advances which accompanied it (E.P. Christensen, 1979).

A clear indication of the low productivity of agriculture around the birth of Christ is the extensive gathering of the seeds of wild plants. This gathering must have been practised outside the cultivated areas, on fallow and harvested fields. Prehistoric man has probably always supplemented his diet with the seeds of wild plants. For the centuries around the birth of Christ, it must still be presumed that a very considerable percentage of the vegetable food was made up of the seeds of wild plants. It must be remembered that agriculture demanded time-consuming labour for weeding the fields, and not until the harrow and more advanced plough types came into use was this labour gradually diminished.

Thus, far into the first millennium AD, agriculture was not very productive. A large investment of labour resulted in a relatively small yield, and even though a number of innovative agricultural methods were introduced, the effects were minimal. A threefold or fourfold harvest was probably the maximum attained. (S. Nielsen, 1980). Only the expansion of animal husbandry could make a notable increase in productivity.

This assumption finds partial corroboration in the excavated villages and can moreover be illustrated by some of the calculations which have been made regarding the average yield of a farmstead in the centuries around the birth of Christ. If a household kept 8–9 large head of cattle and 10–12 head of young cattle and calves over the winter, then the annual yield would have been about 500 kilogrammes of meat. Adding to this the dairy products from the milch cows as well as meat from a number of smaller domesticated animals such as pigs and sheep, the total amount of food would hardly have sufficed to cover more than half of the calorie requirements of a family of 7–8 people (including children and the elderly). The remainder had to be supplied by vegetable food. But here too there were serious limitations. With a yield of threefold or fourfold, a cultivated area of about 3 hectares could produce exactly enough to supply the remaining calorie requirements. However this condition is only fulfilled if there is a three-field system. With a two-field system the area would have had to be considerably greater. But here the labour capacity set a natural limitation. Imitative experiments have shown that it takes 8–9 days to plough and about 10 days to harvest one hectare with a hand sickle. In addition there is a considerable labour input in the form of weeding the cultivated area. Thus an average family could hardly have kept more than about 3 hectares under plough.

In view of the cultivation methods employed it is not possible to expect that the amount of vegetable foods could have been increased to any great degree. Only an expansion of the cattle population could have efficiently ensured a yield increase. This situation first changed during the Viking Age and the early Middle Ages, when the prehistoric farming based mainly on animal husbandry was transformed to a farming based on cereal cultivation as a result of a series of technological changes. The result was an expansion of the cultivated area and a corresponding decrease in the size of the grazing areas.

In the above, an attempt has been made to describe some of the main tendencies of the agrarian communities through the Iron Age. In the fifth and sixth centuries AD there was undeniably a connection with the economic and demographic decline which much of the European continent suffered at that time. In the seventh century, in central Europe, this development changed course; the population now expanded considerably; a strong economic boom took place. Denmark too showed signs of increased growth. But still the ancient tradition of animal husbandry seems to have persisted as late as the Viking Age. Technological improvements must have made their mark during the Iron Age. But as long as our knowledge of land management from 500–800 AD is so poor, it must suffice to note that from the eighth century the size of the village complexes and the growing differentiation of subsistence forms indirectly bear witness to the fact that activity had not stagnated in the intervening period.

Iron

The devélopment of secondary occupations is one of the factors which most clearly illustrates the growth of the productivity of the farming communities through the last millennium of the Iron Age. Of particular importance in this connection is the refinement of the craft of smithing and of the complicated technology required for iron extraction.

The gradual advance of iron technology from central Europe can be illustrated with a distribution map of iron objects from the archaeological finds prior to c. 500 BC (Figure 75). The finds are seen to be concentrated along the central Elbe and the central and lower Oder. Further to the north, that is in northernmost Germany and Denmark, the finds are still quite scarce. To be sure, finds of iron do not necessarily indicate the existence of smithing based upon local iron extraction. A look at the nature of the iron finds from the seventh and sixth centuries BC shows that in fact most of them are small objects such as ornamental pins or toilet articles such as razors, tweezers and the like. Proper tools of iron are quite rare, as also holds true of smithing slags. A true iron production probably took place only in Saxony and Silesia, which were regions bordering directly on the iron-producing central European zone.

It is therefore surprising that in Denmark traces are found of smithing and possibly of local iron extraction shortly after 500 BC. Yet this does in fact seem to be the case, although interpretation of the finds is still being debated.

The precondition for this production was – aside from the capacity to produce charcoal – the bog iron ore which could be extracted in bogs and along streams. Bog iron is plentiful in Denmark, namely in south and west Jutland. Here iron is found as an impure ore which is usually blue-black. Bog iron ore from Jutland seems to have been exploited as early as the fifth century BC and until as late as the seventeenth century AD. In any case this seems to be the conclusion which can be drawn from the most recent finds.

In 1976–7, a settlement, probably from the fifth or fourth century BC, was excavated at Bruneborg in the eastern part of central Jutland. Less than one kilometre from the settlement there is a natural deposit of bog iron ore, and from here the raw material was transported to the settlement, where it has been found in abundance, both in its raw state and as roasted granulated ore. One particularly significant find was that

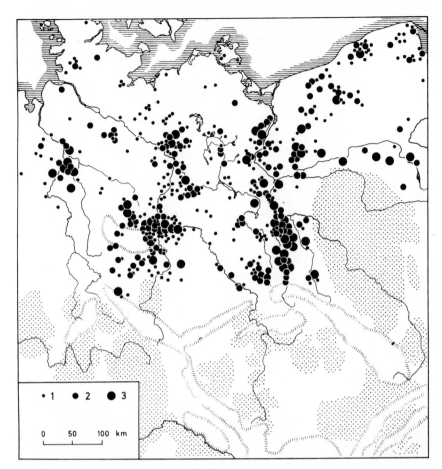

Figure 75 Distribution of iron objects during the 8th – 6th centuries BC in the north European lowland, i.e. period V–VI of the Nordic Bronze Age. The dotted areas show the central European Iron Age Hallstatt culture. 1: 1 object. 2: 2–4 objects. 3: 5 or more objects.

of a smithy in a pit. This contained the forge and other remnants from the fashioning of the iron. The smithing slags were of a type also known from Viking Age settlements; this attests to a smithing technique nearly 1500 years old. Doubtless, smithing took place at the site. But it is somewhat more uncertain whether iron extraction also took place. Iron smelting furnaces have not been found, but worked bog iron has. There are indications that iron extraction may have been carried out in a type of furnace known from other finds from around the birth of Christ. Such furnaces appear today as horseshoe-shaped structures with a mantle of red-burnt clay. Outside the opening there is frequently a pit with slags. Whether these furnaces had a superstructure cannot be known for certain.

Probably the iron extraction which took place in Denmark during the first five centuries of the Iron Age was most modest in extent. It may also have been supplemented with imported iron, although this theory is unsubstantiated. Not until the centuries around the birth of Christ do larger iron objects begin to turn up frequently in the finds. At the same time it is seen how, for example in the village Hodde, the craft of smithing became a part-time speciality in some households.

The landslide in iron production took place a couple of centuries after the birth of Christ in connection with the introduction of more advanced technological methods, such as shaft furnaces.

Shaft furnaces are built over a pit roughly ¾ metre deep, which is intended to hold the melted slags. The shaft itself consists of a conical clay shaft with holes at the bottom for air (Figure 76). It took a long time to heat the furnaces. They were filled with charcoal and straw, and the ore was added little by little in layers alternating with charcoal.

At a temperature of about 1200°C, the slag melted and ran down into

Figure 76 Schematic representation of the stages of prehistoric iron production. 1: extraction of ore. 2: ore piled in a heap for drying. 3: crushing of ore into suitable sizes for the furnace. 4: construction of the furnace. 5: the furnace is preheated and filled with ore and charcoal. 6: when the iron has been reduced from ore, the shaft is broken down and the bloom, a lump of iron and slag, is removed. 7: the bloom is repeatedly heated up in a smithing pit. 8: the bloom is cleansed of as much slag as possible.

the pit. The iron formed in the shaft had a very low content of carbon, less than 2 per cent. It was therefore like a spongey mass which often stuck to the sides of the furnace. When the slag had run down into the pit and the oxidation had ceased, the bloom was broken out of the shaft, which could then be moved to a new slag pit and re-used.

Furnaces of this type are found from the period after *c.* 200 AD at many of the large settlements. They are often situated in groups of eight or ten, and always at some distance from the dwelling area due to the danger of fire. In some villages such as Drengsted in southern Jutland, finds have been made of up to 200 shaft furnaces, some of which contained slags weighing 500 kilogrammes.

Iron production on this scale by far exceeded the needs of the village. Production must have been intended for a larger local area. Moreover, it must have diverted a good deal of labour from food production.

The expansion of iron production seems to have taken place concurrently with the striking restructuring of the village communities – and there is reason to believe that iron extraction was not the only craft which achieved this degree of specialization. Thus the incipient differentiation of production must have been a noteworthy feature during the two or three centuries after the birth of Christ.

17

The development of the economic institutions

Exchange systems

Since the second millennium BC, a developing prestige-goods economy had linked the agrarian societies in Denmark to an extensive network of exchange systems. By means of this network, which covered large parts of the European continent, Denmark was for 1500 years supplied with central European bronze, which was used in domestic circulation to indicate status. For the reproduction of social formations in the Bronze Age, this prestige-goods economy doubtless had decisive importance. But then, in the seventh and sixth centuries BC, metal supplies from central Europe diminished greatly. The reasons for this are unknown but a certain degree of contraction of the interregional trade must have been the result. Then, in the last couple of centuries BC, the exchange of goods rose again; once more northern Europe was bound closely to the more highly developed economic systems in central and southern Europe.

At first contacts were established mainly with the Roman civilization, but later also with its offshoots: the early feudal states which evolved in western Europe from the sixth century AD and later. The prestige-goods economy first culminated a couple of centuries after the birth of Christ. Until then it had developed from rather small local political structures but in time it led to more extensive political unifications, which were reflected in increasingly hierarchical formations. Competition among centres at the local level, disruptions and changes of the trade routes were recurring phenomena and resulted through the centuries in repeated shiftings of the foci of trade and consequently also of the political centres. This occurred synchronously with numerous attempts to unify ever larger local regions. At the threshold to the Viking Age this process had come so far that it resulted in the formation of the first centres with an urban character, that is, with a developed craft specialization. In this way the preconditions were created for the market trade which was to evolve in the coming centuries.

This process is an example of a general phenomenon which social anthropology has discovered in many societies in similar structural positions. In later years the theory has also been applied within the study of prehistoric societies in Denmark (L. Hedager, 1978b and c). At the core of this theory is the assumption that every low-technology society produces a surplus of goods and labour. The purpose of this surplus production is the maintenance of social relations. In this way a circulation of goods arises which most often takes place in connection with events of social or ritual character.

It is important to bear in mind that at this stage of development land and foodstuffs are virtually never included in the circulation. This seems to be a general phenomenon. As pointed out by Maurice Godelier, by excluding from competition problems related to the means of production (land) and the means of existence, the primitive society ensures the physical existence of its members; and by allowing competition for goods which are difficult to obtain it ensures its own existence as a society.

Control of the exchange of goods implies, as we have seen, control over the access to those foreign goods and wealth objects which indicate status and are thus determinant for the development of political power. An internal system arises, based upon redistribution, in which tribute in the form of domestic surplus is passed up through the system to the dominant chief. At the same time wealth objects, often acquired through external trade, are passed down through the same system through a variety of social transactions. These transactions serve to maintain the social reproduction of the involved parties. A differential access to prestige goods thus creates contacts among the political leaders of the local centres, thus creating a network of exchange connections through which goods can be transported over great distances.

Up to about 500 BC this prestige-goods system had functioned in northern Europe without major disturbances. Since the second millennium BC it had given rise to numerous specialized workshops which produced prestige and status items on the basis of, for example, imported bronze and gold. These items were included in a so-called social production withdrawal system (W.L. Rathje, 1975), in which wealth objects are withdrawn from circulation by the élite and through various ritual transactions are converted into status. In the beginning this is achieved by depositing the wealth objects in the graves, later mainly by depositing them in sacrificial hoards in, for example, wet lands or other inaccessible areas.

To understand the further course of events it is necessary to distinguish some general features of the prestige-goods economy. First of all, changes easily occur in the network of exchange if the economic system is linked to another system based on more complicated principles. The adversary will often tend to play the local competing centres against one another. The result will be a number of shifting foci for trade and consequently also for political power. In this way a continuous and conflicting process of evolution and devolution is created. This is apparently what happened in the relationship between the central European centres and their Mediterranean trade partners in the seventh to fifth centuries BC (S. Frankenstein and M.J. Rowlands, 1978). For northern Europe this situation seems to have resulted in the drying up of the flow of bronze from around 600 BC.

The system is also very vulnerable to economic changes within the foreign regions upon which it depends for the supply of valuable goods. This was the case for long periods of the Iron Age, when the northern European areas were bound to economic systems, such as the Roman civilization, which maintained a considerable production for exchange. Changes of production within these core centres normally have a marked effect in the economically less-developed regions.

It is characteristic of production within a core centre that at some point it will change over to mass-produced goods which experience has shown to be particularly popular in the peripheral 'barbarian' areas. The mass production of drinking equipment in the Roman provinces in the centuries after the birth of Christ is one of the most well-known examples of this. Such a production will often create a group of middlemen traders (C. Renfrew, 1975) who take charge of the primary distribution of the products. In the so-called buffer zone outside of the Roman Limes there was probably a group of such middleman traders in the centuries AD.

Finally, there also exists a natural connection between the increasing demand for the exploitation of the resources in the local centres and the ability of social formations to reproduce themselves. If conditions are continually deteriorating, then hierarchization becomes problematic and a sort of devolution can be anticipated, creating a situation with a more competitive economy in which all available surplus is channelled into the horizontal circuits. This cycle can only be broken by a new growth of productivity and this is probably what occurred in the centuries around the birth of Christ in Denmark.

Exchange until 800 AD

The period around 600 BC was a turning point in the history of Europe. Along the Mediterranean coasts political and economic activity began to accelerate, and in the areas north of the Alps a more intensive interaction with the Mediterranean city states led to profound changes in social formations. In the north Alpine zone there now arose a number of economic centres of shifting political importance. These centres, each of which must have been the seat of a paramount, seem to have been surrounded by a system of vassal sub-centres, which through tribute contributed to a centralized production at the paramount centres of such things as bronze and iron objects. Interregional trade seems to have been controlled from these paramount centres. At the same time a redistribution of status objects to the sub-centres seems to have taken place from here. The course of events in central Europe in the sixth and fifth centuries BC is thus an exemplary model of the significance which the control of the exchange of goods may have for political and social reproduction in a chiefdom society.

The city states and colonies of the Mediterranean showed great interest in the central European area, most likely because they wished to attain access to its resources. For this purpose, connections were established to the far-reaching exchange network which for many centuries had existed on the continent. By means of this network raw materials such as iron, copper, salt, amber, wool, hides and presumably also slaves could be obtained and sold on the domestic market. In exchange, the Mediterranean world supplied exotic goods such as bronze objects and other luxury items which entered into circulation north of the Alps, where they were used to indicate political rank.

Baltic amber was one of the raw materials which in these centuries became a part of the widespread exchange. Already in the eighth century BC great quantities of amber had begun to flow to the Mediterranean world via eastern contacts. Unfortunately it is not yet possible to ascertain whether the amber came from the entire Baltic zone, including Denmark, or whether only a single area, namely the eastern part of the Baltic, contributed to the exchange of goods. The latter alternative is the most likely one. For amber seems to have been channelled southward by way of connections which lay further to the east than those which brought bronze to Scandinavia.

The influx of amber to the regions around Caput Adriae culminated in the seventh and sixth centuries BC. In northern and central Italy, a flourishing amber industry now arose, the refined craft products of which in several cases were re-exported to central Europe. Fluctuations in the influx of amber reflect the effect which the increasingly antagonistic relations among the Mediterranean city-states had on contact between the north and the south. In the mid-fifth century, concurrent with the growing crisis in the Mediterranean, the influx of amber stagnated. At the same time central Europe also suffered a period of political instability, thus reflecting the region's heavy dependency upon the more highly developed economic systems in the south.

Exactly what significance these events had for socio-economic development in northern Europe is not entirely clear. In any case, the interaction between the north European and the central European sectors of the exchange system through the seventh and sixth centuries was diminished. The central European surplus production of metal was now channelled southwards instead of northwards, and from the fifth century BC very few central European goods circulated in northern Europe.

For an area like Denmark, which was utterly dependent upon imported metal, this state of affairs had a profound impact. The scarcity of wealth objects must have made it difficult to maintain the earlier hierarchization, and this situation lasted until the first century BC. The extravagant sacrificial rites by which the élite had previously converted surplus into status were modified. Certainly, status symbols continued to be sacrificially deposited in Danish peat bogs, but now the sacrifices consisted almost exclusively of single sets of neck-rings, pins, brooches or other accessories of local fabrication. The metal quantities which went into making these objects come nowhere near the enormous quantities of metal which had been withdrawn from circulation in the first half of the first millennium BC. The few central and southern European wealth objects which did manage to reach Denmark in the period after 500 BC often remained in circulation all the way up to the first century BC. One example of this long circulation is a series of Campanian and Etruscan bronze products (P.J. Riis, 1959) from the fifth to third centuries BC which have been found in Danish graves from the first century BC. These wealth objects must have circulated for three or four hundred years.

About a century before the birth of Christ, new currents were felt. These changes coincided with the development of the town-like settlements, oppidae, which since the second century BC had been established in a wide zone across central Europe from France in the west to Czechoslovakia in the east. After the foregoing centuries of thorough decentralization with division into numerous small chiefdoms, central Europe now moved toward larger unifications, perhaps incipient state formations. There are many similarities between the oppidum civilization and the settlements with an urban character which had arisen about 400 years earlier as a result of the contact between the central Europeans and the Mediterranean city-states. The central European oppidae, like their predecessors in the sixth and fifth centuries BC, were with their specialized production placed in nodal points for trade. Their rise seems to have been catalysed by the desire of the Mediterranean people to gain access to central European resources such as iron. However, the Roman civilization was a considerably more stable trading partner than the Mediterranean city-states of the sixth and fifth centuries BC. At the same time, the central European oppidae civilization represents a more advanced economic stage of development which contained the first seeds of a market economy. As a result, in less than a century, a far-reaching trade network was re-established throughout northern and central Europe.

The first indications of this new situation in Denmark date from the

Figure 77 The Gundestrup cauldron, probably 1st century BC. The cauldron has often been considered a product from a northern Gaulish workshop. However, in light of recent research on silverworks from the Thracian Black Sea region it seems more likely that the cauldron was made in south-east Europe.

first century BC. Once more wealth objects were deposited in the earth as a part of ritual sacrifices. This held true of such objects as precious cauldrons, which had originated in central or south-east Europe. The Gundestrup silver cauldron, most probably the work of a south-east European artisan, perhaps a Thracian, is one of the best-known examples (Figure 77). Another piece, the Brå cauldron, came from a central European workshop in the third century BC, but may not have been buried until the first century BC. At the same time this socio-economic development also curtailed the circulation time of foreign wealth objects, which were now deposited in the graves. The wealth objects included wagons of central European origin (Figure 78) and drinking equipment from the Mediterranean region.

These finds, which plainly indicate an intensified exchange of goods, continued after the birth of Christ, when Roman luxury wares were now dispersed over the entire northern part of the continent as a result of the intimate interaction of at least three different economic systems: the Roman system, that of the buffer zone just beyond the Limes, and that of the rest of northern Europe. In order to understand this exchange we must re-examine the exchange of goods in northern and central Europe. Various analyses (L. Hedager, 1978c) have in recent years been able to clarify the situation further. By measuring the distance from the Roman border, the Limes (Figure 79), at which finds were made of imported

Figure 78 The Dejbjerg wagon from the Pre-Roman Iron Age, found in a bog near Ringkøbing, western Jutland.

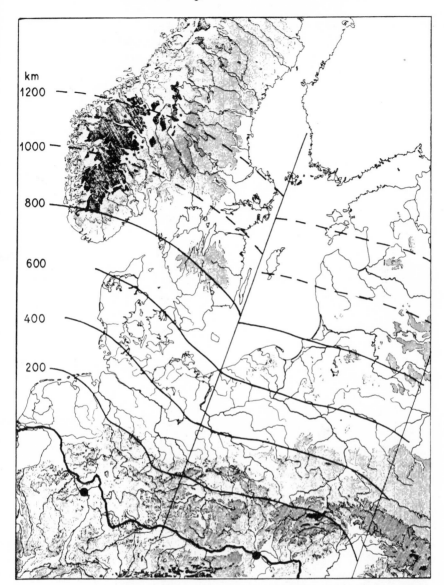

Figure 79 Europe north of the Limes, divided into 200-kilometre units along a borderline separating the area into an eastern and a western part.

Roman objects such as goods made of bronze, glass and silver, or weapons, pottery and brooches, an unmistakable trend emerges as illustrated in Figure 80. The histograms reveal that for one group of objects, the number of finds increases proportionally with the distance

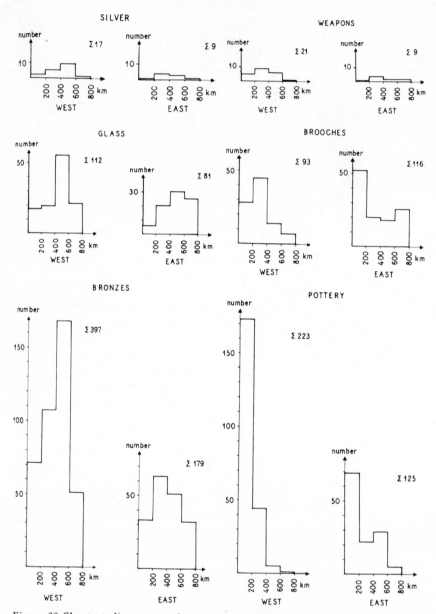

Figure 80 Shortest distance to the western and the eastern Roman border for finds of Roman imports such as silver, weapons, glass, brooches, bronzes, and pottery measured within 200-kilometre intervals.

from the Roman border, but for another group of objects, the number of finds decreases. The objects which increase in number with the distance from the Roman border (up to 600 kilometres) are luxury goods such as bronze, glass and probably also silver and weapons. Objects which decrease in number relative to the distance from the boundary are everyday articles such as pottery and brooches.

This general pattern endured from the first to the fourth centuries AD, although there were some exceptions. Through the first and second centuries AD, for example, there is an extremely large concentration of luxury goods in the zone just beyond the eastern Limes, reflecting the economic importance of the Marcomannian kingdom. After this 'kingdom' lost its political importance, the distribution pattern of the luxury goods again reverted to normal. In the long run, the distribution pattern was quite stable. It may be described thus: just beyond the Limes there was a zone, about 200 kilometres wide, in which Roman luxury goods were rarely deposited as grave-goods. Instead Roman everyday articles were in common use. This may be attributed to two factors: first, the economic trend toward a market economy was more advanced here than further up north, probably because this was the region of the late Celtic oppidae, who had created a more commercially oriented exchange system. Second, the élite of this region had probably been removed from the political system and replaced by Roman influence (L. Hedager, 1978c).

Beyond this 200-kilometre-wide buffer zone, however, there existed a prestige-goods economy based upon a very ancient tradition. Here great quantities of Roman luxury goods functioned in an extremely different context based on a far-flung net of connections among political centres involved in a continuous process of evolution and devolution. No market economy was found here, as may be seen by the finds of Roman coins which indicate monetary functions decreasing in relation to the growing distance from the Roman border (J. Wielowiejski, 1970).

No unambiguous description of this situation can be gleaned from the written sources. However, Tacitus' *Germania*, written at the end of the first century AD, does present a picture of a number of societies seemingly on the chiefdom level of social integration. Judging from Tacitus' rather vague information, the economy of the Germanic chiefdoms was characterized primarily by reciprocity and redistribution; no true market economy is mentioned. Within the individual local communities the functions of the chieftain included the collection of surplus (cattle are named in several connections) and the subsequent redistribution of this surplus to the warriors. A circulation of prestige objects within the élite stratum seems to have played an essential role, often in connection with various social transactions. Tacitus furthermore mentions that drinking rituals of religious, social and political significance were common among the Germanic people. This may explain the enormous circulation of Roman drinking equipment which took place in the centuries following the birth of Christ. Yet another striking feature of the economic functions is that cattle seem to have functioned as special-purpose money, which could be used for paying a fine or a bride price. This description complements the picture presented here of the northern European chiefdoms in the period around the birth of Christ.

The distribution of Roman goods has been interpreted thus: beyond the Roman Limes there were three different zones. In the first zone, the buffer zone which lay 0–200 kilometres from the border, the transports of Roman luxury goods from the border and the northern provinces were organized. The men delegated to take charge of the transports also acquired everyday necessities of Roman origin such as brooches, which were distributed mainly in zone 1 and only rarely in zone 2 and beyond. This may indicate that the further transport to zone 3, of which Denmark was a part, was organized from zone 2, which was an area lying 200–400 kilometres from the Roman border. In any case, this seems to have held true in the western regions. In the eastern regions, the zone 1 middlemen may have traded in both zones 2 and 3, that is up to 600 kilometres from the Limes. The various zones thus represent areas with political and economic centres among which the exchange of goods was carried on.

Of course, only brief glimpses of this exchange of goods can be obtained, for the archaeological record reveals very little about which categories of goods were traded. The most popular goods were drinking equipment of glass and bronze, and weapons. Archaeological and written sources also attest to amber, wine, coins and the silver goblets which were sometimes included in the drinking equipment. Finally, linguistic evidence indicates that wagons, articles of clothing, geese, soap and hides were also traded. In Figure 81 the three postulated economic systems are presented horizontally and the various categories of goods vertically.

The picture drawn by newer research thus shows a complicated network of connections through which various goods were transported over vast distances. Long-distance 'trade routes' in the conventional sense, however, did not develop until sometime during the second and third centuries AD. This fact refutes the once-so-common theories of a trans-European amber route from the eastern Baltic to the northern Adriatic. Pliny's remarks on a journey made by a Roman horseman to the Baltic regions (Pliny's *Natural History* 37:45) have often been used to

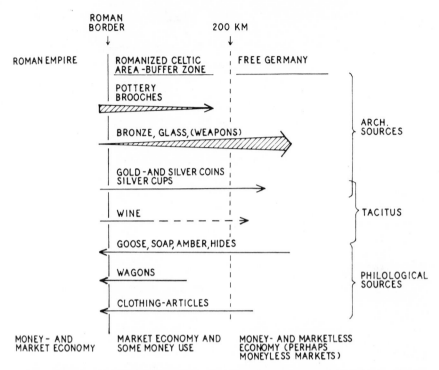

Figure 81 Schematic representation of commodities included in the exchange between the Roman Empire, the buffer zone, and *Germania Libera*.

prove the existence of a long-distance trade route. But in all probability the journey was a never-repeated event and amber, like all other wares, was transported via a long-established network of connections from north to south.

After the amber influx to the south had been considerably curtailed as a result of the economic instability of the Mediterranean region in the fifth century BC, there was again a rise in the first century BC. The reason for this was clearly the renewed growth of settlements of urban character in central Europe, which in turn depended upon intensified interaction with the Mediterranean area. The Celtic oppidum Staré Hradisko in Moravia, for example, was an important place of collection for Baltic amber in the first century BC (C.W. Beck, 1978). Throughout the next two centuries, amber continued to flow by way of the European exchange network to the south, to Carnuntum in Pannonnia, whence the transports continued to Aquileia by the Caput Adriae, the heart of the Roman amber industry. Both the archaeological and the written evidence indicate that Baltic amber was brought to Pannonnia by Germanic middlemen and continued to be brought here until the end of the second century AD, when the eastern contacts were disrupted by the Marcomannian wars. After this time, amber transports to the south declined considerably. Instead, in the third and fourth centuries, amber experienced a renaissance in northern Europe. Here its distribution pattern and its presence in richly equipped graves indicate that exchange among the élite of society was still the means of diffusion.

The many Roman luxury goods which reached Denmark in the centuries after the birth of Christ were spread primarily to the élite in the densely populated agricultural regions along the east coast of Jutland and on the Danish islands. Around 200 AD the exchange of goods intensified. This took place together with a burgeoning mercantilism, particularly in Gaul and lower Germania. At the same time, the Roman production of wealth objects intended for the Germanic regions developed into mass production. Up to the sixth century AD multitudes of Roman provincial and Frankish mass-produced wares circulated among the élite in southern Scandinavia; in time, a large import of gold also followed.

One of the regions in which this trend can most easily be observed is eastern Denmark. Recent fieldwork and re-examinations of the archaeological record have revealed the changes which Roman imports underwent around 200 AD. These changes can be illustrated with the aid of histograms (Figure 82), which show the proportionate wealth in the graves of the region and the distribution of the Roman imports in relation to this. Figure 82 shows how in the first two centuries after the birth of Christ the imports in east Denmark are concentrated within a rather small segment of the Iron Age population. The Roman luxury goods are found in relatively few graves and almost exclusively in graves which, also on the basis of locally produced grave-goods, must be described as very rich. The majority of the graves are far more modestly furnished. This situation more closely resembles the one which we described for the chiefdom societies of the second millennium BC than the situation in the following centuries. For at the end of the second century AD this situation changed drastically (Figure 83). At this time Roman import not only increased in quantity, but was also distributed far more widely among the total number of graves. This observation can thus indicate an increased hierarchization, which may in turn be related to a new distribution pattern of the graves in Denmark (L. Hedager, 1978b).

Figure 82 shows the distribution of the grave finds of Roman imports in east Denmark during respectively the early and late Roman periods.

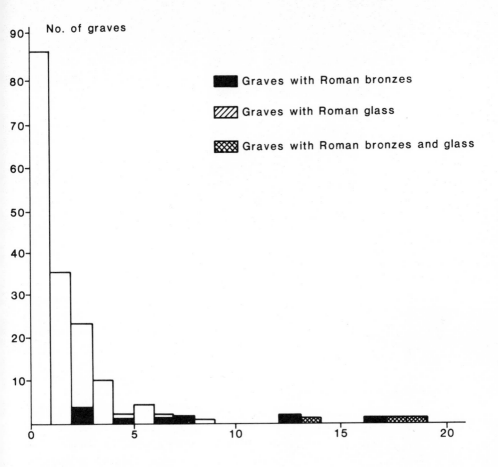

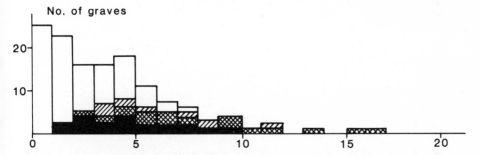

Figure 82 Histogram indicating the proportions of wealth in graves in eastern Denmark during the early Roman Iron Age (above) and the late Roman Iron Age (below). During the early Roman Iron Age the wealth objects were concentrated within a rather small segment of the Iron-Age population. During the later period this situation changed drastically: the Roman imports were now distributed far more evenly among the total number of graves.

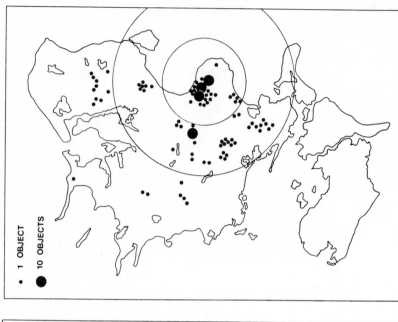

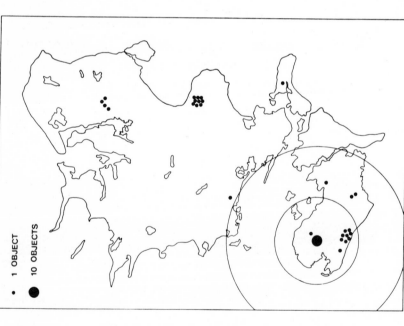

Figure 83 Distribution of grave finds with Roman imports in eastern Denmark. Left: early Roman Iron Age. Right: late Roman Iron Age.

In the early period, most rich graves are found in the south, on the island of Lolland, clustered around the famous Hoby grave, which included the two unique Augustean silver skyphoi (Figure 84). On Zealand the finds are more scattered, although a little concentration of Roman imports does exist in the Stevns region. In the late period, there are no rich graves on Lolland; instead we see a major concentration on east Zealand, where most of the Roman import goods, which had greatly increased in number, are also found.

Figure 84 Augustean grave goods from the famous Hoby grave on the island of Lolland, 1st century AD.

These observations have been interpreted to mean that in the early period, in the first two centuries AD, an exchange system prevailed in which the Roman luxury goods circulated within a very small segment of society and were manifest in the so-called princely graves of the Lübsow type (H.-J. Eggers, 1950). These graves are known everywhere in northern Europe beyond the buffer zone bordering up to the Limes. In the late period, a change set in as a result of the increased hierarchization of society in northern Europe. In Denmark the richest graves were now concentrated on Stevns, Zealand. The sub-centres forming a semi-circle around this centre were not quite as wealthy, but there is evidence of a high concentration of prosperity, including Roman luxury goods. Outside this semi-circle, the sum of wealth is far lower. The distribution and composition of the finds thus indicate that the exchange of goods on Zealand and the surrounding islands was controlled from a centre in eastern Zealand and that this centre exercised control over the long-distance trade.

What we observe here may be an example of a so-called administered trade (K. Polanyi, 1963). By this is meant an exchange based upon tractate relations among the parties concerned. In this way, the extent, composition, quality and prices of the goods exchanged were established. This was thus not a case of a market-created determination of price. The exchange of goods does not generate profit beyond the mutual advantage which both parties derive from it. According to Karl Polanyi, this form of exchange first appeared in Europe, specifically in Greece, about the beginning of the first millennium BC. In central Europe, the epoch of the fortified settlements of urban character in the sixth and fifth centuries BC was probably a manifestation of the same situation. In the Baltic area, including Denmark, administered trade seems to have appeared first with the establishment of economically and politically strong chiefdoms in eastern Denmark just before 200 AD.

According to the general theory we have proposed concerning the connection between the control of external trade and social hierarchization, a development such as the one evident here is not necessarily related to an intensification of subsistence pursuits, for example the introduction of new crop complexes in order to increase surplus. In Denmark, however, administered trade and more hierarchical social patterns arose concurrently with an increase of production, as shown above in the description of the village communities. However, the nature of the relationship between production increase and contemporaneous socio-economic changes in Denmark is still a puzzle.

As already mentioned, a prestige-goods economy in general and administered trade in particular involve very few categories of goods.

These rarely include foodstuffs, because with the weak communication lines it would simply be too risky to depend upon external supplies. Instead, trade will include types of goods necessary for the élite to maintain a certain standard of living. We cannot know to what degree they were distinguished from the rest of the community, but to judge by excavations of village communities from the second and third centuries AD, we may presume that the élite of the Iron Age society were still commoners who tilled their own fields and owned few slaves, if any.

The origin of the presumed administered trade in east Denmark around 200 BC is rather indistinct. It has been related to such goods as hides, which on archaeological grounds have been considered important export articles from the Baltic islands Öland and Gotland (U.E. Hagberg, 1967). In this case Zealand would have played the middleman role in an exchange system which, on one hand, brought Roman luxury goods to southern Scandinavia, and, on the other hand, supplied the Roman army with basic necessities.

As described in the general model, these centralizations of political power based upon control of the exchange of goods cannot have been very stable. Throughout the Roman Iron Age, northern Europe witnessed the continuous evolution and devolution of such centres. Around the fourth century AD the importance of eastern Zealand diminished. Later, other centres arose, for example by the coast of south-west Jutland and on Funen.

In the large settlement Dankirke in south-west Jutland described above, there is an abundance of luxury goods which can best be explained by an exchange of goods at the site, managed by a local magnate. For example, the majority of the glass finds, found at the west end of a house which had burnt down, probably comprised a stock of trade goods. Finds of leaden scale weights in the refuse layers of the same house also indicate trade. The majority of the rich import finds in Dankirke are somewhat later than those of eastern Denmark, being from the fourth and fifth centuries AD.

As in eastern Denmark, however, no indisputable reason can be indicated for the trade at Dankirke. Agricultural productivity was relatively high and a large cattle population must have belonged to the settlements of south-west Jutland. But it is equally important to observe the strong growth of secondary occupations in this era. In Drengsted, not far from Dankirke, traces have been found of a large production of iron. The place included nearly 200 shaft furnaces, so production must have exceeded the local consumption by far. Thus this find attests to an increased domestic exchange probably encompassing many categories of goods.

In the following centuries, the archaeological record fails badly. Future analyses of the only rich find category, the gold finds, will assuredly lead us to new centres for the exchange of goods. It cannot be doubted that south-east Funen in the fifth and sixth centuries AD played an important role in controlling the external exchange of goods. But by and large, our knowledge of the final phase of prehistory, the seventh and eighth centuries AD, is very meagre indeed.

For these last centuries before the beginning of the Viking Age, various attempts have been made to trace the long-distance trade routes on the basis of the very few and scattered finds. Some years ago (C.J. Becker, 1953) a route was drawn through the Limfjord, over the Kattegat and further to the eastern part of the Baltic. The decisive role in the exchange of goods within the Danish territory was thus thought to have been played by northern Jutland. However, recent investigations have indicated that instead it was southern Jutland which functioned as a centre for mercantile contacts between western Europe and the Baltic. New coin finds from Dankirke, excavations in the earliest Ribe and finally the finds from the Hedeby area all indicate that in the eighth century, and perhaps even earlier, power concentrations in southern Jutland administered trade across the Jutland peninsula. A contemporary centre also seems evident in the easternmost part of Denmark, namely on the island of Bornholm (C.J. Becker, 1975).

In this connection, one frequently overlooked aspect of trade ought to be pointed out: its parasites. For in fact insight into the role of trade parasites can provide us with valuable background for the later Viking expeditions. At the end of the eighth century, written sources began to report Viking raids, and Charlemagne, even before his coronation by the Pope in 800 AD, issued orders to guard the coasts of Friesland and the Channel. These actions must have been responses to the growing trade activity which had taken place especially in the seventh and eighth centuries AD. These earliest Viking raids do not yet seem to have been part of any planned military activity. Rather they must have been incidental cases of ordinary piracy.

This early stage also saw the development of that all-important prerequisite for piracy: the ship. From the fourth century AD and onward we have sporadic traces of the development of a vessel with a fixed construction: a double-pointed hull with a very curved keel and curved bow and stern, clinker-laid deck ribs placed symmetrically across the bottom and a thwart or cross-beam for each rib. The earliest known stage of this development was the Nydam boat from around 400 AD (Figure 85). This boat was 23 metres long and could be rowed by thirty men. The next stage was the Gredstedbro ship, found in southern

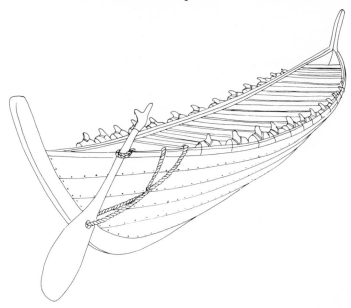

Figure 85 The Nydam boat, *c.* 400 AD, from the large sacrifical weapon find
excavated at Nydam bog, southern Jutland.

Jutland near Ribe (O. Crumlin-Petersen, 1967). A radiocarbon dating
shows that this ship was built around 600–650 AD, with a 100-year
margin to each side. The Gredstedbro ship displayed both older and
newer features (Figure 86). For example, like the Nydam boat it has a
keel scarf, whereas the ribs were fastened with wooden treenails just as
on the later Viking ships from Skuldelev. In general, the overall picture
best corresponds to the 26-metre-long ship from Sutton Hoo in Suffolk
in England. The Gredstedbro ship was probably built as a rowing vessel;
in any case, the keel was not extended to make the keel of a proper
sailing ship. In the seventh and eighth centuries these Scandinavian
ships adopted the mast and sails of the vessels of western Europe. Thus
there evolved a ship which was quick and manoeuvrable, eminently
well suited for piracy and military raids.

Yet there is reason to emphasize that both in this era and in the first
centuries of the Viking Age, piracy reflected the still unsteady basis of
the trade connections. Regular trade involving the frequent transportation of goods begets a specialized piracy. However, if trade is less than
regular, the piracy which accompanies it will be entirely different and
extremely versatile.

The maximal versatile trade parasite carries on his activities part-

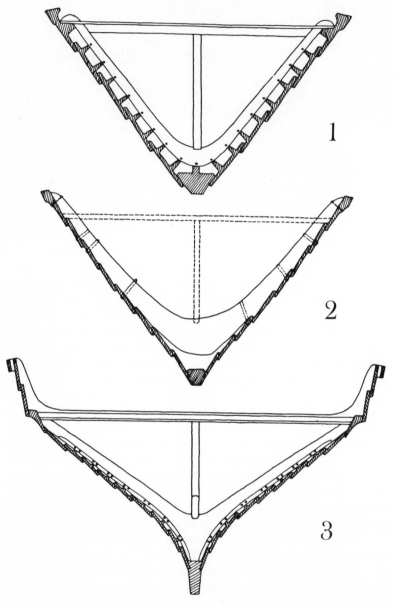

Figure 86 Cross-sections of: 1. the Nydam boat. 2. the Gredstedbro ship. 3. the Oseberg ship.

time, for example in connection with farming. He will steal from all forms of subsistence, both on land and at sea and over as large a geographical area as the means of transportation allows. (K. Lunden, 1972)

This definition applies to the early Viking raids which, indirectly, can attest to a growing but as yet quite limited trade activity.

The same impression also emerges of the earliest settlements of urban character in Denmark and adjacent regions: in Ribe and Hedeby close to the modern Danish–German border. Discussion about these and similar settlements has often been diverted because of historians' wish to frame practical definitions of a town. These definitions, especially those based upon the administrative functions of the town formations, can be of great operative significance in the study of medieval towns. But for the earlier north European settlements of urban character, they are often meaningless. It is far more important to ascertain which types of trade characterized the Iron Age communities up to the beginning of the Viking Age.

In the eighth century, the stage called administered trade had probably not yet been passed. Great emphasis should therefore be placed upon the security required for trade in the period before a general pacification of the regions involved had been achieved. Administered trade seeks to fulfil these security requirements in what Polanyi calls a port of trade. By this is meant a site that offers security to the foreign trader, facilities of anchorage and debarkation, storage and agreement on the goods to be traded. The locality is protected by the local political authority, who ensures his own vital interests in administering the exchange of goods. This exchange is therefore characterized by administrative decisions and cannot, as stressed above, be considered an actual market trade. The potential importance of the port of trade as an administrative centre for the surrounding region is thus of minor importance, which is one of the reasons why the so-called ports of trade are frequently moved. This may explain a statement in the Frankish Annals that in the year 808 AD the Danish king Godfred compelled the merchants of the Slavic town of Reric, as well as those Wismar in northern Germany, to move to his own 'portus' Slesvig, just south of the modern Danish–German border.

The conclusion of the above must be that the long-distance trade was the basis for the earliest trading centres of urban character such as Hedeby and Ribe. However, it could not create any permanent integration of a larger area. This development first took place during the Viking Age and the early Middle Ages. However, through the last 500 years before the Viking Age it may be seen how the growth of secondary occupations led to an increased domestic exchange of goods. From the eighth century there are remains at several large villages by the Limfjord (Bejsebakken, Lindholm Høje and Aggersborg) of workshops and production which attest to a far-reaching occupational differentiation and a growing productivity. Gradually some·of the preconditions were created for the market economy which later came to supplant the archaic prestige-goods economy. This development had still not culminated at the beginning of the Viking Age. Not until the tenth and eleventh centuries can coin finds, for example, show how a market economy was slowly emerging in the urban centres, even as the exchange of goods outside these centres was probably still being carried out according to ancient economic patterns.

18
Political and social development

Economy and social development

One of the first written sources which sheds a faint light upon Denmark dates from the threshold to the Viking Age. In the year 808, the Frankish Annals (*Annales Regni Francorum*) reported on the Danish king Godfred and his plundering of the Slavic town Reric by the Baltic. Moreover the annals relate that King Godfred had the southern boundary of his kingdom fortified against the land of the Saxons by erecting an earthwork at the place where even today the Danish–German border runs. Unfortunately the annals tell nothing about the size of Godfred's kingdom. But judging by the role allotted him by the Frankish chroniclers, it may be concluded that Godfred represented no insignificant political and military power, probably controlling all of southern Denmark, if not more.

The question which arises here is, what sort of political power concentrations existed prior to the mention of King Godfred's realm around the year 800 AD? More specifically, one may enquire whether the political situation manifest in King Godfred's strategy regarding Charlemagne's Frankish empire, for example his fortification of the border, was the result of a brief spontaneous situation provoked by external pressure, or whether it was the result of a situation which had existed for centuries?

From a historian's viewpoint, based on the few written sources which have survived, the first-named alternative has often been accepted. The written sources are taken to imply that the extensive political power concentrations of the Viking Age were of relatively recent date. But from the archaeologist's point of view, matters appear quite different. The description presented here of the economic and demographic development of the agrarian society indicates that throughout the Iron Age in Denmark attempts were being made to unify ever-larger regions under one central authority.

Little insight into this process can be obtained from the more general theories on the evolution of social stratification and community orga-nization. To be sure, Iron Age Denmark included societies on the chiefdom level of socio-cultural integration. Nor can there be any doubt that here and there in Denmark in the course of the Iron Age there arose stratified societies, in which some members had unhindered access to the strategic resources, whereas other members were denied or res-tricted access to the same fundamental resources. This conclusion may be drawn because we know the preliminary end product of this process, namely the state formation of the Viking Age and the early Middle Ages.

The term 'state' as applied here implies an autonomous, political unit equipped with a centralized political power, which has the authority for example to collect taxes, conscript men for war or work, and to issue and enforce laws. The state is thus regarded as a collection of specialized institutions and agencies, some formal and others informal, which maintain an order of stratification (M.H. Fried, 1967). The development of a market economy and the presence of urban centres are also considered decisive traits. If one accepts this definition, then a true state formation in Danish territory first appeared in the course of the late Viking Age and the early Middle Ages. On the other hand, if one chooses a more structural definition, which regards the state as a political instrument basing its function on a legitimate power, then it is probable that already before the Viking Age, Iron Age society developed a complexity which in many respects contained state-like elements (see for example L. Hedager, 1978b).

The definitions of such evolutionary categories as bands, tribes, chiefdoms and states are valuable mainly as heuristic tools. Yet in fact they are nothing more than lists of static traits of different levels of societal organization. They tell very little about the dynamics of social reproduction, that is, about the conditions which caused the system to develop from one social form to another. It is therefore important to describe the Iron Age as a period whose particular structure emerged and was transformed throughout the period.

Yet this approach is rarely encountered in north European archaeo-logy. One of the reasons for this is that many of the evolutionary concepts being used by archaeologists have been developed by the study of the so-called 'early civilizations'. These were formations which depended upon the productive capacity of the very large areas from which they acquired their raw materials. Research has often concentrated upon the core areas of these civilizations, often more or less neglecting the special structural properties which characterize the peripheral areas. However, in recent years important studies have been able to describe how the interaction between, for example, the Mediterranean city-states and the areas north of the Alps in the centuries prior to the birth of Christ led to a commercialization of the latter area before the emergence of any centralized state control (S. Frankenstein and M.J. Rowlands, 1978). They have also pointed out that the particular form assumed by these tribal societies was directly determined by the role which they played within a larger geographical division of labour centred round the Mediterranean world.

This approach, which ought not be confused with more conventional diffusionistic approaches, can prove most fruitful in clarifying the later feudal development in medieval Europe. This is the reason why the present work has so strongly emphasized the importance of identifying the forms of exchange which functioned in Denmark up to the beginning of the Viking Age.

Political and economic power concentrations

Up to the middle of the first millennium BC, the agrarian communities in Denmark had been closely integrated with a far-reaching European exchange network system, which had brought a multitude of prestige goods to the country. These exotic wares became part of the chiefdom's consumption of status symbols and were thus vital for social reproduction. When the influx of these goods ceased around 500 BC, the hierarchization which until then had prevailed in the chiefdoms was hindered, and we must presume that the following centuries were marked by some form of devolution (K. Kristiansen, 1978a). The segmentary hierarchy must have been weakened; the chieftain's control of production must have been modified so that the earliest Iron Age societies developed a decentralized structure. The same phenomenon seems to appear everywhere in the vast north European lowland region. It may therefore logically be associated with the political and economic instability from which central and southern Europe suffered at this time.

For the first three or four centuries of the Iron Age, this basic pattern seems to have dominated. However, the archaeological record for the period shows a considerable population pressure, which led to expanded settlement and the intensification of subsistence pursuits. Excavations of village communities in particular confirm this impression. They show communities whose population fluctuated between fifty and several hundred inhabitants, considerably higher numbers than in the previous period. These statistics are confirmed by the excavated cemeteries which display only faint differences in the distribution of wealth. Objects which can be interpreted as indicators of differential ranking are by and large known only from the sacrificial deposits, particularly in the bogs. Specialized workshops which produced these insignia, for example complicated types of neck-rings (Figure 87), must therefore have continued to exist, just as a more restricted exchange must have been carried out, especially with the areas along the southern borders of the Baltic.

As one might expect in an era highlighted by devolution, population pressure and territorial expansion, traces of warfare are also found. The Hjortspring find from the island of Als in southern Denmark is the most prominent example of this. This find, which dates from around the third and second centuries BC, is the oldest sacrificial weapon find known in Denmark. A vessel, or rather a war canoe, 16 metres long, consisting of five wide boards, one at the bottom and two at each side, had been deposited in a very small bog (Figure 88). Along with the boat, a great

Figure 87 Neck ring from the Pre-Roman Iron Age found in a bog at Væt, Randers county.

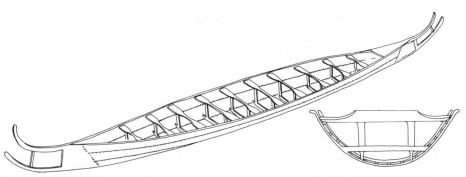

Figure 88 The Hjortspring boat from the Pre-Roman Iron Age, period II, found in a bog on the island of Als, southern Denmark.

number of iron and wooden weapons were also deposited: swords, spears, shields, knives and chain-mail. The boat, which did not carry a sail, could accommodate a crew of 22–24 men. This find must be interpreted in the same way as the sacrificial weapon hoards deposited three or four hundred years later as the possessions of a defeated army, deliberately destroyed by the victor.

Not until the first century BC can a change in the socio-economic situation be discussed. The local prerequisites for this included an intensification of the subsistence pursuits which had taken place through the preceding five centuries, as well as the population pressure which is for instance manifest in the first century BC in the village of Hodde (see p. 206ff), whose relatively light soil supported a population of about 200 with a proportionately large cattle population. The increased strain on the resources can also be observed in the pollen diagrams and in the settlement expansion which concurrently commenced in the boulder clay areas.

Everywhere in the north European lowland, there are contemporaneous indications that a hierarchization of society had been reestablished. It is logical to see this process in the light of the evolving commercialization in the north Alpine zone with the concurrent growth of the oppida civilization. Once again, central and northern Europe joined the system which the Mediterranean civilization drew upon for raw materials and probably also for slaves. One sign of the reestablishment of a far-reaching exchange network is that once more Baltic amber came into circulation and flowed abundantly to the Mediterranean area.

Again it became possible to accumulate foreign prestige goods, and consequently in the first century BC we find in Denmark a group of richly equipped graves which are distinguished from the more modestly furnished majority of graves. Social status was now indicated ever more strongly in the funeral rites. A similar development can be observed over large parts of northern Germany and Poland.

The male graves with weapons are especially striking. Here we find swords, lances, shields and knives. Sometimes the grave furnishings include foreign prestige goods such as central European chariots and Mediterranean bronze works, some of which had been in circulation for several hundred years.

Unfortunately, analyses have not yet been undertaken either of the proportion of these rich graves to the poor graves, or of the spatial distribution of the graves. In some cases the graves of the élite were established at special places, separate from the more modestly furnished graves. This holds true of the richest cemetery of the period, Langå on the island of Funen, where a small group of very rich graves was found at some distance from a large cemetery with approximately 100 modestly equipped graves. The Langå cemetery lies in a region of eastern Funen which was strategically placed for communications with both eastern and western Denmark and which at the same time lay central in relation to Funen as well as the surrounding islands of Langeland, Ærø, and Tåsinge. Through the following centuries in Denmark, this centre remained one of the leading economic, demographic and strategic centres in southern Denmark. Here, in the centuries after the birth of Christ, we also find Møllegårdsmarken, the largest Iron Age cemetery in Denmark with more than 2000 graves, only 6–7 kilometres from Langå. Other centres of wealth may be observed in southern and northern Jutland, although these are not yet so evident in the archaeological record as the centre on Funen.

Alongside this demonstration of high status in the graves, a number of very costly votive deposits also were made, including more or less fragmented bronze cauldrons of central European origin. The most striking of the cauldron finds is the huge silver cauldron from Gundestrup. The village communities also display distinct signs of increased hierarchization. The magnate's farmstead in Hodde is an example of this, as regards both the size and the quality of the finds, especially pottery.

The contemporaneous features here include both an intensified exchange of goods over all the north European region and an increased hierarchization of the communities provoked both by an increased demographic pressure and by an increased control of the growing production by the leaders.

These tendencies continued in the centuries after the birth of Christ. Everywhere in Denmark, but especially in the areas with good agricultural soil, the grave finds continue to show a distinct hierarchization. This is seen above all by the presence of Roman imports, most of which were made in southern Italy. Later the predominant goods were the mass-produced glass and bronze goods from the provincial Roman work-shops in lower Germania and Gaul. A special role seems to have been played by the prestigious drinking equipment. Just as in the earlier centuries, it was probably used for drinking rituals by the élite.

As mentioned earlier, the acquisition of foreign luxury goods seems to have been dependent upon high status – and in the first two centuries AD exchange still seems to have taken place within a relatively small segment of society. At this time there clearly existed in Denmark societies organized on the chiefdom level of socio-cultural integration, but the distribution pattern of such things as foreign prestige goods indicates that we are still dealing with rather small local political structures.

About 200 AD, this picture slowly began to change. One of the reasons for this change may have been the appearance of an administered trade. This can be most clearly observed in eastern Denmark, where the number of burials of high-ranking persons increased strikingly. Often these rich graves are found singly or clustered in small groups. They were kept separate from the cemeteries which contained the burials of the lower strata, in itself an indication of a rather hierarchical organiza-tional form. Of utmost importance, of course, is the distribution of status symbols which was controlled by the political centres. The new pattern can best be discerned in the Stevns area on eastern Zealand. Here, a close correlation is seen between the increased influx of Roman imports and political development (L. Hedager, 1978b and c). A centre with a great accumulation of wealth now arose on Stevns, where the graves show a degree of hierarchization hitherto unknown. Round the centre there was a group of dependent sub-centres, probably with vassal chiefs, which received a considerable part of the trade goods. There seems to have been a development of several specialized functions in the power apparatus, a situation which persisted at least up to the fourth century AD, when Roman imports disappeared from eastern Denmark and instead appeared in western Denmark. Throughout this period there probably existed a political centre controlling all of Zealand and the surrounding islands. Less developed centres, also marked by growing hierarchization, can be seen elsewhere in the country. There is much to indicate that Funen and its surrounding islands comprised a unified whole. In Jutland, the situation is as yet quite murky, as analyses of the grave finds and their contents of, in particular, weapons and wealth symbols have not yet been undertaken.

As may be expected, this evolution is not stable geographically. A direct consequence of the spatial shifts in centres and the conflicts which they occasioned may be seen in the so-called weapon-sacrificial finds which range from the centuries before the birth of Christ up to the seventh century AD. The majority were deposited between 200–400 AD.

The sacrificial deposits of weapons in bogs constitute the largest find group from the Iron Age. A total of nineteen large and small finds from Denmark are known (Figure 89), with ten in Jutland, four on Funen, four on Zealand and Lolland, and one on Bornholm. The weapon sacrifices were always deposited on a meadow or bog surface or cast out from the shore of a small lake. These were clearly not abandoned battlefields, because the objects were often arranged in bundles or packed together in cloth. The areas must have been sacred, as indicated by the fact that the site where the objects were placed was sometimes marked off with poles or wattle.

The weapon sacrifices might include more than just weapons; there might be clothing, personal items, tools, agricultural implements, wagons or boats. Very often, the objects bear traces of fighting and of consequent destruction for the unmistakable purpose of rendering them unusable. This clearly indicates a ritual background for the deposits, a

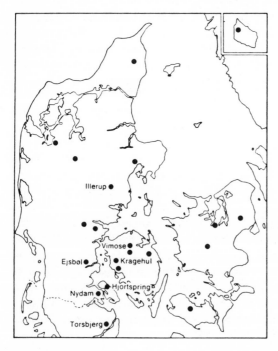

Figure 89 Distribution of the sacrifical deposits of weapons in bogs.

situation corroborated in Caesar's *Gallic Wars*, which describes similar sacrificial customs in Gaul.

Some of the weapon finds include deposits from a number of battles. The find from Illerup in eastern Jutland, for instance, is comprised of at least three sacrifices of war booty. In Ejsbøl in southern Jutland, finds were made of the arms of a large defeated army, along with a couple of smaller deposits. The number of objects found shows that about 200 men had participated in the conflict, and that about 60 foot soldiers and 9 horsemen were killed (Figure 90). Such forces may imply that major power concentrations existed, at least in conflict situations when the élite could gather a considerable force of dependants around them.

More detailed analyses of the contents of the weapon-sacrifice finds will undoubtedly be able to determine the origin of the warriors who fought. Until then it must suffice to associate generally the weapon-sacrifice finds and the military conflicts which they represent with the development of rival centres of political power which arose in Denmark in the centuries following 200 AD. More specifically, the weapon-sacrifice finds have been related to the formation of a political centre in eastern Denmark which up to about 400 AD attempted to extend its power

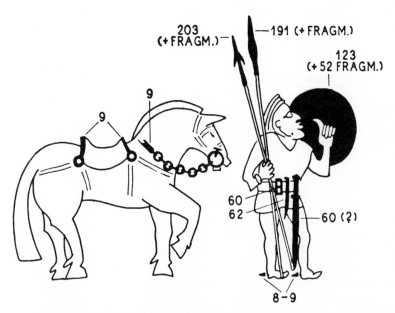

Figure 90 The number of objects found in the sacrificial weapon find at Ejsbøl, southern Jutland, shows that about 200 men had participated in the battle which took place before the sacrifice.

further to the west, 'an attempt which seems to have failed' (L. Hedager, 1978b).

Thus from the second and third centuries AD a number of small 'kingdoms' with shifting political power and vaguely defined territories seem to have existed in Denmark. This development took place along with the growing differentiation in the power apparatus, which can be discerned in the grave finds, and with the appearance of larger farm-steads, as evident in the settlement finds. At the same time the archaeological record shows a considerable population growth and an increasing distance between the top and the bottom in the social system.

One serious impediment to the tracing of this development is the fact that the years from the fifth to the eighth centuries AD comprise one of the most curious periods in the prehistory of Denmark: most of the find groups are very meagre and the archaeological record does not allow for much interpretation.

To be sure, from the fifth and sixth centuries AD there is an over-whelming number of gold finds, many of which may be interpreted as status symbols. The distribution of the gold finds also shows that in southern Denmark, probably on Funen, there existed a centre which played a decisive role in the distribution of the wealth symbols. Analyses of this important find group, however, have not yet been published. The gold finds are of great interest in other respects as well. They have sometimes been regarded as the manifestation of a general gold monetary standard. However, this interpretation contradicts the conclusions hitherto suggested regarding the development of the econo-mic institutions. Instead, an analysis more than 50 years old, by the Norwegian archaeologist A.W. Brøgger, of the weights of the gold may still be valid. Brøgger proved that the Danish gold rings, like the Norwegian ones, were made according to a weight standard based upon the Roman libra corresponding to 12 øre and that the gold had probably functioned as special-purpose money used, for example, to pay wer-geld, a compensation primarily for the killing of a man. Indirectly, then, gold may indicate the presence of a formalized legal system similar to contemporary Germanic law on the continent.

With a number of other exotic materials, gold can also testify to the existence of specialized workshops, which must have been associated with the economic centres whose surplus was converted to prestige symbols. From around 400 AD and up to the Viking Age, we may speak of a special Nordic style. The knowledge of this style rapidly spread throughout Scandinavia, probably via wandering craftsmen, of whom there is evidence beginning in the fifth century AD. The political and social unrest in Gaul at this time is assuredly the explanation of this phenomenon.

Yet for the seventh and eighth centuries, it is still impossible for us to define the political and administrative centres which must have existed in Denmark. Newer studies of the development of the Nordic style plainly show that in this last era before the Viking Age, Denmark was not isolated, as earlier archaeologists often believed it to have been. On the contrary, seventh- and eighth-century Denmark was an integral part of a larger cultural region extending from an Anglo-continental region in the Channel region via the Dutch–Frisian coastal areas to Denmark and thence to the Baltic areas. This eastward contact may have many causes. One of them is probably that administered trade took place between political and economic centres.

One of these centres most likely lay in southern Denmark. Here, by the modern Danish–German border, are the remains of the gigantic fortification structure called the Danevirke. The first building phase of this fortification is in historical sources attributed to King Godfred, from the period around 800 AD. However, the newest radiocarbon and dendrochronological datings of the building timber in the north rampart and the oldest part of the main rampart of the Danevirke have shown that the wood was felled in 737 AD, three generations before King Godfred. Thus at this time there existed a political power capable of erecting this 7-kilometre-long rampart with a 2-metre-high, vertical front palisade and a moat about 1.5 metres deep (Figure 91).

We do not know how much of Denmark was united under this

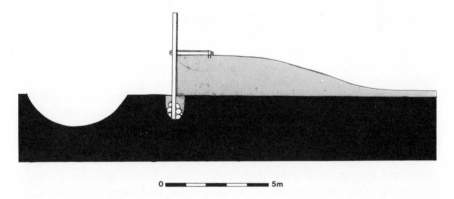

0 ▬▬ ▬▬ ▬▬ 5m

Figure 91 Cross-section through the oldest part of the rampart at Danevirke. Dendrochronological analysis has shown that the wood included in the construction was felled in 737 AD.

political power. The Frankish Annals from 782 mention a Danish king named Sigfred. It is not unreasonable to extend this royal power some decades back in time and regard one of Sigfred's and Godfred's predecessors as the builder of the first rampart.

In this context reference has been made to a Frankish report written about 800 AD which deals with the Frisian missionary Willibrord. This missionary died in 739 AD after having visited 'the very wild people of the Danes' where a certain King Ongendus – or Angantyr – ruled. It is not inconceivable that this king may have ordered the earliest building of the Danevirke.

Elsewhere in Denmark, there are also impressive constructions most likely carried out by a royal power early in the eighth century. For example, there is the several-kilometre-long Kanhave canal, which bisects the island of Samsø at its most narrow part (Figure 92). A navy based in the Stavns Fjord, into which the canal runs, would have been able to control navigation on both sides of this strategically placed island. The sides of the canal were secured with a plank construction formed by oblique oak planks – and these planks were recently radiocarbon-dated to roughly the same period as the earliest part of the rampart at Danevirke.

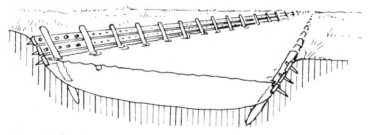

Figure 92 The Kanhave canal on the island of Samsø, constructed in the 8th century AD.

Of course, on this slight basis it is not possible to trace connections from the fifth and sixth centuries AD up to the beginning of the Viking Age, when for the first time the written sources inform us about extensive concentrations of power on Danish territory. But, as shown, the archaeological record indicates that around 800 AD Godfred's kingdom was not the first substantial political unification of large parts of Denmark. The social, political, demographic and economic preconditions for this sort of concentration of power seem to have been present even earlier.

Processes towards the early Danish state

Up to the beginning of the Viking Age, which marked the end of the prehistoric epoch, Danish society was transformed profoundly. The preconditions for this change may be traced sporadically through the Iron Age and it seems clear that the rise of cultural activity which took place in Viking Age Denmark was not created by Viking raids and expanding trade alone. The centuries preceding the Viking Age must have witnessed major changes in the power structure of the society, meaning a development of the relationships of dependency and exploitation.

From a Danish point of view, there are many structural similarities with developments in several neighbouring areas. In England, for example, in the sixth to eighth centuries AD there is sufficient evidence to reveal the existence of many competing kingdoms which were sometimes integrated within larger 'empires' or overlordships. There are several instances in which kings who were firmly incorporated into the kinship system either became monarchs who attained a singular power or were subjected to one (R. Hodges, 1978). An example of the first alternative is that of King Offa, who in the eighth century called himself *rex totius Anglorum patriae*. This may be compared with the Danish king, Harald Bluetooth, who in the tenth century called himself 'he who won all of Denmark and Norway'.

These structural similarities in the pre-Viking Age have been somewhat neglected by Danish historians. Instead the period around 800 AD has been viewed as a sort of cultural breach and has been explained more or less as a direct result of the growth of long-distance trade. In this way the Viking Age has come to appear as a period which decisively broke with the continuity extending far back through prehistoric society. This situation can also be explained by the fact that traditional historians have rarely applied the concepts of social and economic anthropology as well as the evidence of the archaeological record from the Viking period. Therefore the concept of state formation – the phenomenon which definitively terminated archaic Danish society – has not received as much attention from historians as it deserves.

Even though the completion of the process of state formation in Denmark lies beyond the range of the present work, it has been possible to indicate the rise of a number of state-like traits, particularly from the third to the eighth centuries AD. This has been done by depicting some of the main features of socio-economic development, which indeed contributed to the creation of these elements. One of the important prerequisites for this was the attempt to distinguish the economic institutions underlying the exchange of goods in the Iron Age society. The course of development sketched here, contemporary with the commercial flourishing in the Roman provinces around 200 AD, extended an archaic prestige-goods economy to include a so-called administered trade. The origin of administered trade must be presumed to have been social competition and the need of a relatively small social group to maintain a certain standard of living. This implies that through most of the Iron Age, long-distance trade must have been motivated by status. It was directed only towards a relatively small population group at the top of society.

At the same time, an attempt has also been made to demonstrate how throughout the final centuries of prehistory social competition caused a growing accumulation of political and economic power within various parts of the country. This process created the basis for the port-of-trade localities associated with administrated trade, here regarded as preliminary phases of the more town-like settlements which arose in the course of the Viking Age and the early Middle Ages.

What remains to be explained is the relation between this trade activity and the increase of production which seems to have taken effect in Iron Age society from around 200 AD. As mentioned earlier, primitive trade lacks that combination of external and internal trade which is necessary for maintaining a balance in the more complex market economy. This is most likely the reason why the development of secondary occupations occurred at a relatively slow pace through the Iron Age. Nor does the development of the economic means of exchange seem to have exceeded the special-purpose money stage before the eighth century at the earliest. The relatively modest extent of trade activity is also confirmed by the present interpretation of the first Viking expeditions about the eighth century as simply the expression of a very versatile sort of piracy.

To explain this process there is every reason to pay heed to the transformations of not only the primary but also the secondary occupations which took place within the village communities in the period after c. 200 AD. Above, the Vorbasse village was used to exemplify this: it presents a clear-cut picture of an expanding agrarian society. The growing size of the farm plots, the appearance of large multi-functional farmsteads, the undeniable traces of co-operative labour, the numerous workshop buildings and many other features hint that through the latter part of the Iron Age a considerable development of productivity took place as well as an increase in the circulation of domestic goods. As yet, we lack knowledge of a great many details in this process, but there is hope that new archaeological excavation methods can before long fill in the gaps.

None the less the present archaeological record can suggest a number of features of the social organization in the societies which existed from c. 500 BC and up to the beginning of the Viking Age. These societies have been termed chiefdoms, by which is meant hierarchical societies whose internal relations were based upon redistribution and whose central authorities were responsible for political, ritual and economic functions. At the same time it has also been proved that at times there was also considerable social competition among these societies – competition which in periods resulted in armed conflicts. Evidence of this is probably provided by the great sacrificial weapon finds from southern Denmark.

Attempts to enlarge this very rudimentary picture of social and political organization in Iron Age Denmark seen in retrospect from the Viking Age are strikingly rare in Danish archaeology and history. This of course is attributable to the problematic nature of the sources pertaining to the social history of the Viking Age. This holds true above all of the legendary history of the Scandinavians, which has been called 'the morning world of half-remembered dreams' (G. Jones, 1968).

Modern Danish historians have to a great extent rejected the evidence of legendary history with regard to social structure. And it is quite true that these written sources, most of which were recorded in the twelfth century and later, offer a very distorted and idealized picture especially of the uppermost social levels, the élite. At the same time they ignore social relations existing within the remaining sector of society. Moreover, many of the concrete episodes in the early literature can be traced to continental history, in particular the events in the struggles between the Goths and the Huns in the Migration period, celebrated in Germanic heroic poetry. Thus these events cannot be regarded as episodes in Danish history.

Furthermore the other sources related to the social history of the Viking Age, the runic stones, the laws and the archaeological sources, reveal only the most general social categories. These can perhaps help reconstruct the basic features of society but not much more.

One of the most frequently encountered assumptions about social relations in the Viking Age is that the most important boundaries were the ones dividing the ruling caste, the aristocracy, from the free peasants, peasant proprietors, smallholders, or whatever they may be called, on one side – and the free peasants from the slaves on the other side. The free men are often thought to have been the backbone of society, and the slaves (the thralls) to have been inferior and to have lacked rights in relation to the free men. This simplified picture has often been projected back in time onto earlier periods, namely the Iron Age society, as it developed after the birth of Christ. This viewpoint may be found in the works both of historians (E. Arup, 1925) and of archaeologists (G. Hatt, 1937).

This assumption, however, has been modified in the present description of the structure of the Iron Age society. In this connection it is also interesting that newer research into the early law texts has shown that there existed a complex hierarchy of status positions ranging from the slaves to the aristocracy. The concept of 'the free peasants' as a 'class' with common legal and political rights must have been maintained for ideological reasons.

On the basis of the archaeological finds the present work attempts to present a more subtle view of society in the Iron and Viking Ages in describing the societies as hierarchical systems in which the social position of the individual was determined by his position in the family. This position determined the rights to which the individual was entitled and the functions he had to exercise. At the top of the system were the leading families, and at the bottom were the slaves – at least from the end of the seventh century, when the written sources suggest that Denmark was a slave society. Between the top and the bottom it seems that, particularly from the second and third centuries AD, an ever greater differentiation of status positions may be observed.

A closely related phenomenon is the development of political power concentrations which can be followed through the centuries of the Iron Age. There seems to be both a strengthening of the positions of authority in the various communities and an integration in over-lordships or smaller 'kingdoms' comprising, for example, areas the size of Zealand.

As yet it is difficult to say anything about the nature of situations in which the authority of the ruling families was mobilized. With regard to the latter problem, however, the picture can be enlarged on a number of points. For example, it may be seen that as late as the Viking Age the exercise of ritual practice was not carried out by a professional priesthood. The celebration of the communal cult was not a profession in itself but was carried out by the élite of society. It is logical to conclude that the priesthood of the 'big men' (the Godi institution) had roots in a sacred chiefdom system which extended very far back into prehistory. It has also been stressed above that in the chiefdoms sacred as well as secular offices were inherited, often within the same family line, just as priest and chief were often one and the same person.

The authority of the chieftains was also foremost in a number of cases related to the exercise of the economic functions. This held true, for example, in connection with the development of society's exchange of goods, not only the local redistribution and gift trade but also the administered trade, which can already be glimpsed in the second and third centuries. Typically, the chieftain's role in this connection is also intimately related to political, military and social contexts.

It has been suggested above that the appearance of the warrior graves around the birth of Christ may indicate the beginnings of the 'hird' system which later in the Viking period had such a marked effect. However, it is important to remember that the dependent peasants whom the magnates could gather by virtue of the redistributive economic system could hardly have comprised any special warrior class. Economically the warriors were probably still commoners in that they tilled their own fields and owned few, if any, slaves.

This same observation may be applied to the rest of the population, which can hardly be said to have constituted a 'middle class', that is a broad spectrum of equal families. A characteristic trait of all chiefdoms is the thorough inequality among individuals as well as groups. Individuals and groups each had their own position in society, determined by their genealogical relationship to the chief. Thus there were families of high descent and those of low descent. This is the most likely explanation for the graduated distribution of wealth evident both within Iron Age village communities and in the grave finds. This sort of graduated distribution of wealth can in fact be traced as far back as the second millennium BC.

A hierarchical structure of society in the sense described here makes it difficult to use the word 'class' in the sense which it later acquired. In a chiefdom inequality is primarily social and to a much smaller degree economic. Families themselves are split up and can theoretically form a graduated rank order from the top to the bottom of society. One exception to this is the slaves, if there are any. For the reasons named it is logical to reserve the term 'class' for true state formations.

There are two groups whose relationship to the local communities cannot be determined: the merchants and the craftsmen, both probably foreigners originally. Itinerant free craftsmen must have existed in prehistoric Danish society, certainly from the fifth century AD and perhaps even earlier. Their impact must have been considerable in disseminating styles of metal-crafting, especially the so-called Nordic animal styles from the period c. 400–800 AD. With the incipient growth of secondary occupations during the third and fourth centuries, it may be presumed that the importance and size of the craftsmen group had increased. Yet its status in relation to what must have been a rather closed kinship society cannot be known.

This same lack of factual insight also undermines our ideas about those active in trade. It does seem that a group of middlemen traders must already have existed from the third century, when administered trade seems to have commenced. From the beginning they seem to have been foreigners, but it cannot be denied that local part-time traders gradually participated in the exchange of goods. At the beginning of the Viking Age Carolingian law mentions guilds consisting of itinerant merchants, but the question remains whether this sort of institutional form would also apply to Danish conditions. With the picture sketched here of the development of trade in prehistoric Denmark, it seems doubtful whether the origin of the Danish guilds known from a later period can be traced further back in time than the close of the Viking Age.

The last population group to be touched upon is that of slaves (thralls). According to the written sources, slavery probably existed in Denmark from around the seventh century. As late as the thirteenth century, Denmark was a slave society in the widest sense of the phrase. But there is no way of determining how far back in time this institution extended. Apparently, a slave system can arise under such widely varying conditions that it is impossible to postulate one from any particular stage in the general socio-economic course of development. In addition, the archaeological sources up to the Viking Age offer not the slightest indication of the origin of the system or its existence.

In describing the prehistoric society as a kinship-oriented society, it ought to be added that to all appearances the kinship system was patrilinear, though with a certain tendency to bilaterality. This is evidenced both by the runic stones from the early Viking Age and by the Danish words for inheritance, as shown by Aksel E. Christensen. In the early medieval laws the tendency toward bilaterality is emphasized very clearly. The genesis of this tendency towards bilaterality cannot be determined, although it does seem to be of very ancient date. In this regard the studies quoted on page 170ff on the distribution of wealth in men's and women's graves from the second millennium BC are thought-provoking indeed. In any case, the bilateral tendencies must have augmented the opportunities for creating kinship alliances – also over large geographic areas. As it has been pointed out (K. Odner, 1973), the kinship system created ideal conditions for a rapid transference of cultural features. The homogeneity of cultural development over much of Scandinavia in the late Iron Age perhaps ought to be viewed on just this background.

About 800 AD the prehistoric era in Denmark drew to a close. The archaic chiefdom society had then set a course which during the Viking

Age and the early Middle Ages would lead to the birth of a class society on Danish territory. Some of the foundations for this development have been depicted in this work. To be sure, the gaps in the archaeological record have been sadly apparent. But the long perspective of prehistory and the knowledge which we possess today about other forms of society do make it possible to achieve something of a holistic view. Through this

Figure 93 King Gorm's runic stone, here a painted copy photographed in the garden of the National Museum. With its runic inscription this stone symbolizes the formation of the Danish state and the close of Danish prehistory.

we have been able to follow the development of the ancient Danish society up to the point at which the kinship society was slowly losing the basis of its existence due to new relationships of dependency and exploitation. This change was far from complete at the beginning of the Viking Age. Several hundred years were to pass before socio-economic conditions created the ecclesiastical and royal hierarchy which marked the mature state formation and with it the rise of the class society.

In this period the term 'Denmark' first appears in the written sources. Around 890 King Alfred the Great of England had made an Anglo-Saxon translation of Orosius' *History of the World*. To this work he added a geographic description of northern Europe, including two travel accounts: one by the Norwegian Ottar (Othere), one by the Englishman Wulfstan. The former had travelled from the North Cape to the Schlei by the present-day Danish–German border; the latter had journeyed along the southern coast of the Baltic.

The work of Ottar relates that when he sailed from Sciringesheal (Skiringsal in Vestfold, Norway) he had Denemearc on the port side. Wulfstan writes that when he sailed eastwards in the Baltic he had Weonodland (Venderland) on the starboard side, and on the port side he had Langaland, Læland, Falster and Sconeg (Scania): 'All this land belongs to Dene mearcan'.

Less than one century later, we find the name Denmark on two Danish runic stones, namely the stones which King Gorm and King Harald Bluetooth erected in Jelling, Jutland (Figure 93). One of the stones is inscribed, 'King Gorm made this memorial to his wife Thyra, amender (*or* glory *or* adornment) of Denmark'. On the other stone is written, 'King Harald had this memorial made in memory of Gorm his father and Thyra his mother, that Harald who won for himself Denmark and Norway and made the Danes Christian'. The two inscriptions confirm one another – and they relate with all clarity that the throne of Denmark was now hereditary, that Christianity had become a powerful factor, and that the last step had been taken out of prehistory and towards the early feudal state.

19

Finds and interpretations

The archaeological record which elucidates the last major epoch of Danish prehistory, the Iron Age, consists first of all of grave finds and settlement finds. The latter also include a great many traces of prehistoric field systems. Aside from these finds, there are many others which are, however, difficult to classify systematically. For example, the group of finds from wetlands, primarily bogs and meadowlands, is very extensive. The interpretation of these finds is often problematic but their source value lies in the indications they give us of a wide spectrum of civil and military activities in prehistoric society: religious practices, transportation, army organization, and so on. A final group comprises valuable objects often made of gold or silver, the so-called hoards, a source group which is particularly significant in the Late Iron Age.

Settlements from the Iron Age are known in great number, ranging from finds of a few refuse pits to entire villages covering many hectares. The majority of these finds date from the Early Iron Age. From the Late Iron Age, after approximately 400 AD, only few settlement finds are known, a fact which has not yet been satisfactorily explained.

The study of Iron Age settlements has in recent years grown rapidly. This is mainly due to new excavation methods – the uncovering of large surfaces by machines – which have opened new perspectives in the study of settlement finds. Whereas older excavation methods allowed only limited parts of the settlement area to be uncovered, it is today possible to uncover far larger areas and thereby gain an impression of the settlement structure as a whole. It is obvious that mechanical uncovery is possible only in cases where later ploughing has destroyed all traces of floors, hearths, remains of burnt buildings, etc. The large uncovered surfaces normally reveal only traces of holes from posts, hearths and refuse pits in the otherwise undisturbed subsoil. The original surface layer from prehistory will in most cases be completely ploughed away. Examples of such extensive excavations of whole villages from the Iron Age are Grøntoft and Hodde from the centuries before Christ, and Vorbasse, also in Jutland, from the fourth and fifth centuries AD.

One major problem in the study of Iron Age settlements is the uneven distribution of the finds. Almost all the finds come from Jutland and many are in fact from parts of the country which must have been marginal areas during the Iron Age. Thus our impression of the Iron Age settlement pattern on the heavy soils in the eastern areas of Denmark is based upon a very flimsy foundation. However there are indications that the development of house types in eastern Denmark by and large followed the same lines as in the western part. The house type of the Late Bronze Age, the three-aisled longhouse, has now been identified on both Funen and Zealand. The further development of this house type, the longhouse of the Early Iron Age, is also known on *Funen* (Sarup, N.H. Andersen unpublished), *Lolland* (Naglesti, K.H. Snedker, 1959) and *Bornholm* (Dalshøj, O. Klindt-Jensen, 1957). Thus there is little reason to expect major differences between eastern and western Denmark as regards house construction (see also C.J. Becker, 1980b).

As we have mentioned before, the majority of settlement finds in Jutland date from the Early Iron Age. Up till about 200 AD the number of finds is quite impressive; later, the finds become more scattered. From the early period, which lasted about 700 years, well over one hundred find localities are known, some of the most important of which are: *Borremose* (J. Brøndsted, 1960), *Ginderup* (G. Hatt, 1935; H. Kjær, 1928a), *Grønheden* (P. Friis and P. Lysdahl Jensen, 1966), *Grøntoft* (C.J. Becker, 1965, 1968a, b and c, 1971b), *Gørding* (H. Andersen, 1951), *Hodde* (S. Hvass, 1973, 1975, 1976, 1977b), *Holmsland* (G. Hatt, 1953), *Hurup* (A.K. Rasmussen, 1968), *Kjærsing* (N. Thomsen, 1953), *Mariesminde* (G. Hatt, 1960), *Myrthue* (N. Thomsen, 1964), *Nørre Fjand* (G. Hatt, 1960), *Over-bygård* (J. Lund, 1976a and b), *Sjælborg* (N. Thomsen, 1959), *Skærbæk* and *Østerbølle* (G. Hatt, 1938). A locational analysis of the numerous settlement mounds in Thy was published by S. Jensen (1976a).

In connection with many Early Iron Age settlements, there are also the so-called Celtic fields, a source group which in 1949 was treated as a whole by Gudmund Hatt (see also M. Müller-Wille, 1965; J.A. Brongers, 1976; R. Bradley, 1978). A number of new observations made since Hatt's studies have also been published by V. Nielsen (1970a and b) and C.J. Becker (1971). Of special importance are the observations made by the latter of the relationship between the Celtic fields and mobile settlements.

Only a few of the Late Iron Age settlements will be named. One of the most interesting of the early settlements is the large village at *Vorbasse* (S. Hvass, 1977a, 1978, 1980). From southern Jutland there are also finds from *Esbjerg* (H.C. Vorting, 1973), *Oksbøl* (G. Hatt, 1958), *Dankirke* (E. Thorvildsen, 1972) and *Drengsted* (O. Voss, 1976). All of these have only been partially excavated. See also S. Jensen (1980).

The production of iron at the Iron Age settlements has not yet been studied comprehensively. Various technological aspects have been treated by O. Voss (1962, 1971), who suggests that a local iron production began relatively late in Denmark, namely in the period around the birth of Christ (see also M. Strömberg, 1981). This conclusion seems to be contradicted by settlement finds with traces of iron production from as early as the fifth or fourth centuries BC (J.A. Jacobsen, 1979). For iron production at the settlements of south-west Jutland and the rise of secondary occupations, see S. Jensen (1980).

To date, all the important settlements from the last few centuries preceding the Viking Age are available only in the form of preliminary reports. This holds true of *Bejsebakken* (M. Ørsnes, 1974), *Lindholm høje* (T. Ramskou, 1976) and *Aggersborg* (C.G. Schultz, 1949). In *Ribe* (M. Bencard, 1973, 1974) the investigations have not yet been completed. A comprehensive report on many years of excavation in *Hedeby* was published in 1972 by H. Jankuhn.

Grave finds from the first five centuries of the period, the Pre-Roman Iron Age, are to a fairly large degree available in print. The finds from southern and central Jutland were published by C.J. Becker in 1961; those from Funen were published by E. Albrectsen in 1954 with supplements in 1973. The finds from northern Jutland and the strikingly few finds east of the Storebaelt, however, have not yet been discussed as a whole in any publication. Important supplements to this find group include works of C.J. Becker (1957b, 1962), O. Klindt-Jensen (1950, 1957), and E. Jørgensen (1968). The latter treats the important group of weapon graves from the last century BC. See also J.L. Nielsen (1975).

From the four centuries of the Roman Iron Age there are a great number of finds distributed in both eastern and western Denmark. Yet this abundant source material has been little studied. Johannes Brøndsted's major work on Danish prehistory offers a general outline which can give some impression of the wealth of material, but there are very few systematic, topographical publications. First and foremost there is E. Albrectsen's publication of all the finds from Funen (1956, 1968, 1971) – including the noteworthy site *Møllegårdsmarken* with its 2000 and more graves. A catalogue of the abundant material from Århus county was commenced in 1954 (H. Norling-Christensen) but never completed. A catalogue of the grave finds from the Early Roman Iron Age on Zealand has been published by D. Liversage (1980) while the finds from the Late Roman Iron Age in the same area have been published by L. Hedager (1980). From Bornholm there are significant but rather out-dated surveys by E. Vedel (1886, 1897) from the close of the last century; see also K.A. Larsen's general outline from 1949.

Thus an impression of the find material of the period must be pieced together from treatises large and small, and written from widely differing selective viewpoints. The most thoroughly studied group is that of the graves containing imported goods, treated by H.-J. Eggers in 1951. A number of popular works which convey a general impression of the topographically widely varying grave forms include the following. For northern Jutland there are two important works, P. Friis (1963) and P.V. Glob (1937). Both of these discuss the grave forms of the region, which probably reveal a rather pronounced social stratification. From central Jutland, there are studies of the numerous so-called pottery graves in Århus and Randers counties (C. Neergaard, 1928). Unfortunately this significant material is found only in preliminary excavation reports. From south Jutland there is a detailed publication of the rich double grave from *Dollerup* (O. Voss and M. Ørsnes-Christensen, 1948), together with a complete catalogue of the cemetery *Over Jersdal* (F. Tischler, 1955); see also works by H. Neumann (1953) and E. Lomborg (1964).

The material from Zealand and the surrounding islands is also relatively little published. Here, emphasis has been placed upon the richly equipped inhumation graves whose contents provide an idea of the pronounced social stratification which existed in the Roman Iron Age. This holds true, for example, of *Borritshoved* (H. Norling-Christensen, 1952), *Himlingøje* (H. Norling-Christensen, 1951; U. L. Hansen, 1978), *Hoby* (K. Friis Johansen, 1923), *Juellinge* (S. Müller, 1911), *Nordrup* (H. Petersen, 1890), *Læbrogård, Kildemarksvej* and *Skyttemarksvej* in Næstved as well as *Nesteløgård* (H.C. Broholm, 1954), *Udby* (M.B. Mackeprang, 1944), *Uggerløse* (H. Thrane, 1967) and *Harpelev* (U.L. Hansen, 1976).

The grave finds from the last period of the Iron Age, the Germanic Iron Age, are strikingly few in number. The reason for the meagreness of this source group cannot be determined. However, the first centuries of the period are represented by a fairly large material; see for example publications by H. Norling-Christensen (1956) and E. Albrectsen (1973). This odd find situation is particularly evident in the final two centuries of the period, when rather more than half of the known finds come from the small island of Bornholm. But the few grave finds known from elsewhere in Denmark contain rich equipment which bears witness to an advanced social stratification (M. Ørsnes, 1956b; C.J. Becker, 1953, 1955). A catalogue of all the finds containing metal was published by M. Ørsnes in 1966.

Bog finds from the Iron Age constitute a very extensive find group which includes both the so-called sacrificial-weapon finds and a number of deposits of a more civil nature. The group of sacrificial-weapon finds presents a number of special problems. The majority of these finds were excavated in the nineteenth century and published with admirable rapidity. However, these early excavations employed methods which in certain respects hinder modern interpretation of the finds. Two large excavations in recent times, *Ejsbøl* near Haderslev and *Illerup* near Skanderborg, both in eastern Jutland, have since augmented the material. However, it has become apparent that not all of the finds can be interpreted on the basis of the same model. Both military and civil sacrificial rites, often repeated over a considerable length of time, have been identified at every single site. In the *Illerup* river valley (H. Andersen, 1956; J. Ilkjær, 1973, 1975b, 1977) there seem to have been three sacrifices of equipment from a conquered army, two of which took place about 200 AD, the third about 400 AD. In *Ejsbøl* bog (M. Ørsnes, 1963, 1968) there seems to have been an impressive sacrificial deposit in the fourth century, while in *Vimose* (C. Engelhardt, 1869; J. Ilkjær, 1975a) a large deposit was apparently made in the third century. The *Nydam* find (C. Engelhardt, 1865) possibly contains two or three major sacrificial deposits made in the fourth or fifth centuries. *Kragehul* (C. Engelhardt, 1867) is a single deposit from the beginning of the fifth century, while the *Thorsbjerg* find (C. Engelhardt, 1863; K. Raddatz, 1957) is of a more complex character. Here the deposits can be traced continuously from about the birth of Christ up to the fifth century. This find also contains a large number of civilian objects and ought perhaps be interpreted as sacrificial acts repeatedly carried out in a sacred area over a very long period. Yet it must be emphasized that all the other bog finds also have quite a wide chronological distribution.

The *Hjortspring* find (G. Rosenberg, 1937) is unique. To be sure it is the result of one single sacrificial act, but chronologically it dates from about the third or second centuries BC – that is, far earlier than most other weapon sacrifices.

Regarding the civil finds, comprising a very heterogeneous group mainly of pottery, the majority of the finds date from the period from c. 100 BC to 400 AD (C.J. Becker, 1968b, 1971a). Moreover two other important find groups of another type can be distinguished, namely one consisting of wheels and other wagon parts, yokes and whole or fragmented parts of ploughs (P.V. Glob, 1951a; G. Kunwald, 1970), and another consisting of human skeletal parts and so-called bog corpses (P.V. Glob, 1965).

This remarkable group of finds derives mainly from raised bogs in northern and eastern Denmark. In all, more than 160 finds are known (A. Dieck, 1965); however, few of these are preserved. The best-known finds are the bog corpses from *Tollund* (Figure 94), *Elling*, *Grauballe* and *Borremose* (C. Fischer, 1979). Newer radiocarbon datings seem to show that the bog corpses date primarily from the period from *c.* 750 BC to 100 AD, the closing phase of the Bronze Age and the Pre-Roman Iron Age. The find group has formed the basis for important studies of Iron Age

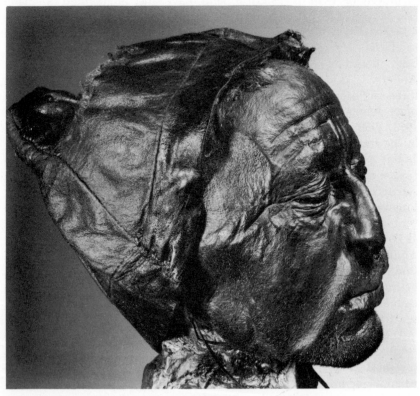

Figure 94 The Tollund Man, a bog corpse found near Silkeborg, central Jutland. The corpse has been radiocarbon-dated to 220 AD. (calibrated) i.e. the Roman Iron Age.

diet (H. Helbæk, 1958) including carbon-13 analyses which show that marine food played only a slight role in the diet (H. Tauber, 1979).

The finds from the wetlands include the roads, which have been particularly well studied on Zealand (H. Nielsen and V. Hansen, 1977). Traces have been found of an extensive and well-maintained road network, which reached its maximum on east Zealand in the late Roman Iron Age.

One last group of finds is that of the hoards, a term covering the group of deposits of valuables, especially of gold, which are known from the fifth and sixth centuries in Denmark. The majority of these finds were published in catalogue form by H. Geisslinger in 1967. A more limited topographical survey exists for the finds from Funen (E. Albrectsen, 1960). Within the hoards the so-called bracteates constitute a significant role. The bracteates were published as a whole by M.B. Mackeprang in 1952. Important analyses of selected hoards have been made by O. Voss (1954) and E. Munksgaard (1953, 1955).

In Danish archaeology the time span, c. 500 BC to 800 AD, is divided into three periods: the Pre-Roman Iron Age (500 BC to 0), the Roman Iron Age (0–400 AD) and the Germanic Iron Age (400–800 AD). In the other Scandinavian countries the term Germanic Iron Age is not used. In Norway and Sweden the period from c. 400–550 is often called the Migration Period, while the span of time c. 550–800 is called in Norway the Merovingian Period and in Sweden the Vendel Period or the late Migration Period. The historical development of the archaeological systems of chronology has been outlined by Bo Gräslund (1974b).

The archaeological datings of the finds from the Pre-Roman Iron Age are in Denmark based upon the three phases into which this age was divided by C.J. Becker in 1961. The basis for this division was primarily a typological classification of the pottery.

For the Roman Iron Age a similar chronological system is still lacking. In 1874 Sophus Müller divided the period into an early and late phase, later termed by Oscar Montelius periods IV and V. From 1897 more detailed datings became possible on the basis of Oscar Almgren's classification of the so-called fibulae. A chronological analysis of the imported Roman objects in Germania Libera, including Denmark, was published in 1951 (H.-J. Eggers). Together with Oscar Almgren's fibula typology, this latter analysis still forms the backbone of the chronological systems. According to the chronology of imports, the Early Roman Iron Age can be divided into phases B 1 and B 2, while the Late Roman Iron Age can be divided into phases C 1, C 2 and C 3 (see also E. Albrectsen, 1968, 1971).

The borderline up to the following period, the early Germanic Iron

Age, has been discussed a good deal – see for example works by H. Norling-Christensen (1949, 1956), O. Voss (1954), U.L. Hansen (1969) and S. Jensen (1978, 1979). The subsequent centuries are divided on the basis of a number of stylistic criteria. The transition between the early and the late Germanic Iron Age is dated to about 550 AD, and from this period till the beginning of the Viking Age three stylistic phases are distinguished: phase 1, c. 550–650; phase 2, c. 650–725; and phase 3, c. 735–800 AD (M. Ørsnes, 1966).

The datings of the Iron Age finds is thus based upon an extremely diversified basis depending, of course, on the variations of the archaeological record within the individual periods.

Very few general outlines have been published of the cultural –historical development through the thirteen centuries of the Iron Age up to the Viking Age. One basic work is volume III (Iron Age) of Johannes Brøndsted's *Danmarks oldtid*, published both in a Danish and a German revised edition in 1960. Later, more popular books (J. Brøndsted, 1977; L. Hvass, 1980) have to a certain extent added new aspects to the picture as a whole.

An up-to-date summary in English of the natural history of Denmark till the Viking Age was published by J. Iversen in 1973. In Sweden, attempts have been made to incorporate observations about vegetational history, and in particular man's influence on the ecosystem, in a more general scheme comprising all of southern Scandinavia (B.E. Berglund, 1969). Yet many problems remain unsolved, especially certain stagnation phenomena observed about the middle of the first millennium AD (see for example E. Nylén, 1962), which have been linked by some scholars to the Justinian bubonic plague (B. Gräslund, 1973). In much archaeological literature, however, the main interest has been focused upon the climatic change at the beginning of the Iron Age; see for example works by G. Sörbom (1966) and T. Bergeron (1956). In 1961, the Danish finds were compared with the evidence of natural history known to date (C.J. Becker, 1961). It was claimed that older theories of crop failure and famine in the first part of the Iron Age were not confirmed by the archaeological record. This viewpoint has since been further strengthened, for example, by modification of R. Sernander's (1910) dramatic theory of climatic deterioration. Thus, as mentioned above, investigations of Danish raised bogs show that over the last 5500 years a series of cyclical climatic variations can be observed (B. Aaby, 1974) whose rhythm correlates very little with changes in the subsistence and settlement patterns of the agrarian societies.

There have been only few studies made of the settlement form of the agrarian societies, and especially of their choice of arable land in the period from 500 BC to 800 AD. T. Mathiassen's major landscape studies from 1948–59, which for the Iron Age are quite insufficient, were up to the 1960s (along with E. Albrectsen's investigations of the finds from Funen) the only systematic attempts. In 1970 and 1974 E. Albrectsen presented a summary of his views on the development of settlement on Funen, with special regard to the relationship between settlement and the earliest place-name types, which are thought to date back to the early Iron Age. A similar evaluation was attempted in 1969 by A.E. Christensen for Denmark as a whole. The basis for the comparisons was, among other things, H.V. Clausen's maps of the oldest place-name types from 1916.

All older research on the subject was strongly influenced by the theory of a systematic regulation of settlement at some unspecified time in the Late Iron Age. This theory originated in a history of Denmark written by Erik Arup in 1925 and has since appeared intermittently in archaeological literature. One example is G. Hatt's work of 1937, where the difference between the village types of the Early Iron Age and the Middle Ages was explained as a result of a state initiative about the middle of the first millennium AD. This theory has also played a large role in the works of A.E. Christensen (1969) and E. Albrectsen (1974).

For a new evaluation of the problems linked to the development of agrarian settlement, the evidence of the so-called mobile village has had great significance. In Denmark this phenomenon was discovered for the first time in connection with the extensive excavations made in Grøntoft, in west Jutland (C.J. Becker, 1965, 1968a, 1971b, 1976, 1980b), at the same time as similar observations were made south of the border, in Germany (R. Schindler, 1957).

On the basis of this and other new observations, good progress has been made in the course of the 1970s, both by the ambitious excavations at Hodde and Vorbasse (S. Hvass, 1973, 1975, 1976, 1977a and b, 1978, 1980) and by a major research project carried out on Funen (T.G. Jeppesen, 1978, 1981; E.P. Christensen, 1979). The problem has also been studied in other regions of Denmark, sometimes in connection with place-name studies (see for example H. Nielsen, 1978, 1979) and in connection with the more permanent settlement form in northern Jutland (S. Jensen, 1976a).

In summary, Danish archaeologists have now abandoned the theory that a 'regulated' village arose sometime during the Late Iron Age. Instead, interest is now focused on the limited territories within which the villages seem to have been moved periodically throughout the Iron Age. From c. 1000–1200 AD a new settlement pattern seems to have arisen as a result of the introduction of the three-field system (E.P.

Christensen, 1979). Yet some of the elements of economic co-operation known from the village societies in historic times must already have existed in the village societies of the Early Iron Age.

In this connection the question of the subsistence form and productivity of the agrarian societies is of great importance. Calculations of the average yield in an Early Iron Age household have been made by W. Abel (1967) and in several areas there are helpful analyses of the quantity and type of animal as well as plant foods (see works of C.F.W. Higham, 1968; H. Helbæk, 1958). To aid understanding of the technology of the agrarian society there is also a rather comprehensive material (P.V. Glob, 1951a; A. Steensberg, 1943, 1973, 1974; M. Müller-Wille, 1965, 1977; H.O. Hansen, 1969). But in general our knowledge covers only the village society of the Early Iron Age. Whatever technological innovations lay behind, for example, the large farm complexes which came into use at various places in southern Scandinavia at the end of the Early Iron Age (B. Myhre, 1975), we have little knowledge of them. The scarcity of settlement finds has so far prevented more wide-reaching conclusions.

The problems concerned with the exchange of goods in agrarian societies have in the present work been formulated on the basis of viewpoints deriving from economic anthropology, especially from the works of K. Polanyi (1957, 1963, 1968), G. Dalton (1961, 1965, 1967, 1969), M. Nash, (1966), M.D. Sahlins (1958, 1963, 1965, 1968, 1974), and H.K. Schneider (1974). Scandinavian archaeologists have until now refrained from allowing terms from economic anthropology to enter into archaeological syntheses. Yet there are exceptions, such as the Norwegian Knut Odner's work of 1973 (compare his 1974 work), in which the cultural development in western Norway in the Migration Period has been explained on the basis of such aspects as redistribution and reciprocal economic patterns. In later years, however, there has been increasing interest in the theories of Karl Polanyi relating to the nature of early trading places (K. Polanyi, 1978). One work (K. Lunden, 1972) provides a deeper analysis of the possibilities of employing the concepts of economic anthropology in the study of the Viking Age and the early Middle Ages. A brief introduction to the theories of K. Polanyi in particular has been published by C.-A. Moberg and U. Olsson (1973).

Of the extensive literature on the exchange of goods in the Early Iron Age, mention will be made only of works of H.-J. Eggers (1951) and G. Ekholm (1956, 1958). For more restricted areas in connection with a postulated administered trade, see works such as those of U.E. Hagberg (1967) and W. Slomann (1959, 1968). A number of important recent studies, U.L. Hansen (1976, 1978b, 1980) and L. Hedager (1978a, b and c, 1980) have shed light upon the vigorous socio-economic development in eastern Denmark in the Late Roman Iron Age. L. Hedager's studies deal with the theoretical framework established by scholars such as J. Friedman and M.J. Rowlands (1978), a framework of decisive importance for the understanding of the rise of the first state-like elements in Denmark from around 200 AD. There is an abundance of literature on later trade activity, including works by C.J. Becker (1953, 1955) H. Jankuhn (1953), J. Werner (1961) and D. Ellmers (1972). These latter studies discuss various aspects of the exchange of goods from the middle of the first millennium AD.

In the attempt to describe the social integration level in the final phase of Danish prehistory, the Iron Age, reference has been made several times to evolutionistic social anthropology, including the works of Morton H. Fried (1960), Marshall D. Sahlins (1968) and Elman R. Service (1971, 1975). On the basis of these scholars' theories of social development, Iron Age society is described as having consisted of chiefdoms, that is kinship-oriented societies, which were non-egalitarian in their social organization and which in time absorbed ever more state-like elements. Chiefdoms of this character gradually seem to have developed ever more numerous positions of authority and a growing degree of centralized leadership. These societies were typified by unequal access to control of goods and production. Social differences based primarily upon rank existed, but there were no clear-cut socio-economic or political classes.

The presumed culmination of this process was the formation of a true state, the class society. This differed from even the highly developed chiefdoms in that it was integrated by means of institutional forms which employed the legalized use of power. A state constitutes itself legally by explicitly declaring in what way and under what circumstances it may employ power, and at the same time it forbids others to employ power by legal interference in conflicts between individuals and groups in society.

In sum, the course of development through the final millennium of Danish prehistory saw the transition from an archaic chiefdom society to a true state formation. At the beginning of the Viking Age in Denmark, this transition was still not complete. The conditions necessary for elucidating the details of this development in its various stages do not yet exist in the archaeological record. This is due not only to a source material often full of gaps but also to the fact that essential analyses of the Iron Age finds remain to be made. In recent years sporadic attempts have been made in north European archaeology to develop such analytical forms, for example, in the works of M. Gebühr (1974), R.

Köhler (1975) and W. Schlüter (1970). These works indicate some of the more fruitful directions which will, hopefully, be taken in Danish archaeological research in the future.

Bibliography

The following bibliography includes all the works referred to in the text. A good part of the literature has been published in Danish with an English or German summary. This holds true of all articles from the leading Danish journals such as *Årbøger for nordisk oldkyndighed og historie*, *Kuml* and *Antikvariske Studier* as well as the major series of monographs such as *Nordiske Fortidsminder, Nationalmuseets Skrifter* and *Jysk arkæologisk selskabs skrifter*. The joint Scandinavian journal *Acta Archaeologica* publishes its articles exclusively in English, German or French. The magazine *Skalk* is a popular little newsletter, written in Danish and issued six times annually, which presents brief reports on the most recent finds and excavations. A complete bibliography of Scandinavian literature on prehistory and the Middle Ages, *Nordic Archaeological Abstracts (NAA)* has been published since 1976 with one annual issue.

Aaby, B. (1974) 'Cykliske klimavariationer i de sidste 7500 år påvist ved undersøgelser af højmoser og marine transgressioner,' *Danmarks geologiske undersøgelser, Årbog 1974*, 91–107.

Aaris-Sørensen, K. (1980a) 'Depauperation of the Mammalian Fauna of the Island of Zealand during the Atlantic Period,' *Vidensk. Medd. dansk naturhist. Foren.*, 142, 131–8.

Aaris-Sørensen, K. (1980b) 'Atlantic Fish, Reptile, and Bird Remains from the Mesolithic Settlement at Vedbæk, North Zealand,' *Vidensk. Medd. dansk naturhist. Foren.*, 142, 139–49.

Aaris-Sørensen, K. (1980c) 'The Subfossil Wolf, Canis lupus L., in Denmark,' *Vidensk. Medd. dansk naturhist. Foren.*, 142, 131–8.

Abel, W. (1967) 'Geschichte der deutschen Landwirtschaft vom frühen

Mittelalter bis zum 19. Jahrhundert,' *Deutsche Agrargeschichte*, ii, Stuttgart.

Acsádi, G. and Nemeskéri, J. (1970) *History of Human Life Span and Mortality*, Budapest.

Albrectsen, E. (1946) 'Fyns bebyggelse i den ældre jernalder,' *Årbøger for nordisk oldkyndighed og historie*, 1–72.

Albrectsen, E. (1951a) 'Fyns bebyggelse i oldtiden,' *Fynske årbøger*.

Albrectsen, E. (1951b) 'Ein Gräberfeld der jüngeren Eisenzeit auf Fünen,' *Acta Archaeologica*, xxi, 234–53.

Albrectsen, E. (1954) *Fynske jernaldergrave*, i, Odense.

Albrectsen, E. (1956) *Fynske jernaldergrave*, ii, Odense.

Albrectsen, E. (1960) 'Fynske guldfund,' *Fynske Studier*, iii, Odense.

Albrectsen, E. (1968) *Fynske jernaldergrave*, iii, Odense.

Albrectsen, E. (1970) 'Den ældre jernalders bebyggelse på Fyn,' *Kuml*, 123–44.

Albrectsen, E. (1971) *Fynske jernaldergrave*, iv, Odense.

Albrectsen, E. (1973) *Fynske jernaldergrave*, v, Odense.

Albrectsen, E. (1974) 'Fyn i oldtiden,' *Odense University Studies in History and Social Science*, xx.

Albrethsen, S.E. (1976) 'De levede og døde ... for 7000 år siden,' *Nationalmuseets arbejdsmark*, 5–23.

Albrethsen, S.E. and Street-Jensen, J. (1964) 'En højgruppe i Vojens,' *Årbøger for nordiske oldkyndighed og historie*, 1–31.

Albrethsen, S.E. *et al.* (1976) 'Excavation of a Mesolithic Cemetery at Vedbæk, Denmark,' *Acta Archaeologica*, xlvii, 1–28.

Almgren, O. (1897) *Studien über nordeuropäische Fibelformen*. Stockholm.

Althin, C.A. (1954) 'The Chronology of the Stone Age Settlement in Scania, Sweden: The Mesolithic Settlement,' *Acta Archaeologica Lundensia*, i.

Ammermann, A.J. and Cavalli-Sforza, L.L. (1973) 'A Population Model for the Diffusion of Early Farming in Europe,' in Renfrew, C. (ed.) *The Explanation of Culture Change: Models in Prehistory*, London.

Andersen, A. (1966) 'Geologi og arkæologi i Draved mose,' *Meddelelser fra Dansk Geologisk Forening*, xvi, 255–8.

Andersen, H. (1951) 'Et landsbyhus på Gørding hede,' *Kuml*, 40–64.

Andersen, H. (1952) 'Fra tomten af en sløjfet høj,' *Kuml*, 144–86.

Andersen, H. (1956) 'Afsked med ådalen,' *Kuml*, 7–23.

Andersen, H. Hellmuth (1960) 'Køkkenmøddingen ved Mejlgård,' *Kuml*, 25–35.

Andersen, H. Hellmuth (1976) 'Danevirke,' *Jysk arkæologisk selskabs skrifter*, xiii.

Andersen, K. (1951) 'Hytter fra Maglemosetid: Danmarks ældste boliger,' *Nationalmuseeets arbejdsmark*, 69–76.

Andersen, K. (1960) 'Verupbopladsen: En Magelmoseboplads i Åmosen,' *Årbøger for nordisk oldkyndighed og historie*, 118–51.

Andersen, Niels H. (1974) 'Sarup: Et befæstet neolitisk anlæg på Sydvestfyn,' *Kuml*, 109–20.

Andersen, Niels H. (1975) 'Die neolitische Befestigungsanlage in Sarup auf Fünen,' *Archäologisches Korrespondenzblatt*, v, 11–14.

Andersen, Niels H. (1976) 'Keramikgruber fra to bebyggelsesfaser,' *Kuml*, 11–46.

Andersen, Niels H. (1980) 'Sarup: Befæstede neolitiske anlæg og deres baggrund,' *Kuml*, 63–103.

Andersen, Steen Wulff (1981) 'Huset under højen,' *Skalk*, 1981, 2.

Andersen, Søren H. and C. Malmros (1965) 'Norslund: En kystboplads fra ældre stenalder,' *Kuml*, 35–114.

Andersen, Søren H. (1969a) 'Flintægdolken fra Flynderhage,' *Kuml*, 91–5.

Andersen, Søren H. (1969b) 'Brovst: En kystboplads fra ældre stenalder,' *Kuml*, 67–90.

Andersen, Søren H. (1970) 'Senglaciale bopladser ved Bro,' *Fynske Minder*, 85–100.

Andersen, Søren H. (1971) 'Gudenåkulturen,' *Holstebro museums årsskrift*, 14–32.

Andersen, Søren H. (1972) 'Bro: En senglacial boplads på Fyn,' *Kuml*, 7–60.

Andersen, Søren H. (1973) 'Overgangen fra ældre til yngre stenalder i Sydskandinavien set fra en mesolitisk synsvinkel,' *Tromsø museums skrifter*, xiv.

Andersen, Søren H. (1974) 'Ringkloster, en jysk indlandsplads med Ertebøllekultur,' *Kuml*, 11–108.

Andersen, Søren H. (1976) 'Norsminde Fjord undersøgelsen,' *Skrifter fra Institut for historie og samfundsvidenskab, Odense Universitet*, xvii, 18–61.

Andersen, Søren H. (1978) 'Aggersund: En Ertebølleplads ved Limfjorden,' *Kuml*, 7–75.

Andersen, S. Th. (1974) 'The Eemian Freshwater Deposits at Egernsund, South Jutland and the Eemian Landscape Development in Denmark,' *Danmarks Geologiske Undersøgelse, Årbog*.

Andersen, S. Th. (1979) 'Brown Earth and Podzol: Soil Genesis Illuminated by Microfossil Analysis,' *Boreas*, viii, 59ff.

Aner, E. (1963) 'Die Stellung der Dolmen Schleswig-Holsteins in der nordischen Megalithkultur,' *Offa*, xx, 9–38.

Aner, E. and Kersten, K. (1973ff) *Die Funde der älteren Bronzezeit in Dänemark, Schleswig-Holstein und Niedersachsen*, 1 (1973), 2 (1976), 3

(1977), 4 (1978), 5 (1979). Series in progress.

Arup, E. (1925) *Danmarks Historie*, I: *Land og Folk til 1282*, Copenhagen.

Bagge, A. and Kaelas, L. (1950) *Die Funde aus Dolmen und Ganggräbern in Schonen, Schweden*, Lund.

Bailey, G.N. (1978) 'Shell Middens as Indicators of Postglacial Economies: A Territorial Perspective,' in Mellars, P. (ed.) *The Early Postglacial Settlement of Northern Europe*, London.

Bantelmann, A. (1955) *Tofting, eine vorgeschichtliche Warft an der Eidermündung*, Neumünster.

Bantelmann, A. (1975) *Die frühgeschichtliche Marschensiedlung beim Elisenhof in Eiderstedt*, Frankfurt/M.

Bath, B.H. Slicher van (1963) *The Agrarian History of Western Europe, AD 500–1850*, London.

Baudou, E. (1960) *Die regionale und chronologische Einteilung der jüngeren Bronzezeit im Nordischem Kreis*, Stockholm.

Bay-Petersen, J.L. (1978) 'Animal Exploitation in Mesolithic Denmark,' in Mellars, P. (ed.) *The Early Postglacial Settlement of Northern Europe*, 115–45, London.

Beck, Curt W. (1965) 'Infrared Spectra of Amber and the Chemical Identification of Baltic Amber,' *Archaeometry*, VIII, 96–109.

Beck, Curt W. (1970) 'Amber in Archaeology,' *Archaeology*, XXIII, 1, 7–11.

Beck, Curt W. *et al.* (1975) 'Die Herkunft der Bernsteinfunde vom Hagenauer Forst,' *Bericht der Staatlichen Denkmalpflege im Saarland*, XXII, 5–17.

Beck, Curt, W. *et al.* (1978) 'The Chemical Identification of Baltic Amber at the Celtic Oppidum Staré Hradisko in Moravia,' *Journal of Archaeological Science*, V, 343–54.

Becker, C.J. (1936) 'Enkeltgravskulturen på de danske øer,' *Årbøger for nordisk oldkyndighed og historie*, 145–231.

Becker, C.J. (1945) 'En 8000-årig stenalderboplads i Holmegårds mose,' *Nationalmuseets arbejdsmark*, 61–72.

Becker, C.J. (1947) 'Mosefundne lerkar fra yngre stenalder,' *Årbøger for nordisk oldkyndighed og historie*, 1–318

Becker, C.J. (1950a) 'Den grubekeramiske kultur i Danmark,' *Årbøger for nordisk oldkyndighed og historie*, 153–274.

Becker, C.J. (1950b) 'Die Maglemosekulter in Dänemark: Neue Funde und Ergebnisse,' *Actes de la IIIe Session, Zürich*, 180–3.

Becker, C.J. (1951) 'Late Neolithic Flint Mines at Aalborg,' *Acta Archaeologica*, XXII, 135–53.

Becker, C.J. (1953) 'Zwei Frauengräber des 7.Jahrhundert aus Nørre Sandegård, Bornholm,' *Acta Archaeologica*, XXIV, 127–55.

Becker, C.J. (1954) 'Die mittelneolitischen Kulturen in Südskandina-vien,' *Acta Archaeologica*, xxv, 49–150.

Becker, C.J. (1955) 'Smykkefundet ved Ørby,' *Nationalmuseets arbe-jdsmark*, 26–34.

Becker, C.J. (1957a) 'Den tyknakkede flintøkse,' *Årbøger for nordisk oldkyndighed og historie*, 1–27.

Becker, C.J. (1957b) 'Førromersk jernaldergrav fra Try skole i Vendsys-sel,' *Kuml*, 49–67.

Becker, C.J. (1958) '4000 årig flintminedrift i Thy,' *Nationalmuseets arbejdsmark*, 77–82.

Becker, C.J. (1959) 'Stendyngegrave fra mellemneolitisk tid,' *Årbøger for nordisk oldkyndighed og historie*, 1–90.

Becker, C.J. (1961) *Førromersk jernalder i Syd- og Midtjylland*, Copenhagen.

Becker, C.J. (1962) 'Das eisenzeitliche Gräberfeld Nörre Sandegård auf Bornholm,' *Germania*, xl, 317–30.

Becker, C.J. (1964a) 'Sen-neolitikum i Norden: Aktuelle problemer,' *Tor*, 121–34.

Becker, C.J. (1964b) 'Neue Hortfunde aus Dänemark mit frühbronzezeit-lichen Lanzenspitzen,' *Acta Archaeologica*, xxxv, 115–52.

Becker, C.J. (1965) 'Ein früheisenzeitliches Dorf bei Gröntoft, Westjüt-land: Vorbericht über die Ausgrabungen 1961–63,' *Acta Archaeologi-ca*, xxxvi, 209–22.

Becker, C.J. (1967a) 'The Interrelationship of the TRB and the Battle-axe Culture in Denmark,' *Palaeohistoria*, xii, 33–40.

Becker, C.J. (1967b) 'Gådefulde jyske stenaldergrave,' *Nationalmuseets arbejdsmark*, 19–30.

Becker, C.J. (1968a) 'Zum Problem der ältesten eisenzeitlichen Dörfer in Jütland,' *Studien zur europäischen Vor- und Frühgeschichte*, 74–83.

Becker, C.J. (1968b) 'Zur Frage der eisenzeitlichen Moorgefässe in Dänemark,' *Vorgeschichtliche Heiligtümer und Opferplätze in Mittel- und Nordeuropa: Bericht über ein Symposium in Reinhausen bei Göttingen*, 119–66.

Becker, C.J. (1968c) 'Haus und Siedlung der jüngsten Bronzezeit und älteren Eisenzeit in Jütland,' *Die Kunde*, xix, 152–4.

Becker, C.J. (1968d) 'Das zweite früheisenzeitliche Dorf bei Grøntoft, Westjütland. 2. Vorbericht: Die Ausgrabungen 1964–66,' *Acta Archaeologica* xxxix, 235–55.

Becker, C.J. (1968e) 'Bronzealderhuse i Vestjylland,' *Nationalmuseets arbejdsmark*, 79–88.

Becker, C.J. (1969) 'Grav eller tempel?,' *Nationalmuseets arbejdsmark*, 17–28.

Becker, C.J. (1971a) '"Mosepotter" fra Danmarks jernalder: Problemer omkring mosefundne lerkar og deres datering,' *Årbøger for nordisk oldkyndighed og historie*, 5–60.

Becker, C.J. (1971b) 'Früheisenzeitliche Dörfer bei Gröntoft, Westjütland. 3. Vorbericht: Die Ausgrabungen 1967–68,' *Acta Archaeologica*, XLII, 79–110.

Becker, C.J. (1971c) 'Late Palaeolithic Finds from Denmark,' *Proceedings of the Prehistoric Society*, XXXVII, 131–9.

Becker, C.J. (1972a) 'Hal og hus i yngre bronzealder,' *Nationalmuseets arbejdsmark*, 5–16.

Becker, C.J. (1972b) 'Ein Hausgrundriss der späten Bronzezeit aus Westjütland,' *Bonner Hefte zur Vorgeschichte*, III, 13–17.

Becker, C.J. (1973) 'Studien zu neolitischen Flintbeilen,' *Acta Archaeologica*, XLIV, 125–86.

Becker, C.J. (1974) 'Jernalder-landsbyen i Jylland: Aktuelle problemer omkring dens oprindelse,' *Kuml*, 294–6.

Becker, C.J. (1975) 'Hovedlinier i Bornholms oldtidshistorie,' *Bornholmske samlinger*, 1–41.

Becker, C.J. (1976) 'Bosættelsesproblemer i bronze- og jernalder,' *Skrifter fra Institut for historie og samfundsvidenskab, Odense Universitet*, XVII, 70–83.

Becker, C.J. (1980a) 'Hvad sker der i dansk arkæologi? Grundvidenskaben i dag,' *Det kgl. danske videnskabernes selskabs pjeceserie*, Copenhagen.

Becker, C.J. (1980b) 'Bebyggelsesformer i Danmarks yngre bronzealder,' in Thrane, H. (ed.) *Bronzealderbebyggelse i Norden, Skrifter fra Historisk Institut, Odense Universitet*, XXVIII.

Behrens, H. and Schlette, F. (1969) 'Die neolitischen Becherkulturen im Gebiet der DDR und ihre europäische Beziehungen,' *Veröffentlichungen d. Landesmus. f. Vorgeschichte in Halle*, XXIV.

Behrens, H. (1973) 'Die jungsteinzeit im Mittelelbe-Saale-Gebiet,' *Veröffentlichungen d. Landesmus. f. Vorgeschichte in Halle*, XXVII.

Bekmose, J. (1978) 'Megalitgrave og megalitbygder,' *Antikvariske studier*, I, 47–64.

Bencard, M. (1973) 'Ribes vikingetid: En foreløbig redegørelse for udgravningerne 1972–73,' *Mark og Montre*, 28–48.

Bencard, M. (1974) 'Ribes ældste udvikling,' *Mark og Montre*, 20–7.

Berg, H. (1951) 'Tre langelandske megalitgrave,' *Meddelelser fra Langelands Museum*.

Berg, H. (1956) 'Langdolmen bei Pæregård,' *Acta Archaeologica*, XXVII.

Bergeron, T. (1956) 'Fimbulvinter,' *Fornvännen*, 1–18.

Berglund, B.E. (1966a) 'Late-Quaternary Vegetation in Eastern Blekinge, Southeastern Sweden: A Pollen-Analytical Study, Late Glacial

Time.' *Opera Botanica*, xii, 1.

Berglund, B.E. (1966b) 'Late-Quaternary Vegetation in Eastern Blekinge, Southeastern Sweden: A Pollen-analytical study, Post-Glacial Time,' *Opera Botanica*, xii, 2.

Berglund, B.E. (1968) 'Vegetationsudviklingen i Norden efter istiden,' *Sveriges Naturs Årsbok*, 31–53.

Berglund, B.E. (1969) 'Vegetation and Human Influence in South Scandinavia during Prehistoric Times,' *Oikos*, xii, 9–28.

Berglund, B.E. (1971a) 'Late Glacial Stratigraphy and Chronology in South Sweden in the Light of Biostratigraphic Studies on Mt. Kullen,' *GFF*, xciii, 11–45.

Berglund, B.E. (1971b) 'Litorina Transgressions in Blekinge, South Sweden,' *GFF*, xciii, 625–52.

Binford, L.R. (1962) 'Archaeology as Anthropology,' *American Antiquity*, xxviii, 217–25.

Binford, L.R. (1968a) 'Post-Pleistocene Adaptions,' in Binford, S.R. and Binford, L.R. (eds) *New Perspectives in Archaeology*, Chicago.

Binford, L.R. (1968b) 'Archaeological Perspectives,' in Binford, S.R. and Binford, L.R. (eds) *New Perspectives in Archaeology*, Chicago.

Binford, L.R. (1971) 'Mortuary Practices: Their Study and Their Potential,' in Brown, J.E. (ed.) *Approaches to the Social Dimensions of Mortuary Practices, Memoirs of the Society for American Archaeology*, xxv.

Blankholm, R.E. and Andersen, S.H. (1967) 'Stallerupholm: Et bidrag til belysning af Maglemosekulturen i Østjylland,' *Kuml*, 61–115.

Boas, N.A. (1980) 'Egehøjbopladsen fra ældste bronzealder,' in Thrane, H. (ed.) *Bronzealderbebyggelse i Norden, Skrifter fra Historisk Institut, Odense Universitet*, xxviii.

Boaz, N.T. and Hampel, J. (1978) 'Strontium Content of Fossil Enamel and Diet in Early Hominids,' *Journal of Paleontology*, lii, 4, 928–33.

Boserup, E. (1965) *The Conditions of Agricultural Growth*, London.

Boserup, E. (1972) Boserup symposium (see *Peasant Studies Newsletter: History, Politics, and Economy of Traditional Societies*, i, 2, 34–65, Pittsburg.

Boye, V. (1896) *Fund af egekister fra bronzealderen i Danmark*, Copenhagen.

Bradley, R. (1978) 'Prehistoric Field Systems in Britain and North-West Europe: A Review on Some Recent Work'. *World Archaeology*, ix, 265–80.

Broholm, H.C. (1924) 'Nye Fund fra den ældste stenalder. Holmegård og Sværdborg fundene'. *Årbøger for nordisk oldkyndighed og historie*, 1–144.

Broholm, H.C. (1943–9) *Danmarks Bronzealder*, i–iv.

Broholm, H.C. (1954) 'Fra yngre romertid i Sydsjælland'. *Nationalmuseets arbejdsmark*, 95–107.

Broholm, H.C. and Hald, M. (1939) 'Skrydstrupfundet'. *Nordiske Fortidsminder*, III, 2.

Broholm, H.C. and Rasmussen, J.P. (1931) 'Ein steinzeitlicher Hausgrund bei Strandegård'. *Acta Archaeologica*, II.

Brongers, J.A. (1976) 'Air Photography and Celtic Field Research in the Netherlands'. *Nederlandse Oudheden*, VI.

Brown, A.B. (1974) 'Bone Strontium as a Dietary Indicator in Human Skeletal Populations'. *University of Wyoming, Contributions to Geology*, XIII, 47–8.

Bruce-Mitford, R. (1972) *The Sutton Hoo Ship Burial*, London.

Brøgger, A.W. (1921) 'Ertog og Øre'. *Videnskapselskapets skrifter*, II, 3.

Brøndsted, J. (1934) 'Ein nordjütisches Steingrab aus römischer Zeit'. *Acta Archaeologica*, V, 167–75.

Brøndsted, J. (1957) *Danmarks oldtid I. Stenalderen*, Copenhagen.

Brøndsted, J. (1958) *Danmarks oldtid II. Bronzealderen*, Copenhagen.

Brøndsted, J. (1960a) *Danmarks oldtid III. Jernalderen*, Copenhagen.

Brøndsted, J. (1960b) *Nordische Vorzeit I. Steinzeit*, Neumünster.

Brøndsted, J. (1962) *Nordische Vorzeit II. Bronzezeit*, Neumünster.

Brøndsted, J. (1963) *Nordische Vorzeit III. Eisenzeit*, Neumünster.

Brøndsted, J. (1977) *Danmarks historie indtil år 600*. Politikens Danmarkshistorie, 2nd rev. edn, Copenhagen.

Brøste, K. and J.B. Jørgensen (1956) *Prehistoric Man in Denmark. A study in physical anthropology*, I-II, Copenhagen.

Burgess, C. and Miket, R. (eds) (1976) 'Settlement and Economy in the Third and Second Millennia BC'. *British Archaeological Reports*, XXXIII.

Butler, J.J. (1963) 'Bronze Age Connections across the North Sea'. *Palaeohistoria*, IX.

Caneiro, R.L. (1970) 'A Theory of the Origin of the State', *Science*, CLXIX.

Childe, V. Gordon (1935) *New Light on the Most Ancient Near East*, London.

Christensen, Aksel E. (1966) 'Mellem vikingetid og valdemarstid'. *Historisk Tidsskrift*.

Christensen, Aksel E. (1969) *Vikingetidens Danmark*, Copenhagen.

Christensen, E. Porsmose (1979) 'Bebyggelse, kulturlandskab og driftsmåder på overgangen mellem yngre jernalder og ældre middelalder,' *Skrifter fra Historisk Institut, Odense Universitet*, XXVII.

Claiborne, R. (1970) *Climate, Man, and History*, New York.

Clark, J.G.D. (1936) *The Mesolithic Settlement of Northern Europe*, Cambridge.

Clark, J.G.D. (1954) *Excavations at Starr Carr*, Cambridge.

Clark, J.D.G. (1972) 'Starr Carr: A Case Study in Bioarchaeology,' *Module*, x, 1–42.

Clark, J.G.D. (1975) *The Earlier Stone Age Settlement of Scandinavia*, Cambridge.

Clarke, David (1972) *Models in Archaeology*, London.

Clarke, David (1976) 'Mesolithic Europe: The Economic Basis,' in Sieveking, G. de G. (ed.) *Problems in Economic and Social Archaeology*, 449–81, London.

Clason, A.T. (1971) 'Die Jagd und Haustiere der mitteldeutschen Schnurkeramik,' *Jahresschrift für mittledeutsche Vorgeschichte*, LV, 105–12.

Clausen, H.V. (1916) 'Studier over Danmarks oldtidsbebyggelse,' *Årbøger for nordisk oldkyndighed og historie*, 1–226.

Coles, John M. (1976) 'Forest Farmers: Some Archaeological, Historical and Experimental Evidence Relating to the Prehistory of Europe,' *Dissertationes Archaeologicae Gandenses*, XVI, 59–66.

Cowgill, G.L. (1975) 'On Causes and Consequences of Ancient and Modern Population Changes,' *American Anthropologist*, LXXVII, 505–25.

Crumlin-Petersen, O. (1967) 'Gredstedbro-skibet,' *Mark og Montre*, 11–15.

Dalton, G. (1961) 'Economic Theory and Primitive Society,' *American Anthropologist*, LXIII, 1–25.

Dalton, G. (1965) 'Primitive Money,' *American Anthropologist*, LXVII, 44–65.

Dalton, G. (1967) 'Tribal and Peasant Economies,' *Readings in Economic Anthropology*, Garden City, N.Y.

Dalton, G. (1969) 'Theoretical Issues in Economic Anthropology,' *Current Anthropology*, x, 70–3.

Davidsen, K. (1972) 'Valbykeramik und Kugelamphorenkultur,' *Offa*, XXIX, 133ff.

Davidsen, K. (1974) ''Tragtbægerkulturens slutfase: Nye C-14 datering-en *Kuml*, 165–78.

Davidsen, K. (1975) 'Relativ kronologi i mellemneolitisk tid,' *Årbøger for nordisk oldkyndighed og historie*, 42–77.

Davidsen, K. (1978) 'The Final TRB Culture in Denmark: A Settlement Study,' *Arkæologiske Studier*, V.

Dayton, J.E. (1971) 'The Problem of Tin in the Ancient World,' *World Archaeology*, III, 49–70.

Degerbøl, M. (1933) *Danmarks pattedyr i fortiden*, Sammenligning med recente former, Copenhagen.

Degerbøl, M. and Fredskild, B. (1970) *The Urus and Neolithic Domesticated Cattle in Denmark*, Copenhagen.

Dennell, R.W. (1979) 'Prehistoric Diet and Nutrition: Some Food for Thought,' *World Archaeology*, XI, 121–35.

Dieck, A. (1965) *Die europäischen Moorleichenfunde*, Neumünster.

Donath, P. and Ullrich, H. (1971) 'Einwohnerzahlen und Siedlungsgrösse der Merowingerzeit,' *Zeitschrift für Archäologie*, V, 234–65.

Earle, T. and Ericson, J. (1977) *Exchange Systems in Prehistory*, London.

Ebbesen, K. (1975) 'Die jüngere Trichterbecherkultur auf den dänischen Inseln,' *Arkæologiske Studier*, II.

Ebbesen, K. (1978) 'Tragtbægerkultur i Nordjylland,' *Nordiske Fortidsminder*, ser. B, V.

Ebbesen, K. and Mahler, D. (1979) 'Virum: Et tidligneolitisk bopladsfund,' *Årbøger for nordisk oldkyndighed og historie*, 11–61.

Ebbesen, K. and Petersen, E. Brinch (1973) 'Fuglebæksbanken: En jættestue på Stevns,' *Årbøger for nordisk oldkyndighed og historie*, 73–106.

Eggers, H.-J. (1950) 'Lübzow, ein germanischer Fürstensitz der älteren Kaiserzeit,' *Prähistorische Zeitschrift*, XXXIV/XXXV, 58–111.

Eggers, H.-J. (1951) *Der römische Import im Freien Germanien*, Hamburg.

Eggers, H.-J. (1955) 'Zur absoluten Chronologie der römischen Kaiserzeit im Freien Germanien,' *Jahrbuch des römisch germanischen Zentralmuseums Mainz*, II.

Ehrlich, P.R. and Holdren, J.P. (1971) 'Impact of Population Growth,' *Science*, CLXXI, 1212–17.

Ekholm, G. (1956) 'Orientalische Gläser in Skandinavien während der Kaiser- und frühen Merowingerzeit,' *Acta Archaeologica*, XXVII, 35–59.

Ekholm, G. (1958) 'Westeuropäische Gläser in Skandinavien während der Kaiser- und frühen Merowingerzeit,' *Acta Archaeologica*, XXIX, 21–50.

Ekholm, K. (1972) *Power and Prestige: the Rise and Fall of the Kongo Kingdom*, Uppsala.

Ellmers, D. (1972) *Frühmittelalterliche Handelsschiffahrt in Mittel- und Nordeuropa*, Neumünster.

Ember, M. (1967) 'The Emergence of Neolocal Residence,' *Transactions of the New York Academy of Sciences*, XXX, 291ff.

Ember, C. and Ember, M. (1973) *Cultural Anthropology*, Englewood Cliffs, N.J.

Ember, M. and Ember, C. (1971) 'The Conditions Favoring Matrilocal versus Patrilocal Residence,' *American Anthropologist*, LXXIII, 571ff.

Engelhardt, C. (1863) *Thorsbjerg mosefund*, Copenhagen.

Engelhardt, C. (1865) *Nydam mosefund*, Copenhagen.

Engelhardt, C. (1867) *Kragehul mosefund*, Copenhagen.

Engelhardt, C. (1869) *Vimosefundet*, Copenhagen.

Engelhardt, C. (1970) *Nydam Fundet*, Ørsnes, M. *(ed.) Sønderjyske Mosefund*, II, reprinted, Copenhagen.

Eriksen, P. and Thorsen, S. (1980) 'Begravet langdysse,' *Skalk* 1980/2, 29.

Es, W.A. van (1967) *Wijster: A Native Village beyond the Imperial Frontier, 125–450 AD*, Groeningen.

Faber, O. (1976) 'Hus eller grav? Et anlæg fra yngre stenalder ved Vejle,' *Mark og Montre*, 5–11.

Fischer, A. (1978) På sporet af overgangen mellem palæolitikum og mesolitikum i Sydskandinavien,' *Hikuin*, IV, 27–50.

Fischer, Chr. (1975) 'Tidlig neolitiske anlæg ved Rustrup,' *Kuml*, 29–72.

Fischer, Chr. (1979) 'Moseligene fra Bjældeskovdal,' *Kuml*, 7–44.

Flannery, K.V. and F. Hole (1969) 'Origins and Ecological Effect of Early Domestication in Iran and the Near East,' in Ucko, P.J. and Dimbleby, D.W. (eds) *The Domestication and Exploitation of Plants and Animals*, London.

Fleming, A. (1972) 'The Genesis of Pastoralism in European Prehistory,' *World Archaeology*, IV.

Fleming, A. (1973) 'Models of the Development of the Wessex Culture,' in Renfrew, C. (ed.) *The Explanation of Culture Change: Models in Prehistory*, London.

Forssander, J.E. (1936) *Der ostskandinavische Norden währnd der ältesten Metallzeit Europas*, Lund.

Frankenstein, S. and Rowlands, M.J. (1978) 'The Internal Structure and Regional Context of Early Iron Age Society in South Western Germany,' *Institute of Archaeology Bulletin*, no. 15, London.

Fried, Morton H. (1960) 'On the Evolution of Social Stratification and the State,' in Diamond, S. (ed.) *Culture in History: Essays in Honor of Poul Radin*, New York.

Fried, Morton H. (1967) *The Evolution of Political Society*, New York.

Fried, Morton H. (1968) 'On the Concept of "Tribe" and "Tribal Society".' in Helm, J. (ed.) *Essays on the Problem of the Tribe*, American Ethnological Society.

Friedman, J. (1975) 'Tribes, States, and Transformations,' in Bloch M. (ed.) *Marxist Analysis and Social Anthropology: ASA Studies*, London, 161– 202.

Friedman, J. and Rowlands, M.J. (1978) 'Notes towards an Epigenetic Model of the Evolution of "Civilization",' in Friedman, J. and Rowlands M.J. (eds) *The Evolution of Social Systems*, London.

Friis, P. (1963) 'Jernaldergrave ved Gjurup med teltformede dødehuse,' *Kuml*, 42–59.

Friis, P. and Lysdahl Jensen, P. (1966) 'En jernalderhustomt med kælder på Grønhedens mark,' *Kuml*, 31–58.

Gebühr, M. (1974) 'Zur Definition älterkaiserzeitlicher Fürstengräber vom Lübzow-Typ,' *Prähistorische Zeitschrift*, XLIX, 82–128.

Geisslinger, H. (1967) 'Horte als Geschichtsquelle,' *Offa Bücher*, XIX.

Gejvall, N.-G. (1955) 'The Cremations at Vallhagar,' in *Vallhagar: A Migration Period Settlement on Gotland, Sweden*, II, 700–23.

Gejvall, N.-G. (1960) *Westerhus: Medieval Population and Church in the Light of Skeletal Remains*, Stockholm.

Gejvall, N.-G., (1968) 'Mangehøje: Ældre bronzealders gravhøje på åsen ved Kårup,' *Museet for Holbæk og omegn, årsberetning*, 15–48.

Glob, P.V. (1937) 'Neues aus Vendsyssels älterer Eisenzeit,' *Acta Archaeologica*, VIII, 186–204.

Glob, P.V. (1944) 'Studier over den jyske enkeltgravskultur,' *Årbøger for nordisk oldkyndighed og historie*, 1–282.

Glob, P.V. (1949) 'Barkær: Danmarks ældste landsby,' *Nationalmuseets arbejdsmark*, 5–16.

Glob, P.V. (1951a) *Ard og plov i Nordens oldtid*, Århus.

Glob, P.V. (1951b) 'Jyllands øde agre,' *Kuml*, 136–44.

Glob, P.V. (1965) *Mosefolket*, Copenhagen. (English edn (1969) *The Bog People: Iron-Age Man Preserved*, London.

Glob, P.V. (1967) *Danske oldtidsminder*, Copenhagen.

Glob, P.V. (1969) *Helleristninger i Danmark*, Copenhagen.

Glob, P.V. (1970) *Højfolket*, Copenhagen.

Glob, P.V. (1975) 'De dødes lange huse,' *Skalk*, 1975/6.

Godelier, M. (1977) *Perspectives in Marxist Anthropology*, Cambridge.

Granlund, E. (1932) 'De svenska högmossernas geologi,' *Sv. Geol. Unders.*, ser. C, no. 373.

Gräslund, B. (1973) 'Äring, näring, pest och salt,' *Tor*, 274–93.

Gräslund, B. (1974a) 'Befolkning-bosättning-miljö,' *Fornvännen*, 3–13.

Gräslund, B. (1974b) 'Relativ datering: Om kronologisk metod i nordisk arkeologi,' *Tor*, XVI.

Grierson, P. (1959) 'Commerce in the Dark Ages,' *Transactions of the Royal Historical Society*, 5th ser, IX.

Grierson, P. (1977) 'The Origins of Money,' *The Creighton Lecture in History, University of London*.

Groenmann-van Wateringe, W. (1979) 'Nogle aspekter af jernalderens landbrug i Holland og Nordvesttyskland,' *Skrifter fra Historisk Institut, Odense Universitet*, XXVII.

Haarnagel, W. (1961) 'Zur Grabung auf der Feddersen Wierde 1955–59,' *Germania*, 42–69.

Haarnagel, W. (1963) 'Die Ergebnisse der Grabung Feddersen Wierde im Jahre 1961,' *Germania*, 280–317.

Haarnagel, W. (1969) 'Die Ergebnisse der Grabung auf der ältereisenzeitlichen Siedlung Boomborg/Hatzum in den Jahren 1965 bis 1967,' *Neue Ausgrabungen und Forschungen in Niedersachsen*, IV.

Hachmann, R. (1957a) 'Zur Gesellschaftsordnung der Germanen in der Zeit um Christi Geburt,' *Archaeologica Geographica*, V/VI.

Hachmann, R. (1957b) 'Die frühe Bronzezeit im westlichen Ostseegebiet und ihre mittel- und südosteurapäischen Beziehungen,' *6th Beiheft zum Atlas der Urgeschichte*, Hamburg.

Hagberg, U.E. (1967) *The Archaeology of Skedemosse*, I-II, Stockholm.

Hansen, H.O. (1969) 'Experimental Ploughing with a Døstrup Ard Replica,' *Tools and Tillage*, I, 2.

Hansen, U.L. (1969) 'Kvarmløsefundet- en analyse af Söstalastilen og dens forudsætninger,' *Årbøger for nordisk oldkyndighed og historie*, 63–102.

Hansen, U.L. (1972a) 'A Mesolithic Grave from Melby in Zealand, Denmark,' *Acta Archaeologica*, XLIII, 239–49.

Hansen, U.L. (1972b) 'Mellem-neolitiske jorddgrave fra Vindinge på Sjælland,' *Årbøger for nordisk oldkyndighed og historie*, 5–70.

Hansen, U.L. (1976) 'Das Gräberfeld bei Harpelev, Seeland,' *Acta Archaeologica*, XLVII, 91–160.

Hansen, U.L. (1978a) 'Himlingøje-gravpladsens høje,' *Antikvariske Studier*, II, 47–80.

Hansen, U.L. (1978b) 'International stormagt kontra randområder: Handel i romersk og ældre germansk jernalder,' *XV Nordiske arkeologmötet, Förtryck av mötesföredrag*.

Hansen, U.L. (1980) 'Zur jüngeren römischen Kaiserzeit auf Seeland unter besonderer Berücksichtigung chronologischer Probleme der Grabbeigaben,' *Studien zur Sachsenforschung*, II, 261–73, Hildesheim.

Harner, M.J. (1970) 'Population Pressure and the Social Evolution of Agriculturalists,' *Southwestern Journal of Anthropology*, XXVI, 67–86.

Hatt, G. (1935) 'Jernalderbopladser ved Ginderup i Thy,' *Nationalmuseets arbejdsmark*, 37–51.

Hatt, G. (1937) *Landbrug i Danmarks oldtid*, Copenhagen.

Hatt, G. (1938) 'Jernalders bopladser i Himmerland,' *Årbøger for nordisk oldkyndighed og historie*, 119–266.

Hatt, G. (1949) 'Oldtidsagre,' *Videnskabernes selskab, arkæologisk kunsthistoriske skrifter*, II, 1.

Hatt, G. (1953) 'An Early Roman Iron Age Dwelling Site in Holmsland,

West Jutland,' *Acta Archaeologica*, xxiv, 1–25.

Hatt, G. (1957) 'Nørre Fjand: An Early Iron Age Village Site in West Jutland,' *Videnskabernes selskab, arkæologisk kunsthistoriske skrifter*, ii, 2.

Hatt, G. (1958) 'A Dwelling Site of Early Migration Period at Oxbøl, Southwest Jutland,' *Acta Archaeologica*, xxiv, 142–54.

Hatt, G. (1960) 'The Roman Iron Age Dwelling Site at Mariesminde, Vestervig,' *Acta Archaeologica*, xxxi, 31–85.

Hayden, B. (1972) 'Population Control among Hunter–Gatherers,' *World Archaeology*, iv, 205–21.

Hedager, L. (1978a) 'Bebyggelse, social struktur og politisk organisation i Østdanmark i ældre og yngre romertid,' *Fortid og Nutid*, xxvii, 246–58.

Hedager, L. (1978b) 'Processes towards State Formation in Early Iron Age Denmark,' *Studies in Scandinavian Prehistory and Early History*, i, 217–23.

Hedager, L. (1978c) 'A Quantitative Analysis of Roman Imports in Europe North of the Limes (0–400 AD), and the Question of Roman–Germanic Exchange,' *Studies in Scandinavian Prehistory and Early History*, i, 191–216.

Hedager, L. (1980) 'Besiedlung, soziale Struktur und politische Organization in der älteren und jüngeren römischen Kaiserzeit Ostdänemarks,' *Prähistorische Zeitschrift*, lv, 38–109.

Helbæk, H. (1951) 'Ukrudtsfrø som næringsmiddel i førromersk jernalder,' *Kuml*, 65–73.

Helbæk, H. (1954) 'Prehistoric Plants and Weeds in Denmark,' *Danmarks Geologiske Undersøgelse*, ii, 80.

Helbæk, H. (1958) 'Grauballemandens sidste måltid,' *Kuml*, 83–116.

Helbæk, H. (1970) 'Da rugen kom til Danmark,' *Kuml*, 279–96.

Helle, K. (1964) *Norge blir en stat*, Oslo.

Henriksen, B.B. (1976) *Sværdborg I. (Excavations 1943–44) – A Settlement of the Later Maglemose-Culture in South Zealand*, Copenhagen.

Higham, C.F.W. (1967) 'Stock Rearing as a Cultural Factor in Prehistoric Europe,' *Proceedings of the Prehistoric Society*, 84–103.

Higham, C.F.W. (1968) 'The Economy of Iron Age Vejleby (Denmark),' *Acta Archaeologica*, xxxviii, 222–41.

Higham, C.F.W. (1969) 'The Economic Basis of the Danish Funnel-Necked Beaker (TRB) Culture,' *Acta Archaeologica*, xl, 200–9.

Hingst, H. (1971) 'Eine befestigte jungsteinzeitliche Siedlung in Büdelsdorf,' *Offa*, xxviii, 90–3.

Hodges, R. (1978) 'State Formation and the Role of Trade in Middle Saxon England,' *British Archaeological Reports, International Series (Supplementary)*, xlvii, 439–55.

Hole, F. Flannery K.V. and Neely, J.A. (1969) *Prehistory and Human Ecology of the Deh Luran Plain*, Ann Arbor.

Holmqvist W. (1976) 'Die Ergebnisse der Grabungen auf Helgö,' *Prähistorische Zeitschrift*, LI, 127–77.

Horst, F. (1971) 'Hallstattimporte und -einflüsse im Elb-Havel-Gebiet,' *Zeitschrift für Archäologie*, V, 192–214.

Hundt, H.-J. (1955) 'Versuch zur Deutung der Depotfunde der nordischen jüngeren Bronzezeit,' *Jahrbuch des römischgermanischen Zentralmuseums Mainz*, II.

Hvass, L. (1980) *Jernalderen*, I-II, Copenhagen.

Hvass, S. (1973) 'Hodde: En vestjysk jernalderlandsby med social deling,' *Mark og Montre, Fra sydvestjyske museer*, 10–21.

Hvass, S. (1975) 'Hodde: Et 2000-årigt landsbysamfund i Vestjylland,' *Nationalmuseets arbejdsmark*, 75–85.

Hvass, S. (1976) 'Das eisenzeitliche Dorf bei Hodde, Westjütland,' *Acta Archaeologica*, XLVI, 142–58.

Hvass, S. (1977a) 'Udgravningerne i Vorbasse,' *Fra Ribe amt*, 345–86.

Hvass, S. (1977b) 'Jernalderlandsbyens udvikling i Hodde og Vorbasse,' *Skrifter fra Institut for historie og samfundsvidenskab, Odense Universitet*, XXII, 39–48.

Hvass, S. (1978) 'Die völkerwanderungszeitliche Siedlung Vorbasse, Mitteljütland,' *Acta Archaeologica*, XLIX, 61–111.

Hvass, S. (1980) 'Die Struktur einer Siedlung der Zeit von Christi Geburt bis ins 5. Jahrhundert nach Christus,' *Studien zure Sachsenforschung*, II, 161–80.

Højlund, F. (1974) 'Stridsøksekulturens flintøkser og -mejsler,' *Kuml*, 179–96.

Højlund, F. (1979) 'Stenøkser i Ny Guineas højland: Betydningen af prestigesymboler for reproduktionen af et stammesamfund,' *Hikuin*, 31–48.

Ilkjær, J. (1973) 'Tilbage til ådalen,' *Skalk*, 1973/3, 14–15.

Ilkjær, J. (1975a) 'Et bundt våben fra Vimose,' *Kuml*, 117–56.

Ilkjær, J. (1975b) 'Nye udgravninger i Illerup ådal,' *Kuml*, 99–116.

Ilkjær, J. (1977) 'Illerup ådal: Udgravningen 1976,' *Kuml*, 105–17.

Iversen, J. (1937) 'Undersøgelser over Litorinatransgressionerne i Danmark,' *Meddelelser fra Dansk Geologisk Forening*, VII, 223–32.

Iversen, J. (1941) 'Landnam i Danmarks stenalder,' *Danmarks geologiske undersøgelse*, II, 66.

Iversen, J. (1949) 'The Influence of Prehistoric Man on Vegetation,' *Danmarks geologiske undersøgelse*, IV, 3.

Iversen, J. (1954) 'The Late Glacial Flora of Denmark and its Relation to

Climate and Soil,' *Danmarks geologiske undersøgelse*, II, 80.

Iversen, J. (1967) 'Naturens udvikling siden sidste istid,' *Danmarks Natur*, I, 345–448.

Iversen, J. (1969) 'Retrogressive Development of a Forest Ecosystem Demonstrated by Pollen Diagrams from Fossil Moor,' *Oikos. Acta Oecologica Scandinavica, supplementum*, XII, 35–49.

Iversen, J. (1973) 'The Development of Denmark's Nature since the Last Glacial,' *Geol. Survey of Denmark*, V, series no. 7-C.

Jacob-Friesen, G. (1967) 'Bronzezeitliche Lanzenspitzen Norddeutschlands und Skandinaviens,' *Veröffentl. d. urgesch. Sammlungen d. Landesmuseums zu Hannover*, XVII, Hildesheim.

Jakobsen, B. (1973) *Skovens betydning for landbrugets udvikling i Danmark indtil 1300*, Copenhagen.

Jacobsen, J.A. (1979) 'Bruneborg, en tidlig førromersk boplads med jernudvinding,' *Skrifter fra Historisk Institut, Odense Universitet*, XXVII, 4–14.

Jankuhn, H. (1952) 'Klima, Besiedlung und Wirtschaft in der älteren Eisenzeit im westlichen Ostseebecken,' *Archaeologia Geographica*, III, 28ff.

Jankuhn, H. (1953) 'Der fränkisch-friesische Handel zum Ostseegebiet im frühen Mittelalter,' *Zeitschrift für Sozial-und Wirtschaftsgeschichte*, XL, 193ff.

Jankuhn, H. (1969) 'Vor- und Frühgeschichte vom Neolitikum bis zur Völkerwanderungszeit,' in *Deutsche Agrargeschichte*, I, Stuttgart.

Jankuhn, H. (1972) 'Haitabu,' *Ein Handelsplatz der Wikingerzeit*, Neumünster.

Jazdzewski, K. (1973) 'The Relations between Kujawian Barrows in Poland and Megalithic Tombs in Northern Germany, Denmark, and Western European Countries,' in Daniel, G. and Kjærum, P. (eds) *Megalithic Graves and Ritual*, Copenhagen.

Jensen, J. (1965) 'Bernsteinfunde und Bernsteinhandel der jüngeren Bronzezeit Dänemarks,' *Acta Archaeologica*, XXXVI, 43–86.

Jensen, J. (1966a) 'Griffzungenschwerter der späten nordischen Bronzezeit,' *Acta Archaeologica*, XXXVII, 25–51.

Jensen, J. (1966b) 'Arkæologi og kulturforskning,' *Historisk Tidsskrift*, 1–30.

Jensen, J. (1967a) 'Voldtofte-fundet: Bopladsproblemer i yngre bronzealder i Danmark,' *Årbøger for nordisk oldkyndighed og historie*, 91–154.

Jensen, J. (1967b) 'Zwei Abfallgruben von Gevninge, Zeeland,' *Acta Archaeologica*, XXXVII, 187–202.

Jensen, J. (1968) 'Et jysk ravfund: Ravhandelen i den yngre bronzealder,'

Kuml, 93–110.

Jensen, J. (1969) 'Ein thrako-kimmerischer Goldfund aus Dänemark,' *Acta Archaeologica*, xxx, 159–84.

Jensen, J. (1970) 'Et bronzealderanlæg fra Fyrkat,' *Årbøger for nordisk oldkyndighed og historie*, 78–93.

Jensen, J. (1971) 'Rammen,' *Skalk*, 1971/5.

Jensen, J. (1972) 'Ein neues Hallstattschwert aus Dänemark: Beitrag zur Problematik der jungbronzezeitlichen Votivfunde,' *Acta Archaeologica*, xliii, 115–64.

Jensen, J. (1979a) *Bronzealderen*, i-ii, Copenhagen.

Jensen, J. (1979b) 'Oldtidens samfund: Tiden indtil 800 e. Kr.', *Dansk Socialhistorie*, i, Copenhagen.

Jensen, J. (1982) *Nordens guld*. Copenhagen.

Jensen, J., Cullberg, C. and Mikkelsen, E. (1978) 'Udvekslingssystemer i Nordens forhistorie,' *XV Nordiska arkeologmötet. Förtryck av mötesföredrag*.

Jensen, J.Å. (1972) 'Bopladsen Myrhøj: 3 hustomter med klokkebægerkeramik,' *Kuml*, 61–122.

Jensen, S. (1976a) 'Byhøjene i Thy og aspekter af samfundsudviklingen i ældre jernalder,' *Museer i Viborg Amt (MIV)*, vi, 64ff.

Jensen, S. (1976b) 'Fynsk keramik i gravfund fra sen romersk jernalder,' *Kuml*, 151–90.

Jensen, S. (1978) 'Overgangen fra romersk till germansk jernalder,' *Hikuin*, iv, 101–16.

Jensen, S. (1979) 'En nordjysk grav fra romersk jernalder: Sen romersk jernalders kronologi i Nordeuropa,' *Kuml*, 167–98.

Jensen, S. (1980) 'To sydvestjyske bopladser fra ældre germansk jernalder: Jernalderbebyggelsen i Ribeområdet,' *Mark og Montre*, 23–36.

Jeppesen, T. Grøngård (1978) 'Oldtidsbebyggelse- middelalderbebyggelse: Kontinuitet eller brud,' *Hikuin*, iv, 117–24.

Jeppesen, T. Grøngård (1979) 'Bebyggelsesflytninger på overgangen mellem vikingetid og middelalder,' *Skrifter fra Historisk Institut, Odense Universitet*, xxvii, 99–117.

Jeppesen, T. Grøngård (1981) 'Middelalderlandsbyens opståen,' *Fynske Studier*, xi, Odense.

Jessen, K. (1935) 'Archaeological Dating in the History of North Jutland's Vegetation,' *Acta Archaeologica*, v, 185–214.

Jessen, K. (1937) 'Litorinasænkningen ved Klintesø i pollenfloristisk belysning,' *Meddelelser fra Dansk geologisk forening*, ix, 2.

Jessen, K. (1938) 'Some West Baltic Pollen Diagrams,' *Quartär*, i, 129–39.

Jessen, K. (1939) 'Bundsø: En yngre stenalders boplads på Als,' *Årbøger for nordisk oldkyndighed og historie*, 65–84.

Jessen, K. (1951) 'Oldtidens korndyrkning i Danmark,' *Viking*, xv, 25–37.

Jochim, M.A. (1976) *Hunter–Gatherer Subsistence and Settlement: A Predictive Model*, New York.

Johansen, E. (1975) 'Øster Hassing huset: En hustomt fra yngre stenalder,' *Hikuin*, ii, 57–66.

Johansen, K. Friis (1917) 'Jordgrave fra Dyssetid,' *Årbøger for nordisk oldkyndighed og historie*, 131–47.

Johansen, K. Friis (1919) 'En boplads fra den ældste stenalder i Sværdborg mose,' *Årbøger for nordisk oldkyndighed og historie*, 106–235.

Johansen, K. Friis (1923) 'Hoby-fundet,' *Nordiske Fortidsminder*, ii, 3.

Johansson, A. (1964) 'Sydsjællands oldtidsbebyggelse: En foreløbig meddelelse,' *Historisk Samfund for Præstø Amt, Årbog*, 245–328.

Jones, Gwyn (1968) *A History of the Vikings*, London.

Jørgensen, E. (1968) 'Sønder Vilstrup fundet: En gravplads fra ældre jernalder,' *Årbøger for nordisk oldkyndighed og historie*, 32–80.

Jørgensen, E. (1977a) *Hagebrogård-Vroue-Koldkur: Neolitische Gräberfelder aus Nordwest Jütland*, Copenhagen.

Jørgensen, E. (1977b) 'Brændende langdysser,' *Skalk*, 1977/5.

Jørgensen, G. (1976) 'Et kornfund fra Sarup: Bidrag til belysning af Tragtbægerkulturens agerbrug,' *Kuml*, 47–64.

Jørgensen, G. (1977) 'Acorns as a Food-Source in the Later Stone Age,' *Acta Archaeologica*, xlviii, 233–8.

Jørgensen, S. (1953) 'Skovrydning med flintøkse,' *Nationalmuseets arbejdsmark*, 36–43.

Jørgensen, S. (1956) 'Kongemosen: Endnu en Åmose-boplads fra den ældste stenalder,' *Kuml*, 23–40.

Jørgensen, S. (1961) 'Zur Frage der ältesten Küstenkultur in Dänemark,' *Bericht über den V. internationalen Kongress für Vor- und Frühgeschichte, Hamburg*, 440–7.

Jørgensen, S. (1963) 'Early Postglacial in Åmosen: Geological and Pollen-Analytical Investigations of Maglemosian Settlements in the West-Zealand Bog Åmosen i-ii,' *Danmarks Geologiske Undersøgelse*, ii, 87.

Kaelas, L. (1967) 'The Megalithic Tombs in South Scandinavia: Migration or Cultural Influence?', *Palaeohistoria*, xii, 287–321.

Keely, Lawrence H. (1980) *Experimental Determination of Stone Tool Uses: A Microwear Analysis*, Prehistoric Archaeology and Ecology Series, University of Chicago.

Kjær, H. (1902) 'Et nyt fund fra Nydam mose,' *Nordiske Fortidsminder*, i, 4.

Kjær, H. (1928a) 'Oldtidshuse ved Ginderup i Thy,' *Nationalmuseets arbejdsmark*, 7–20.

Kjær, H. (1928b) 'Var Boeslunde et oldtids helligsted?,' *Årbog for Historisk Samfund Sorø.*

Kjærum, P. (1954) 'Striber på kryds og tværs: Om plovfurer under en jysk stenalderhøj,' *Kuml*, 18–29.

Kjærum, P. (1955) 'Tempelhus fra stenalderen,' *Kuml*, 7–32.

Kjærum, P. (1957) 'Storstensgrave fra Tustrup,' *Kuml*, 9–23.

Kjærum, P. (1967a) 'The Chronology of the Passage Graves in Jutland,' *Palaeohistoria*, XII, 323–33.

Kjærum, P. (1967b) 'Mortuary Houses and Funeral Rites in Denmark,' *Antiquity*, XLI, 190–6.

Kjærum, P. (1969) 'Jættestuen Jordhøj,' *Kuml*, 9–66.

Kjærum, P. (1977) 'En langhøjs tilblivelse,' *Antikvariske Studier*, I, 19–26.

Klindt-Jensen, O. (1950) *Foreign Influences in Denmark's Early Iron Age*, Copenhagen.

Klindt-Jensen, O. (1957) 'Bornholm i Folkevandringstiden,' *Nationalmuseets skrifter, større beretninger*, II.

Klindt-Jensen, O. (1959) 'To krigergrave fra Bornholms jernalder,' *Nationalmuseets arbejdsmark*, 90–100.

Köhler, R. (1975) *Untersuchungen zu Grabkomplexen der älteren römischen Kaiserzeit in Böhmen unter Aspekten der religiösen und sozialen Gliederung*, Neumünster.

Königsson, L.-K. (1969) 'Natural and Cultural Factors in the Landscape Development in Oland,' *Oikos, Acta Oecologica Scandinavica, Supplementum*, XII, 50–9.

Kossack, G. (1964) 'Trinkgeschirr als Kultgerät der Hallstattzeit,' *Varia Archaeologica, Schriften der Sektion für Vor- und Frühgeschichte d. Deutschen Akademie der Wissenschaften*, 96–105.

Kristiansen, K. (1974) 'En kildekritisk analyse af depotfund fra Danmarks yngre bronzealder (periode IV-V): Et bidrag til arkæologisk kildekritik,' *Årbøger for nordisk oldkyndighed og historie*, 119–60.

Kristiansen, K. (1978a) 'Bebyggelse, erhvervsstrategi og arealudnyttelse i Danmarks bronzealder,' *Fortid og Nutid*, XXVII, 320–45.

Kristiansen, K. (1978b) 'The Consumption of Wealth in Bronze Age Denmark: A Study in the Dynamics of Economic Processes in Tribal Societies,' *Studies in Scandinavian Prehistory and Early History*, I, 158–190.

Kroll, H.J. (1975) *Ur-und Frühgeschichtliche Ackerbau in Archsum auf Sylt*, Kiel.

Kunwald, G. (1962) 'Broskovvejene,' *Nationalmuseets arbejdsmark*, 149–67.

Kunwald, G. (1964) 'Oldtidsveje,' *Turistforeningen for Danmarks årbog,* 18–36.

Kunwald, G. (1970) 'Der Moorfund in Rappendam auf Seeland,' *Prähistorische Zeitschrift,* XLV, 42–88.

la Cour, V. (1927) *Sjællands ældste bygder,* Copenhagen.

Larsen, K.A. (1949) 'Bornholm i ældre jernalder,' *Årbøger for nordisk oldkyndighed og historie,* 1–214.

Larsen, K.A. (1957) 'Stenalderhuse på Knardrup Galgebakke,' *Kuml,* 24–41.

Lasko, P. (1971) *The Kingdom of the Franks,* London.

Lassen, Aksel (1965) *Fald og Fremgang: Træk af befolkningsudviklingen i Danmark 1645–1960,* Århus.

Lee, R.B. (1968) 'What Hunters do for a Living, or How to Make out on Scarce Resources,' in Lee, R.B. and DeVore, I. (eds) *Man the Hunter,* Chicago.

Leeds, A. and Vayda, A.P. (1965) 'Man, Culture and Animal: The Role of Animals in Human Ecological Adjustments,' *Publications of the American Association for the Advancement of Science,* no. 78, Washington, DC.

Lévi-Strauss, C. (1962) *La pensée sauvage,* Paris.

Lichardus, J. (1976) *Rössen-Gartesleben- Baalberge: Ein Beitrag zur Chronologie des mitteldeutschen Neolitikums und zur Entstehung der Trichterbecher Kulturen,* Bonn.

Liversage, D. (1964) 'En hellekiste ved Gerdrup, Københavns amt,' *Årbøger for nordisk oldkyndighed og historie,* 32–62.

Liversage, D. (1970) 'Stendyssens forløber,' *Skalk,* 1970/1, 5–11.

Liversage, D. (1980) 'Material and Interpretation: The Archaeology of Sjælland in the Early Roman Iron Age,' *Publications of the National Museum: Archaeological Historical Series 1,* XX.

Lomborg, E. (1960) 'Donauländische Kulturbeziehungen und die relative Chronologie der frühen nordischen Bronzezeit,' *Acta Archaeologica,* XXX, 51–146.

Lomborg, E. (1963) 'Grav und fra Stubberup, Lolland: Menneskeofringer og kannibalisme i bronzealderen,' *Kuml,* 14–32.

Lomborg, E. (1964) 'Myrthue-graven: Ældre romertids jordfæstegrave i Sydvestjylland,' *Kuml,* 31–51.

Lomborg, E. (1968) 'Den tidlige bronzealders kronologi,' *Årbøger for nordisk oldkyndighed og historie,* 91–157.

Lomborg, E. (1973a) 'Die Flintdolche Dänemarks,' *Nordiske Fortidsminder,* ser. B in quarto, I.

Lomborg, E. (1973b) 'En landsby med huse og kultsted fra ældre bronzealder,' *Nationalmuseets Arbejdsmark*, 5–15.

Lomborg, E. (1975) 'Klokkebæger: og senere Beaker-indflydelser i Danmark,' *Årbøger for nordisk oldkyndighed og historie*, 20–41.

Lomborg, E. (1977) 'Udgravningerne ved Skamlebæk,' *Antikvariske Studier*, I, 123–30.

Lund, J. (1976a) 'Overbygård-landsbyen fra ældre romersk jernalder,' *Vendsyssel nu og da*, I, 53–62.

Lund, J. (1976b) 'Overbygård, en jernalderlandsby med neddybede huse,' *Kuml*, 129–50.

Lund, N. and Hørby, K. (1980) 'Samfundet i vikingetid og middelalder,' *Dansk socialhistorie* II, Copenhagen.

Lunden, K. (1972) *Økonomi og samfunn, Synspunkt på økonomisk historie*, Oslo.

Løppenthin, B. (1967) 'Danske ynglefugle i fortid og nutid,' *Acta Historica Scientarum Naturalium et Nedicinalium: Editet Bibliotheca Universitatis Hauniensis*, XIX, Copenhagen.

Mackeprang, M.B. (1943) *Kulturbeziehungen im nordischen Raum des 3.-5. Jahrhunderts*, Copenhagen.

Mackeprang, M.B. (1944) 'En bronzespand med billedfrise i en grav fra 3.århundrede,' *Nationalmuseets arbejdsmark*, 61–72.

Mackeprang, M.B. (1952) 'De nordiske guldbrakteater,' *Jysk arkæologisk selskabs skrifter*, II, Arhns.

Madsen, A.P. (1900) *Affaldsdynger fra Stenalderen i Danmark: Undersøgelser for Nationalmuseet*, Copenhagen.

Madsen, T. (1971) 'Grave med teltformet overbygning fra tidlig neolitisk tid,' *Kuml*, 127–50.

Madsen, T. (1974) 'Tidlig neolitiske anlæg ved Tolstrup,' *Kuml*, 121–54.

Madsen, T. (1975) 'Stendyngegrave ved Fjelsø,' *Kuml*, 73–82.

Madsen, T. (1977) 'Toftum ved Horsens, et "befæstet" anlæg tilhørende Tragtbægerkulturen,' *Kuml*, 161–84.

Madsen, T. (1978a) 'Bebyggelsesarkæologisk forskningsstrategi: Overvejelser i forbindelse med et projekt over Tragtbægerkulturen i Østjylland,' *Skrifter fra Historisk Institut, Odense Universitet*, XXIII, 64–76.

Madsen, T. (1978b) 'Perioder og periodeovergange i neolitikum,' *Hikuin*, 51–60.

Madsen, T. (1979a) 'Earthen Long Barrows and Timber Structures: Aspects of the Early Neolithic Mortuary Practice in Denmark,' *Proceedings of the Prehistoric Society*, XLV, 301–20.

Madsen, T. (1979b) 'En tidlig neolitisk langhøj ved Rude i Østjylland. *Kuml*, 79–108.

Malmer, M.P. (1962) *Jungneolitische Studien*, Lund.

Malmros, C. and Tauber, H. (1975) 'Kulstof-14 dateringer af dansk enkeltgravskultur,' *Årbøger for nordisk oldkyndighed og historie*, 78–95.

Marseen, O. (1959) 'Lindholm Høje,' *Kuml*, 53–68.

Marseen, O. (1960) 'Ferslevhuset,' *Kuml*, 36–55.

Mathiassen, T. (1973) 'Gudenå-kulturen,' En mesolitisk indlandsbebyggelse i Jylland,' *Årbøger for nordisk oldkyndighed og historie*, 1–186.

Mathiassen, T. (1939) 'Bundsø: En yngre stenalders boplads på Als,' *Årbøger for nordisk oldkyndighed og historie*, 1–54.

Mathiassen, T. (1940) 'Havnelev-Strandegård,' *Årbøger for nordisk oldkyndighed og historie*, 3–82.

Mathiassen, T. (1942) 'Dyrholmen: En stenalderboplads på Djursland,' *Det kongelige danske videnskabernes selskab: Arkæologisk kunsthistoriske skrifter*, I, 1.

Mathiassen, T. (1943) 'Stenalderbopladser i Åmosen,' *Nordiske Fortidsminder*, III, 3.

Mathiassen, T. (1946a) 'En senglacial boplads ved Bromme,' *Årbøger for nordisk oldkyndighed og historie*, 121–97.

Mathiassen, T. (1946b) 'En boplads fra ældre stenalder ved Vedbæk boldbaner,' *Søllerødbogen*, 19–35.

Mathiassen, T. (1948) *Studier over Vestjyllands oldtidsbebyggelse*, Copenhagen.

Mathiassen, T. (1959) *Nordvestsjællands oldtidsbebyggelse*, Copenhagen.

Mathiessen, H. (1942) *Det gamle land: Billede fra tiden før udskiftningen*, Copenhagen.

Mauss, M. (1969) *The Gift: Forms and Function of Exchange in Archaic Societies*, London.

Mellars, P. (1975) 'Ungulate Populations, Economic Patterns, and the Mesolithic Landscape,' *The Council for British Archaeology, Research Report*, no. 11.

Moberg, C.-A. (1956) 'Till frågan om samhällsstrukturen i Norden under bronsåldern,' *Fornvännen*, 65–79.

Moberg, C.-A. and Olsson, U. (1973) *Ekonomisk historisk början: Forsörjning och samhälle*, Stockholm.

Montelius, O. (1885) *Om tidsbestämning inom bronsåldern*, Stockholm.

Montelius, O. (1896) 'Den nordiske jernålders kronologi,' *Svenska Forminnesföreningens Tidsskrift*, IX.

Müller, S. (1897) *Vor Oldtid*, Copenhagen.

Müller, S. (1898) 'De jyske enkeltgrave fra stenalderen,' *Årbøger for nordisk oldkyndighed og historie*, 158–282.

Müller, S. (1904) 'Vej og bygd i sten- og bronzealderen,' *Årbøger for nordisk oldkyndighed og historie*, 1–64.

Müller, S. (1911) 'Juellinge-fundet og den romerske periode,' *Nordiske Fortidsminder*, II, 1.

Müller, S. (1912) 'Vendsyssel-studier,' *Årbøger for nordisk oldkyndighed og historie*, 83–142.

Müller, S. (1919) 'Bopladsfund fra bronzealderen,' *Årbøger for nordisk oldkyndighed og historie*, 35–105.

Müller-Karpe, H. (1968) 'Jungsteinzeit,' *Handbuch der Vorgeschichte*, II, Munich.

Müller-Wille, M. (1965) 'Eisenzeitliche Fluren in den festländischen Nordseegebieten,' *Siedlung und Landschaft in Westfalen*, V.

Müller-Wille, M. (1977) 'Bauerliche Siedlungen der Bronze- und Eisenzeit in den Nordseegebeieten,' in Jankuhn, H., Schützeichel, R. and Schwind, F. (eds) *Das Dorf der Eisenzeit und des frühen Mittelalters*, Göttingen.

Munksgaard, E. (1953) 'Collared Gold Necklets and Armlets: A Remarkable Danish Fifth Century Group,' *Acta Archaeologica*, XXIV, 67–80.

Munksgaard, E. (1955) 'Late-Antique Scrap Silver Found in Denmark: The Hardenberg, Høstentorp, and Simmersted Hoards,' *Acta Archaeologica*, XXVI, 31–67.

Myhre, B. (1975) 'Gårdshusenes konstruksjon og funksjon i jernalderen,' *Arkæologiske Skrifter, Historisk Museum, Universitetet i Bergen*, II, 73–106.

Myhre, B. (1978) 'Agrarian Development, Settlement History, and Social Organization in Southwest Norway in the Iron Age,' *Studies in Scandinavian Prehistory and Early History*, I, 224–71.

Møhl, U. (1957) 'Zoologisk gennemgang af knoglematerialet fra jernalderbopladserne Dalshøj og Sorte Muld, Bornholm,' in Klindt-Jensen, O. (ed.) *Bornholm i Folkevandringstiden*, 279–318.

Møhl, U. (1961) 'Rislevfundets dyreknogler,' *Kuml*, 96–105.

Møhl, U. (1970) 'Fangstdyrene ved de danske strande: Den zoologiske baggrund for harpunerne,' *Kuml*, 297–329.

Nash, M. (1966) *Primitive and Peasant Economic Systems*, San Francisco.

Navarro, J.M.de (1925) 'Prehistoric Routes between Northern Europe and Italy Defined by the Amber Trade,' *Geographical Journal*, LXVI, 481–507.

Neergaard, C. (1916) 'Sønderjyllands jernalder,' *Årbøger for nordisk oldkyndighed og historie*, 255–310.

Neergaard, C. (1928) 'Jernalder-gravpladsen ved Lisbjerg,' *Nationalmuseets arbejdsmark*, 21–37.

Neergaard, C. (1931) 'Nogle sønderjyske fund fra den ældre jernalder,' *Nationalmuseets arbejdsmark*, 63–80.

Neumann, H. (1953) 'Et løveglas fra Rhinlandet,' *Kuml*, 137–54.

Newell, R.R., Constandse-Westermann, T.S. and Meikeljohn, C. (1979) 'The Skeletal Remains of Mesolithic Man in Western Europe: an Evaluative Catalogue,' *Journal of Human Evolution*, VIII, 1.

Nielsen, H. (1970) 'Oldtids- og middelalderveje ved Stevns og Tryggevælde åer,' *Køge Museum 1970–73*, 27–40.

Nielsen, H. (1978) 'Det tilfældige fundstofs anvendelse i bebyggelsesarkæologien med Østsjælland som eksempel,' *Skrifter fra Historisk Institut, Odense Universitet*, XXIII.

Nielsen, H. (1979) 'Jernalderfund og stednavnetyper, en sammenligning af fynske og sjællandske forhold,' *Skrifter fra Historisk Institut, Odense Universitet*, XXVII, 87–98.

Nielsen, H. and Hansen, V. (1977) 'Oldtidens veje og vadesteder, belyst ved nye undersøgelser ved Stevns,' *Årbøger for nordisk oldkyndighed og historie*, 72–117.

Nielsen, J.L. (1975) 'Aspekter af det førromerske våbengravsmiljø i Jylland,' *Hikuin*, II, 89–96.

Nielsen, J.N. (1980) 'En jernalderboplads og -gravplads ved Sejlflod i Østhimmerland,' *Antikvariske Studier*, IV, 83–102.

Nielsen, P.O. (1977a) 'De tyknakkede flintøksers kronologi,' *Årbøger for nordisk oldkyndighed og historie*, 5–71.

Nielsen, P.O. (1977b) 'Die Flintbeile der frühen Trichterbecherkultur in Dänemark,' *Acta Archaeologica*, XLVIII, 61–138.

Nielsen, S. (1979) 'Den grubekeramiske kultur i Norden,' *Antikvariske Studier*, III, 23–48.

Nielsen, S. (1980) 'Nogle bemærkninger om de forhistoriske landbrug med særligt henblik på agerjordens beskaffenhed,' *Antikvariske Studier*, IV, 103–34.

Nielsen, V. (1970a) 'Agerlandets historie,' *Danmarks Natur*, VIII, Copenhagen.

Nielsen, V. (1970b) 'Iron Age Plough-Marks in Store Vildmose, North Jutland,' *Tools and Tillage*, I, 3, 151–72.

Nordman, C.A. (1917a) 'Jættestuer i Danmark,' *Nordiske Fortidsminder*, II, 2.

Nordman, C.A. (1917b) 'Studier öfver gånggriftkulturen i Danmark,' *Årbøger for nordisk oldkyndighed og historie*, 269–332.

Nordman, C.A. (1935) *The Megalithic Culture of Northern Europe*, Helsinki.

Norling-Christensen, H. (1945) 'Skeletgraven fra Korsør Nor: Et menneskefund fra ældre stenalder,' *Nationalmuseets arbejdsmark*, 5–17.

Norling-Christensen, H. (1949) 'Germansk jernalders bebyggelse i Norden,' *Viking*, XIII, 1–16.

Norling-Christensen, H. (1951) 'Jernaldergravpladsen ved Himlingøje,'

Nationalmuseets arbejdsmark, 39–46.

Norling-Christensen, H. (1952) 'Gravfund fra Borritshoved med romerske glas og bronzekar,' *Kuml*, 84–90.

Norling-Christensen, H. (1954) 'Katalog over ældre romersk jernalders grave i Århus amt,' *Nordiske Fortidsminder*, IV, 2.

Norling-Christensen, H. (1956) 'Haraldstedgravpladsen og ældre germansk jernalder i Danmark,' *Årbøger for nordisk oldkyndighed og historie*, 14–143.

Nylén, E. (1962) 'Bebyggelsesproblem i Norden förhistoria,' *Tor*, 169–85.

Odner, K. (1973) 'Økonomiske strukturer på Vestlandet i eldre jernalder,' *Historisk Museum, Universitetet i Bergen*.

Odner, K. (1974) 'Economic Structures in Western Norway in the Early Iron Age,' *Norwegian Archaeological Review*, VII, 104–12.

Odum, E.P. (1969) 'The Strategy of Ecosystem Development,' *Science*, CLXIV, 262–70.

Olsen, O. (1975) 'Nogle tanker i anledning af Ribes uventet høje alder,' *Fra Ribe Amt*, 225–58.

Paludan-Müller, C. (1978) 'High Atlantic Food Gathering in Northwestern Zealand: Ecological Conditions and Spatial Representation,' *Studies in Scandinavian Prehistory and Early History* I, 120–57.

Peeples, C.S. and Kus, S.M. (1977) 'Some Archaeological Correlates of Ranked Societies,' *American Antiquity*, XLII.

Petersen, C.G.J. (1922) 'Om tidsbestemmelse og ernæringsforhold i den ældre stenalder i Danmark,' *Det kongelige danske videnskabernes selskab, Biologiske meddelelser*, III, 9.

Petersen, E. Brinch (1966) 'Klosterlund–Sønder Hadsund–Bøllund: Les trois sites principaux du Maglemosien Ancien en Jutland,' *Acta Archaeologica*, XXXVII, 77–185.

Petersen, E. Brinch (1970a) 'Ølby-Lyng: En østsjællandsk kystboplads med Ertebøllekultur,' *Årbøger for nordisk oldkyndighed og historie*, 5–42.

Petersen, E. Brinch (1970b) 'Le Bromméen et le cycle de Lyngby,' *Quartär*, XXI, 93–5.

Petersen, E. Brinch (1971) 'Sværdborg II: A Maglemose Hut from Sværdborg Bog, Zealand, Denmark,' *Acta Archaeologica*, XLII, 43–77.

Petersen, E. Brinch (1973) 'A Survey of the Late Palaeolithic and the Mesolithic of Denmark,' in Kozlowski, S.K. (ed.) *The Mesolithic in Europe*, Warszawa.

Petersen, E. Brinch (1974) 'Gravene fra Dragsholm,' *Nationalmuseets arbejdsmark*, 112–20.

Petersen, E. Brinch (1976a) 'Vedbækprojektet', Søllerødbogen, 97–122.
Petersen, E. Brinch (1976b) 'De levede og døde ... for 7000 år siden: En undersøgelse af gravpladsen på Bøgebakken i Vedbæk,' National-museets arbejdsmark, 5–23.
Petersen, E. Brinch (1979) 'Vedbækprojektet,' Søllerødbogen, 1979.
Petersen, E. Ladewig (1980) 'Fra standssamfund til rangssamfund,' Dansk socialhistorie, III, Copenhagen.
Petersen, H. (1890) 'Gravpladsen fra den ældre jernalder på Nordrup Mark ved Ringsted,' Nordiske Fortidsminder, I, 1–14.
Phillips, A.P. (1973) 'The Evolutionary Model of Human Society and its Application to Certain Early Farming Populations of Western Europe,' in Renfrew, C. (ed.) The Explanation of Culture Change: Models in Prehistory, London.
Piggott, S. (1966) '"Unchambered" Long Barrows in Neolithic Britain,' Palaeohistoria, XII, 381–94.
Polanyi, K. (1957) 'The Economy as Instituted Process,' in Polanyi, K., Arensberg, C.M. and Pearson, H.W. (eds) Trade and Market in the Early Empires, New York.
Polanyi, K. (1963) 'Ports of Trade in Early Societies,' The Journal of Economic History, XXII, 30–45.
Polanyi, K. (1968) 'Primitive, Archaic and Modern Economies,' in Dalton, G. (ed.) Essays, New York.
Polanyi, K. (1978) 'Trade, Markets, and Money in the European Early Middle Ages,' Norwegian Archaeological Review, II, 92–117.
Polgar, S. (ed.) (1975) 'Population, Ecology, and Social Evolution', World Anthropology, The Hague, Paris.
Price, B. (1978) 'Secondary State Formations: An Explanatory Model,' in Cohen, R. and Service, E.R. (eds) Origins of the State, Philadelphia.

Raddatz, K. (1957) 'Der Thorsberger Moorfund,' Offa Bücher, XIII.
Ramskou, T. (1976) Lindholm Høje, Gravpladsen, Copenhagen.
Randsborg, K. (1967) '"Aegean" Bronzes in a Grave in Jutland,' Acta Archaeologica, XXXVIII, 1–27.
Randsborg, K. (1968) 'Von Periode II zu III,' Acta Archaeologica, XXXIX, 1–142.
Randsborg, K. (1970) 'Zwei Peschiera Dolche aus Südskandinavien,' Acta Archaeologica, XLI, 191–5.
Randsborg, K. (1972) From Period III to Period IV: Chronological Studies of the Bronze Age in Southern Scandinavia and Northern Germany, Copenhagen.
Randsborg, K. (1973) 'Wealth and Social Structure as Reflected in Bronze

Age Burials: A Quantitative Approach,' in Renfrew, C. (ed.) *The Explanation of Culture Change.*

Randsborg, K. (1974a) 'Befolkning og social variation i ældre bronzealders Danmark,' *Kuml*, 197–208.

Randsborg, K. (1974b) 'Social Stratification in Early Bronze Age Denmark: A Study in the Regulation of Cultural Systems,' *Prähistorische Zeitschrift*, XLIX, 38–61.

Randsborg, K. (1974c) 'Prehistoric Populations and Social Regulations: The Case of Early Bronze Age Denmark,' *Homo*, XXV, 59–67.

Randsborg, K. (1975) 'Social Dimensions of Early Neolithic Denmark,' *Proceedings of the Prehistoric Society*, 105–18.

Randsborg, K. (1979a) *The Viking Age in Denmark*, London.

Randsborg, K. (1979b) 'Resource Distribution and the Function of Copper in Early Neolithic Denmark,' in Ryan, M. (ed.) *Proceedings of the 5th Atlantic Colloquium, Dublin*, 303–18.

Rappaport, R.A. (1968) *Pigs for Ancestors*, New Haven, London.

Rasmussen, A.K. (1968) 'En byhøj i Thyland,' *Nationalmuseets arbejdsmark*, 137–44.

Rathje, W.L. (1975) 'Last Tango at Mayapan: A Tentative Trajectory of Production-distribution Systems,' in Sabloff, J. and Lamberg-Karlovsky, C.C. (eds) *Ancient Civilization and Trade*, Albuquerque, 409–48.

Redman, Charles, L. (1978) *The Rise of Civilization: From Early Farmers to Urban Society in the Ancient Near East*, San Francisco.

Renfrew, C. (1969) 'Trade and Culture Process in European Prehistory,' *Current Anthropology*, X, 151–69.

Renfrew, C. (1971) 'Europe's Creative Barbarians,' *The Listener*, LXXXV, 12–15.

Renfrew, C. (1972) *The Emergence of Civilization*, London.

Renfrew, C. (1973a) 'Monuments, Mobilization and Social Organization in Neolithic Wessex,' in Renfrew, C. (ed.) *The Explanation of Culture Change*, London.

Renfrew, C. (1973b) *Before Civilization*, London.

Renfrew, C. (1975) 'Trade as Action at a Distance: Questions of Integration and Communication,' in Sabloff, J. and Lamberg-Karlovsky, C.C. (eds) *Ancient Civilization and Trade*, Albuquerque.

Renfrew, C. (1976) 'Megalith, Territories and Populations,' in de Laet, S.J. (ed.) *Acculturation and Continuity in Atlantic Europe*, 198–220.

Renfrew, C. (1978) 'Space, Time and Polity,' in Friedman, J. and Rowlands, M.J. (eds) *The Evolution of Social Systems*, London.

Riis, P.J. (1959) 'The Danish Bronze Vessels of Greek, Early Campanian and Etruscan Manufactures, *Acta Archaeologica*, XXX, 1–50.

Rosenberg, G. (1929) 'Nye Jættestuefund,' Årbøger for nordisk oldkyndighed og historie, 245–62.

Rosenberg, G. (1937) 'Hjortspringfundet,' Nordiske Fortidsminder, III, 1.

Rostholm, H. (1977) 'Nye fund fra yngre stenalder fra Skarrild Overby og Lille Hamborg,' Hardsyssels årbog, 91–112.

Rowlands, M.J. (1973) 'Modes of Exchange and the Incentives for Trade with Reference to Later European Prehistory,' in Renfrew, C. (ed.) The Explanation of Culture Change.

Russel, J.C. (1958) 'Late Ancient and Medieval Populations,' Transactions of the American Philosophical Society, NS, 48, 3.

Russel, J.C. (1968) 'That Earlier Plague,' Demography, V.

Rust, A. (1937) Das altsteinzeitliche Rentierlarger Meiendorf, Neumünster.

Rust, A. (1943) Die alt- und mittelsteinzeitlichen Funde von Stellmoor, Neumünster.

Rønne, P. (1979) 'Høj over høj,' Skalk, 1979/5.

Sahlins, M.D. (1958) Social Stratification in Polynesia, American Ethnological Society Monograph, Seattle.

Sahlins, M.D. (1963) 'Poor Man, Rich Man, Big Man, Chief: Political Types in Melanesia and Polynesia,' Comparative Studies in Society and History, V, 285–303, The Hague.

Sahlins, M.D. (1965) 'On the Sociology of Primitive Exchange,' in Banton, M. (ed.) The Relevance of Models for Social Anthropology, New York.

Sahlins, M.D. (1968) Tribesmen, Foundation of Modern Anthropology Series, New York.

Sahlins, M.D. (1974) Stone Age Economies, Social Science Paperbacks, London.

Salmonsson, B. (1964) 'Découverte d'une habitation du Tardiglaciaire à Segebro, Scania, Suede' Acta Archaeologia, XXXV.

Sarauw, G.F.L. (1903) 'En stenalders boplads i Maglemose ved Mullerup sammenholdt med beslægtede fund,' Årbøger for nordisk oldkyndighed og historie, 148–315.

Sawyer, Peter H. (1977) 'Kings and Merchants,' in Sawyer, P.H. and Wood, I.N. (eds) Early Medieval Kingship, Leeds.

Scheffrahn, W. (1967) 'Paläodemograpischi Beobachtungen and den Neolitikern von Lenzburg, Kt. Aargau,' Germania, XLV, 34–42.

Schild, R. (1976) 'The Final Palaeolithic Settlement of the European Plain,' Scientific American, Feb. 1976, 88–99.

Schindler, R. (1957) 'Siedlungsprobleme im Stormarngau im Anschluss an die Ausgrabungen Hamburg-Farmsen,' Archaeologica Geographica, 25ff.

Schlüter, W. (1970) 'Versuch einer sozialen Differenzierung der jungkaiserzeitlichen Körpergräbergruppe von Hassleben-Leuna anhand einer Analyse der Grabfunde,' *Neue Ausgrabungen und Forschungen in Niedersachsen*, VI.

Schmid, P. and Zimmermann, W.H. (1976) 'Flögeln: Zur Struktur einer Siedlung des 1. bis 5. Jhs. n. Chr. im Küstengebiet der südlichen Nordsee,' *Probleme der Küstenforschung im südlichen Nordseegebiet*, XI, 1–77.

Schneider, H.K. (1974) *Economic Man: The Anthropology of Economics*, New York.

Schultz, C.G. (1949) 'Aggersborg, vikingelejren ved Limfjorden,' *Nationalmuseets arbejdsmark*, 91–108.

Schultz- Klinken, K.R. (1976) 'Ackerbausystem des Saatfurchen und Saatbettbaues in urgeschichtlicher und geschichtlicher Zeit sowie ihr Einfluss auf die Bodenentwicklung,' *Die Kunde*, 5–68.

Schwabedissen, H. (1967) 'Ein horizontierter Breitkeil aus Sarup und die manigfachen Kulturbeziehungen des beginnenden Neolitikums im Norden und Nordwesten,' *Palaeohistoria*, XII, 409–68.

Schwabedissen, H. (1968) 'Der Übergang vom Mesolitikum zum Neolitikum in Schleswig Holstein,' *Führer zu vor- und frühgeschichtlichen Denkmalern*, 9, Schleswig.

Sernander, R. (1910) *Die schwedischen Torfmoore als Zeugen postglazialer Klimaschwankungen*, Stockholm.

Service, E.R. (1966) *The Hunters*, Englewood Cliffs, N.J.

Service, E.R. (1971) *Primitive Social Organization: An Evolutionary Perspective*, New York.

Service, E.R. (1975) *Origins of the State and Civilization: The Process of Cultural Evolution*, New York.

Sherratt, A.G. (1972) 'Socio-economic and Demographic Models for the Neolithic and Bronze Age of Europe,' in Clarke, D. (ed.) *Models in Archaeology*, London.

Sherratt, A.G. (1976) 'Resources, Technology, and Trade: An Essay in Early European Metallurgy,' in Sieveking, G. de G. and Wilson, K.E. (eds) *Problems in Economic and Social Archaeoloy*, London.

Sherratt, A.G. (1980) Plough and Pastoralism: Aspects of the Secondary Products Revolution,' in *Pattern of the Past: Studies in Honour of David Clarke*, Cambridge.

Skårup, J. (1973) *Hesselø-Sølager: Jagdstationen der südskandinavishen Trichterbecherkultur*, Copenhagen.

Skårup, J. (1975) *Stengade: Ein langeländischer Wohnplatz mit Hausresten aus der frühneolitischen Zeit*, Copenhagen.

Slomann, W. (1959) 'Sætrangfundet: Hjemlig tradisjon og fremmed indslag,' *Norske oldfunn*, IX 1–62, Oslo.

Slomann, W. (1968) 'The Avaldnes Find and the Possible Background for the Migration Period Finds in Southwest and West Norway,' *Norwegian Archaeological Review*, I.

Smith, C.A. (1976) 'Exchange Systems and the Spatial Distribution of Elites: The Organization and Stratification in Agrarian Societies,' in . Smith, C.A. (ed.) *Regional Analysis*, II, *Social Systems*, New York, San Francisco, London.

Smith, Ph. E.L. (1970) 'Changes in Population Pressure in Archaeological Explanation,' *World Archaeology*, II, 6–18.

Snedker, K.H. (1959) 'Naglesti bondesamfund gennem 4000 år,' *Årbog Lolland Falster*, 166–206.

Sörbom, G. (1966) 'Rutger Sernanders klimaförsämringsteori,' *Tor*, XI, 83–115.

Spooner, B. (1971) 'Report on Colloquium Entitled "Population, Resources and Technology",' *Current Anthropology*, XII, 254–55.

Spooner, B. (1972) *Population Growth: Anthropological Implications*, Cambridge, Mass.

Steensberg, A. (1943) *Ancient Harvesting Implements*, Copenhagen.

Steensberg, A. (1973) *Den danske landsby gennem 6000 år*, Copenhagen.

Steensberg, A. (1974) *Den danske bondegård*, Copenhagen.

Steensberg, A. (1979) *Draved: An Experiment in Stone Age Agriculture – Burning, Sowing and Harvesting*, Copenhagen.

Sterum, N. (1978) 'Nogle C-14-frie synspunkter på den Beckerske kontakthypothese,' *Hikuin*, IV, 61–76.

Stjernqvist, B. (1963) 'Präliminarien zu einer Untersuchung von Opferfunden,' *Meddelanden från Lunds Universitets Historiska Museum*, 5–64.

Stjernqvist, B. (1966) 'Models of Commercial Diffusion in Prehistoric Times,' *Kungl. Hum. Vetenskapssamfundet i Lund, Scripta Minora*, no. 2.

Stjernqvist, B. (1969) 'Beiträge zum Studium von bronzezeitlichen Siedlungen,' *Acta Archaeologica Lundensia*, no. 8.

Stjernqvist, B. (1970) 'Zur Frage der Siedlungskontinuität der Völkerwanderungszeit,' *Meddelanden från Lunds Universitets Historiska Museum*, 99–149.

Strömberg, M. (1961) 'Untersuchungen zur jüngeren Eisenzeit in Schonen,' *Acta Archaeologica Lundensia*, ser. in 4°, no. 4.

Strömberg, M. (1968) 'Der Dolmen Trollasten in St. Köpinge, Schonen.' *Acta Archaeologica Lundensia*, ser. in 8°, no. 7.

Strömberg, M. (1971a) 'Senneolitiske huslämningar i Skåne,' *Fornvännen*, 237–54.

Strömberg, M. (1971b) 'Die Megalithgräber von Hagestad: Zur Problematik von Grabbauten und Grabriten,' *Acta Archaeologica Lundensia*, ser. in 8°, no. 9.

Strömberg, M. (1981) *Järn i österlenska forntidsfynd*, Simrishamn.

Struever, S. (ed.) (1971) *Prehistoric Agriculture*, Garden City, N.Y.

Struve, K. W. (1955) *Die Einzelgrabkultur in Schleswig-Holstein*, Neumünster.

Sturdy, D.A. (1975) 'Some Reindeer Economies in Prehistoric Europe,' in Higgs, E.S. (ed.) *Palaeoeconomy*, Cambridge.

Stürup, B. (1965) 'En jordgrav fra tidlig-neolitisk tid,' *Kuml*, 13–22.

Suess, H.E. (1970) 'Bristle-cone Pine Calibration and the Radiocarbon Time–Space 5200 BC to the Present,' in Olsson, I.V. (ed.) *Radiocarbon Variations and Absolute Chronology*, Wiley, N.Y.

Sussmann, R. (1972) 'Child Transport, Family Size and the Increase in Human Population During the Neolithic,' *Current Anthropology*, XIII, 258–67.

Tauber, H. (1965) 'Differential Pollen Dispersal and the Interpretation of Pollen Diagrams, with a Contribution to the Interpretation of the Elm Fall,' *Danmarks geologiske undersøgelse*, II, 89.

Tauber, H. (1966) 'Copenhagen Radiocarbon Dates VII,' *Radiocarbon*, VIII, 212–34.

Tauber, H. (1970) 'The Scandinavian Varve Chronology and C-14 Dating,' in Olsson, I.U. (ed.) *Nobel Symposium 12, Radiocarbon Variations and Absolute Chronology*, Stockholm.

Tauber, H. (1972) 'Radiocarbon Chronology of the Danish Mesolithic and Neolithic,' *Antiquity*, XLVI, 106–10.

Tauber, H. (1973) 'Copenhagen Radiocarbon Dates X,' *Radiocarbon*, XV, 86–112.

Tauber, H. (1979) 'Kulstof-14 datering af moselig,' *Kuml*, 73–8.

Terray, E. (1970) *Den historiska materialismen och de 'primitiva samhällena'*, Zenithserien no. 9, Stockholm.

Thompson, E.A. (1960) 'Slavery in Early Germany,' in Finley, M.I. (ed.) *Slavery in Classical Antiquity*, Cambridge.

Thomsen, N. (1953) 'Om en vestjysk stald,' *Kuml*, 171–81.

Thomsen, N. (1959) 'Hus og kælder i romersk jernalder,' *Kuml*, 13–27.

Thomsen, N. (1964) 'Myrthue, et gårdsanlæg fra jernalder,' *Kuml*, 15–29.

Thorsen, S. (1980) 'Klokkehøj ved Bøjden: Et sydvestfynsk dyssekammer med bevaret primærgrav,' *Kuml*, 105–46.

Thorvildsen, E. (1972) 'Dankirke,' *Nationalmuseets Arbejdsmark*, 47–60.

Thorvildsen, K. (1941) 'Dyssetidens gravfund i Danmark,' *Årbøger for nordisk oldkyndighed og historie*, 22–87.

Thorvildsen, K. (1946) 'Grønhøj ved Horsens. En jættestue med offerplads', *Arbøger for nordisk oldkyndighed og historie*, 73–120.

Thrane, H. (1962) 'The Earliest Bronze Vessels in Denmark's Bronze Age,' *Acta Archaeologica*, XXXIII, 109–63.

Thrane, H. (1965) 'Dänische Funde fremder Bronzegefässe der jüngeren Bronzezeit,' *Acta Archaeologica*, XXXVI, 157–207.

Thrane, H. (1967a) 'Stenalders fladmarksgrave under en bronzealderhøj,' *Årbøger for nordisk oldkyndighed og historie*, 27–90.

Thrane, H. (1967b) 'Fornemme fund fra en jernaldergrav i Uggeløse,' *Nationalmuseets arbejdsmark*, 67–80.

Thrane, H. (1968) 'Eingeführte Bronzeschwerter aus Dänemarks jüngerer Bronzezeit,' *Acta Archaeologica*, XXXIX, 143–218.

Thrane, H. (1971) 'En bronzealderboplads ved Jyderup skov i Odsherred,' *Nationalmuseets arbejdsmark*, 141–64.

Thrane, H. (1973a) 'Urnenfeldermesser aus Dänemarks jüngerer Bronzezeit,' *Acta Archaeologica*, XLIII, 165–228.

Thrane, H. (1973b) 'Bebyggelseshistorie: En arkæologisk arbejdsopgave,' *Fortid og Nutid*, XXV, 299–321.

Thrane, H. (1975) *Europæiske forbindelser: Bidrag til studiet af fremmede forbindelser i Danmarks yngre bronzealder*, Copenhagen.

Thrane, H. (1976) 'Lusehøj ved Voldtofte,' *Fynske Minder*, 17–32.

Tischler, F. (1955) 'Das Gräberfeld Oberjersdal, Kreis Hadersleben,' *4. Beiheft zum Atlas der Urgeschichte*, Hamburg.

Troels-Smith, J. (1942) 'Geologisk datering af Dyrholm-fundet,' in T. Mathiassen *et al.*, *Dyrholmen: En stenalderboplads på Djursland*, Copenhagen.

Troels-Smith, J. (1953) 'Ertebøllekultur-bondekulter: Resultater af de sidste 10 års undersøgelser i Åmosen,' *Årbøger for nordisk oldkyndighed og historie*, 5–62.

Troels-Smith, J. (1955) 'Senglacialtidens jægere,' *Nationalmuseets arbejdsmark*, 129–53.

Troels-Smith, J. (1956) 'Nulevende rensdyrjægere,' *Nationalmuseets arbejdsmark*, 23–40.

Troels-Smith, J. (1957a) 'Maglemosetidens jægere og fiskere,' *Nationalmuseets arbejdsmark*, 101–33.

Troels-Smith, J. (1957b) 'Muldbjerg-bopladsen, som den så ud for 4500 år siden,' *Naturens Verden*, VII, 1–32.

Troels-Smith, J. (1959a) 'The Muldbjerg Dwelling Place,' *Annual Report of the Smithsonian Institution*, Washington, DC.

Troels-Smith, J. (1959b) 'En elmetræs-bue fra Åmosen og andre træsager fra tidlig neolitisk tid,' *Årbøger for nordisk oldkyndighed og historie*, 91–145.

Troels-Smith, J. (1960a) 'Ertebølletidens fangstfolk og jægere,' *Nationalmuseets arbejdsmark*, 95–119.

Troels-Smith, J. (1960b) 'Ivy, Misteltoe and Elm. Climate Indicators – Fodder Plants: A Contribution to the Interpretation of the Pollen Zone Border VII-VIII,' *Danmarks geologiske undersøgelse*, IV, 4.

Troels-Smith, J. (1967) 'The Ertebølle Culture and its Background,' *Palaeohistoria*, XII, 505–28.

Tromnau, G. (1975) 'Die jungpaläolitischen Fundplätze im Stellmoorer Tunneltal im Überblick,' *Hammaburg*, NF, II, 9–20.

Ussinger, H. (1975) 'Pollenanalytische und stratigraphische Untersuchungen zn zwei Spätglazial-Vorkommen in Schleswig-Holstein,' *Mitteilungen der Arbeitsgemeinschaft Geobotanik in Schleswig-Holstein und Hamburg*, XXV, Kiel.

Vallois, H.V. (1960) 'Vital Statistics in Prehistoric Populations as Determined from Archaeological Data,' in Heizer, R.F. and Cook, S.F. (eds) *The Application of Quantitative Methods in Archaeology*, Viking Fund Publications in Archaeology, XXVIII.

Vedel, E. (1886) *Bornholms oldtidsminder og oldsager*, Copenhagen.

Vedel, E. (1897) *Efterskrift til Bornholms oldtidsminder og oldsager*, Copenhagen.

Vorting, H.C. (1973) 'Endnu en bopladsforekomst fra germansk jernalder i Esbjerg,' *Mark og montre, Fra sydvestjyske museer*, 22–7.

Voss, O. (1954) 'The Høstentorp Silver Hoard and its Period,' *Acta Archaeologica*, XXV, 171–217.

Voss, O. (1962) 'Jernudvinding i Danmark i forhistorisk tid,' *Kuml*, 7–32.

Voss, O. (1966) 'Langdysserne i Steneng ved Abterp,' *Sønderjysk Månedsskrift*, VIII, 268–75.

Voss, O. (1971) 'Eisenproduktion und Versorgung mit Eisen in Skandinavien vor der Wikingerzeit,' *Antikvarisk Arkiv*, XL.

Voss, O. (1976) 'Drengsted: Et bopladsområde fra 5. årh. e. Kr. f. ved Sønderjyllands vestkyst,' *Iskos*, I, Helsingfors.

Voss, O. and Ørsnes-Christensen, M. (1948) 'Der Dollerupfund: Ein Doppelgrab aus der römischen Eisenzeit,' *Acta Archaeologica*, XIX, 209–71.

Waals, J.D. van der (1964) 'Prehistoric Disc Wheels in the Netherlands,' *Palaeohistoria*, X, Groningen.

Wallace, A. (1966) 'Religion: An Anthropological View,' New York.

Waterbolk, H.T. (1964) 'The Bronze Age Settlement of Elp,' *Helinium*, IV, 97–131.

Waterbolk, H.T. (1974) 'L'archéologie en Europe: Une réaction contre la "New Archaeology",' *Helinium*, XIV.

Watson, Patty Jo *et al.* (1971) *Explanations in Archaeology: An Explicitly Scientific Approach*, New York.

Webb, M.C. (1975) 'The Flag Follows the Trade: An Essay on the Necessary Interaction of Military and Commercial Factors in State Formation,' in Sabloff, J.A. and Lamberg-Karlovsky, C.C. (eds) *Ancient Civilization and Trade*, Albuquerque.

Welinder, S. (1977) 'Ekonomiska processer i förhistorisk expansion,' *Acta Archaeologica Lundensia*, ser. in 8°, VII.

Wells, C. (1967) *Diagnose 5000 Jahre später: Krankheiten und Heilkunst in der Frühzeit des Menschen.*

Werner, J. (1951) 'Zur Entstehung der Reihengräberzivilization,' *Archaeologica Geographica*, I.

Werner, J. (1961) 'Fernhandel und Naturalwirtschaft im östlichen Merowingerreich,' *Bericht d. Röm. Germ. Kom.*, XLII, 307–46.

Westerby, E. (1927) *Stenalderbopladser ved Klampenborg: Nogle bidrag til studiet af den mesolitiske periode*, Copenhagen.

Wielowiejski, J. (1970) *Kontakty Noricum i Pannonii z ludami Polnoçnymi*, Wroclaw, Warszawa, Krakow.

Winther, J. (1926–8) *Lindø* I-II, Rudkøbing.

Winther, J. (1935) *Troldebjerg, en bymæssig bebyggelse fra Danmarks yngre stenalder*, Rudkøbing.

Winther, J. (1943) *Blandebjerg*, Rudkøbing.

Wüstemann, H. (1974) 'Zur Sozialstruktur im Seddiner Kulturgebiet,' *Zeitschrift für Archaeologie*, VIII, 67–107.

Yellen, J. and Harpending, H. (1972) 'Hunter–Gatherer Populations and Archaeological Inference,' *World Archaeology*, IV, 2, 244–53.

Zeist, W. van (1955) 'Some Radio-Carbon Dates from the Raised Bog near Emmen, Netherlands,' *Palaeohistoria*, IV, 113–18.

Ørsnes, M. (1956a) 'Om jættestues konstruktion og brug,' *Årbøger for nordisk oldkyndighed og historie*, 221–32.

Ørsnes, M. (1956b) 'Kyndby: Ein seeländischer Grabplatz aus dem 7–8. Jahrhundert nach Christus,' *Acta Archæologica*, XXVI, 69–162.

Ørsnes, M. (1958) 'Borbjerg-fundet,' *Årbøger for nordisk oldkyndighed og historie*, 1–107.

Ørsnes, M. (1963) 'The Weapon Find in Ejsbøl Mose at Haderslev: Preliminary Report,' *Acta Archaeologica*, XXXIV, 232–47.

Ørsnes, M. (1966) *Form og Stil i Sydskandinaviens yngre germanske jernalder*, Copenhagen.

Ørsnes, M. (1968) 'Der Moorfund von Ejsbøl bei Hadersleben und die

Deutungsprobleme der grossen germanischen Waffenopferfunde,' *Vorgeschichtliche Heiligtümer und Opferplätze in Mittel- und Nordeuropa: Abhandlungen der Akademie der Wissenschaften in Göttingen.*

Ørsnes, M. (1974) 'Bejsebakken,' In *Hoops Reallexikon der germanischen Altertumskunde*, II, 173–5.

Åkerlund, H. (1963) *Nydamskeppen*, Göteborg.

Index

A-landnam, 76
Aaby, B., 135, 186, 282
Aaris-Sørensen, K., 60, 62
Abel, W., 284
Acsádi, G., 24, 83, 126
administered trade, 248, 253, 261, 268
Adriatic, 242
aerial phtotography, 199
Aggersborg, 254
Aggersund, 61
agriculture, earliest, 68
Albrectsen, E., 277, 278, 281,
Albrethsen, S.E., 24, 61, 182
alder, 196
Alfred the Great, 274
Allerød period, 12, 13, 36
Almgren, O., 281
Als, 119
Amager, 45
amber route, 242
amber, 95, 103, 104, 109, 113, 156, 158, 161,
    162, 235, 242, 243, 259,
Anatolia, 72
Andersen, A., 125
Andersen, H., 182, 276, 279
Andersen, H.H., 61
Andersen, K., 59, 60
Andersen, N.H., 96, 119, 276
Andersen, S.H., 60, 61, 63, 64, 66, 124
Andersen, S.T., 75
Andersen, S.W., 181
Aner, E., 120, 182, 183
Angantyr, 266
animal styles, 271, 282
Annales Regni Frankorum, 255
annual territory, 40
Aquileia, 243

arctic willow, 12
ards, 99, 100, 224
ard-ploughing, 143, 151, 223
arrows, 41, 48, 50, 53
arrowheads, 66
Arup, E., 270, 283
ash, 17
aspen, 15, 17
Atlantic forest, 46
Atlantic period, 18, 19, 30, 32, 56, 60
aurochs, 16, 17, 19, 39, 41, 42, 43
axes, 41, 48

B-landnam, 76, 77
badges, 173
Bailey, G.N., 61, 62
Balkan peninsula, 72
Baltic Ice Lake, 13, 17
band society, 69
Barkær, 90, 113, 119
barley, 153, 225
barn, 218
Barren Grounds, 30
barrows, Bronze-Age, 168
base camp, 33
battle axes, 170
Baudou, E., 182, 183, 185
Bay-Petersen, J.L., 62
beadmakers, 222
beans, 153
beavers, 13, 40
Beck, C.W., 161, 188, 243
Becker, C.J., 59, 60, 66, 120, 121, 123, 124,
    125, 126, 180, 181, 183, 185, 187, 188, 250,
    276, 277, 281, 282, 283, 285
Bejsebakken, 254, 277
Bekmose, J., 85

Berg, H., 117, 120
Bergeron, T., 186, 282
Berglund, B.E., 61, 125
Big Men, 106, 270
bilaterality, 272
Binford, L.R., 51, 170
birch trees, 12, 15
bird cherries, 12
bison, 13
Bjerg, 150, 181
Bjerre, 102
Black Sea, 237
Blandebjerg, 117, 118
Blankholm, R.E., 60, 66
Bloksbjerg, 61
Blomstervænget, 122
bloom, 230
blubber lamps, 47
blue hares, 13
blue whales, 13
boars, 43
Board of Ancient Monuments, 4
boats, 42, 53
Boeslunde, 183
bog corpses, 280
bog finds, Iron Age, 279
bog iron, 228
boomerang, 50
Boreal period, 17, 32, 34, 39
Bornholm, 201, 223, 278, 279
Borremose, 276, 280
Borritshoved, 278
Borum Eshøj, 172
Boserup, E., 79, 80, 126
boundary horizon, 134, 135, 137, 186
bows, 41, 50, 53
bowls, wooden, 173
bracteates, 281
Bradley, R., 276
Brandenburg, 166
Brendekroggård, 122
bride purchase, 166
Brinch Petersen, E., 60, 61, 62, 66
Broholm, H.C., 182, 183, 185, 186, 278
Bromme, 64
Brongers, J.A., 276
Bronze Age graves, 139
bronze technology, 161
bronze, 163
brooches, Roman, 239
Brovst, 60
brown bears, 13
Brown, A.B., 62
Bruneborg, 228
Brøgger, A.W., 264
Brøndsted, J., 120, 156, 185, 188, 197, 282

Brøste, K., 126
Brå cauldron, 238
Büdelsdorf, 119
buffer zone, 234
bullocks, 101
Bundsø, 117, 118
burial customs, Neolithic, 111
butchering places, 40
Butler, J.J., 188
Bygholm Nørremark, 111, 112, 120
byre, 224
Bøgebakken, 24, 25, 60, 61
Bølling oscillation, 12
Bølling period, 13

Caesar, 262
calibration of radiocarbon datings, 123
Campania, 236
canoe, 258
Capeshøj, 122
Caput Adriae, 235, 243
carbon-13, 281
Carnuntum, 243
Carolingian law, 272
cattle raising, 93, 100
cauldron, 165
causewayed camp, 93
Cavalli-Sforza, L.L., 123
celtic field, 195, 206, 223, 276
Celtic, 241
central site, 91, 92, 93, 97, 115
cereal cultivation, 70
cereal pollen, 50
ceremonial flint axes, 105
chain-mail, 259
charcoal, 228
chariot of the sun, 176
Charlemagne, 250, 255
chiefdom, 106, 131, 158, 169, 236, 241, 256, 285
Child-bearing capacity, 27, 51
childbirth, 26
Childe, V.G., 123
children's graves, 169
Christensen, A.E., 272, 283
Christensen, E.P., 200, 226, 283, 284
chronology, Iron Age, 281
chronology, Mesolithic period, 62
chronology, Neolithic, 124
circulation of goods, 103
city states, Mediterranean, 235
Clark, J.G.D., 30, 34, 36, 62, 64
class division, 271
Clausen, H.V., 283
climate, 12, 19, 73, 134, 196
climatic change, 136, 282

climatic development, 186
climatic fluctuations, 134
climax forest, 52
clothing, Mesolithic, 41
clubs, 41
coastal settlements, 46
cod, 13, 43, 46, 153
coins, Frankish, 250
coins, Roman, 241, 242
combs, 222
common elk, 13
commons, 208
copper, 235
Cowgill, G.L., 126
cremation, 170, 174
crop rotation, 226
Crumlin-Petersen, O., 251
cult house, 121

daggers, 163
Dalshøj, 276
Dalton, G., 187, 284
Danevirke, 265, 266
Dankirke, 210, 214, 249, 250, 277
Davidsen, K., 117, 125, 185
Degerbøl, M., 62, 126
Dejbjerg wagon, 238
demographic decline, 227
demographical control, 107
dendrochronology, 3, 265
Denmark, 274
Dennell, R.W., 62
Dieck, 280
diet, Iron-Age, 281
diffusionism, 3, 5
division of labour, 29, 55
dogs, 42
dogfish, 43
Dollerup, 278
dolmen, rectangular, 85
dolmens, 120
Donneruplund, 225
Draved bog, 186
Draved forest, 125
Drengsted, 210, 214, 220, 231, 249, 277
drinking equipment, 238
dwarf birch, 12
dwarf willow, 12
Dyrholm, 61
Døstrup, 152

Earle, T., 187
Early Bronze Age, 170
earth graves, 92, 111, 113, 118, 120
Ebbesen, K., 120, 124
economy, Neolithic, 107

ecosystem, 22
egalitarian band society, 110
egalitarian society, 114
Egebak, 155
Egehøj, 150
Eggers, H.-J., 248, 278, 281, 284
Egtved, 172
Ehrlich, P.R., 62
Ejsbøl, 262, 263, 279
Ejsing, 48
Ekholm, G., 284
Ekholm, K., 158
elk, 16, 19, 39, 41, 42
Elling, 280
Ellmers, D., 285
elm fall, 76
elm, 17
Engelhardt, C., 279
environmental laws, 3
Ericson, J., 187
Ertebølle culture, 43, 66
Ertebølle, 61
Esbjerg, 277
Etruscans, 236
exchange of goods, Neolithic, 106
exchange of goods, Iron Age, 284
exchange systems, 132, 155, 187, 231
exchange, 104, 163
exchange, concepts of, 157

Faber, O., 120
fall-off-pattern, 104
fallow periods, 200
farmstead, Bronze Age, 146
farmstead, Iron-Age, 204
female mortality, 26
fences, 208
fertility, 24, 26, 81
figurines, 176
Fischer, A., 60, 64, 66
Fischer, C., 120, 280
fish hooks, 50
fish trap, 47
fishing, 212
Flannery, K.V., 71, 123
Fleming, A., 187
flint dagger, 140, 182
flint daggers, typology, 171
flint, 103, 156, 158
flint-mines 101, 103, 106, 183,
  Flögeln, 220
flounder, 153
folding stool, 173
food production, incipient, 81
forge, 229
Forssander, J., 188

fox, 40
Frankenstein, S., 158, 162, 234, 257
Frankish Annals, 253, 255, 266
Frankish Empire, 255
Fredskild, B., 62
free peasants, 269
Fried, M.H., 109, 110, 127, 128, 256, 285
Friedman, J., 158, 285
Friesland, 250
Friis, P., 276
Fuglebæksbanken, 122
Funnel-Necked Beaker culture, 50, 72, 122,
    131, 138, 183
furnaces, 215, 229

Gallic Wars, 263
Gaul, 261
Gebühr, M., 285
geest, 210
Geisslinger, H., 281
Gejvall, N.-G., 83, 182
Gerdrup, 182
Germania Libera, 243, 281
Germania, 261
Ginnerup, 140, 182
glass, 239, 245, 249
Glob, P.V., 119, 120, 181, 183, 186, 278, 280,
    284
goats, 100
Godelier, M., 233
Godfred, 253, 255, 265, 266
Godi, 270
gold bowls, 176
gold, 163, 166, 167, 170, 172, 233, 244, 264
Gorm, 273, 274
Goths, 269
Gotland, 201, 249
grain impressions, 50
Granlund, F., 186
Gräslund, B., 185, 281, 282
grass pasture, 132
Grauballe, 280
grave finds, Iron Age, 277
grave finds, Mesolithic, 61
grave finds, Neolithic, 119
grave finds, Bronze Age, 182; Late
    Neolithic, 182; Single Grave culture, 181
Gredstedbro ship, 250, 251, 252
Greenland whale, 13
grey seal, 46
Grønheden, 276
Grøntoft, 151, 204, 206, 212, 276, 209
Gudenå culture, 63
guilds, 272
Guldhøj, 173
Gundestrup cauldron, 237, 260

Gørding, 276

haddock, 153
Hagberg, U.E., 249, 284
Hald, 11
Hallstatt culture, 229
Hamburg culture, 36
Hansen, H.O., 99, 284
Hansen, U.L., 61, 120, 278, 282, 284
Hansen, V., 202, 281
Harald Bluetooth, 267, 274
Harner, M.J., 123
Harpelev, 278
harpoons, 50
harrow, 226
Hatt, G., 270, 276, 283
hawthorn, 223
hay-making, 210
Hayden, B., 62
hazel nuts, 40
hazel, 17
Hedager, L., 232, 238, 244, 256, 261, 264,
    278, 284
Hedeby, 220, 253, 277
Helbæk, H., 284
Henriksen, B.B., 66
Herrup, 120
Hesselø, 119
hides, 41, 235, 242
hierarchization, 234
High Atlantic period, 44, 73
Higham, C.F.W., 131, 187, 284
Himlingøje, 278
Himmelev, 122
Hingst, H., 119
Historical Archaeological Experimental
    Centre, Lejre, 205
History of the World, 274
Hjortspring, 258, 279
hoards, 259
hoards, Bronze Age, 166, 174, 182
hoards, Late Neolithic, 183
Hoby, 247
Hodde, 206, 208, 209, 210, 212, 214, 215,
    217, 220, 230, 259, 260, 276, 283
Hodges, R., 267
Holdren, J.P., 62
Hole, F., 123
Holland, 149
Holmegård, 59, 60
Holmsland, 276
honey, 163
hook ards, 224
horses, 153
Hov, 101, 102
Hovergårde, 149, 181

Huns, 269
hunters and gatherers, Atlantic period, 42, 52; mobility, 33
hunting places, Neolithic, 93
Hurup, 212, 276
huts, 40
Hvass, S., 209, 276, 282, 283
Hvorslev, 152
Højlund, F., 104, 182

Ilkjær, J., 279
Illerup 279, 262
import, central European, 163
import, Frankish, 244
imports, Roman, 240
infant mortality, 24, 83
infanticide, 27
infra-red spectoscopy, 161
inhumation, 174
invasion, 5, 81, 138, 143, 152, 154, 183
Irish elk, 13
iron extraction, 195
iron production, 215, 228, 277
iron, 235, 249
Iversen, J., 61, 75, 125, 126, 186, 282

Jacob-Friesen, G., 185
Jacobsen, J.A., 277
Jankuhn, H., 277, 285
Jazdzewski, K., 120
Jelling; 274
Jensen, J., 180, 181, 183, 185, 187, 188
Jensen, J.S., 182
Jensen, S., 210, 276, 283
Jeppesen, T.G., 283
Jessen, K., 61, 125, 126
Johansen, E., 117
Johansen, K.F., 60, 120
Jones, G., 269
Justinian bubonic plague, 194, 282
Jørgensen, E., 120, 277
Jørgensen, G., 126
Jørgensen, J.B., 126
Jørgensen, S., 59, 61, 66, 125

Kaelas, L., 120
Kanhave canal, 266
Kersten, K., 182
Kertinge Mark, 175
Kildemarksvej, 278
killer whale, 13
kingdoms, 264, 270
kinship alliances, 166
kitchen midden commission, 61
Kjær, H., 183, 276
Kjærsing, 276

Kjærum, P., 120, 121
Klampenborg, 45
Klindt-Jensen, O., 276, 277
Klintebakken, 117, 118
Klosterlund, 60
Köhler, R., 286
Kolding Fjord, 48
Kolind, 61
Kongemose culture, 43, 60, 66
Kongemosen, 59
Kragehul, 279
Kristiansen, K., 144, 167, 183, 186, 187, 189, 257
Kroll, H.J., 224
Kunwald, G., 280
Kærholm, 181

land management, 151, 200
landnam phase, 98, 186, 194
Langeland, 118
Larsen, K.A., 278
Late Dryas, 12
Late Glacial Ice Sea, 13
Late Glacial period, 35, 38, 39
Late Neolithic period, 132, 170
leather goods, 222
Lee, R.B., 57, 62
Leeds, A., 62
Lejre, 205
lemming, 13
Lévi-Strauss, C., 55
libra, 264
Lichardus, J., 124
Liebig, J., 27
life expectancy, 83
lime trees, 17, 74
Limes, 238
limestone deposits, 102
Limfjord, 250
Lindholm Høje, 254, 277
Lindø, 117, 118
Linear pottery culture, 72
Listleby, 152
Litorina transgressions, 19, 61, 73
Litorina-Tapes transgressions, 7
Liversage, D., 120, 182, 278
loincloth, 172
Lomborg, E., 181, 182, 183, 185, 186, 188 278
long barrow with timber structure, 113
long barrows, 87, 90
long dolmens, 97
long-tailed ducks, 13
longhouse, 146, 181; development of, 218
Lübsow, 248
Lund, J. 276

Lundby, 59
Lunden, K., 187, 252, 284
Lüneburg, 167, 167
lur, 176
Lusehøj, 176
lynx, 13
Læbrogård, 278
Læsø, 13
Løppenthin, B., 62

Mackeprang, M.B., 278, 281
Madsen, A.P., 61
Madsen, H.J., 182
Madsen, T., 91, 113, 119, 120, 124, 185
Maglemose culture, 39, 60, 66
Maglemosegårds Vænge, 47, 48
Mahler, D., 124
Main stationary line, 6
maintenance site, 92
male-female relationship, 173
Malmer, M.P., 183, 186
Malmros, C., 61, 125, 185
Malthus, T.R., 29
manuring, 224
Marcomannian kingdom, 241
Mariesminde 212, 276
markets, 157; economy, 157
marriage alliance, 55, 105
marsh, North Sea, 195
marshland shores, 8
marten, 40
Mathiassen, T., 60, 61, 63, 117, 186, 203, 283
Mecklemburg, 162, 167
medieval villages, 200
Mediterranean trade, 234
megalith graves, 87, 91, 92, 97, 110, 111, 113, 120, 138
Mejlgård, 45, 61
Mellars, P., 32
Merovingian period, 281
Mesolithic chronology, 31
metal ingots, 163
metal technology, 132, 154
metal, 104, 170
metal, Neolithic, 95
metalcasters, 222
microliths, 41, 65
Middle Neolithic chronology, 124
middlemen traders, 234
Migration period, 269, 281
millet, 153
Moberg, C.-A., 187, 284
mobile settlements, 204
mobile village, 206, 283
molluscs, 45, 153

monetary standard, 264
monoculture, 99
Montelius, O., 185
moraine flats, 8
mortality rate, 26
mortality, 24, 81
mortuary house, 111
mould, 75, 99; under Bronze-Age borrows, 144
mouldboard, 225
mountain avens, 12
Muldbjerg, 119
Müller, S., 149, 180, 181, 183, 187, 281
Müller-Karpe, H., 123
Müller-Wille, M., 276
Mullerup, 60
Munksgaard, E., 281
Mycenaean shaft graves, 156, 162
Myhre, B., 284
Myrhøj, 147, 150, 181
Myrthue, 276
mythology, 176
Møhl, U., 62
Møllegårdsmarken, 260, 277

Naglesti, 276
naked barley, 153
Nash, M., 284
National Museum, Danish, 2
Neergaard, C., 278
Nemeskéri, J., 24, 126
Nesteløgård, 278
net fishing, 47
Neumann, H., 278
New Guinea, 104
Newell, R.R., 61
Nielsen, H., 202, 203, 281, 283
Nielsen, J.L. 277
Nielsen, P.O., 121, 138, 185
Nielsen, S., 99, 125, 126, 143, 186, 226
Nielsen, V., 276
Nisset Nørremose, 154
Nissum Bredning, 85
Nivå, 45
non-egalitarian ranked societies, 131
non-megalithic graves, 112, 120
non-megalithic pottery, 124
Nordman, C.A., 120
Nordrup, 278
Norling-Christensen, H., 61, 278, 282
Norrland, 163
Norslund, 61
North Sea, 17
nuclear family, 40
Nydam boat, 250, 251
Nydam bog, 251

Nydam, 279
Nygård, 122
Nylén, E., 282
Nørre Fjand, 212, 276

oak coffin, 172
oak, 16, 74
oats, 153, 225
Odner, K., 188, 272, 284
Offa, 267
oil plant, 153
Öland rock rose, 12
Öland, 201, 249
Older Dryas, 12
Olsson, U., 187, 284
Ongendus, 266
oppidum, 236, 241
Ormø, 21
Orosius, 274
Oseberg ship, 252
Ottar, 274
Over Jersdal, 278
over-population, 83
Overbygård, 276

paddle, 41, 49, 50
palaeodemography, 25
Palaeolithic hunters, 30
palisade, 207
Paludan-Müller, C., 44, 51, 61, 62, 66, 124
Pannonnia, 243
paramounts, 235
park tundra, 12
passage graves, 87, 114, 120
patrilineal band, 53
patrilocal band, 53
peas, 153
pedology, 126, 186
perch, 13
Petersen, C.C.J., 62
Petersen, E.J., 204
Petersen, H., 278
Phillips, A.P., 123
pigs, 100, 153; domesticated, 74
Piggott, S., 120
pike, 13, 40
pine, 12
piracy, 250, 251, 268
pithouses, 217, 218
pitted ware culture, 125
place names, 202, 203
plant food, 17
Pleistocene, 11
Pliny, 242
plough marks, 122
ploughs, 79, 227, 280

Polanyi, K., 157, 187, 248, 253, 284
pollen analysis, 3, 75, 133, 186
pollen diagrams, 15
population balance, 20, 29; crisis, 26, 50,
    204; density, 31, 174; equilibrium, 73;
    growth, 78, 200, 264; pressure, 79, 143;
    size, 44, 50, 27, 204
porpoise, 43
port of trade, 253
Post-Pleistocene theory, 51
pottery, 163
pottery, Mesolithic, 47, 49, 51
pottery-making, 219
Pre-Boreal period, 15, 16, 39, 60
prestige chains, 162
prestige goods, 166, 182, 259
prestige symbols, 104
prestige-goods economy, 162, 232, 234,
    248, 268
priesthood, 270
Prinsens Palæ, 4
Præstehøj, 122

quaking aspen, 12

Raddatz, K., 279
radio carbon dating, 3, 64, 183
raised bog, 135, 223, 280
ramparts, 265
Ramskou, 277
Randsborg, K., 104, 126, 170, 185, 188, 189
ranked society, 156, 169
ranking, 109, 110, 169
Rappaport, R.A., 106, 158
Rasmussen, A.K., 276
Rathje, W.L., 233
reciprocity, 157, 241
rectangular dolmen, 111
red deer, 19, 39, 43, 45
redistribution, 157, 233, 241
Redman, C.L., 123, 127
reindeer hunters, 35
reindeer, 6, 12, 15, 16, 30, 35, 36
Renfrew, C., 63, 87, 162, 188, 234
reproductive capacities, 26
Reric, 253
resource crisis, 70, 108
resource territories, 199, 204, 209
Rhône, 162
Ribe, 211, 220, 222, 250, 253
Riis, P.J., 236
Ring Kloster, 61
ringed seals, 13
Riss-Saale glaciation, 7
Ristoft, 181
roads, 201

roe deer, 19, 39, 43, 45
Roman civilization, 232
Roman Empire, 243
rorqual, 13
Rosenberg, G., 120, 279
Rostholm, H., 185
round barrows, 87
round dolmen, 97
rowan, 12
Rowlands, M.J., 158, 163, 234, 257, 285
Royal antiquities commission, 1
rubbish pits, 224
runic stones, 273
Russel, J.C., 194
Rust, A., 64
rye, 200, 225
Rønne, P., 111, 120
Røsnæs, 194

sacrificial deposits, 176
sacrificial deposits, Neolithic, 139
Sahlins, M.D., 158, 187, 284, 285
Salmonsson, B., 66
salt, 163, 235
Samland, 103
Samsø, 266
Sarauw, G.F.L., 60
Sarup, 93, 96, 117, 119, 276
Saxons, 255
Saxony, 228
scabbards, 172
Scheffrahn, W., 126
Schlüter, W., 286
Schmid, P., 220
Schneider, H.K., 284
Schultz-Klinken, K.R., 225
Schwabedissen, H., 124
scrub pasture, 132
sea buckthorn, 12
sea mammals, 36, 40
seals, 36, 43, 93
seasonal camps, 46
secondary occupations, 210, 228
Seddin, 166
sedentarism, 80
semi-agrarian culture, 107
Sennels, 103
Senon flint, 103
Sernander, R., 186, 282
Service, E.R., 109, 127, 128, 169, 285
settlement pattern, Bronze Age, 138, 187
settlement pattern, Ertebølle culture, 44;
    Iron Age, 198; Mesolithic, 41; Neolithic,
    90
settlements, Bronze Age, 179; Iron Age,
    275; Late Neolithic, 179; Single Grave

culture, 146
shaft furnace, 230
sharing, 55
sheep, 100, 153
shell mounds, 45
shellfish, 43
Sherratt, A., 123, 126, 140
shields, 164, 259
ships, 250
shirts, 172
sickles, 163
Siegerslev, 98
Sigfred, 266
Sild, 224
Silesia, 228
silver, 239
Single Grave culture, 75, 83, 88, 108, 125,
    131, 138, 139, 156, 163, 181, 183, 186, 188
Sjælborg, 276
Skallerup, 165
Skamlebæk, 181
skeletal remains, Late Neolithic, 182;
    Neolithic, 111, 126; Single Grave culture,
    182
Skibshøj, 122
Skiringsal, 274
Skuldelev, 251
skyphoi, 247
Skyttemarksvej, 278
Skærbæk, 276
Skårup, J., 61, 117, 119, 124, 126
slag, 230
slash and burn, 77, 79, 80, 89
slaughtering age, 101
slave society, 270
slaves, 235, 269, 272
Slesvig, 253
Slomann, W., 284
Smith, P.E.L., 62, 126
smithing, 214, 219, 228
smithy, 215, 229
Snave, 122
Snedker, K.H., 276
soap, 242
social territory, 34
soil exhaustion, 99
Sörbom, 186, 282
spears, 41, 163, 259
special-purpose money, 242, 264
specific activity camps, 40, 92
Spjald, 150, 181
Spooner, B., 62, 123
stall partition, 148
stalls, 148
Stallerupholm, 60
Staré Hradisko, 243

state formations, 236, 271
state, 256, 267
status symbols, 174, 236
staves, 173
Steensberg, A., 125, 126, 284
Steneng, 122, 126
Stengade, 117, 119
Sterum, N., 185
Stevns, 247, 248
Stjernqvist, B., 180, 187, 188
stock raising, 70, 89, 143, 177
stone-heap grave, 114
Store Bælt, 17
storehouses, 206
string skirts, 172
Strömberg, M., 120, 181, 277
Struever, S., 123
Struwe, K.W., 182
Sturdy, D.A., 62
Stürup, B., 120
sub-arctic climate, 22
subsistence patterns, Iron Age, 222
summer camps, 40
sumptuary rules, 158
survival chart, 82
Sussmann, R., 123
Sutton Hoo, 251
Sværdborg, 60
swidden agriculture, 143
swiddening, 77
swords, 164, 259
Sølager, 61, 119
Sønder Hadsund, 60
Sønderup, 164
Sørup, 164

Tacitus, 241
tanged-point techno complex, 36
Tauber, H., 123, 125, 183, 185, 281
techno-complex, 34
techno-territory, 34
territory, 33
territory, Neolithic, 97
textiles, 163
Theissen polygon, 96
thick-butted axes, 124
thin-butted flint axes, 98
Thomsen, C.J., 1
Thomsen, N., 276
Thorsbjerg, 279
Thorsen, S., 114, 120
Thorvildsen, E., 277
Thorvildsen, K., 120
Thracian, 237
thralls, 269, 272
Thrane, H., 166, 180, 182, 185, 186, 188, 278

three-aisled longhouses, 146, 205
three-field system 200, 226, 283
three-period system, 2
threshing floors, 218
Thy, 276
Thyra, 274
Tischler, F., 278
Toftum, 93, 119
Tollund bog, 14
Tollund, 280
topography of Denmark, 6
towns, 220
trade, 188; long-distance, 166, 250; market, 253
trade, Roman, 242
transhumance, 131
transit camps, 40
traps, 154
Trappendal, 148, 181
trend surface analysis, long dolmens, 86
tribal organisation, 69
tribal society, 109
tribute, 233
Troels-Smith, J., 30, 61, 62, 64, 66, 119, 124, 126
Troldebjerg, 117, 118
tundra, 12, 13, 22
turf walls, 205
Tybrind Vig, 49

Udby, 278
Uggerløse, 278
Ulkestrup, 60
University of Copenhagen, 4
University of Århus, 4
urban communities, 222
urban settlements, 253

Vadgård, 150, 181
Vallois, H.V., 126
van Es, 220
vassals, 235
Vayda, A.P., 62
Vedbæk boldbaner, 60
Vedbæk, 24, 45, 60, 61
Vedel, E., 278
Vejstrup Forest, 11
Vendel period, 281
Venderland, 274
Verup, 60
Vestervig, 212
Viking raids, 250
Viking ships, 251
villages, 151
villages, Bronze Age, 146; Iron Age, 204
Villingebæk, 45

Vimose, 279
Voldtofte, 151, 166, 177
Vorbasse, 212, 216, 219, 220, 268, 277, 283
Vorting, H.C., 277
Voss, O., 126, 277, 278, 281
votive finds, Neolithic, 121

Wadden Sea, 85
wagons, 238
walrus, 13
wandering craftsmen, 264
wandering village, 210
Wateringe, W.G. van, 224
wealth objects, 158, 233
weapon sacrifices, 262
wear analysis, 167
weaving, 219
weeding, 226
weight standard, 264
Welinder, S., 189
Weonodland, 274
Werner, J., 285
Westerby, E., 61
whales, 38
wheel ploughs, 225, 226, 200
Wijster, 220
wild boar, 19
wild horses, 133
wild pigs, 40, 45
Willibrord, 266
wine, 242
winter settlements, 40

Winther, J., 117
Wismar, 253
wolves, 13
wolverine, 13
wool, 235
workshop, 217, 220, 222, 254, 258
Worsaae, J.J.A., 2
worship of the dead, 110
Wulfstan, 274
Würm-Weichsel glaciation, 6, 7
Wüstemann, H., 166

Younger Dryas, 38

Zagros Mountains, 71
Zimmermann, W.H., 220

Ærø, 47

Ølby Lyng, 61
øre, 264
Ørsnes, M., 120, 277, 279
Ørsnes-Christensen, M., 278
Øster Jølby, 60
Østerbølle, 210, 276
Østerå, 165

Ålborg, 102
Åmosen, 59, 119
Årup, J., 181
Årupgård, 95

clarity. The cultural region in which the hunting peoples in Denmark were integrated expanded in comparison to that of the Late Glacial period. In archaeological literature this territory or techno-complex is termed the Maglemose culture. For nearly 1500 years there was a striking unity in subsistence form and technology over much of the great north European lowland, the area which today includes England, Denmark, central and southern Sweden, northern Germany and parts of northern and western Poland. In all, this region covered about 300,000 km². To be sure, the hunting communities varied in behavioural forms within this vast region. The seasonally determined migrations of the communities were of course intimately related to the meat animals which still comprised the chief source of protein – and in fact the movements of these animals in the terrain were determined in great part by the topography of the country. In this regard there is a clear-cut difference between a lowland region such as Denmark and a region with more distinct surface relief such as England. Yet although certain differences in the seasonal pattern of the hunting peoples are evident, the material is too meagre to permit sweeping generalizations.

The same uncertainty also holds true of attempts to define the annual territory. Most often, the hunter–gatherer communities of the Pre-Boreal and Boreal are depicted as typical inland cultures. But this view may be challenged due to the one-sidedness of the source material. The coastlines of the Pre-Boreal and Boreal (Figure 7) lie mostly beneath the sea today, so traces of any possible coastal settlement sites are necessarily few. Even if the coastal zone in the Pre-Boreal and Boreal period did not offer quite the same biological richness as later during the Atlantic with the rise of the sea level, it is logical to assume that the exploitation of the resources of the coastal zone was also part of the seasonal life pattern of the hunter-gatherer communities, for example during the critical spring months; in fact, seal hunting has been documented. In evaluating the significance of the coastal zone it must be remembered that even in later periods, for while intensive exploitation of the coast has been documented, we find only few traces of coastal hunting at the inland settlement sites.

The accessible evidence of the hunter–gatherer communities' exploitation of the resources, particularly in the seventh millennium BC, shows a broad exploitation of the biological potential of the forest. All species of large meat animals were hunted. Among these, elk and aurochs could yield about 500 kilogrammes of meat. Both of these large meat animals were present from the beginning of the period but gradually played out their role as game in the course of the following millennia in pace with the increasing density of the forest. The plentiful red deer and roe deer were also hunted. In fact, living conditions for these animals improved in the course of the period. The same holds true of the wild pig, which during the period played an ever-larger role as a source of protein. The preferred fur-bearing animals were the beaver, the marten, the fox and the badger. Inland fishing was dominated by the catching of pike, for which fishing spears and lines were used. There is but poor evidence of the gathering of plant foods; the gathering of hazel nuts and a few other fruits and seeds is the only indication of this vital aspect of the subsistence pattern.

Due to the marked lopsidedness of the archaeological record, knowledge of the annual migrations of the hunter-gatherer communities, and consequently of their annual territory in the Pre-Boreal and Boreal, is limited. The best-known aspects are the camps of the summer season, which were made primarily by inland fresh-water streams and lakes. From a number of these localities there are finds of small rectangular huts apparently built of branches rammed in round a floor and pulled together at the top to make a roof. These small huts were inhabited by small groups of people – probably just a single nuclear family. The summer huts were the base camp for many activities such as hunting, fishing and gathering of plant food. To judge from what we know of present-day hunting societies we can presume that gathering was largely carried out by the women.

The settlement sites of the winter months are, in contrast, virtually unknown. A few localities indicate that during the cold period settlement was made on dryer land, although still near fresh water. It is an important observation that the winter settlements seem to have been comprised of larger groups than those of the summer. Winter settlements were apparently based upon the advantages of co-operative hunting.

Little is known of how the hunter–gatherer bands moved between these two settlement types. Presumably exploitation of the coastal zone took place in the late autumn and early spring months; both periods seem to be advantageous for the hunting of sea mammals, as indicated by a few finds. Aside from the more permanent summer and winter settlements, we know of a number of specific activity camps seemingly more transitory in character, such as butchering-places, where big game such as elk and aurochs were quartered before transport back to the base camp. The fishing sites also found were probably connected to the summer settlement. Finally there are some sites which may have functioned as transit camps on the way between the seasonal settlement sites of the coast and the inland sites. The picture is still dim, but it does seem certain that the strategy of the hunter–gatherer communities entailed a mobile settlement pattern and that segments of the bands split off temporarily during certain seasons in order to exploit especially favourable ecological niches of the territory.

The material equipment of the hunter–gatherer communities in this phase shows a varied exploitation of the accessible resources. The hunters used the bones of the aurochs and the elk for making at least fifteen different types of tools; the hides were used for clothing. The tool types include spearheads, which seem to have been widely used in hunting as well as fishing. Fishing hooks are also known. The hunter's bow and arrows attest a highly developed woodworking technique. The bow is accompanied by several different kinds of specialized arrows (Figure 14). Wooden spears and clubs are also known, as well as a number of specialized axes for purposes such as woodworking. Other implements include paddles, which imply the use of boats (probably hollowed-out tree trunks). The boat type is still only known from the fringes of the techno-territory. Aids in hunting may also have included the dog, which already seems to have been domesticated in eastern Europe in the Late Glacial period.

Hunters and gatherers of the Atlantic period

Improved living conditions in the Boreal created the preconditions for a population increase which presumably culminated around the middle of the seventh millennium BC. But because in the following period the dense shady virgin forest gained ever more ground, it is conceivable that a certain impoverishment of the fauna of the forest began during the sixth millennium BC. Both for the elk and the aurochs, but also for the deer species, the density of the forest meant a certain decline in living conditions. During this period the land began to shrink in area (Figure 8) as a result of the rise of the sea-level. Stratigraphical observations have shown that this occurred in four stages, probably separated by intervals in which the sea-level sank slightly. The last two of these four rises were particularly extensive. It is logical to assume that the rises of sea-level gradually encroached upon the territory of the hunter–gatherers, thus resulting in both a greater permanence of settlement and a more severe strain on the resources. For a time the richer and more varied biological environment at the coasts could relieve the growing population pressure, but in the long run the situation was untenable.

If this theory is correct, it may explain some of the changes in the behaviour of the hunter–gatherers during the sixth and fifth millennia BC. As yet the nature of these changes is not clear, but in light of the environmental situation it is understandable that gradually the productive coastal zones were thoroughly exploited. In contrast to the view

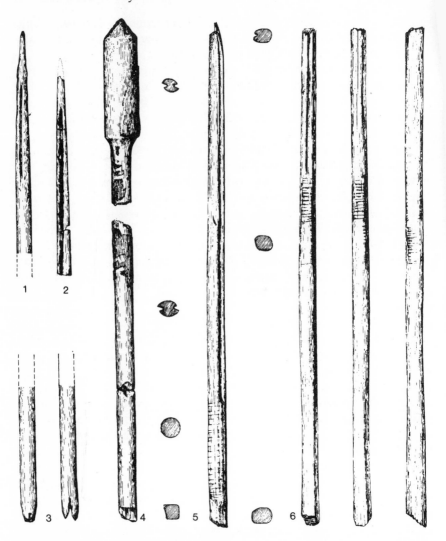

Figure 14 Wooden arrows and spears found at the Maglemosian settlement Holmegård IV, Zealand. Both arrows and spears have furrows intended for insertion of flint microliths.

frequently put forward in older archaeological literature, we must assume that the inland regions were also exploited to some degree. Earlier ideas of the all-dominating role of the coastal zone for the hunter–gatherer communities are due in some degree to a onesidedness favoured by the selection of sites chosen for excavation by earlier